FIFTH EDITION

Orientation to the THEATER

Theodore W. Hatlen

University of California, Santa Barbara

D1119555

 Prentice Hall, Englewood Cliffs, New Jersey 07632

Library of Congress Cataloging-in-Publication Data

Hatlen, Theodore W.
    Orientation to the theater / Theodore W. Hatlen. -- 5th ed.
        p.   cm.
    Filmography
    Includes bibliographical references and index.
    ISBN 0-13-638883-3
    1. Drama. 2. Theater.   I. Title.
PN1655.H3 1992
    808.2--dc20   91-28020
                                                                       CIP

**Thanks to my wife, Dorcas,
without whose assistance, encouragement, and advice,
this revision would never have come to print.**

Acquisitions editor: Steve Dalphin
Editorial/production supervision
   and interior design: Serena Hoffman
Cover design: Patricia Kelly
Cover photo: Hank Kranzler,
   Oregon Shakespeare Festival Theater
Prepress buyer: Kelly Behr
Manufacturing buyer: Mary Ann Gloriande
Copy editor: Judith Ashkenaz

© 1992, 1987, 1981, 1972, 1962 by Prentice-Hall, Inc.
A Simon & Schuster Company
Englewood Cliffs, New Jersey 07632

Printed in the United States of America
10 9 8 7 6 5 4 3 2 1

ISBN 0-13-638883-3

PRENTICE-HALL INTERNATIONAL (UK) LIMITED, *London*
PRENTICE-HALL OF AUSTRALIA PTY. LIMITED, *Sydney*
PRENTICE-HALL CANADA INC., *Toronto*
PRENTICE-HALL HISPANOAMERICANA, S.A., *Mexico*
PRENTICE-HALL OF INDIA PRIVATE LIMITED, *New Delhi*
PRENTICE-HALL OF JAPAN, INC., *Tokyo*
SIMON & SCHUSTER ASIA PTE. LTD., *Singapore*
EDITORA PRENTICE-HALL DO BRASIL, LTDA., *Rio de Janeiro*

Contents

six
Traditional Modes   153

seven
Realism   181

eight
Theatricalism and the New Theater   210

fourteen
Playwriting 392

Preface

Theatrical production, like all creative expression, is a reminder that a culture is not to be judged by its material accomplishments alone, but also by the aspirations and ideals that motivate conduct. In dealing with significant choices and actions, dramatists have at their disposal special means of illuminating the human condition. Thus, a play is more than an evening's diversion in the theater, more than pages of a text; it is a personal statement of the playwright and a clue to the culture that produced it. The objective of this work is to provide students with the tools of analysis that will give them insight into the total imaginative process that makes up theater.

Since *Orientation to the Theater* first appeared in print in 1962, there have been a great many changes in our world—and in the theater too. Always leading a precarious life, this "magnificent invalid" continues to survive in a variety of unexpected ways. Despite the changes, certain basic elements persist from one generation to the next. It has been the author's purpose to define and illustrate these essentials.

I wish to express my gratitude to my students and colleagues over the years from whom I learned so much. I also want to thank many helpful people and institutions for their friendly cooperation in the preparation of this text: Dr. Jaromir Svoboda of the Prague National Theater; Dr. Eckart Nolle of the Munich Theatermuseum; the Victoria and Albert Museum; Dimitrios Harissiadis; the Guthrie Theater; George Street Playhouse; Oregon Shakespeare Festival; La Jolla Playhouse; Paper Mill Playhouse; the Cleveland Play House; the Arena Stage; the Mark Taper Forum; Pacific Conservatory of Performing Arts; the Hartford Stage; Asolo State Theater; American Conservatory Theater; St. Louis Repertory Theater; Cincinnati Playhouse in the Park; the Goodman Theater; South Coast Repertory Theater; Royal Shakespeare Company; Théâtre du Soleil; Steppenwolf Theater Company; Trinity Square Theater; New York Museum of Modern Art; New York Public Library; Walker Art Center; Berliner Ensemble; Stadt Theater, Bern. I am also grateful to the Theater Arts Departments of the universities of California at Berkeley, California at Santa Barbara; Colorado, Cornell, Michigan, Minnesota, North Carolina, Stanford, Toledo, U.C.L.A., and Yale.

Thedore W. Hatlen

one
The Background

A view through the entrance gate to the orchestra circle during a modern performance in the ancient theater at Epidaurus. Drama had its origin in Greece during the sixth century B.C. as a part of the celebration in honor of the god Dionysus.

YOU AND THE THEATER

Theater exists because of your special ability to make real and imaginary connections. You can instantly direct your mind to recall an event from your own experience.

Suppose you begin with the words *high school graduation*. You immediately call up a cluster of memories: where the ceremony was held, who was there, what you wore, and the party afterwards. With no effort at all, you can put together an album of recollections.

You also have an amazing facility for projecting yourself into an imaginary situation. What can you do with this idea? Here are the car keys and a wad of cash. Out in front is a nice, red convertible, all gassed up, waiting for you. Where do you want to go? Care for company? You deserve a break. Be my guest. No doubt you can fill in the scenario from there. If you prefer, make it a cruise ship, or a tropical island, or a cabin in the snowy mountains. It is easy to get carried away.

In addition, for the theater, your gift for illusion allows you to enter into the experience of someone else. Have you ever shared the embarrassment of an actor who forgot his lines? A waitress who spilled a tray of dishes? A shortstop who

In Alfred Uhry's prize-winning play *Driving Miss Daisy*, **the middle-class elderly lady and her chauffeur are brought together reluctantly, but they gradually reach a warm understanding.** *(George Street Playhouse, New Brunswick, New Jersey)*

dropped a routine pop fly? Can you recall celebrating a total stranger's triumph at Wimbledon? Or the disappointment of a favored candidate who lost an election? Or the grief of parents, standing over a flag-draped casket?

Even more importantly for the theater, you have an extraordinary aptitude for projecting yourself into a make-believe experience, with a group of strangers, in a situation completely foreign to you.

Here is an elderly Jewish lady who has wrecked her car. Her son hires an old black chauffeur so she can get about. She is totally against the arrangement, and you sympathize with her spirit of independence. Yet, little by little, the playwright Alfred Uhry, in *Driving Miss Daisy*, leads her and you through a series of encounters to the point where she says, "You know, Hoke, you're my best friend."

Through our gift for illusion, we can span the centuries to Renaissance Verona and find a kinship with Romeo and Juliet, who fall madly in love with one another. They learn that their two families are deadly enemies and that to continue with their love would be a revolt against parental authority. We share with them their anxiety and determination when they attempt to free themselves from the tragic net of circumstances in which they are caught and which ulti-mately results in their untimely deaths. Or, for the space of an evening, we are able to join in the beauty-and-the-beast fantasy of the disfigured Phantom in his ill-fated infatuation with Christine.

Experienced playwrights are aware of your capacity for projecting yourself imaginatively into the plays and productions they create. They depend on your ability to make connections. If you remain aloof, bored, or uncaring, the produc-tion will fail. Every aspect of the performance is aimed at getting you involved.

Histrionic Sensibility

Another way of describing theatrical response is found in Francis Fergusson's term *histrionic sensibility*—the theatergoer's ability to perceive and discriminate actions and visual symbols, just as the trained ear discriminates sounds. It is a learned process that we employ when we judge behavior. When we communicate with one another on important issues, we prefer face-to-face contact, which enables us to make judgments about others because of the way they act. Consider a familiar episode from life that may have the quality of drama:

You apply for a job. You go through a process that generates a certain amount of tension, because the outcome is in doubt, and it is vitally important to you to succeed.

You are obliged to follow a specific procedure. You fill out a form; perhaps you submit letters of recommendation or your service record elsewhere; you make an appointment for an interview. When you meet your prospective em-ployer, she turns out to be an attractive, mature woman with an air of competence about her. You make every effort to create a favorable impression, so that your words and actions will help you to achieve your objective. She consults what you have written on the forms and your other papers and listens to your answers. With a bit of luck, the job is yours.

This lively quarrel in the Oregon Shakespeare Festival production of *Two Gentlemen of Verona* shows the actors fully involved in a way that clearly communicates the emotional content of the scene.

Why the interview? Because it gave the employer and you an opportunity to assess each other. When you entered the boss's office, you got certain impressions from the room, the furniture, the decor, the things on the desk. And you made tentative judgments about the person based on her appearance, manner of speaking, and way of looking at you as you answered questions.

What you were both doing during this sizing-up process was evaluating each other by histrionic sensibility. We have learned to read body language; we are responsive to others' "vibrations"; we communicate on a subliminal or visceral level that sometimes can be more intense than the spoken word. This kind of communication is essential for understanding the impact of the theater. The actors' shrug of a shoulder or lifting of an eyebrow, the pace of the action, the cadence of sounds, the reaction of one character to another—all constitute an eloquent vocabulary of a universal language, even though the signals may be ephemeral and ambiguous, vanishing at the moment of creation.

Experienced playwrights are aware of these multifaceted forces, and they create their actions to make optimum use of them. Here, in the opening scene of Arthur Miller's *Death of a Salesman,* you see a dramatist making full use of theatrical materials:

> *(From the right, Willy Loman, the Salesman, enters, carrying two large sample cases. The flute plays on. He hears but is not aware of it. He is past sixty years of*

An exhausted Willy Loman returns home after an unsuccessful business trip in Arthur Miller's *Death of a Salesman.* *(Munich Kammerspiele)*

age, dressed quietly. Even as he crosses the stage to the doorway of the house, his exhaustion is apparent. He unlocks the door, comes into the kitchen, and thankfully lets his burden down, feeling the soreness of his palms. A word-sigh escapes his lips—it might be "Oh boy, oh boy." He closes the door, then carries his cases out into the living-room, through the draped kitchen doorway. Linda, his wife, has stirred in her bed at the right. She gets out and puts on a robe, listening.)

Linda: *(Hearing Willy outside the bedroom, calls with some trepidation)* Willy!

Willy: It's all right. I came back.

Linda: Why? What happened? *(Slight pause)* Did something happen, Willy?

Willy: No, nothing happened.

Linda: You didn't smash the car, did you?

Willy: *(With casual irritation)* I said nothing happened. Didn't you hear me?

Linda: Don't you feel well?

Willy: I'm tired to death. *(The flute has faded away. He sits on the bed beside her, a little numb.)* I couldn't make it. I just couldn't make it, Linda![1]

In this brief excerpt, Miller combines all elements of the drama—music, costume, lighting, scenery, dialogue, and action—to create a specific effect. In just eight lines of dialogue, our attention is captured, and we begin to be involved. What is wrong with Willy? The entire evening will be spent in answering this question. We want to know what is behind the façade of words—the *subtext*, which Stanislavski defined as "a web of innumerable, varied, minor patterns inside the play . . ."

During your interview for a job, you and the boss were studying each other, looking for signs that would tell you something about your future relationship. You listened to her words and the way she said them, and you looked for any other clues that might be behind the conversation . . . the subtext. You also looked for signs in her behavior. Was her manner friendly, cool, direct, sincere? Was she attentive, willing to listen, or preoccupied and brusque? Did you feel that you would be comfortable working with her? In real life, many social situations are trivial and inconsequential. Dialogue is small talk, actions are without any serious purpose or meaning. On stage, however, the playwright and the director have selected only significant material. Every exchange of dialogue, every piece of business is there for a purpose. As spectators, we try to be aware of what is going on, because everything counts.

In the theater, as in life, we constantly make an assessment of the characters on stage, and the performers in turn provide us with a steady barrage of dialogue, actions, and clues that will help us understand them and the play. It has been said that the job of the playwright is to put the spectator to work. And that is precisely what we do, as we try to connect with the play through histrionic sensibility.

Empathy

Your facility for entering into the experience of others may be called *empathic.* *Empathy* means "feeling into." It may also be defined as "imitative motor response." Notice the word *motor.* An empathic response is more than sympathy; it involves physical identification and participation as well. When Willy sets the heavy sample cases down and feels the soreness in his hands, we share in his feeling. Our hands and shoulders and back are relieved to set the burden down.

Watch bystanders near the high-jump pit, and you will see some of them trying to help the jumper over the bar. When the bride feeds the groom the first piece of cake, many of the onlookers will open their mouths empathically. Take a ride with a reckless driver, and your foot will be tired from trying to apply the brakes from the passenger's side.

In Anton Chekhov's *The Three Sisters*, **Masha and the Colonel are caught up in their last desperate embrace when his regiment is transferred. The spectator responds empathetically to the body language of the actors.** *(Gorki Theater, Berlin)*

In the sports world, the largest crowds are attracted to those contests that involve vigorous physical action to which the spectator responds empathically. When you go through an overtime "cliffhanger" game, you may be exhausted because of the physical tension of feeling yourself involved in the action. Similarly, film and television fare that exploits violence and action, such as in melodramas and farces, is the most popular because it elicits a strong empathic response.

The art of the theater depends on your ability to be a willing partner in illusion. Drama has always been a shared, group experience.

Appeal of the Theater

Why do people go to the theater?

Why did the citizens of ancient Athens arise in the cold hours of dawn, scale the steep slope of the Acropolis, and sit on the hard seats of the Theater of Dionysus while they watched a trilogy such as Aeschylus' *Oresteia*—three plays of unrelieved suffering and seriousness? Why did a London chimney sweep of Elizabethan times make his way across the Thames to the Globe Theater to stand for hours in the pit to see a play like *Hamlet*—a work so perplexing in language

The theater's appeal to the senses comes through in the La Jolla Playhouse's world premiere musical *80 Days*. (*Directed by Des McAnuff*)

and content that literary scholars still argue about its meaning? Why did our forefathers find the lure of theatrical performance so appealing that they journeyed for several days to see second-rate actors in a makeshift showboat production of *The Rivals*? Why do people today, after a hectic day's work in the office, submit themselves to the ordeal of fighting their way through snarled traffic, rushing through dinner, and paying for expensive seats in a dark cavern so they can see the latest Broadway hit? What is the secret of theatrical appeal so compelling that we find it necessary to install electronic boxes in nearly every living room, so that we can huddle in the dark, night after night, giving ourselves to make-believe characters going through make-believe actions?

The sources of the theater's appeal are many, and no doubt the theatrical experience is often a blend of several. Let us suggest four.

First, the theater offers us an effective means of expanding our range of experience. From very primitive times, storytellers have entertained their companions around the fire with vivid accounts of the triumphs of heroes and heroines over adversity. Likewise, in the theater, we enjoy a stirring contest between two well-matched opponents. Through our imaginations, we enter into the experience and are moved by the give and take of the struggle, the excitement of the chase, the surprise of discovery, and the final resolution of the conflicts.

When we were children, we not only learned by imitation, but also, through imaginative participation, we extended the borders of our experience. We engaged in daring adventures that enabled us to escape from the narrow confines of our immediate surroundings. We fought battles, became exotic creatures, soared aloft on wings of imagination. This capacity for fanciful life continues with us into adulthood. Sometimes we project ourselves into the past by recalling our earlier experiences or by reliving the myths and legends of our ancestors. We become associated with Rosalind or Cyrano, with Orestes or Juliet. Sometimes, we pursue imaginary adventures into the unknown: exploring strange waters, crossing over into undiscovered country, scaling a precipitous mountain, shooting for the moon. Sometimes, we attempt to gain strength, and perhaps immortality, by linking ourselves with supernatural powers. Through the theater, or with other arts, we participate in illusions that carry us beyond the here and now. Small wonder that plays that enable those caught up in the rat-race to escape from the daily routine are heavily favored at the box office. One of the distinguishing marks of a fine play is that it provides satisfactions on many levels—one of which may be narrative.

Second, the audience finds pleasure in the skill of execution. Sports enthusiasts at the Olympic Games may marvel at a pole-vaulter as he swings his body up and over the bar more than nineteen feet above the ground. Or they may enjoy the incredible balance and timing of a gymnast working on the parallel bars, or the precision of a diver as she lofts her body into the air, executes a complicated figure, and enters the water with scarcely a splash.

In the arts, one derives pleasure from the mastery of materials—the painter's brushwork, the sculptor's ability to shape stone and metal, the musician's control of a voice or instrument, the dancer's use of space. We enjoy the repetition of familiar music at least in part because of the skills of those who play it. Certainly, one of the chief attractions of musical comedy comes from the excellence of the dancing and singing. In straight plays, the viewer enjoys memorable performances of outstanding actors and actresses, such as Maggie Smith's delightful mugging in *Lettice and Lovage,* Derek Jacobi's tour de force in the multi-faceted role of *Kean,* Michael Crawford's virtuoso playing in *The Phantom of the Opera,* and Dustin Hoffman's incisive revelation of new aspects of Willy in *Death of a Salesman* and Shylock in *The Merchant of Venice.* In Japan, for example, the spectator of the Kabuki theater may compare an actor's performance in a role with that of his father or grandfather, as each generation follows precisely in the footsteps of the one before. As a knowledgeable spectator, you learn to note the effectiveness of the ensemble acting, the director's adroit use of pace and rhythm, the actor's ability to react as well as to speak, the expressive use of movements and

One of the appeals of the theater is responding to the fine execution by the performers, as in this dance from *Jerome Robbins' Broadway.*

business, the emotional content implied by the groupings of characters, and the dramatist's use of symbols. You find pleasure also in the skill of a designer, such as Santo Loquasto or Ming Cho Lee, in providing a setting that exactly suits the emotional and visual needs of a play. Other examples would be the exuberant and extravagant settings, costumes, and effects of Maria Björnsen for *The Phantom of the Opera* or Tommy Tune's sophisticated choreography for *Grand Hotel*. One of the rewards of seeing a Peter Brook production is to be confronted with astonishing theatricalism that is fresh and highly original. To a student of the theater, one of the most enjoyable aspects of drama is to experience a play that has been expertly crafted, so that it becomes a genuine theater piece—alive, vigorous, and compelling.

A third satisfaction of the theater is that it gives us opportunities for gaining fresh perceptions. Aristotle suggested that one of the greatest pleasures in life is learning. The theater is an excellent way to extend ourselves to a wide variety of experiences and contacts that we can never make in reality. In a play, we can go back twenty-five centuries and share the varied conflicts of well-intentioned characters in *Antigone*.

Think of the range of characters we can get to know personally in Shakespeare alone: from country bumpkins to kings and queens; from romantic young ladies and gentlemen to drunkards, villains, and bawds; soldiers, usurpers, murderers, parasites, priests, and clowns. The theater introduces us to all kinds of characters we would never meet in our small worlds. Oedipus, on stage, is no murky, remote king, but a man of flesh and blood, torn asunder by his guilt and suffering. *Equus* gives us insight into the life and motivations of a boy whose psyche has been disturbed by his fixation on horses. We spend a couple of hours becoming acquainted with characters whose distorted personalities would probably make us avoid them in real life, such as Blanche DuBois in *A Streetcar Named Desire*, Ibsen's *Hedda Gabler*, August Strindberg's *Miss Julie*, or Duerrenmatt's Madame Zachanassian in *The Visit*. We can probe into all kinds of problems dealing with justice, greed, responsibility, prejudice, and inequality. And by virtue of its way of working, the theater opens us up to intense and dynamic questions. The theater offers us extraordinary opportunities for insightful experiences.

Fourth, the dramatic experience can also be a spiritual one. As Aristotle suggested, comedy may show us to be worse than we are, but tragedy shows us to be better. It is serious, elevated in scale, and of a certain magnitude. At its best, tragedy evokes a catharsis—a purging away, a cleansing of the ignoble, the mean, the base. Great works of drama depict great characters exploring the great issues of life. In them, humans are tested to the utmost, and although their bodies may be broken, their spirit triumphs. Through suffering, they transcend their physical limitations and affirm the dignity of humankind and its resilient spirit. Greek tragedy was a declaration of faith; it exalted humankind. "Wonders are many, and none is more wonderful than man," sang Sophocles. The trials and sufferings of Antigone, Oedipus, and Prometheus were positive statements about the Greek way of life and of humans' potential grandeur. Our loftiest ideas and aspirations have been the significant content of drama, and spiritual stimulation one of its enduring achievements. Comic writers like Molière and George Bernard Shaw have attacked and exposed hypocrisy and chicanery. Likewise, those concerned with humans as a social animal, writers like Ibsen, Rabe, Miller, and August Wilson, have stripped away the façade of social pretense and have forced us to see reality. Thus the theater has often been a salutary social weapon for dealing with the truth.

In addition to these venerable appeals, the new theater has given many of us fresh insights into ways of responding to extraordinary stimuli. We have been exposed to audacious use of language and astonishing images, sometimes shocking, sometimes painful, sometimes fabulous. We have been battered by sounds, temporarily blinded by lights, and startled by assaults on our nervous system. Although on occasion we may be bewildered by these symbols, actions, and images that come at us in spurts and spasms, and which we cannot really identify with or relate to, we may enjoy expanding our awareness, stretching our minds and emotional capacities, and sharing in the excitement of exploring new territory.

Let us see how it all began.

THESPIS

The time: Sixth century B.C. It is the vintage season.
The place: A circular threshing floor of hard-packed earth, just outside the city wall in Icaria, near Marathon.
The cast: A chorus of fifty men and boys performing before their fellow citizens.

The onlookers gather about the circle; some stand at the sides, but most of them sit on the sloping hillside. All eyes are on the chorus, singing and dancing in unison—their voices clear and bright in the crisp morning air, their familiar steps performed with an easy grace, the flow of the dance and the rhythm of the music and movement felt by all who watch.

The stricken hero is carried aloft by the Chorus in Euripides' tragedy *Hippolytus*, produced at the theater in Epidaurus, Greece.

Suddenly, a solitary figure breaks away from the chorus and mounts an altar stone in the center of the circle. The crowd is startled when he begins to speak, his voice cutting off the chant of the chorus. Instead of the cadence of the dancing and singing, he speaks in the accents of a storyteller, recalling the adventures of an ancient hero. The sunlight catches the chalky white makeup of his face; his body is animated and his voice is charged with emotion. This is no ordinary storyteller: This is the hero himself, brought by the audacious act of impersonation from the distant past into the living present.

The chorus, momentarily transfixed by the miraculous appearance of the hero, now draws toward him as he enacts the ordeal of suffering. He seems to be wounded; he struggles mightily and dies. The chorus responds in mimetic action, sometimes singing and dancing, bodies and voices following the hero. During his suffering, the chorus sings a hymn of supplication; when he dies, they gather about the altar in lamentation, take up his body, and move in a solemn recessional, circling the ring, while the onlookers are involuntarily caught up in the stirring atmosphere of the performance.

When Thespis made the daring leap from narration to impersonation, he changed the manner of presentation from *recitation* to *enactment*. Before Thespis, when Greek rhapsodists recited stories of legendary heroes, their performance was in the form of narration. With Thespis, the performer *became* the character. He lost his own identity and became another person. It was no longer Thespis dancing—it was the god. Theatrical performance ever since has created the illusion of imaginary characters in action. Thespis' innovation had a profound effect on the Chorus, too, because when the hero appeared in the flesh, the Chorus was compelled to respond to him in a new way. Its lamentations were not for some remote figure in the dim past, but for a living character, suffering before its eyes. In essence, the Chorus became actors, too. Although the individual members did not become distinct individuals, they did assume roles of elders, handmaidens, warriors, suppliants, and so on; and they responded and reacted as actors involved in the fate of the hero.

So it may have been with Thespis in ancient Greece—Thespis, who is thought to have been the first actor. After he perfected his art and wrote plays to suit his innovation, he took his show to Athens, where he quickly won approval and the flattery of imitation. Others followed his example; and the ruler, Pisistratus, was so impressed by "tragedies," as they now came to be called, that he set up contests in them in 534 B.C. as a part of the City Dionysia, a festival in homage to Dionysus, god of wine, vegetation, and fertility. Most appropriately, Thespis was the first to win the prize.

AN EASTER TROPE

Move ahead to the tenth century at Winchester, England. It is Easter morning and the cathedral is filled with worshipers. As the Mass begins, the faithful notice that something different has been added. A tomb has been placed before the altar

At a performance of the Easter trope in a church, the three Marys meet the angels and discover the empty tomb.

steps, but it is open. All at once, from the side of the altar, two figures appear—angels, so their folded wings seem to say. Next come three women down the aisle, carrying cloths and ointments. These must be the three Marys. As they near the tomb, one of the angels steps forward, puts up a restraining hand, and speaks:

First Angel: Whom do you seek in the tomb, worshipers of Christ?

The Women: Jesus of Nazareth who was crucified, O dweller of Heaven.

Angel: He is not here, he has risen as he foretold; go announce that he has risen, saying:

The Women: Hallelujah! The Lord has risen today, a brave lion, Christ the son of God.

First Angel: *(Pointing to the tomb)* Come and see the place where the Lord was laid, hallelujah! hallelujah!

Second Angel: Go quickly and tell the disciples that the Lord has risen, hallelujah!

Women: *(Singing in unison with shouts of joy)* The Lord was hung upon the cross for us, has risen from the tomb, hallelujah![2]

Now the congregation joins in singing "Hallelujah, hallelujah, He is risen." This little trope, known as *Quem Quaeritis* ("Whom do you seek?"), the oldest fragment of liturgical drama, shows how the biblical tale came alive: The word became flesh. Salvation is based on victory over death, and one of the strongest discoveries of the gospel is the discovery of the empty tomb. So on Easter morning, when the three Marys approach the tomb to anoint the body, their hearts are heavy after the agony of the Crucifixion. At the sight of the angels, they might at first be apprehensive, but when they hear the good news and see the evidence, sorrow is turned to joy. The discovery brings a reversal that shows the change of fate for the hero.

In the medieval church, the clergy's objective was to convey to their flocks the message of salvation; but since most of the people were illiterate and services were conducted in Latin, the impact of the worship service left something to be desired. Attempts were made to present graphic representations of the gospel in mosaics, sculptures, and stained glass windows. The introduction of enacted material into the Mass was an extension of the effort to make the biblical story more compelling.

The dramatic action of the tropes in medieval times led to the evolution of full-scale theatrical pieces, until some cycle plays required three days for performances and included dozens of incidents and characters. As liturgical plays grew more complex and secular, medieval drama broke away from the church and developed a remarkably flexible style of playwriting and staging, which was to profoundly influence the nature of English Renaissance theater.

These two instances illustrate the beginnings of theater in the Western world. When Thespis made the daring leap from narration to impersonation, he changed the *manner* of presentation from recitation to enactment. Before Thespis, when Greek rhapsodists recited stories of legendary heroes, primarily from Homer, their performance consisted of description and narration. With Thespis, the performer became the character; he assumed a complete identity. The effect was to create dramatic action that seemed to be happening here and now. Theatrical performance ever since has had the quality of an ongoing experience. Similarly, when the angels and the three Marys acted out the discovery at the tomb, the incident came to life before the eyes of the worshipers. The event was given immediacy by dramatic action.

HAMLET'S "MOUSETRAP"

Thus far we have seen elementary examples of dramatic action. Now let us turn to a more complicated situation, in which Hamlet tried his hand at playwriting. Hamlet is grieved by the sudden death of his father and the hasty marriage of his mother to his uncle, Claudius. Early in the play, Hamlet confronts his father's

Sir John Gilbert's drawing of "The Mousetrap" at the moment when Claudius reveals his guilt in poisoning the King to Hamlet.

ghost, who tells him that he has been murdered by Claudius. The dead king gives Hamlet the burden of avenging his murder. For a time Hamlet delays, not altogether sure of the new king's guilt. So when the traveling players arrive to perform at court, Hamlet persuades them to play *The Murder of Gonzago,* to which he adds "a dozen or sixteen lines" of his own. This interjection, which he calls "The Mousetrap," shows a reenactment of the murder of King Hamlet by pouring poison into his ears. Hamlet devises this scene to see whether or not Claudius is actually guilty of murder. "The play's the thing/Wherein I'll catch the conscience of the King."

At the performance before the court, Hamlet stations himself so that he can see Claudius' face. Here then is a dramatic action performed to produce a very specific effect on one member of the audience.

The play begins with a dumb show in which the poisoning is enacted, but Claudius does not respond. Then Lucianus recites the lines that Hamlet wrote:

Lucianus: Thoughts black, hand apt, drugs fit, and time agreeing,
Confederate season, else no creative seeing,
Thou mixture of rank, of midnight weeds collected,
With Hecate's ban thrice blasted, thrice infected,

Thy natural magic and dire property
On wholesome life usurps immediately.

(Pours the poison in his ears)[3]

At this action, King Claudius blanches, rises, and flees from the room. Hamlet's play has produced the desired effect. The bait was taken. The trap was sprung.

"The Mousetrap" is a major advance over *Quem Quaeritis*. Both are discovery scenes, but the medieval trope is relatively passive, for we do not see the climactic moment when Jesus breaks the seal and emerges from the tomb. Instead, we are presented with the circumstantial evidence of his departure.

In *Hamlet,* the discovery is a double one: Claudius' murder of King Hamlet is apparent from his guilty reaction to the simulated poisoning. He discovers that his crime is known, which means that he must take action against the prince. Hamlet also discovers what he needed to know. The ghost of his father was an honest one; his Uncle Claudius did indeed commit murder. The revelation of Claudius' guilt culminates the rising tension that preceded it. The audience, as well as Hamlet, is in on the psychological ambush of Claudius, and once the discovery is made, the emotional momentum surges forward toward the next action.

Hamlet's "Mousetrap" is a good example of the dramatic method. A sequence of words and actions is created to be performed to evoke a response, namely, that the King reveals his connection with the murder of Claudius.

DRAMATIC ACTION

In its simplest form, *action* refers to the physical movement of the play: the entrances and exits; the stage business of the characters; the larger movements of the ensemble; the quarrels, love scenes, reunions, and partings—all the overt action essential for the plot. Like every other element of the play, the dramatist includes this kind of action because it is significant and pertinent.

The year 1989 was an extraordinary one because of the astonishing dramatic events in the world: the confrontation of students and the military in Tiananmen Square, the rallies and protests in the name of freedom in Prague and Budapest, and the tearing down of the Berlin Wall. Like the action in a good play, these happenings were vivid, exciting, and charged with emotion. Moreover, the actions were significant, because they had meaning. Symbolically, the actions were evidence of deep-seated frustrations and a hunger for freedom and opportunity.

The playwright may use a strong action to set the plot in motion. Charles Fuller began his Pulitzer Prize-winning play, *A Soldier's Play*, with a violent action, which becomes the focus of attention for all that follows.

The scene is at Fort Neal, Louisiana, in 1944.

(As the play opens, the stage is black. In the background, rising in volume, we hear the song "Don't Sit Under the Apple Tree," sung by the Andrews Sisters. Quite

Cyrano de Bergerac is a romantic play filled with dynamic action and sword play. *(Directed by James Edmondson, Oregon Shakespeare Festival Theater)*

suddenly, in a sharp though narrow beam of light, in limbo, Tech/Sergeant Vernon C. Waters, a well-built, light-brown-skinned man in a World War II winter army uniform, is seen down on all fours. He is stinking drunk, trying to stand and mumbling to himself.)

Waters: *(Repeating)* They'll still hate you! They still hate you. . . . They still hate you!

(Waters is laughing as suddenly someone steps into the light. We never see this person. He is holding a .45 caliber pistol. He lifts it swiftly and ominously toward Water's head and fires. Waters is knocked over backward. He is dead. The music has stopped and there is a strong silence onstage.)

Voice: Let's go!

(The man with the gun takes a step, then stops. He points the gun at Waters again and fires a second time. There is another silence as limbo is plunged into darkness, and the barracks is just as quickly lit.)[4]

From this initial action, the play is developed as an investigation of the murder, which turns out to have more to do with the character of the victim than

In *The Caucasian Chalk Circle,*
**Grusha's escape generates suspense
and involvement despite Brecht's
wish to avoid emotional attachment.**
*(Directed by Theodore Hatlen,
University of California, Santa Barbara)*

with finding the guilty party. *A Soldier's Play* is more than a whodunit; Fuller has written a biting exploration of racial tensions among blacks and between blacks and whites.

Although Bertolt Brecht, the remarkable creator of the "epic theater," denied any interest in evoking an emotional response, many of the actions in his plays, which reveal the nature of his characters, also arouse feeling.

In *The Caucasian Chalk Circle,* Grusha, a kitchen maid, rescues the governor's abandoned child during a rebellion, after the governor has been slain and his head impaled on a lance before the palace gates. Everyone leaves except Grusha and the child. She tries to tear herself away.

The Story Teller:

(She walks a few steps toward the child and bends over it.)

. . . she went back for one more look at the child.
Only to sit with him for a moment or two,
Only till someone should come,
Its mother, perhaps, or anyone else.

(Leaning on a trunk, she sits facing the child.)

Mark Antony's famous oration over the dead body of Julius Caesar is an example of speech as action. Notice the emotional involvement of the mob in this production by the Duke of Saxe Meiningen's company, which toured European countries.

    Only till she would have to leave, for the danger was too great,
The city was full of flame and crying.

(The light grows dimmer, as though evening and night were coming on.)

    Terrible is the seductive power of goodness!

(Grusha now settles down to watch over the child through the night. . . .)

    A long time she sat with the child
Till evening came, till night came, till dawn came.
Too long she sat, too long she saw
The soft breathing, the little fists,
Till toward morning the temptation grew too strong
And she rose, and bent down and, sighing, took the child
And carried it off.

(She does what the Story Teller says as he describes it.)[5]

    Brecht shows his audience that even waiting is an action. Samuel Beckett, of course, built an entire play on waiting in his *Waiting for Godot.* He makes the point that the two lonely tramps are waiting because there is no place for them to go. The meaning comes from *inaction,* from the excruciatingly painful ordeal of two lost souls, with no resources of their own, trying to ignite a spark of faith in the empty darkness.

Since plays are brought to their completed form by directors, actors, and designers, playwrights are at the mercy of those who interpret their work, and although their text and directions may be faithfully followed, playwrights cannot possibly control the production of their plays, even if they direct them themselves. Actors bring the text to life, and their legitimate contribution to their performance is their way of speaking, moving, and reacting, as they (and the director) interpret the play. The actors enter, walk, sit, argue, make love, eat, drink, and exit—and all these movements reflect the performer's way of responding to the playwright's text. Indeed, the *manner* in which the actors perform is their creative contribution to the production—the legitimate and necessary extension of the playwright's script in theatrical terms. Thus, the physical action of the play is a combination of the dramatist's original creation and the enrichment of the actors' and director's interpretation.

Speech itself is a form of action. It can be a way of doing, of creating tension and momentum to move the play forward. Implicit in most dramatic dialogue is an underlying pattern of action as a character strives for a goal, seeks to influence the behavior of others, searches for the meaning of his or her experience, or becomes embroiled in a vigorous clash of wills. Good dramatic dialogue is action.

Mark Antony, in his famous speech over the slain body of Julius Caesar, stirs the mob to action with the following words—notice the action implied in Shakespeare's dialogue:

Antony: You will compel me then to read the will?
          Then make a ring about the corpse of Caesar,
          And let me show you him that made the will.
          Shall I descend? and will you give me leave?

Citizens: Come down.

Second Citizen: Descend.

Third Citizen: You shall have leave.

Fourth Citizen: A ring; stand round.

First Citizen: Stand from the hearse; stand from the body.

Second Citizen: Room for Antony; most noble Antony.

Antony: Nay, press not so upon me; stand far off.

Citizens: Stand back! room! bear back!

Antony: If you have tears, prepare to shed them now.
          You all do know this mantle; I remember
          The first time ever Caesar put it on;

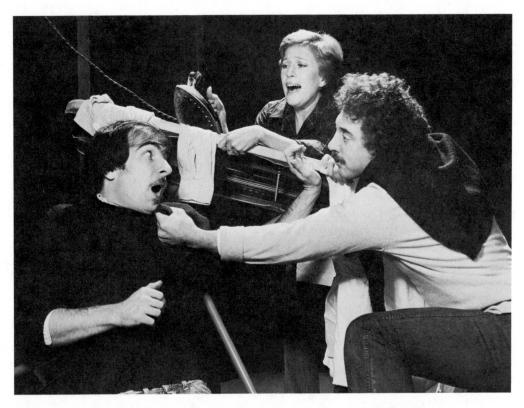

In John Osborne's pivotal play *Look Back in Anger,* a bit of friendly horseplay turns sour when Alison burns herself. *(Cleveland Play House)*

'Twas on a summer's evening, in his tent,
That he overcame the Nervii.
Look! in this place ran Cassius' dagger through:
See what a rent the envious Casca made;
Through this the well-beloved Brutus stabb'd;
And as he pluck'd his cursed steel away
Mark how the blood of Caesar follow'd it,
As rushing out of doors, to be resolv'd
If Brutus so unkindly knock'd or no;
For Brutus, as you know, was Caesar's angel;
Judge, O you gods! how dearly Caesar lov'd him.
This was the most unkindest cut of all;
For when the noble Caesar saw him stab,
Ingratitude more strong than traitor's arms,
Quite vanquish'd him: then burst his mighty heart;[6]

John Osborne's *Look Back in Anger* (1956) was a pivotal play in postwar British theater because of its scathing attack on class distinctions and social inertia in general. Jimmy Porter, the protagonist, was the first of the "angry young men" who brought about sweeping changes in playwriting, acting, and production. As the play opens, Jimmy and his friend Cliff are reading the Sunday paper, while Jimmy's wife, Alison, is ironing. Jimmy, who castigates everyone and everything, turns his attention to Alison in this verbal assault, which nearly has the effect of physical blows:

Alison: Really, Jimmy, you're like a child.

Jimmy: Don't try and patronize me. *(Turning to Cliff)* She's so clumsy. I watch for her to do the same things every night. The way she jumps on the bed, as if she were stamping on someone's face, and draws the curtains back with a great clatter, in that casually destructive way of hers. It's like someone launching a battleship. Have you ever noticed how noisy women are? *(Crosses below chairs to L. C.)* Have you? The way they kick the floor about, simply walking over it? Or have you watched them sitting at their dressing tables, dropping their weapons and banging down their bits of boxes and brushes and lipsticks?

(He faces her dressing table.)

I've watched her doing it night after night. When you see a woman in front of her bedroom mirror, you realise what a refined sort of a butcher she is. *(Turns in)* Did you ever see some dirty old Arab, sticking his fingers into some mess of lamb fat and gristle? Well, she's just like that. Thank God they don't have many women surgeons! Those primitive hands would have your guts out in no time. Flip! Out it comes, like the powder out of its box. Flop! Back it goes, like the powder puff on the table.

Cliff: *(Grimacing cheerfully)* Ugh! Stop it!

Jimmy: *(Moving upstage)* She'd drop your guts like hair clips and fluff all over the floor. You've got to be fundamentally insensitive to be as noisy and as clumsy as that.[7]

Jimmy's dialogue reveals the deep, smoldering rage that animates him.

The total play may be regarded as an action, or perhaps a "system of actions," to use Aristotle's term—an organic whole with nothing missing or irrelevant, a cohesive beginning, middle, and end. Until recent years, such unity was considered essential for structuring a play. And although an orderly progression of incidents no longer describes the form of many current plays, the need for action, for a dynamic quality to the shaping of material, is still fundamental to playwriting.

Playwrights create organized patterns of words and movement. Although initially they set down the play in written terms, what they actually produce is a barrage of sensory stimuli—concrete, objective signals that can come to life in the theater. The audience can respond only to what it sees and hears in performance. And what it sees and hears are actions.

THEATER AS AN ART

1. Theater is *mimetic—representational.* It imitates people and actions from life. The primary source material is human experience. Painting and sculpture may represent life in portraits, landscapes, and figures of people and animals, but it may also be completely abstract, with no direct reference to observed experience. Although experimentalists in the theater have attempted at times to deviate from recognizable characters and situations, in general the theater takes its cue from life.

2. Theater is *temporal* and *transient,* like music. The audience gets the impression that what is happening on stage is happening now. Dramatic action is in the present tense. The stage directions always read: Willy, or Nora, *enters*— never *entered.* As a result of its ephemeral quality, production in the theater is limited in time. And it is never the same twice. The visual arts have no connection with passing time. They are fixed and stationary.

3. Like music, the theater is *interpretive.* Between the composer and the listener there are musicians. Between the playwright and the spectator, there are a director, actors, and designers. The work of a painter or sculptor is seen in its original state by the viewer without an interpreter. The poet's work may be read directly. Because dramatic art requires the contribution of so many interpreters, the original conception of the playwright may be distorted or enhanced by varied interpretations.

4. The theater is a *collaborative effort* that is incomplete until there is a synthesis of text, performance, and audience response. The poet and visual artist work alone. Dramatic art places a premium on the cooperation of all elements of the production, plus the receptivity of a living audience.

5. Theater art is *communal.* It grew out of a public celebration as a shared experience. Music, poetry, and the visual arts may be enjoyed in isolation, but dramatic art is incomplete without the interrelationship of the play in performance before an audience.

Because of these five characteristics, the theater is a complex and expensive art that demands enormous individual talents, plus the ability to work together.

THEATRICAL CONVENTIONS

Theatrical production, like all forms of art, is conventionalized. That is, there are certain common agreements between spectator and theater worker concerning the manner of creation and production—certain "ground rules" that determine how the game is to be played. In easel painting, there is the convention that colored pigments are applied to a flat surface within a regular framework. Music is a conventionalized combination of sounds and rhythms, which make almost no pretense of imitating nature. Spectators, as they enter the theater, become a partner to conventions governing time, space, and the manner of playing.

The conventions of realistic production that dominated the theater during the latter part of the nineteenth century and for much of the twentieth attempted to foster the illusion of actuality through lifelike representation of characters and setting. There was tacit agreement that performer and spectator would remain separate from one another. The separation was facilitated by the darkened auditorium and the lighted stage and by the architectural features of the raised stage, which could be closed off by a curtain and the proscenium arch. There was also a psychological barrier known as the "fourth wall," a convention in which the actors pretended that the audience did not exist and avoided direct communication across the footlights. Dramatic structure was usually linear and tied to a story line. Scenery was designed to give the illusion of a genuine environment, with practical doors and windows and properties and furniture that seemed a part of real life. Actually, there was a good deal of license in the arrangement of furniture and exits and entrances so that the setting would "open out" to the audience and the actors could be readily heard and seen.

Artistic conventions are susceptible to change. Just as we had remarkable innovations in painting and music in the twentieth century, we have had rebellion in theatrical conventions. Many theater workers have rejected the limitations of the proscenium arch and are finding ways, such as the thrust or arena stages, to bring the spectator and the performer into a closer relationship. More recently, performances are given in "found spaces," such as warehouses, garages, store buildings, and street corners, abandoning conventional theaters altogether. Scenery has become frankly theatrical instead of illusionistic. As an example of this tendency, a fragment of a wall or a skeletal framework picked out of the darkness by light serves as a setting, which a generation ago would have required a complete interior with three walls, a ceiling, and a room full of furniture. Playwrights have rejected the conventions of realism in an effort to gain more freedom. Acting is often quite stylized; the separation between spectator and performer has broken down. Indeed, in some instances, the theater worker actively seeks to involve the audience in the action. Modern theatergoers are no longer sure whether the performance will remain onstage or end up in their lap. Nor does the play necessarily have a well-defined plot, or even clear language and sharp delineation of character.

Fashions in theatrical conventions have differed from time to time, and to understand the drama of any period, it is essential to know the conventions that influenced the production. In the Greek theater, for example, only three speaking characters appeared at one time; there was little or no violence onstage; actors wore masks, special footgear, and headpieces; the plays were written in verse, dramatizing ancient legends and myths and were presented usually in a single, permanent setting, with a simple story that occurred in a short space of time; and a Chorus of twelve or fifteen members was usually visible throughout the performance.

In the Elizabethan theater, as in the Greek, all roles were played by male actors in an outdoor theater in the daytime, with little or no illusionistic scenery. The plays, written in verse, were quite different in form and content from Greek drama. The play usually was a complicated one, involving several plot lines; comedy material was mixed with serious, highborn characters with low; and the playwright ransacked history and literature for material that would tell an exciting story. The plays were performed by professional actors in theaters whose dimensions and arrangement placed the actor in close proximity to the spectator and allowed the subtleties of the language to be exploited. The convention of the large, unlocalized platform gave the dramatist a great deal of freedom in staging an animated and complicated narrative.

In each age, theater conventions have varied according to the influences of the playwrights, actors, audiences, and physical theaters; the conventions in turn have affected all elements of the drama. It is essential to recognize these conventions in evaluating any drama because of their pressure in shaping the play and its production.

It is unfortunate that most of us are initially exposed to the arts in a secondhand way. Before we visit an important museum, we see reproductions of paintings. Before we attend a concert of a first-rate orchestra, we listen to recordings. Before we go to an excellent theatrical production, we see films and television, or perhaps we read the script of a play.

Although motion pictures and television shows can be genuinely entertaining and informative, they are not the same as spoken drama, played before an audience of live actors in a theater. A fine film offers exceptional opportunities for the full play of creative imagination, but the names of film writers are scarcely known to us, and few of us can recall a single line of dialogue—unless the script was based on a good play. Film has its own merits, but it is not the same as live theater.

Television, which relies heavily on film, is a marvelous means of showing us our world. It has a remarkable capacity for bringing us news, almost instantaneously, into the intimacy of our own living rooms. On the other hand, the medium suffers from the enormous pressure of becoming a device for producing a standardized, commercial product, aimed at what the sponsors consider the widest possible market.

Although reading a play can be a rewarding experience, it is like trying to make a journey by studying a map, or like looking at a stuffed animal instead of going on a safari. Experiencing a play has a special quality to it because of the "circular response" that is built up in performance. The actors stimulate the audience who, in turn, stimulate the performers, and a spell is woven between the two. This response is at the root of the power that makes theater a special kind of experience. And it is all made possible by your special ability to make imaginary connections.

Responding to a play is an *active* process, a fascinating exploration. You are invited to participate with such sensitivity and imagination as you possess. You will need to respond and make judgments from a welter of words, signals, and actions that are constantly in flux; and you must keep track of the action, as the eye follows a moving object. You are called on to respond to your fellow human beings—to their follies, problems, and aspirations—when they are caught up in the most telling moments of their lives. As you see and hear the action onstage, you are challenged to search out the meanings behind the characters' actions and words. Theatergoing is an opportunity to come to terms with life.

PLAYS TO READ AND SEE

F = Film Available; V = Videotape available

F	V	Arthur Miller, *Death of a Salesman*
F	V	William Shakespeare, *Hamlet* (Olivier/Williamson)
F	V	*Julius Caesar* (Brando)
F	V	John Osborne, *Look Back in Anger*
F	V	Charles Fuller, *A Soldier's Play* (*A Soldier's Story*)

BIBLIOGRAPHY

FERGUSSON, FRANCIS. *The Idea of a Theater*. Princeton, N.J.: Princeton University Press, 1949.

GASSNER, JOHN, and RALPH G. ALLEN. *Theater and Drama in the Making*, 2 vols. Boston: Houghton Mifflin, 1964.

NAGLER, ALOIS M. *Source Book in Theatrical History*. New York: Dover Publications, 1952.

NICOLL, ALLARDYCE. *The Development of the Theater*. New York: Harcourt Brace Jovanovich, 1966.

ROWE, KENNETH THORPE. *The Theater in Your Head*. New York: Funk & Wagnalls, 1960.

STYAN, J. L. *The Dramatic Experience*. Cambridge: Cambridge University Press, 1965.

WILLIAMS, RAYMOND. *Drama in Performance*. London: F. Muller, 1954.

NOTES

1. Arthur Miller, *Death of a Salesman* (New York: Viking Press, 1949). Copyright © 1949; renewed © 1977 by Arthur Miller. Used by permission of Viking Penguin, Inc., a division of Penguin Books USA, Inc.

2. *Quem Quaeritis*, 10th century manuscript in Winchester Cathedral.

3. William Shakespeare, *Hamlet*, Act III, Scene 2.

4. Charles Fuller, *A Soldier's Play* (New York: Hill and Wang, 1981). Copyright © 1981 by Charles Fuller. Reprinted by permission of Hill and Wang, a division of Farrar, Straus and Giroux, Inc.

5. Bertolt Brecht, *The Caucasian Chalk Circle*, trans. Eric Bentley and Maja Apelman (New York: Grove Press, 1947). Copyright © 1947 by University of Minnesota Press.

6. William Shakespeare, *Julius Caesar*, Act III, Scene 2.

7. John Osborne, *Look Back in Anger* (Chicago: Dramatic Publishing Company, 1959). Copyright © 1957 by S. G. Phillips. Reprinted by permission of S. G. Phillips, Inc.

two
The Play
and Its Parts

Agamemnon (458 B.C.), by the first great tragic writer, Aeschylus, tells the story of the homecoming of the triumphant hero and his murder by his wife, Clytemnestra. Here she feigns a warm welcome for her husband and his concubine, Cassandra.

Drama is a lively and complicated creature. It may change its spots while you look at it, or it may vanish behind protective camouflage. Penning it up behind fences of verbal definition does not really give us a good notion of its true character. One may stuff it and mount it with great skill, but the inanimate form does not reveal the élan so essential to its behavior in the natural habitat of the theater.

Perhaps we may avoid a verbal assault and arrive at a sense of the nature of drama by indirection—through description, example, and an examination of its parts and how they work.

Since a play comes alive only in the theater, it must be *compact.* The performance is restricted to a relatively small number of people, played by a limited cast in a moderate number of locales in a short space of time. There have been a number of ingenious ways of coping with these restrictions. Peter Brooks's *Mahabarata,* a condensation from an immense Sanskrit fable, used two dozen actors who played a variety of characters in many areas on an open stage, in a performance that ran for nine hours. (Incidentally, tickets cost $96.00!). The Steppenwolf Theater Company of Chicago managed to put together a cohesive stage version of Steinbeck's novel *The Grapes of Wrath,* and the Royal Shakespeare Company's long production of Dickens's *Nicholas Nickleby* was very effective in the theater, but these are the exceptions to the generally followed strictures that affect theatrical production.

The Greeks usually confined the action of their plays to a single locale, but the Elizabethans moved about freely, without benefit of stage scenery. Modern innovators use an "open stage" (a stage without scenery or with a setting that can be used arbitrarily to represent any locale). Very often, the open stage suggests the environment of the action through changes in costumes, stage properties, or projections. Despite these attempts to achieve a more flexible stage, every theater worker must eventually come to terms with the inherent physical restrictions of the theater, as compared to the freedom of the novelist or of the film script writer.

The initial form of drama is almost always written. The playwright is usually an individual, although two or more writers may collaborate on a work. In Medieval times, individual segments of cycle plays were put together for a production that might last for three days. Experimental pieces in the present-day theater have been improvised or written as a group effort. In general, however, a play is the work of a solitary playwright.

If you glance at the script of a play, you will notice that it consists mostly of lines of dialogue, with minimal stage directions by the playwright. The hand of the writer is not laid on in detailed descriptions of the characters' inner minds. The script itself is incomplete, awaiting the contributions and creative efforts of the performers and the production staff.

Aristotle, in the fourth century B.C., was the first to write about dramatic criticism. Although he lived a century after the golden age of Greek drama and some of his views may seem arbitrary, his *Poetics* is the fountainhead of critical theory, and one cannot discuss the subject very long without referring to him. We will use some of Aristotle's ideas and terminology to discuss the elements of drama.

His analysis of tragedy listed these six parts, in order of importance:

1. Plot
2. Character
3. Thought
4. Diction
5. Music
6. Spectacle

We will follow this hierarchy as a convenient framework for discussion, bearing in mind that it is subject to endless controversy.

PLOT

Plot is the structural element of the play that gives the action its form. Plot is to the playwright what composition is to the painter and musician. Although most plays tell stories, the plot is not the narrative itself, but the *shape* of the action. Plot is made up of a series of incidents, selected and arranged in order, to produce an audience response.

Although Aristotle considered plot the most important element of drama, his priorities are often ignored. A playwright like Anton Chekhov was more interested in character; Bernard Shaw and Bertolt Brecht emphasized thought; high comedy exploits diction; and many musicals rely almost entirely on music and spectacle. But whatever priorities different playwrights observe, their work takes some kind of form, or plot.

Conflict

Most plots are built around *conflict*—actually, a series of conflicts. An individual is confronted by an opposing force, which demands action. Ferdinand Brunetière, nineteenth-century French critic, put it in these words: "Drama is the spectacle of a will striving toward a goal." In essence, the dramatic experience comes from witnessing the clash of two conflicting forces caught up in decisive action. The conflict may be that of an individual against the gods or society, his or her fellow creatures, or the self. In significant plays, the conflicts are played for high stakes, and the leading characters make strong commitments that give the action a sense of urgency. Through the process of striving for important goals, the characters reveal themselves. As we watch the protagonists, we become vicariously involved in their actions, and we find ourselves caught up in the charged emotional situation. Usually, an initial conflict sets off a chain reaction built on more conflicts, until a major climax is reached and there is a resolution. The immediacy of sharing the same room with the performers and the social facilitation of being caught up in the action with other spectators give the theater its special kind of appeal.

In August Wilson's *The Piano Lesson,* Willie tries to get the family piano away from his sister in order to assure his economic future.

In classical drama, conflicts are of immense importance. At stake are not only the lives of the protagonists, but the welfare of the state itself. Playwrights wrote about fundamental issues: What is the relation of the individual to the gods? To the state? To the preservation of his or her own integrity?

These are the conflicts in Sophocles' *Antigone* (442 B.C.) Antigone vainly tries to persuade her sister, Ismene, to defy King Creon's edict by burying the body of their slain rebel brother, Polyneices. Creon clashes with Antigone, who has been caught burying the body. She defies his edict on the grounds that she is fulfilling her sacred obligation. Haemon, in love with Antigone, pleads with Creon for her life, but Creon is adamant. Antigone and Creon argue their case. She acts from religious grounds; he insists on obedience to his rule. Ismene belatedly offers to share in the blame, but Antigone rejects her. The blind seer, Teiresias, attempts to dissuade Creon from his headstrong decision, but the king refuses to reconsider. The Chorus persuades Creon to release Antigone, but it is too late. The conflicts are resolved by the deaths of Antigone, Haemon, and Queen Eurydice.

This example follows the classic pattern of involving important characters in significant conflicts found in most Greek and Elizabethan drama. In the so-called contemporary drama of the last century, characters are engaged in conflicts with ordinary mortals or with society itself. Ibsen's play *A Doll's House* shows the young wife, Nora, struggling to find her identity in the face of her hidebound husband's opposition. In Tennessee Williams's *Streetcar Named Desire*, Stanley clashes with Blanche in his attempt to preserve his relationship with his wife, Stella. The plays of David Mamet dramatize the brutalizing force of greed in the marketplace. August Wilson dramatizes the plight of the blacks in urban conditions.

Not all plays follow an obvious conflict pattern. Playwrights with other fish to fry, such as the absurdists, rebelled against the conflict-centered play and instead wrote plays in which nothing much overt happens. Characters do not make choices, nor do they strive toward clear objectives. Such plays attempt to show a fragmented universe, without meaning or order, so no organic plot structure or emotional involvement is sought after. Our current dramatists no longer follow rigid patterns, but use all manner of plotting techniques. However, a play with strong conflicts is still popular at the box office.

In addition to conflicts, these plot devices are useful in analyzing a play:

A. Exposition
B. Discovery
C. Point of attack
D. Foreshadowing
E. Reversal
F. Climax
G. Denouement

Exposition

Exposition is a part of the process of discovery that appears at the first part of the play. The playwright's initial problem is to capture the attention of the audience by providing a series of clues, so that audience members can identify the characters and follow the action. Marsha Norman, whose 'night, Mother won the Pulitzer Prize in 1983, describes the challenge: "In plays, you have eight minutes at the beginning to let the audience know what's at stake, who this is about, and when they can go home."[1]

Sophocles' *Antigone* begins with an episode between Antigone and her sister, Ismene. In their first two speeches, they bring the audience into the problem by posing the question that faces the heroine: What shall we do about the king's edict that forbids us to bury our brother, Polyneices?

(Enter Antigone and Ismene)

Antigone: Ismene, my dear, my mother's child, my sister,
What part of Oedipus' sad legacy
Has Zeus not laid in full on us who live?
There is nothing bitter, nothing of disaster,
No shame, no humiliation I have not seen
In the number of your sufferings and mine.
And now what is this order which they say
Our leader has announced throughout the city?
Do you know? Have your heard? Or do I have to tell you

Ismene tries in vain to dissuade her sister, Antigone, from defying the King's edict not to bury the body of their slain brother. *(Greek National Theater)*

> That what has happened to our enemies
> Is threatening to fall upon our friends?

Ismene: I have heard no word of friends, Antigone,
>   To bring me comfort or to bring me pain
>   Since the time we two were robbed of our two brothers,
>   Dead in one day, and by each other's hand.
>   And now the Argive army overnight
>   Has disappeared, I am no nearer knowing
>   Whether my luck has changed for good or bad.[2]

While an exchange between two characters is often used in traditional plays, another common expository device is a monologue presented directly to the audience. In Thornton Wilder's *Our Town* (1938), the Stage Manager strolls out on the stage and begins describing the town and the time of the action. Another play that begins with a monologue is Lanford Wilson's *Talley's Folly.* The leading actor takes the spectators into his confidence:

Matt: (*Enters in front of the stage. Matt Friedman is forty-two, dark, and rather large. Warm and unhurried, he has a definite talent for mimicry. In his voice there is still a trace of a German-Jewish accent, of which he is probably unaware. He speaks to the audience.*)

Talley's Folly **is a romantic story dramatizing Talley's efforts to win his bride. The plot begins with a lengthy monologue in which Talley provides the necessary exposition and creates the light atmosphere for the action.** *(University of Kentucky)*

They tell me that we have ninety-seven minutes here tonight—without intermission. So if that means anything to anybody, if you think you'll need a drink of water or anything . . .

You know, a year ago, I drove Sally home from a dance, and while we were standing on the porch up at the house, we looked down to the river and saw this silver flying thing rise straight up and zip off. We came running down to the river, we thought the Japanese had landed some amazing new flying machine, but all we found was the boathouse here, and—uh, that was enough.[3]

Although a monologue can be an effective way of handling the exposition, the more normal practice is to keep the actors within the playing area, apparently ignoring the audience, as, for example, in the opening of *Death of a Salesman* (see Chapter 1, pp. 4–6). The function of exposition is to acquaint the spectator with the characters, their relationships, their backgrounds, and their environment.

Discovery

Most dramas involve a sequence of discoveries. In *Antigone*, we discover that the protagonist faces a decision between her religious duty and the king's edict. We discover that Ismene will not join her in her decision. The guard comes to King Creon, who discovers that the body has been buried. The king discovers that Antigone is guilty and is willing to accept the consequences. We discover that

Haemon is in love with Antigone and that his efforts to dissuade the king are futile. We discover the deaths of Antigone, Haemon, and Queen Eurydice. At the end, the king makes a discovery about himself as he kneels by the corpses of his wife and son.

Creon: Lead me away, I pray you; a rash and foolish man, who have slain thee, oh my son, unwittingly, and thee, too, my wife—unhappy that I am![4]

In the first chapter, we saw how the medieval trope *Quem Quaeritis* was built around the significant discovery of the empty tomb; in Hamlet's play-within-a-play, "The Mousetrap," the discovery of Claudius' guilt is a major turning point in the action. One of the most famous discovery scenes occurs in Molière's *Tartuffe*. The title character masquerades as a priest and worms his way into Orgon's household, scheming to steal not only Orgon's fortune, but also his wife, Elmire. She unmasks the impostor by getting her husband to hide under a table while she pretends to respond to Tartuffe's advances.

Another outstanding example of a discovery scene that combines action and dialogue occurs in Peter Shaffer's *Amadeus*, when Salieri first meets Mozart at the emperor's palace. Salieri, the court musician, has composed a "March of Welcome," which he plays as Mozart enters. It is banal and vague. A few moments later, as they are about to part, this exchange takes place:

Mozart: You're a good fellow, Salieri! And that's a jolly little thing you wrote for me.

Salieri: It was my pleasure.

Mozart: Let's see if I can remember it. May I?

Salieri: By all means. It's yours.

Mozart: *Grazie, Signore. (Mozart tosses the manuscript onto the lid of the pianoforte, where he cannot see it, sits at the instrument, and plays Salieri's "March of Welcome" perfectly, from memory—at first slowly, recalling it, but on the reprise of the tune, very much faster.)* The rest is just the same, isn't it? *(He finishes it with insolent speed.)*

Salieri: You have a remarkable memory.

Mozart: *(Delighted with himself)* Grazie ancora, Signore! *(He plays the opening seven bars again, but this time stops on the interval of the fourth, and sounds it again with displeasure.)* It doesn't really work, that fourth, does it? . . . Let's try the third above. . . . *(He does so—and smiles happily.)* Ah yes! . . . Good! *(He repeats the new interval, leading up to it smartly with the well-known military trumpet arpeggio, which characterizes the celebrated march from the* Marriage of Figaro, *"Non piu andrai." Then, using the interval—tentatively, delicately, one note at a time, in the treble—he steals into the famous tune itself. On and on he plays, improvising happily what is virtually the March we know now, laughing gleefully each time he comes to the amended interval of a third. Salieri watches him* *with an answering smile on his face. Mozart's playing grows more and more exhibitionistic, revealing to the audience the formidable virtuoso he is. The whole time, he himself remains totally oblivious to the offense he is giving. Finally, he finishes the March with a series of triumphant flourishes and chords. An ominous pause.)*

Salieri: *Scusate.* I must go.

Mozart: Really? *(Springing up and indicating the keyboard)* Why don't you try a variation?

Salieri: Thank you, but I must attend the Emperor.

Mozart: Ah.

Salieri: It was delightful to meet you.

Mozart: For me too! . . . And thanks for the march!

> *(Mozart picks up the manuscript from the top of the fortepiano and marches happily offstage. A slight pause. Salieri moves toward the audience. The lights go down around him.)*

Salieri: *(To audience)* Was it then—so early—that I began to have thoughts of murder?[5]

Salieri has made a momentous discovery—he has a gifted rival. This discovery

Queen Jocasta and Oedipus at the moment of discovery, when they learn that he has unknowingly killed his father and married his mother. *(Greek National Theater at Epidaurus)*

precipitates the action and leads Salieri to plan and execute Mozart's destruction.

Discovery is a form of action. Knowing can be the most significant thing that happens to a character. As we have seen in *Antigone*, Creon comes to a self-realization. Similarly, *Oedipus Rex* contains a series of discoveries that the hero makes about himself. When Oedipus knows the complete truth, the play is over and he is destroyed by what he learns. At the end of *King Lear*, Lear has gained knowledge that makes him a far wiser man than the rash ruler who made so many mistakes in judgment. As an audience, making these discoveries from the characters' words and actions, we learn the meaning of the play.

Point of Attack

The point of attack refers to that moment when the mechanism is set in motion—the first pitch is thrown, the football is kicked off, the first blow is landed, the battle is joined. Disequilibrium is created, resulting in a change that continues until a new equilibrium is established, usually at the end of the play.

In *Antigone*, the point of attack occurs in the first episode, when the protagonist announces her decision to defy the king by burying Polyneices.

> ***Antigone:*** I will do my part—and thine, if thou wilt not—to a brother. False to him I will never be found.[6]

The first complication and the point of attack occur when Romeo and Juliet fall in love with one another, despite their parents' enmity. *(Scenography by Joseph Svoboda, Prague National Theater)*

In *Hamlet,* the action is first set in motion when Hamlet confronts his father's ghost and learns of the murder. In *Amadeus,* the point of attack is in the scene just cited between Mozart and Salieri.

The point of attack caused by making an important commitment is used widely in modern drama as well. In the play *A Soldier's Story,* Captain Davenport has the obligation to find out who murdered the sergeant. Shirley Valentine determines to escape from her domestic prison and to find her identity. The Phantom falls in love with Christine. When the elderly, feisty Miss Daisy smashes her car in an accident, her son hires a black chauffeur over her strenuous objections.

The point of attack often occurs with the arrival of a person whose presence disrupts the situation. In *A Streetcar Named Desire,* Blanche comes to visit her sister and brother-in-law in New Orleans, and this threatens their marriage. In *The Visit,* Madame Zachanassian, once an outcast from her impoverished village but now a wealthy widow, returns to avenge her ill-treatment at the hands of her former lover. Petruchio arrives in Padua and determines to tame the shrew, Kate, and to make her his obedient wife. The point of attack precipitates the action.

Foreshadowing

Foreshadowing is the playwright's method of preparing for the action that is to follow. It makes the subsequent action credible, builds suspense and tension, and carries the momentum forward.

In the first episode of *Antigone,* both Ismene and Antigone fear disaster because of their unlucky parentage as daughters of Oedipus, and because of their conflict with King Creon.

Ismene: Alas, unhappy one! How I fear for thee![7]

Within the first thirty lines of *Hamlet,* the guards anticipate the return of "the dreaded sight" that has appeared twice before, thus foreshadowing the ghost's entrance. As we saw earlier in *Death of a Salesman,* playwright Miller establishes Willy's precarious condition immediately, and this prepares us for his ultimate self-destruction. In Wilson's play *The Piano Lesson,* Boy Willie begins the action with his decision to take away the family piano. Very early in *Steel Magnolias,* the diabetic Shelby, who is preparing for her wedding, suddenly goes into shock from taking too much insulin, thus setting up the rationale for her death later in the play. At the end of the scene with Mozart, Salieri foreshadows his rival's destruction.

Eugene O'Neill, one of the foremost American playwrights, begins his one-act *In the Zone* with dramatic action that is a good example of foreshadowing. The title refers to the fact that the ship is in the war zone and in danger of submarine attack.

Strindberg's *Miss Julie* dramatizes an encounter between Miss Julie and her father's manservant. He is about to chop off a bird's head, foreshadowing Julie's suicide.

Scene: *The seamen's forecastle. On the right above the bunks three or four portholes covered with black cloth can be seen. On the floor near the doorway is a pail with a tin dipper. A lantern in the middle of the floor, turned down very low, throws a dim light around the place. Five men, Scotty, Ivan, Swanson, Smitty, and Paul, are in their bunks apparently asleep. It is about ten minutes of twelve on a night in the fall of the year 1915.*

     Smitty turns slowly in his bunk and, leaning out over the side, looks from one to another of the men as if to assure himself that they are asleep. Then he climbs carefully out of his bunk and stands in the middle of the forecastle fully dressed, but in his stocking feet, glancing around him suspiciously. Reassured, he leans down and cautiously pulls out a suitcase from under the bunks in front of him.

     Just at this moment, Davis appears in the doorway, carrying a large steaming coffeepot in his hand. He stops short when he sees Smitty. A puzzled expression comes over his face, followed by one of suspicion, and he retreats farther back in the alleyway, where he can watch Smitty without being seen.

> *All the latter's movements indicate a fear of discovery. He takes out a small bunch of keys and unlocks the suitcase, making a slight noise as he does so. Scotty wakes up and peers at him over the side of the bunk. Smitty opens the suitcase and takes out a small black tin box, carefully places this under his mattress, shoves the suitcase back under the bunk, climbs into his bunk again, closes his eyes and begins to snore loudly.*[8]

Reversal

Many plays follow a pattern of *reversal,* in which the fortunes of the leading characters turn from good to bad or vice versa. King Creon, proud and powerful, is humbled and destroyed at the end. King Claudius, in *Hamlet,* goes from reigning monarch to an ignoble death. In Duerrenmatt's *The Visit,* the villagers rejoice when the wealthy widow Zachanassian returns because they expect to prosper; however, she destroys them by preying upon their greed when she sets a price on the head of her former lover.

Reversal is one of the most common comic devices, often showing a humble person attaining status, such as the woodchopper's becoming physician to the king in Molière's *The Doctor in Spite of Himself,* or the ne'er-do-well impostor's being mistaken for the inspector general by the mayor and other town officials in Gogol's brilliant satire. Another example is the Cockney flower girl in Shaw's *Pygmalion;* she is changed into a "lady of quality" by improving her speech and dressing in finery.

Climax

The climax culminates the course of action. It is "the maximum disturbance of the equilibrium," "the moment of most intense strain," "the point of highest emotional tension." Creon accuses Antigone of undermining his rule, and she insists upon fulfilling her obligation to the gods, even though it means death. The climax comes in Hamlet's "Mousetrap" when the king reveals his guilt during the simulated murder of King Hamlet. In *Quem Quaeritis,* the climax is the discovery of the empty tomb. Another strong climax is the showdown between Troy and his wife in August Wilson's Pulitzer Prize–winning play, *Fences.*

In Miller's *Death of a Salesman,* the strongest emotional scene comes when Biff forces his father, Willy, to face reality.

Willy: *(With hatred, threateningly)* The door of your life is wide open!

Biff: Pop! I'm a dime a dozen, and so are you!

Willy: *(Turning on him now in an uncontrolled outburst)* I am not a dime a dozen! I am Willy Loman, and you are Biff Loman! *Biff starts for Willy, but is blocked by Happy. In his fury, Biff seems on the verge of attacking his father.)*

Biff: I am not a leader of men, Willy, and neither are you. You were never anything but a hard-working drummer, who landed in the ashcan like all

Lee J. Cobb played the lead in the original production of *Death of a Salesman,* **which dramatized the conflicts between a father and his two sons.**

the rest of them! I'm a dollar an hour, Willy! I tried seven states and couldn't raise it. A buck an hour! Do you gather my meaning! I'm not bringing home any more, and you're going to stop waiting for me to bring them home!

Willy: *(Directly to Biff)* You vengeful, spiteful mutt! *(Biff breaks from Happy. Willy, in fright, starts up the stairs. Biff grabs him.)*

Biff: *(At the peak of his fury)* Pop, I'm nothing. I'm nothing, Pop. Can't you understand that? There's no spite in it any more. I'm just what I am, that's all. *(Biff's fury has spent itself, and he breaks down, sobbing, holding on to Willy, who dumbly fumbles for Biff's face.)*

Willy: *(Astonished)* What're you doing? What're you doing? *(To Linda)* Why is he crying?

Biff: *(Crying, broken)* Will you let me go, for Christ's sake? Will you take that phony dream and burn it before something happens?[9]

Most plays involve a series of climaxes growing out of the conflicts, and these keep the dramatic action surging forward.

Denouement

The denouement is the final resolution of the plot, literally the untying of the knot that the conflicts have formed. In tragedies, the protagonists preserve their integrity and achieve their spiritual goal, even though they suffer physical destruction. Antigone and Haemon are united in death, and Creon becomes a broken, chastened man. In *Hamlet*, the hero lies dead, along with the king, the queen, and Laertes, as Fortinbras enters to restore order to the kingdom. In romantic comedies, lovers are united, problems are solved, and misunderstandings are cleared up. In melodramas, the good are rewarded and the bad are punished. The denouement indicates the ultimate disposition of the major characters. Its function is to restore order and to unify and complete the cause of action.

The experimental playwright, who rejects traditional plotting, may leave the resolution ambiguous or incomplete. At the end of Beckett's *Waiting for Godot*, Vladimir and Estragon continue waiting for Godot. Harold Pinter's plays are noted for their vague and sinister atmosphere. Luigi Pirandello, one of the foremost dramatists of the twentieth century, engages his characters in intellectual chases and psychological sorties with no clear-cut guidelines. Most audiences, however, like to know the answers.

Generally, the denouement brings about a clear and ordered resolution. One of the most successful and poignant endings in recent years is the final bit of action in *Driving Miss Daisy*. When Hoke was first hired by Boolie to drive Boolie's elderly mother, she objected strenuously to the intrusion, but over a period of twenty years, the mismatched twosome came to know and respect one another. At the end, Daisy, now "fragile and diminished but still vital," is about to have her Thanksgiving dinner in a nursing home. She enters slowly with her walker and sits at the table.

(*Daisy dozes for a minute in her chair. Then she looks at Hoke.*)

Daisy: Boolie paying you still?

Hoke: Every week.

Daisy: How much?

Hoke: That between me an' him, Miz Daisy.

Daisy: Highway robbery. (*She closes her eyes again. Then opens them.*) How are you?

Hoke: Doin' the bes' I can.

Daisy: Me too.

Hoke: Well, thass all there is to it, then. (*He nods, smiles. Silence. He sees the piece of pie on the table.*) Looka here. You ain' eat yo' Thanksgiving pie. (*She tries to pick up her fork. Hoke takes the plate and fork from her.*) Lemme hep you wid this. (*He cuts a small piece of pie with the fork and gently feeds it to her. Then another as the lights fade slowly out. Curtain.*)[10]

This touching denouement in *Driving Miss Daisy* shows her, frail and elderly, in a convalescent home where Hoke visits her on Thanksgiving Day and feeds her a piece of pumpkin pie. *(George Street Playhouse, New Brunswick, New Jersey)*

CHARACTER

Aristotle, in his *Poetics*, regarded *character* as secondary to plot, thus beginning an argument that continues to this day. Actually, the controversy is a fruitless one, since plot and character are interrelated. Character is defined by what the character says and does. Plot is character in action.

Like other aspects of drama, characterization has varied with fashion. In Greek, Elizabethan, and Japanese drama, the roles of women were played by men. Medieval drama often made use of allegorical figures representing single attributes of character, such as Wisdom, Greed, or Gluttony. High tragedy has dealt primarily with men "as better than we are" and low comedy with men "as worse than we are." Medieval characters ranged from God to the Devil, from the purest saint to the most abject sinner. Some characters have been drawn on a heroic scale, masters of their fate, working out their destinies by their own resources; other characters have been treated as hapless victims of an unfortunate heredity and environment, incapable of taking action, defeated, frustrated, and resigned. Modern dramatists of a realistic or naturalistic persuasion have endeavored to create the illusion of complicated character by piling up a wealth of physical details, by capitalizing on the significant trifle, and by searching for the psychological meaning beneath the act. The expressionists have experimented with split personalities, or have effaced from characters all aspects of individuality, reducing them to X or Mr. Zero. Dramatic literature is filled with a wide variety of portraits.

Novelists can create characters by using a broad range of actions over many years and under many conditions. They can express directly the thoughts coursing through the heads of their creatures, and they have great freedom with time and space. In sharp contrast, playwrights' works are compressed in time and restricted in scope because they have only a short time to present them to an audience. Thus, playwrights must define and delineate characters by their words and actions, which reveal their inner lives. If a character is meant to portray a hero, his heroism must be established for the audience in word and action. Concrete signs are essential if the theatergoer is to believe in or identify with the character.

In the opening episode of *Antigone*, Sophocles reveals the characters and their basic differences in facing the threat of death if they bury their brother.

Antigone: Will you help this hand of mine to lift the dead?

Ismene: You mean to bury him? Against the law?

Antigone: Bury my brother? Yes—and bury yours,
If you will not. No one shall call me faithless.

Ismene: You would not dare, when Creon has forbidden it!

Antigone: He has no right to keep me from my own.[11]

Remember how Arthur Miller, in *Death of a Salesman*, gave us a sharp image of Willy by his entrance and first few lines? Tennessee Williams, in *A Streetcar Named Desire*, quickly reveals the characters of Stanley and Stella in their first appearance:

(*Two men come around the corner, Stanley Kowalski and Mitch. They are about twenty-eight or thirty years old, roughly dressed in blue denim work clothes. Stanley carries his bowling jacket and a red-stained package from the butcher's. They stop at the foot of the steps.*)

Stanley: (*Bellowing*) Hey there! Stella, baby! (*Stella comes out on the first floor landing, a gentle woman about twenty-five, and of a background obviously quite different from her husband's.*)

Stella: (*Mildly*) Don't holler at me like that. Hi, Mitch.

Stanley: Catch!

Stella: What?

Stanley: Meat! (*He heaves the package at her. She cries out in protest but manages to catch it; then she laughs breathlessly.*)[12]

During the last quarter of the nineteenth century, progress in scientific methods and psychology led playwrights to delineate characters with complicated inner lives and complex motivations, often concealed behind a façade of conventional behavior. Part of the appeal of such plays was the gradual revelation of the true character beneath the surface, such as occurs in the plays of Ibsen, Strindberg, and Chekhov. Many twentieth-century plays depend for their appeal on substantial characters who are psychologically complex, as in O'Neill's *Long Day's Journey into Night,* Tennessee Williams's *Streetcar Named Desire,* and Arthur Miller's *Death of a Salesman.*

Some contemporary writers and theorists now reject the psychological aspects of drama in favor of plays that emphasize philosophical or political context, subordinating the individual identity to the larger social scene. The characters may not be defined at all, and little attempt is made to create credible, complex people or to probe beneath the surface. Actors become agents of the action without revealing their inner life; their performance is more like that of dancers or musicians. In avant garde plays, actors may represent states of mind or one aspect of character, rather than a complete person. In innovative productions of the classics, one actor may play several parts, or the character may be entirely changed: Hamlet is played by a woman, Macbeth's witches become three punk teenagers, Peer Gynt is played by six different actors. Novels like *The Grapes of Wrath* and *Nicholas Nickleby* require most of the cast to play several roles. Peter Brooks's gargantuan production of *Mahabharata* involves a couple of dozen actors in a nine-hour performance. Larry Shues's *Wenceslas Square* dramatizes the story of a professor and a photographer on a visit to Prague, where they meet a variety of actors and journalists, all performed by just two actors who create instantaneous transformations. Albert Finney, in a recent London production of *Another Time,* plays the part of the father of a promising young pianist in Act I. In Act II, placed thirty-five years later, he appears as his son, now a middle-aged professional musician. The mainstream of drama, however, relies on credible characters who are recognizable human beings to whom we can relate.

Characterization may be delineated in several ways:

By appearance. The character's physical presence is an immediate stimulus to the spectator because it offers clues to his or her age, occupation, economic level, social status, health, disposition, and so on—all of which have been carefully considered by the director when casting, as well as by the costume and makeup designers. Often, the playwright prescribes a specific image.

The initial appearance of a major character is very important to many playwrights. In *The Phantom of the Opera,* the audience is told about the mysterious figure who haunts the opera house, and they hear him sing before he finally appears out of the darkness, magically seen through Christine's mirror in his stunning white mask. David Hwang's *M. Butterfly* caused a sensation on Broadway when he dramatized the true story of a French diplomat in Beijing who lived for years with his mistress, Soong Liling, a leading lady of the Chinese opera—who turned out to be a man! It is essential to the plot that Soong's first appearance as a woman be absolutely convincing—which it was, thanks to the superb performance of the female impersonator.

Giraudoux's bitter comedy *The Madwoman of Chaillot* shows how a pictur-esque woman combats and destroys the attempts of several businessmen who propose to drill for oil in the Rue de Chaillot near the Eiffel Tower. Giraudoux describes his heroine's first appearance:

> *At this point, the Madwoman enters. She is dressed in the grand fashion of 1885, a taffeta skirt with an immense train—which she has gathered up by means of a clothespin—ancient button shoes, and a hat in the style of Marie Antoinette. She wears a lorgnette on a chain, and an enormous cameo pin at her throat. In her hand she carries a small basket. She walks in with great dignity, extracts a dinner bell from the bosom of her dress, and rings it sharply. Irma appears.*

Countess: Are my bones ready, Irma?

Irma: There won't be much today, Countess. We had broilers. Can you wait? While the gentleman inside finishes eating?

Countess: And my gizzard?

Irma: I'll try to get it away from him.

Countess: If he eats my gizzard, save me the giblets. They will do for the tomcat that lives under the bridge. He likes a few giblets now and again.

Irma: Yes, Countess.

> *(Irma goes back into the cafe. The Countess takes a few steps and stops in front of the President's table. She examines him with undisguised disapproval.)*

The President: Waiter, ask that woman to move on.

Waiter: Sorry, sir. This is her cafe.[13]

By speech. The kind of language used by a person defines a character, as do his or her manner of speaking, voice quality, inflection pattern, pitch, rate, dialect, and general vitality. Most playwrights take great care to write dialogue that establishes character.

Shakespeare had a marvelous facility for writing speeches that produced memorable figures. One of his best known soliloquies opens *Richard III.* It not only delineates the character of one of the most celebrated villains of the theater, but it also foreshadows the actions and sets the play in motion.

> *(Enter Gloucester, later Richard III.)*
>
> Now is the winter of our discontent
> Made glorious summer by this sun of York;
> And all the clouds that lour'd upon our house
> In the deep bosom of the ocean buried. . . .
> Grim-visag'd war hath smooth'd his wrinkled front;
> And now, instead of mounting barbed steeds
> To fright the souls of fearful adversaries,

Laurence Olivier as Richard III at the Old Vic.
(Royal Shakespeare Company)

He capers nimbly in a lady's chamber
To the lascivious pleasing of a lute.
But I, that am not shap'd for sportive tricks,
Nor made to court an amorous looking-glass;
I, that am rudely stamp'd, and want love's majesty
To strut before a wanton ambling nymph;
I, that am curtail'd of this fair proportion,
Cheated of feature by dissembling nature,
Deform'd, unfinish'd, sent before my time
Into this breathing world, scarce half made up,
And that so lamely and unfashionable
That dogs bark at me as I halt by them;
Why, I, in this weak piping time of peace,
Have no delight to pass away the time,
Unless to see my shadow in the sun
And descant on mine own deformity;
And therefore, since I cannot prove a lover,
To entertain these fair well-spoken days
I am determined to prove a villain.[14]

August Wilson has a special ability to characterize by means of dialogue, often in monologues that are full of vivid images. In *Fences*, Troy describes how he was suffering a fever from pneumonia when Death came to him with a sickle in

August Wilson's *Fences* is based on strong conflicts, such as this one between Troy and his son Cory. *(Directed by Lloyd Richards, Yale Repertory Theater)*

his hand. Troy defied him and drove Death away. In Act II, after the death of an "outside woman" who died giving birth to Troy's child, the image of Death haunts him again:

Troy *(with a quiet rage that threatens to consume him):*   All right . . . Mr. Death. See now . . . I'm gonna tell you what I'm gonna do. I'm gonna take and build me a fence around this yard. See? I'm gonna build me a fence around what belongs to me. And then I want you to stay on the other side. See? You stay over there until you're ready for me. Then you come on. Bring your army. Bring your sickle. Bring your wrestling clothes. I ain't gonna fall down on my vigilance this time. You ain't gonna sneak up on me no more. When you ready for me . . . when the top of your list say Troy Maxson . . . that's when you come around here. You come up and knock on the front door. Ain't nobody else got nothing to do with this. This is between you and me. Man to man. You stay on the other side of that fence until you ready for me. Then you come up and knock on the front door. Any time you want. I'll be ready for you.[15]

By action. Behavior and body language offer clues to the understanding of character. We are apt to judge people by what they do, rather than by what they say. Peter Shaffer, in *Amadeus*, introduces Mozart to the audience in a startling fashion. The following action takes place in the Emperor's palace:

(Offstage, noises are heard.)

In *Amadeus,* playwright Peter Shaffer immediately characterizes the two leading players in a scene of comic action that surprises the audience's expectations about the musical genius, Mozart.

Constanze: *(Off)* Squeak! Squeak! Squeak!

> *(Constanze runs on from upstage: a pretty girl in her early twenties, full of high spirits. At this second she is pretending to be a mouse. She runs across the stage in her gay party dress, and hides under the fortepiano. Suddenly a small, pallid, large-eyed man in a showy wig and a showy set of clothes runs in after her and freezes—center—as a cat would freeze, hunting a mouse. This is Wolfgang Amadeus Mozart. As we get to know him through his next scenes, we discover several things about him: he is an extremely restless man; his hands and feet in almost continuous motion; his voice is light and high; and he is possessed of an unforgettable giggle—piercing and infantile.)*

Mozart: Miaouw.

Constanze: *(Betraying where she is)* Squeak!

Mozart: Miaouw! . . . Miaouw! . . . Miaouw!

> *(The composer drops on all fours and, wrinkling his face, begins spitting and stalking his prey. The mouse—giggling with excitement—breaks her cover and dashes across the floor. The cat pursues. Almost at the chair where Salieri sits*

concealed, the mouse turns at bay. The cat stalks her—nearer and nearer—in its knee breeches and elaborate coat.)

I'm going to pounce-pounce! I'm going to scrunch-munch! I'm going to chew-poo my little mouse-wouse! I'm going to tear her to bits with my paws-claws!

Constanze: No!

Mozart: Paws-claws—paws-claws—paws-claws! Oh! *(He falls on her. She screams.)*[16]

One of the most famous actions in Ibsen's *Hedda Gabler* occurs at the end of Act III, when the protagonist reveals her destructive, neurotic nature by burning a valuable manuscript—the product of Lovborg and his helper, Thea.

(Hedda listens for a moment at the door. Then she goes up to the writing table, takes out a packet of manuscript, peeps under the cover, draws a few of the sheets half out, and looks at them. Next she goes over and seats herself in the armchair beside the stove, with a packet in her lap. Presently, she opens the stove door, and then the packet.)

Hedda: *(Throws one of the quires into the fire and whispers to herself.)* Now I am burning your child, Thea! Burning it, curly-locks! *(Throwing more quires into the stove.)* Your child and Eilert Lovborg's. *(Throws the rest in.)* I am burning—I am burning your child.[17]

By the way others speak about him or her, or by the manner in which they react to a character. Sometimes the playwright uses comments about an absent character as a method of revealing the truth. For example, the true character behind the blustering, swaggering barker, Liliom, is indicated by Julie's line: "It is possible, dear, that someone may beat you, and beat you, and beat you—and not hurt you at all." Willy Loman in *Death of a Salesman* is a man who has never seen himself or his motivations accurately. His son Biff expresses the truth about Willy when he says, "He had the wrong dreams. All, all wrong. . . . The man didn't know who he was."

The playwright may deliberately mislead or perplex the spectator by having characters say ambiguous or controversial things. Pirandello delighted in making the point time and again in his plays that it is difficult, if not impossible, to really comprehend the character of another. Hence, his plays are filled with conflicting statements about the characters. In his *Right You Are If You Think You Are*, he dramatizes a series of incidents in which the leading characters tell conflicting stories about one another, so that the audience never knows the truth—thus illustrating the problem of separating illusion from reality.

The sharpness of a character's image is in part dependent on the structure of the drama. Plays written for a theater that permit most of the essential action to appear onstage give the playwright a greater opportunity to create more vivid and complex characters than plays that are confined to a minimum of action.

Hamlet clashes with Ophelia when he suspects that she is spying on him.
(Royal Shakespeare Company)

Antigone does not really have much dimension for us, since we see her only with two other speaking characters—Ismene and Creon—and her death is narrated, not seen on stage. This paucity of exposure was due to the conventions of the Greek theater, which limited the playwrights to three speaking characters, and the practice of keeping the locale of a play in a single place over a short space of time, with a simple plot. Shakespeare's theater, on the other hand, offered great freedom, so that in *Hamlet,* for example, we see the hero in scenes with the Ghost, Horatio, Polonius, the Court, Ophelia, the Players, Laertes, Gertrude, Claudius, and Rosencrantz and Guildenstern.

In most drama, the purpose of showing characters in action is to enlist our interest and involve our emotions. To accomplish this purpose, the dramatist creates characters with whom we have some kind of bond, through either temperament, condition, or destiny. If we do not connect with them, we are apt to remain passive and indifferent, and the action does not fulfill its function. Hence, it is important for us to *believe in* the characters. Sometimes, they leave us cold. Their motivations and sense of values seem incredible; they are confused and incomprehensible; they make no effort to decide their fate; they are too self-centered, or too shortsighted. On the other hand, good playwrights can kindle our interest and sympathy for all kinds of characters, if they give us understanding, particularly if these characters are well played by skillful performers.

Because a play is performed by actors and actresses, another dimension is added to characterization. Inevitably, the personal attributes of the performer influence the way in which the audience perceives the character. Indeed, some players give the effect of playing themselves over and over again as they become associated with a certain role or type of character. Very often, theatergoers are attracted to a play to see a well-known actor, because they like the personality of the performer, which remains constant no matter what the play is about.

THOUGHT

The third element cited by Aristotle is *thought,* the intellectual aspect of the play, as shown by the characters' speech and actions whenever they argue, decide, or reason. Thought is the rationale for behavior.

One does not go to the theater primarily for information. Plays are not objective debates, nor are they mere presentations of facts and logical arguments, leading to a clear decision. As in life itself, characters make decisions out of a network of feelings and thoughts. Like all forms of literature, good drama usually is meaningful. A play is a unified organization of an imaginative experience and insight, and while it provides emotional outlets, it also engages the mind. We go to the theater for delight and discovery. As Eric Bentley says, the effect of seeing a great play is "of a veil lifted, the scales falling from the eyes, in a word, something momentous exhibited—and said."

As we indicated earlier, a basic ingredient in the theater from the very beginning to the present day has been conflict—husband versus wife, children clashing with parents, lovers' quarrels, rebels against society. In dramatizing such collisions, the playwright has found it necessary to show both sides of the argument. Even in medieval drama, written specifically to show the rewards for following the straight and narrow path to salvation, the clergy were obliged for dramatic reasons to include the Devil as well as God, vices as well as virtues, sinners as well as saints. In most plays, the dramatist presents a variety of thoughts and views. Blanche's sensitivity is opposed by Stanley's brutality; Major Barbara's religious convictions are challenged by her father's capitalistic views as a munitions manufacturer; El Teatro Campesino of Luis Valdez shows Chicanos against Anglo growers and extortionists; the disillusioned war veteran in David Rabe's *Sticks and Bones* is shown in opposition to his family's determined efforts to resist his intrusion into their superficial lives. In recent plays, we have seen current issues dramatized in the theater: feminism in Wendy Wasserstein's Pulitzer Prize play of 1988, *The Heidi Chronicles;* greed in the economic jungle, which comes under attack in David Mamet's *Speed the Plow;* the status of black people in the plays of Athol Fugard and August Wilson. The rationale for conflicting points of view constitutes one aspect of thought in drama.

In addition to the varied views of individual characters, thought concerns a play's theme—a "golden text" that summarizes the moral and indicates the symbolic meaning of the play as a whole: "Love conquers all," "Murder will out," "Niceness pays." But drama does not always lend itself to such neat copybook maxims. A given play may convey a variety of interpretations to an audience. Most of Ibsen's contemporaries were profoundly shocked by Nora's decision in *A Doll's House* to leave her husband and children, although her action is entirely credible to most of us today. Some people regard Antigone as headstrong and foolish in openly defying Creon and thus deliberately choosing to die. In his notes while directing *A Streetcar Named Desire*, Elia Kazan clearly shows that he intended to express Williams's point of view: "If we don't watch out, the apes will take over." But in production, the impression conveyed to many spectators by the actors' performance was that Blanche threatened the Kowalski home and that Stanley's brutal treatment of her was justified.

The ideas of great drama have, of course, been sources of endless academic contention. What is the true interpretation of *Hamlet*? Is Shylock a comic or a tragic figure? Is the tragedy of *Antigone* really the tragedy of Creon? Varied versions of a play's meaning indicate that the dramatist has not been explicit in stating a theme. Many great plays have a depth or richness that makes them susceptible to all kinds of interpretations. One of the most interesting aspects of the contemporary theater is the astonishing variety of experimental revival productions of plays from the past. Throughout the year 1990, everywhere, classic plays took on new meanings because of the revolutions in central Europe. Plays classified as "absurd" have been found to be an accurate reflection of today's political and cultural ferment. Inevitably, individual readers and spectators are challenged to search their own minds and experiences in evaluating a play.

Whatever the purpose of the playwright, the action of significant drama is as meaningful as an experience of life itself. The choices that the characters make, their motivation and behavior, their dialogue and the subtext, and the sequence of action are rewarding subjects for investigation. The content of a play is a valid reflector of the time in which it was written. Current drama often mirrors the world in a vivid and compelling way, focusing on our life-styles, our shifting sense of values, our loss of philosophic roots, the plight of minorities, alienation, and our struggles for power, recognition, and security.

August Wilson defines his view of the thought element in his plays:

> All art is political. It serves a purpose. All of my plays are political, but I try not to make them dogmatic or polemical. Theater doesn't have to be agitprop. I hope my art serves the masses of blacks in America who are in desperate need of a solid and sure identity. I hope my plays make people understand that these are African people, that this is why they do what they do.[18]

Wilson's primary focus has been the creation of a cycle of plays chronicling the lives of black Americans in each decade of the century. *Joe Turner's Come and Gone*, set in a boarding house in 1911, is the story of a man looking for his estranged wife after years of forced labor on a southern farm. In the preface to this play, Wilson describes the social and political background of his characters:

It is August in Pittsburgh, 1911. The sun falls out of heaven like a stone. The fires of the steel mill rage with a combined sense of industry and progress. Barges loaded with coal and iron ore trudge up the river to the towns that dot the Monongahela and return with fresh, hard, gleaming steel. The city flexes its muscles. Men throw countless bridges across the rivers, lay roads and carve tunnels through the hills sprouting with houses. From the deep and the near South the sons and daughters of newly freed African slaves wander into the city. Isolated, cut off from memory, having forgotten the names of the gods and only guessing at their faces, they arrive dazed and stunned, their heart kicking in their chest with a song worth singing. They arrive carrying Bibles and guitars, their pockets lined with dust and fresh hope, marked men and women seeking to scrape from the narrow, crooked cobbles and the fiery blasts of the coke furnace a way of bludgeoning and shaping the malleable parts of themselves into a new identity as free men of definite and sincere worth. Foreigners in a strange land, they carry as part and parcel of their baggage a long line of separation and dispersement which informs their sensibilities and marks their conduct as they search for ways to reconnect, to reassemble, to give clear and luminous meaning to the song which is both a wail and a whelp of joy.[19]

Earlier we suggested that language can be a form of action, and while most playwrights combine words and movement, language by itself can be a dynamic force, as in the plays of George Bernard Shaw. In Lee Blessing's play *A Walk in the Woods*, the conflict between the Russian negotiator, Botvinnik, and his American counterpart, Honeyman, is conveyed behind the façade of words. The two delegates to Geneva, frustrated by the progress made at the conference table, take a series of walks in an attempt to resolve their differences. Here is an example of their verbal sparring, against a political background of the Russian rejection of an American arms reduction proposal:

Honeyman: Your government rejected our proposal, didn't they?

Botvinnik: Not exactly.

Honeyman: What do you mean?

Botvinnik: They didn't reject your proposal itself. They rejected what your President has turned the proposal into.

Honeyman: Which is?

Botvinnik: Which is—in their words—a cynical public-relations scheme.

Honeyman: It is not a cynical . . .

Botvinnik: It is. From the moment he announced it to the world.

Honeyman: He had to announce it.

Botvinnik: Why? When we had not agreed to it yet.

Honeyman: You never agree to anything! You accepted one small point, before our election, and since then—nothing, zero, no movement all winter. He couldn't wait any longer.

Botvinnik: You should have stopped him.

The conflict in Lee Blessing's *A Walk in the Woods* pits a Russian delegate against his American counterpart during a Geneva disarmament conference. The action is verbal. *(La Jolla Playhouse)*

Honeyman: I tried. I argued him out of going public on this three times in the past five months. You know that.

Botvinnik: You should have tried again.

Honeyman: I did. But I was running out of ammunition.

Botvinnik: So. In one speech he destroys all the work we have done. Good. Fine. Why not?

Honeyman: You were the ones who destroyed it. By delay.

Botvinnik: Delay does not destroy agreements. One can always renew efforts. But to announce the proposal . . .

Honeyman: He had the right.

Botvinnik: He bears the responsibility!

Honeyman: For what? For telling the world? Why's that so terrible?

Botvinnik: Don't be ridiculous.

Honeyman: No, tell me. Why is it so bad if the world knows what we're discussing?

Botvinnik: Because it makes us look like fools. If we accept your proposal now, what will the rest of the world say? "Ah, the Americans have finally thought of a clever plan. Thank God the unimaginative Russians have agreed."

Honeyman: The rest of the world, if they said anything, would say, "At last—two maniacs have had a moment of sanity."

Botvinnik: Yes, they would say that too, but first they would say it is an American peace, an American security.

Honeyman: Who cares whose peace it is?

Botvinnik: You do. You do not want a Russian peace. Two years ago we announced to the world a plan of our own—just as good as yours. And you rejected it.

Honeyman: There were significant problems with that plan.

Botvinnik: Yes, it was ours. Now please, John—stop pretending. You know neither of our countries can afford to be second in the quest for peace.

Honeyman: What quest for peace? At this rate there is no quest for peace.

Botvinnik: But there's the quest for the appearance of the quest for peace. These are negotiations, John. There are rules. There are forms. You know them as well as I do. Your President knows them, too. When he announced the proposal, he knew we would have to reject it.[20]

DICTION

The fourth element of drama is *diction*—the language of the play, the dialogue the actors speak. The diction provides a system of verbal signs that set the characters and their actions before an audience.

Spoken language in the theater must be immediately apprehended by the listener; there can be no turning back the pages, no pausing to weigh and consider a line before continuing to the next. The dialogue must be interesting, despite the need for simplicity and economy. It should capture the spirit of life and character. As the Irish playwright J. M. Synge put it: "In a good play, every speech should be as fully flavored as a nut or an apple." The diction must be appropriate for the character and the situation. Lines do not exist in the theater as separate entities. They are always in context, growing out of the emotionally charged incidents of the plot. The language of drama must be dynamic. As we have already suggested, speech is a form of action. Dialogue shows the characters' relationship to others; reflects the progression of the action; indicates what is happening inside the characters; reveals their suffering, growth, or decline. It is a means of articulating the clash of wills and conflicting motivations.

The dramatist needs the poet's feeling for language—a rich imagination, a facility with provocative imagery, and awareness of the weight, texture, and arrangement of words. Dramatic dialogue is not contemplative or static; it is harnessed to action and change. Even in the Japanese Noh dramas, which are often plays of reminiscence, the dialogue pulses with the life of the remembered event. It must be speakable, so that it gives the performers sounds and cadences that aid them in projecting the thought and feelings of the characters. For the audience, the dialogue must have audible intelligibility, so that the words are arresting in sound as they stimulate the ear and evoke images that are not only immediately comprehensible, but set up emotional reverberations as well.

Much of the serious drama before the late nineteenth century was linked to poetry. The Greek and Elizabethan masters of drama were poets as well as playwrights, as we have seen in Sophocles' *Antigone* and Shakespeare's *Hamlet* and *Richard III*. Their works, therefore, have an added literary value, and their use of verse and imagery seems particularly appropriate for their elevated tragedies of highborn characters.

In modern times, poetry has given way to prose, as the naturalists and realists bring on stage commonplace figures in everyday pursuits. We have seen examples of colloquial speech in Miller's *Death of a Salesman,* Osborne's *Look Back in Anger,* Shepard's *Curse of the Starving Class,* Giraudoux's *Madwoman of Chaillot,* Wilson's *Fences,* and Blessing's *A Walk in the Woods.*

In the discussion of character, we cited one of Shakespeare's best known soliloquies from *Richard III*. Other soliloquies from his tragedies find characters voicing their innermost thoughts in some of the most familiar passages of English literature. Shakespeare's astonishing contribution to our language is pointed out in this paragraph from Bernard Levin's *Enthusiasms:*

> If you cannot understand my argument, and declare "It's Greek to me," you are quoting Shakespeare; if you claim to be more sinned against then sinning, you are quoting Shakespeare; if you recall your salad days, you are quoting Shakespeare; if you act more in sorrow than in anger, if your wish is father to the thought, if your lost property has vanished into thin air, you are quoting Shakespeare; if you have ever refused to budge an inch or suffered from green-eyed jealousy, if you have played fast and loose, if you have been tongue-tied, a tower of strength, hoodwinked or in a pickle, if you have knitted your brows, made a virtue of necessity, insisted on fair play, slept not one wink, stood on ceremony, danced attendance (on your lord and master), laughed yourself into stitches, had short shrift, cold comfort or too much of a good thing, if you have seen better days or lived in a fool's paradise—why, be that as it may, the more fool you, for it is a foregone conclusion that you are (as good luck would have it) quoting Shakespeare; if you think it is early days and clear out bag and baggage, if you think it is high time and that that is the long and short of it, if you believe that the game is up and that truth will out even if it involves your own flesh and blood, if you lie low till the crack of doom because you suspect foul play, if you have your teeth set on edge (at one fell swoop) without rhyme or reason, then—to give the devil his due—if the truth were known (for surely you have a tongue in your head) you are quoting Shakespeare; even if you bid me good riddance and send me packing, if you wish I was dead as a doornail, if you think I am an eye-sore, a laughing stock, the devil incarnate, a stony-hearted villain, bloody-minded or a blinking idiot, then—by Jove! O Lord! Tut, tut! for goodness' sake! what the dickens! but me no buts—it is all one to me, for you are quoting Shakespeare.[21]

Monologues are not restricted to classical drama or period pieces. They are widely used in contemporary drama in the plays of David Rabe, Samuel Beckett, Harold Pinter, Edwin Albee, Marsha Norman, and Sam Shepard, to cite a few. William Russell, in his *Shirley Valentine,* made a full evening of a one-woman show in which his frustrated housewife bounces her feelings off the wall. When Shirley meets an old school acquaintance, who asks her, "Didn't you used to be Shirley Valentine?" she is suddenly driven to self-analysis in a speech delivered to the kitchen wall:

> On the way home, on the bus, I was cryin'. I don't know why. I'm staring out the window, tears trippin' down me cheeks. An' in me head there's this voice that keeps sayin' . . . I used to be Shirley Valentine. I used to be Shirley Valentine . . . I used to be Shirley . . .
>
> *(She is crying.)*
>
> What happened? Who turned me into this? I don't want this. Do you remember her, wall? Remember Shirley Valentine? She got married to a boy named Joe an' one day she came to live here. An' even though her name was changed to Bradshaw she was still Shirley Valentine. For a while. She still knew who she was. She used to laugh. A lot. Didn't she? She used to laugh with Joe—when the pair of them did things together. Remember wall? Remember when they first painted you an' the silly buggers painted each other as well. Stood here, the pair of them, havin' a paint fight, coverin' each other from head to foot in yellow paint. An' then the two of them, thinkin' they're dead darin', gettin' in the bath— together. And the water was so yellow that he said it was like gettin' a bath in vanilla ice cream. And Shirley Valentine washed his hair . . . and kissed his wet head . . . and knew what happiness' meant . . . What happened wall?[22]

Many people have lamented the absence of poetry in the modern theater; attempts have been made to recapture some of the enrichment of the poetic speech, notably by Maxwell Anderson, Christopher Fry, Bertolt Brecht, T. S. Eliot, and Federico Garcia Lorca. Although modern drama lacks elevated language, however, it would be a mistake to think that all plays written in the poetic form were successful. Indeed, the use of verse in the past was often puerile and ostentatious. Many poets had no sense of dramatic form or theatrical awareness. Often their plays were not stageworthy; their preoccupation with the language retarded the action, and the drama was bogged down with ambiguous clutter.

Among contemporary writers, Harold Pinter's language has the capacity for setting up echoes and vibrations far beyond the façade of words. Pinter's use of rhythm and silence opens up unexpected associations and a surreal sense of menace. As John Lahr says of Pinter, "The story on stage is deeper than the words that explain it, the language mere signposts for an immense and inaudible despair."[23]

The following passage indicates Pinter's remarkable ability to create theatrical effects with the colloquial idiom. In *The Birthday Party,* Stanley has sought

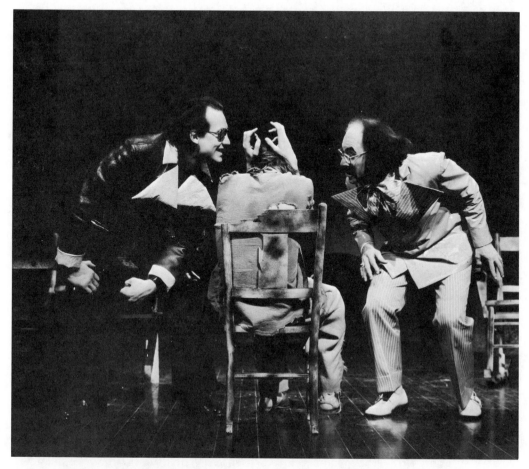

In Pinter's *The Birthday Party,* **a pair of strangers bedevil and threaten Stanley, an innocuous young man who has tried to find a quiet sanctuary at a summer resort.** *(Directed by Weldon Durham, University of Missouri)*

refuge at a seaside resort, but he has been followed by two sinister strangers who undermine and destroy him. When they are about to take Stanley away in their long black car, this dialogue occurs:

McCann: He looks better, doesn't he?

Goldberg: Much better.

McCann: A new man.

Goldberg: You know what we'll do?

McCann: What?

Goldberg: We'll buy him another pair.

   (They begin to woo him, gently and with relish. During the following sequence, Stanley shows no reaction. He remains with no movement, where he sits.)

McCann: Out of our own pockets.

Goldberg: It goes without saying. Between you and me, Stan, it's about time you had a new pair of glasses.

McCann: You can't see straight.

Goldberg: It's true. You've been cockeyed for years.

McCann: Now you're even more cockeyed.

Goldberg: He's right. You've gone from bad to worse.

McCann: Worse than worse.

Goldberg: You need a long convalescence.

McCann: A change of air.

Goldberg: Somewhere over the rainbow.

McCann: Where angels fear to tread.

Goldberg: Exactly.

McCann: You're in a rut.

Goldberg: You look anaemic.

McCann: Rheumatic.

Goldberg: Myopic.

McCann: Epileptic.

Goldberg: You're on the verge.

McCann: You're a dead duck.

Goldberg: But we can save you.

McCann: From a worse fate.

Goldberg: True.

McCann: Undeniable.

Goldberg: From now on, we'll take the hub of your wheel.

McCann: We'll renew your season ticket.

Goldberg: We'll take twopence off your morning tea.

McCann: We'll give you a discount on all inflammable goods.

Goldberg: We'll watch over you.

McCann: Advise you.

Goldberg: Give you proper care and treatment.[24]

Other dialogue devices have been used from time to time in the theater: choral speeches; antiphonal passages between a leader and a group; staccato, telgraphic fragments of speech in expressionistic plays; extensive monologues, prologues, and epilogues for exposition, foreshadowing, or commenting on the action; bits of poetry; and involved conceits and epigrams. But the primary form of diction in most drama is compressed dialogue, which, despite its conventions, gives to the listener the impression of natural conversation.

The use of the vernacular in the modern theater has often resulted in stage speech that is flat, pedestrian, and vulgar, filled with cliches of commonplace conversation. As Elder Olson has said, "The drama has increasingly sought to be articulate in the language of the inarticulate."[25] He goes on to lament the loss of subtle expression and profound thoughts available when poetic diction was more flexible.

On the other hand, the current emphasis on colloquial speech has eliminated the straining for effect in "purple passages" of pretentious rhetoric. With the poet's feeling for language, some contemporary playwrights have created speech that is vivid and evocative. One thinks, for example, of the texture of Sam Shepard's plays, utilizing the imagery of the rock and car-road culture; and the graphic local color in the work of Beth Henley, Preston Jones, Lanford Wilson, and August Wilson. Others have created passages of words and pauses that have the power to stimulate the imagination and suggest hidden and unsuspected meanings.

MUSIC

The fifth element mentioned by Aristotle is *music,* which refers to all of the auditory material, including music and sound effects.

We remember that the Greek drama, in its early association with dithyrambs, made full use of the musical potential in the singing and dancing of the chorus. Sound patterns were also important in the acting of the major characters, who sang, chanted, danced, and spoke with great variety in cadence, texture, and tempo. In the Noh and Kabuki theaters of Japan and in the traditional as well as modern plays of China and India, an orchestra is an essential aspect of the performance, and music is an integral part of the show. Elizabethan drama was rich in lyricism that broke into song. Later, English drama continued the use of music, and in burlettas, the entire performance might have been sung or chanted. (A *burletta* is a combination of burlesque and operetta. It is no more than three acts, each of which includes at least five songs.) Melodrama was originally linked to music, and even though the spoken word came to dominate the genre, musical backgrounds were used to accompany exits and entrances of major characters

In the La Jolla Playhouse's lively musical version of a Jules Verne novel, *80 Days*, the intrepid travellers receive a warm welcome to India. *(Directed by Des McAnuff)*

and to reinforce the mood of emotionally loaded scenes, such as chases, fights, escapes, love scenes, and deaths.

America's major theatrical invention, the musical comedy, grew out of popular entertainment of the nineteenth century. The minstrel show appealed to a wide audience from 1840 onward; its male ensembles usually played in black-face in a medley of comedy, song, and dance. The first musical comedy to become a hit was *The Black Crook* (1866), an extravaganza which featured spectacle and scantily clad chorus girls to set a pattern popular ever since. Other early influences were the operettas by European composers, which used sentimental stories about charming people in make-believe places and which provided opportunities for picturesque scenery and tuneful music—for instance, Lehar's *Merry Widow* (1907) and Oscar Strauss's *Chocolate Soldier* (1910). From France came the influence of "leg" shows like the Folies-Bergère, which combined vaudeville, comedy, and beautiful women in lavish costumes and scenery. Florenz Ziegfeld set the fashion for such display in the United States.

George M. Cohan added the patriotic note in his bright, energetic musicals, such as *Forty-Five Minutes from Broadway*. In 1927, a major change occurred when Jerome Kern and Edna Ferber produced Ferber's book *Showboat*, linking literary material with music. George and Ira Gershwin introduced sophisticated musical forms in early works like *Lady Be Good* (1924), but their landmark was *Porgy and Bess* (1935), a play about southern blacks that created the first successful native folk opera. In 1931, the Gershwins, with Morrie Ryskind, produced the political satire *Of Thee I Sing*, the first musical to win the Pulitzer Prize. In 1943, Rodgers and Hammerstein made another significant change in the musical with their *Oklahoma*, based on Lynn Riggs's folk play *Green Grow the Lilacs*. The dancing of chorus girls was replaced by Agnes de Mille's ballet, and the story and music were melded organically in a plot that dealt with simple, lively country folk instead of dramatizing the frivolous love affairs of upper-class big-city dwellers. Other memorable musicals produced by Rodgers and Hammerstein were *South Pacific* (1949) and *The Sound of Music* (1959). Leonard Bernstein and Stephen Sondheim combined serious subject matter with sophisticated music in *West Side Story* (1957). In the late 1960s, the "American tribal love-rock musical" *Hair,* a brash, formless protest against the established culture, created a new style of show. In 1964, *Fiddler on the Roof* became a phenomenal hit with its warm-hearted treatment of the stories of Sholom Aleichem.

Musical comedies have always been the biggest drawing card at the box office. More than two dozen musicals have enjoyed runs of over a thousand performances on Broadway. The formula of popular music, spectacular scenery, and imaginative choreography continues as standard fare in the commercial theater in such hits as *Cats, Me and My Girl, Jerome Robbins' Broadway, Gypsy, City of Angels,* and *A Chorus Line.*

In recent years, with the emergence of the British producer Andrew Lloyd Webber, "rock opera" has become the popular attraction at the box office. Examples are *Cats, The Phantom of the Opera, Starlight Express, Aspects of Love,* and *Miss Saigon.* In works like these and the Royal Shakespeare Company's production of *Les Miserables,* there is scarcely any spoken dialogue. The emphasis is entirely on music and spectacle, aimed directly at the general public as a marketable product. Consumer response has been phenomenal. *Cats* is reported to have netted over $44 million in the United States alone. *The Phantom of the Opera* cost $8 million to open in New York, but advance ticket sales were over $17 million. Thanks to the success of these shows, Broadway continues to break box office records, even though straight plays and conventional drama are struggling for survival in the commercial theater.

The American answer to the British invaders is Stephen Sondheim, who has a reputation for digging a little deeper and seeing a little farther than his rivals, whose eyes are always focused on the marketplace. He is a master at combining lyrics and music that are a bit too sophisticated for the Tin Pan Alley tradition. Nevertheless, he has worked on a broad spectrum of successful theater pieces, including *A Funny Thing Happened on the Way to the Forum, Follies, Sweeney Todd, Pacific Overtures, Sunday in the Park with George, A Little Night Music,* and *Into the Woods.*

Although motion pictures have always exploited the evocative power of music to heighten emotional effects, naturalistic and realistic drama have usually rejected music as an artificial intrusion. But even in realistic drama, playwrights

Spectacle is usually an important ingredient in musicals, as in the "Peter Pan" sequence in *Jerome Robbins' Broadway*.

have used sound to enhance the mood of their plays. For example, Chekhov was very conscious of the use of sounds in *Uncle Vanya*. In the final act of the play, a melancholy atmosphere is reinforced by the click of counting beads, the scratch of a pen, the chirping of a cricket, the tapping of the night watchman's cane, the soft strumming of a guitar, and the bells of the carriage when Dr. Astrov departs.

As the theater has become freer in recent years, music and sound have often played an increasingly important part in performance. In Jack Gelber's play *The Connection*, a jazz orchestra is a part of the acting company and actually plays approximately thirty minutes of music in each act. Brecht, with his lyrical gifts, uses music as an important part of his epic theater—for example, in *The Caucasian Chalk Circle*, which follows the Eastern practice of having an orchestra onstage and interjecting songs freely into the dialogue.

In C. P. Taylor's play *Good*, a mild German scholar is gradually transformed into a Nazi execution camp administrator. Throughout the action, a five-piece band sits onstage and plays appropriate music, sometimes underscoring the action and sometimes as a counterpoint to it. Taylor's *And a Nightingale Sang* also makes use of expressive music during the action, when one of the characters at the piano plays songs from World War II. In *The Elephant Man*, a cellist in evening clothes is stationed near the wings and intermittently plays music from Elgar and Bach. He is not a character involved in the plot, but his appearance and performance seem aesthetically right.

Another of the present-day dramatists with a keen sense of the power of music in drama is Peter Shaffer. In *Equus*, he called for an "Equus noise"—"a choric effect made up of all the actors sitting around upstage and composed of humming, thumping, and stamping"—an effect that was particularly striking during the scene when the boy is wounding the animals. Of course, Shaffer's stunning use of Mozart's music lifted the action of *Amadeus* to a very high level of production.

In the plays of Sam Shepard, the influence of rock, jazz, and country music is an integral part of his work. It is evident not only in the songs and incidental music, but also in Shepard's language, which is often strident and jumpy, recalling rock jargon. August Wilson acknowledges his debt to the blues in his plays, which often integrate music and dance as an organic part of the action.

In the experimental work of the new theater, many innovators make a sharp break from traditional dramatic practice in placing most of their emphasis on music, sound, and spectacle. Often, conventional dialogue is replaced by disparate fragments, some of which may be recorded. Very often a complex sound track accompanies a series of striking images and actions that do not follow a plot line, but serve to evoke moods and feelings through their sensuous appeal.

Jean-Claude van Itallie, in his *America Hurrah!* (1965), a satire on traditional values, uses highly theatricalized techniques, including nonsense language, the use of impersonal automatons instead of characters, and stylized sound. For example, in the first episode, "Interview," the Telephone Operator suffers from a stomach cramp. She falls over the seat in pain:

> *(The whistling of the telephone circuit becomes a siren. Three actors carry the Telephone Operator over to the boxes, stage left, which now serve as an operating table. Three actors imitate the Telephone Operator's breathing pattern, while four actors behind her make stylized sound and movements as surgeons and nurses in the midst of an operation. The Telephone Operator's breathing accelerates, then stops. After a moment, the actors begin spreading over the stage and making the muted sounds of a cocktail party, music, laughter, talk. The actors find a position and remain there, playing various aspects of a party in slow motion and muted tones. They completely ignore the First Interviewer who, as a Girl at the Party, goes from person to person as if she were in a garden of living statues.*[26]

SPECTACLE

The sixth dramatic element, *spectacle,* includes all visual aspects of the production: scenery, lighting, costuming, makeup, and the stage business of the performers. It also includes the environment of the action, whether it be in an actual playhouse or an adapted site, such as a Greek hillside, a Japanese shrine in a dry riverbed, an opulent hall in a Renaissance palace, an open marketplace, an inn yard, a factory warehouse, or a street. The audience is also a part of the celebration we call theater, because spectators often come to be seen as well as to see, and the communal experience of being eyewitnesses to a stirring event has its own effect.

Because drama is often thought of as *dialogue,* the word threatens to dominate the audience experience. But there is rebellion against this dominance, and today, more than ever, we are conscious of the need to make a theater of images—even at the expense of subordinating the diction and rejecting the conventional playhouse and scenery. By its very nature, dramatic action results in compelling visual experiences. Think of the images called to mind in Chapter 1, even without the benefit of performance, when the Three Marys see the miracle of the empty tomb; or imagine the manner in which Hamlet's "Mousetrap" reveals Claudius' crime; or call to mind Willy Loman's first entrance, when he staggers through the gloom, bone-weary and defeated, carrying his heavy sample cases. The theater has a marvelous facility for filling our heads with rich visual experience.

Throughout history, as we shall see in Chapter 10 on the designer, theaters have appealed to the eye as well as to the ear, whether or not actual scenery was used. In the production of Greek, Elizabethan, and Japanese Noh plays, virtually no representation of locale was required, except that supplied by the architecture, and, of course, the performers themselves. In the Greek and Noh theaters, the use of masks and striking costumes and the dancing of the chorus and actors enriched the spectacle.

During the Renaissance, the proscenium arch was introduced into the theater, separating audience and performers by placing the acting area behind an architectural framework, so that the spectators looked through the opening to the stage. This innovation was quickly exploited as theatrical production came to be dominated by spectacular changeable scenery, which often ran away with the show. Scenic artists vied with one another in creating lavish settings and spectacular effects. The impulse for display often spilled over into the auditorium, and architecture reflected a taste for ornamentation. The proscenium arch, with its use of pictorial scenery, has dominated the theater even to the present day, although its style and function have changed a good deal, as we shall see.

During the nineteenth century, melodrama gained a wide following in the theater; part of its popularity depended on spectacular scenic effects, coupled with vigorous action. As realism and naturalism made their impact on the late-nineteenth-century audience, scenery took on a new importance in production because of the scientifically inspired concern with environment as a conditioning force in determining behavior. Hence, spectacle assumed an organic, psychological role in the performance, as reinforcement of the meaning of the action and as a device relating character to the social milieu.

Tastes have changed considerably in modern times, and although many plays still require a semblance of representational setting, a number of innovators reject not only scenery, but the theater as well. Even in experimental productions, however, the visual aspects of drama are important in the environment of the performance and the action. Visual stimuli of lights and color are fundamental in creating states of mind and atmosphere. Today, scenographers not only work with complete freedom in the use of the stage, but they also have at their hand high-tech equipment for shifting and lighting their settings and a broad range of new materials to work with. The lavish, opulent productions of the present theater testify to the public's taste for show in "show business."

PLAYS TO READ AND SEE

F = Film Available; V = Videotape Available.

F	V	Peter Shaffer, *Amadeus, Equus*
F		Sophocles, *Antigone, Oedipus Rex*
F		Harold Pinter, *The Birthday Party*
F	V	Beth Henley, *Crimes of the Heart*
F	V	Arthur Miller, *Death of a Salesman*
F	V	Henrik Ibsen, *A Doll's House*
F	V	Alfred Uhry, *Driving Miss Daisy*
		August Wilson, *Fences, The Piano Lesson*
		Marsha Norman, *'night, Mother*
F		Thornton Wilder, *Our Town*
F	V	Willy Russell, *Shirley Valentine*
F	V	Tennessee Williams, *A Streetcar Named Desire*

BIBLIOGRAPHY

ESSLIN, MARTIN. *An Anatomy of Drama.* New York: Hill and Wang, 1976.

FERGUSSON, FRANCES. *The Idea of a Theater.* Princeton, N.J.: Princeton University Press, 1949.

NICOLL, ALLARDYCE. *The Theater and Dramatic Theory.* New York: Barnes and Noble, 1962.

ROWE, KENNETH THORPE. *The Theater in Your Head.* New York: Funk & Wagnalls, 1960.

STYAN, J. I. *The Dramatic Experience.* Cambridge: Cambridge University Press, 1965.

NOTES

1. Marsha Norman, *'night Mother* (New York: Hill and Wang, 1981).

2. Sophocles, *Antigone,* trans. Peter D. Arnott (New York: Appleton-Century-Crofts, 1949).

3. Lanford Wilson, *Talley's Folly* (New York: Hill and Wang, 1979). Copyright © 1979 by Lanford Wilson. Reprinted by permission of Hill and Wang, a division of Farrar, Straus and Giroux, Inc.

4. *Antigone.*

5. Peter Shaffer, *Amadeus* (New York: New American Library, 1984).

6. *Antigone.*

7. *Antigone.*

8. Eugene O'Neill, *In the Zone* in *Seven Plays of the Sea* (New York: Random House, 1923). Copyright 1919 and renewed 1974 by Eugene O'Neill. Reprinted by permission of Random House, Inc.

9. Arthur Miller, *Death of a Salesman.* Copyright 1949; renewed © 1977 by Arthur Miller. Used by permission of Viking Penguin, a division of Penguin Books USA, Inc.

10. Alfred Uhry, *Driving Miss Daisy* (New York: Flora Roberts, 1986).

11. *Antigone.*

12. Tennessee Williams, *A Streetcar Named Desire* (New York: New Directions, 1947). Copyright © 1947 by Tennessee Williams. Reprinted by permission of New Directions Publishing Company.

13. Jean Giraudoux, *The Madwoman of Chaillot*. Copyright 1947 by Maurice Valency; copyright renewed 1974 by Maurice Valency. English version by Maurice Valency.

14. William Shakespeare, *Richard III*, Act I, Scene 1.

15. August Wilson, *Fences*. Copyright © 1986 by August Wilson. Used by permission of New American Library, a division of Penguin Books USA, Inc.

16. Peter Shaffer, *Amadeus*.

17. Henrik Ibsen, *Hedda Gabler*, trans. Edmund Gosse and William Archer (New York: Charles Scribner's Sons, 1907). Copyright © 1907 by Charles Scribner's Sons.

18. August Wilson, interviewed by David Savran in *In Their Own Words* (New York: Theater Communications Group, 1989).

19. August Wilson, Preface to *Joe Turner's Come and Gone*. Copyright © 1988 by August Wilson. Used by permission of New American Library, a division of Penguin Books USA, Inc.

20. Lee Blessing, *A Walk in the Woods*. Copyright © 1986 by Lee Blessing. Used by permission of Penguin Books USA, Inc.

21. Bernard Levin, *Enthusiasms* (Philadelphia: Coronet Books, 1983).

22. Willy Russell, *Shirley Valentine* (London: Methuen, 1988).

23. John Lahr, *Casebook on* Pinter's Homecoming (New York: Grove Press, 1971).

24. Harold Pinter, *The Birthday Party*. Copyright © 1959, 1960, 1965 by Harold Pinter. Used by permission of Grove Press, Inc.

25. Elder Olson, *Tragedy and the Theory of Drama* (Detroit: Wayne State University Press, 1961).

26. Jean-Claude van Itallie, *America Hurrah!*. Copyright © 1966 by Jean-Claude van Itallie as unpublished plays. Copyright © 1966, 1967 by Jean-Claude van Itallie.

three
Tragedy

When the tragic hero Oedipus Rex discovers that his guilty actions in the past have caused a plague in the kingdom, he strikes out his eyes, renounces his throne, and condemns himself to exile. Oedipus is shown here in the Greek National Theater production at Epidaurus.

Oedipus Rex (c. 430 B.C.) is one of the greatest tragedies ever written. It is a play of discovery, in which Sophocles' tragic hero gradually unveils the past. The setting is before the royal palace at Thebes. A Chorus of suppliant citizens comes to the king and asks him to save them from the plague that blights the city.

Warned by an oracle that his son would one day murder his father, King Laius of Thebes had given the child, Oedipus, to a shepherd to abandon in the wilderness. Instead, the child was taken out of the country by another shepherd, who raised him in Corinth. As he grew up, Oedipus learned of the prophecy and attempted to escape by going to Thebes. On the way, he became involved in a violent altercation at the crossroads and killed an old man, not suspecting that the victim was Laius, his father. When Oedipus arrived at Thebes, he freed the city from the Sphinx by solving the riddle. He was made king and married Laius' widow, Jocasta, not realizing that she was his mother. He ruled well and had four children. The confident Oedipus assured the Thebans that he would rescue them again by investigating the cause of the plague. Then, step by step, he learned the awful truth that it was Oedipus himself who had blighted the kingdom by fulfilling the prophecy of murder and incest. Jocasta hanged herself, and Oedipus struck out his own eyes. He groped his way out of the palace and stood before his people, blinded and bleeding, but suffering even more within. He bade farewell to his daughters, Antigone and Ismene, and exiled himself from the kingdom that he had once so proudly ruled.

When we first encounter tragedy in dramatic literature, a question arises: How can we find pleasure in a play that involves so much violence and suffering? What satisfaction is there in seeing or reading about death and destruction?

Sophocles was concerned with many ideas, among them the ironic truth that the individual with eyes may be as blind as those without sight. The emphasis is not on the violent actions, which take place in the past or behind the scenes. There is a terrible fascination in the actions that Oedipus takes to save the kingdom, only to learn the truth that destroys him. In tragedy, we do not look for poetic justice or reward and punishment. Tragedy is an aesthetic object, not a moral lesson. We are challenged by the nobility of the character of the tragic hero or heroine in the face of certain physical oblivion, but their integrity remains intact.

THE NATURE OF TRAGEDY

Tragedy is a strange and mysterious country, despite considerable efforts to fix its boundaries, blaze its trails, and establish its configurations. All who venture here must find their own way through an entangling jungle of conjecture and a luxuriant undergrowth of verbiage surrounding a bewildering, semantic swamp. There is no shortcut, no easy, known way, because tragedy is a quality of experience we must all discover for ourselves.

Tragedy is rare. It does not bulk large in the history of the theater, nor does one find it listed in the record of popular attractions on Broadway. Yet tragedy is the most discussed genre, and it was the first kind of drama that the Greeks introduced into the theater. Of the original Greek tragedies we have only seven plays each by Aeschylus and Sophocles and eighteen by Euripides. From the Renaissance, we have the tragedies of the Elizabethans, mostly Shakespeare, and the neoclassical works of Racine and Pierre Corneille. In addition, we have a body of critical theory that is even more diverse and contradictory than the plays themselves.

The first to mark the way was Aristotle, who in the fourth-century B.C. work, the *Poetics*, sought to guide those who followed him. Although he found his direction from limited observation of carefully chosen examples, we may still retrace his steps with profit, so acutely did he designate his landmarks. But we should remember that the *Poetics* is a short analysis of the kind of tragedy that was created a century before, in Athens. His study is, therefore, an investigation of the drama that preceded him, not a set of rules for his contemporaries or followers, even though Renaissance writers misapplied his views as those of a lawgiver. Moreover, there is considerable latitude for misunderstanding Aristotle, partly because of his language, and partly because of the examples he cites as evidence to support his views. Aristotle's *Poetics*, therefore, should be regarded as a lamp in the darkness, not the source of all light.

Aristotle's Definition of Tragedy

Let us turn our attention to Aristotle's *Poetics*, probably the most discussed piece of criticism in dramatic literature. He begins with this definition of tragedy:

> Tragedy, then is an imitation of an action that is serious, complete, and of a certain magnitude; in language embellished with each kind of artistic ornament, the several kinds being found in separate parts of the play; in the form of action, not of narrative; through pity and fear effecting the proper purgation of these emotions.[1]

The origin of the word *tragedy* is a matter of conjecture. *Tragos* in Greek means "goat"; *oide* means "song." The exact connection of goat-song to drama is not clear, although three hypotheses have been advanced: (1) a goat was sacrificed as part of the original improvised ritual honoring Dionysus; (2) the chorus wore goatskins for costumes; (3) a goat was offered as a prize in the early choral contests. In any case, tragedy was associated with goat-song or goat-singer in its early stages. The terms *tragic* and *tragedy*, as we use them in everyday speech, have little to do with "tragedy" as a form of drama. A person may speak of the "tragic" death of a small child in an automobile accident. Although tragedy usually involves catastrophe, it is not the calamity itself on which attention is focused in drama. Death may even seem incidental in *Hamlet* or *Romeo and Juliet* when it occurs to such secondary characters as Polonius or Paris or Tybalt. The validity of genuine tragedy is not concerned with the act of violence but with what that act says about life—the struggle of the protagonist, the issues at stake, the effect of his or her suffering.

An "action" refers to the play as a dynamic organized process intended for

This scene from *Prometheus Bound* at Stanford University shows the chained hero being visited by Oceanus and the Chorus. The scale of Erik Vos's setting suggests the magnitude of Greek tragedy.

presentation in the theater—not a narrative for a solitary reader.

Tragedy is *serious* in nature, not trivial or frivolous. It deals with the most profound problems of humanity—identity and destiny, the nature of good and evil, the mysterious forces of the universe, and the consequences of individual responsibilities. Its purpose is not mere diversion or amusement but an investigation of ethical and spiritual values.

Tragedy attains *magnitude* in the heroic stature of its characters, in the use of poetry, in the universality of its meaning, and in the loftiness of its ideas. Tragedies are elevated; they possess scale and scope beyond the petty vicissitudes of daily existence. Magnitude of character is realized through highborn characters, persons of nobility and prominence who occupy "exposed positions"—people who, as Aristotle said, "are better than we are" or those who achieve greatness.

A tragedy is *complete;* it has a beginning, a middle, and an end—and, according to Aristotle, each of these parts is a well-articulated structure without extraneous material. The course of action is a "necessary and probable" linking of antecedents and consequents. Such unity and wholeness are fundamental to the Greek aesthetic view of life.

The chief difference between the *dramatic* and *narrative form* is a result of the *manner* of presentation. A narrative may be written or told; drama must be presented with impersonation and action—it is "a thing done."

Pity, fear, and *catharsis* are terms that have perplexed and intrigued generations of scholars and critics. This special effect that tragedy aims to produce will be discussed at length later in the chapter. For now, let us recognize that pity goes beyond mere pathos to include the compassion that accompanies shared grief, and that fear transcends sheer fright to convey a sense of anxious concern and profound reverence. Catharsis suggests purgation and purification—a release of emotional tension that results in tranquility.

The idea of tragedy is man-made. There is no ideal tragedy—only a small collection of plays that (with more or less agreement) we refer to when we talk about it. For the moment, we will confine ourselves to "classic" tragedy, which includes the Greeks, the works of Shakespeare and some of his contemporaries, and the French neoclassicists Racine and Corneille. We will deal with modern attempts at tragedy a bit later.

PLOT

Aristotle lays great stress on plot—the "soul of tragedy." He cites the need for a unified and complete sequence of interlocking action; the proper use of reversal, discovery, and recognition; and the obligation of the playwright to make everything "necessary and probable." Most Greek tragedies follow these precepts. They have only a few episodes, with no subplots or extraneous complications, and they do not mix comic matter with the tragic.

The French neoclassicist Racine had no difficulty in plotting his tragedies in the Greek format, but Shakespeare and his fellow Elizabethans composed their plots with utmost freedom. The unities of time, place, and action were of no concern in the flexible playhouses designed to accommodate complex stories that showed all the action. Comic and serious matter were blended together, and highborn characters mixed with lowly ones in complicated plots.

Nevertheless, there are valid generalizations that do apply to the tragic form. Tragedy usually deals with a positive, active protagonist caught in sharp conflict with opposing forces. In the ensuing struggle, he or she suffers greatly and goes from fortune to misfortune. Tragic conflicts are of a particular kind. The issues at stake are not mundane considerations, such as economic or environmental problems. The struggle is ethical, spiritual. Consider the story outline of one of the best known tragedies by Shakespeare—*Hamlet*.

Prince Hamlet comes home from Wittenburg to attend the funeral of his father and learns that his mother, Gertrude, has hastily remarried the old King's brother, Claudius, who is now on the throne. The ghost of Hamlet's father reveals that he was poisoned by Claudius. Hamlet is sworn to avenge the murder. To establish the validity of the ghost, Hamlet composes a dramatic scene that resembles his father's murder, to be played before the court by a traveling troupe of players (see "The Mousetrap" in Chapter 1). Polonius, the king's advisor, thinks

Hamlet is mad for the love of his daughter, Ophelia, whom he and the king use as a decoy to discover Hamlet's motivations. Claudius blanches in guilty fear when he sees the simulated poisoning and knows that Hamlet is a dangerous adversary. While Hamlet is berating his mother for her alliance with Claudius, he hears a noise behind the curtain; he stabs through it and slays the eavesdropping Polonius. Ophelia's mind snaps from the tension, and she drowns herself. Her brother, Laertes, determined to avenge the deaths of Ophelia and his father, is persuaded by Claudius to engage Hamlet in a "friendly" duel, with Laertes' foil tipped with poison. To make doubly sure that Hamlet dies, Claudius prepares a poisoned drink for him. As a result of these machinations, which go awry, Laertes, Gertrude, Claudius, and Hamlet all die. The prince's friend, Horatio, eulogizes,

> Now cracks a noble heart. Goodnight, sweet Prince,
> And flights of angels sing thee to thy rest![2]

Fortinbras, king of Norway, arrives to restore order to the kingdom.

Suzanne K. Langer, in her perceptive book *Feeling and Form,* sees tragedy shaped by a "tragic rhythm"—a pattern transferred from nature, of growth, maturation, and decline. The action of the play shows the hero's "self-realization as under increasing pressure, he reaches the highest potential in the vision of life as accomplished . . . a sense of fulfillment that lifts him above defeat."[3] *Hamlet* and *Oedipus Rex* follow Langer's pattern of the tragic rhythm.

It is apparent that the tragic effect is not a matter of dramatic structure. *Hamlet* is entirely different from *Oedipus Rex.* Shakespeare's play was written for a company of actors, to be played in a playhouse that accommodated its loose structure—more than forty characters, twenty different scenes, and a mixture of highborn characters and low, and of tragedy and comedy. All of the essential actions were put on stage, including the final scene, during which four leading characters die violent deaths. On the other hand, in *Oedipus,* most of the play is about past events, and the suicide and blinding are done behind the scenes. There is only one locale, only eight speaking characters (played by three actors), and a chorus of fifteen.

Yet both plays have tragic plots that are serious, complete, and of a certain magnitude. They have protagonists who suffer mightily and end up with their integrities intact. There are no last-minute reprieves, no escape from catastrophe. Neither Shakespeare nor Sophocles exploits the suffering for pathos. The end result is a catharsis, an enlightenment, a sense of exaltation for witnessing the audacity of the human spirit confronted with adversity.

THE TRAGIC HERO

One of the most discussed aspects of Aristotelian thought is his concept of the tragic hero, who is seen as good but not free from faults—"an intermediate kind of personage," who, though not preeminently virtuous, is not depraved. The

In the denouement of *Romeo and Juliet*, the lovers are united in death as a result of the conflict between the Montague and Capulet families. *(Scenography by Josef Svoboda, Prague National Theater)*

hero's "flaw" (*hamartia*, which means "missing the mark") is a term that has caused endless argument because it is not uniformly applicable to all tragedies, nor does it appear to be consistent in the variety of characters involved in catastrophes.

How does one equate the suffering of Prometheus with that of Oedipus? Antigone or Hippolytus with Medea? Hamlet with Macbeth, Lear with Romeo and Juliet? The degree of guilt seems to have little or nothing to do with justice. All tragic figures suffer, regardless of their degree of guilt or responsibility. Sometimes their fall seems to be a matter of cause and effect rather than crime and punishment. Pity is related not to vengeance but to "undeserved misfortune." Antigone and Hamlet are not evildoers who are punished for their sins. Our attention as we look at tragic protagonists is not on their guilt or innocence but on the quality of their spirit. How do they respond to those "boundary situations" in which they are tested to the limit? What is the effect on them of evil and injustice? Implicit in the Aristotelian concept of the tragic hero is that he or she must be a character of some magnitude—an elevated figure, one who occupies an important position in society so that the fall is from a high place.

Northrop Frye gives us the image of the tragic hero at the top of the wheel of fortune, above humanity and below something greater in the sky, who acts as a "conductor" of power from above. "Tragic heroes are wrapped in the mystery of their communion with that something beyond which we can see only through them and which is the source of their strength and their fate alike."[4]

DICTION

The elevated style of Greek, neoclassical, and Elizabethan tragedy, with its characters and themes of great magnitude, required poetic language. Tragedy is also characterized by the grandeur of the diction. But like all good language for the stage, it is functional, as an appropriate level of speech for the dramatic situation, not as a separate element of the play. In general, tragedy has been written by dramatists who have the poetic gifts to combine dignity with clarity, who speak with an eloquence free from bombast or self-conscious display. Their verse lifts the drama through images and rhythms that have the essential quality of being eminently speakable.

Robert F. Goheen, in his *The Imagery of Sophocles' Antigone*,[5] found in Creon's and Antigone's language clues to their opposing views of the world. Because the king has a materialistic focus, he consistently uses imagery associated with measurable fact, whereas Antigone, with her interior motivation that is emotional and intuitive, expresses herself in recurrent sensory language aligned with pain, pleasure, and tears. On the other hand, Sophocles makes a positive statement graphic through imagery of nature in a choral ode in praise of human achievement:

> Wonders are many, and none is more wonderful than man; the power that crosses the white sea, driven by the stormy south-wind, making a path under surges that threaten to engulf him; and Earth, the eldest of the gods, the immortal, the unwearied, doth he wear, turning the soil with the offspring of horses, as the ploughs go to and fro from year to year.
>
> And the light-hearted race of birds, and the tribes of savage beasts, and the sea-brood of the deep, he snares in the meshes of his woven toils, he leads captive, man excellent in wit. And he masters by his arts the beast whose lair is in the wilds, who roams the hills; he tames the horse of shaggy mane, he puts the yoke upon its necks, he tames the tireless mountain bull.[6]

Caroline Spurgeon's monumental work, *Shakespeare's Imagery and What It Tells Us,* was the first large-scale, systematic investigation of imagery. She discovered that Shakespeare used two prominent categories: images of the English countryside and the homely concerns of domestic life. In *Hamlet* Spurgeon identified 279 images; the dominant one was of sickness, decay, and disease; blemishes of nature and of the body; and the idea of an ulcer or tumor as descriptive of the unwholesome condition of Denmark.[7]

Hamlet, bitterly resenting the hasty marriage of his mother and King Claudius, expresses his dark view in this image:

> How weary, stale, flat and unprofitable
> Seem to me all the uses of this world.
> Fie on't! tis an unweeded garden,
> That grows to seed; things rank and gross in nature
> Possess it merely.[8]

AESTHETIC PLEASURE

The pleasure that tragedy affords is not moral but aesthetic. We admire the grandeur of conception, the ability of the dramatists to create significant action around great themes. And we also enjoy "insight experiences," which show us that despite injustice and evil, excessive pride and passion, violence and tyranny, the human spirit has the capacity to endure. The tragic hero's purpose is defeated, his passion is agonizing, but he comes to terms with his fate through perception. And from that imitation we learn—we attain a clearer awareness of the mystery of our own nature. As Langer suggests, there is aesthetic pleasure in seeing the tragic rhythm completed, the expectation fulfilled, and, within the tragic rhythm, human dignity retained.

There are those who see the universality of tragedy as a way of connecting us to the latent experiences of myth and ritual, which have absorbed the attention of Carl Jung and his followers, in archetypal patterns of thought and behavior—patterns and experiences that Jung said are "deeply implanted in the memory of the race." Gilbert Murray describes the phenomenon in these terms:

> In plays like *Hamlet* or the *Agamemnon* or the *Electra* we have certainly fine and flexible character-study, a varied and well-wrought story, a full command of the technical instruments of the poet and the dramatist; but we have also, I suspect, an undercurrent of desires and fears and passions, long slumbering yet eternally familiar, which have for thousands of years lain near the root of our most intimate emotions and have been wrought into the fabric of our most magical dreams. How far into the past ages this stream may reach back, I dare not even surmise; but it seems to me as if the power of stirring it or moving with it were one of the last secrets of genius.[9]

CATHARSIS

The most significant element that distinguishes tragedy from other forms of drama is the tragic effect. Just what it is in tragedy that gives pleasure through pain is difficult to determine. August Schlegel felt that the tragic tone was one of "irrepressible melancholy" when the audience is consoled and elevated by witnessing human weakness exposed to the vagaries of fate and natural forces. Arthur Schopenhauer saw the meaning of tragedy as resignation and renunciation in the face of a miserable and desolate existence. On the other hand, Henry Myers saw evidence of a just order in tragedy:

> Since it is positive and affirmative, great tragic poetry satisfies our deepest rational and moral inclinations. As rational beings, we are always looking for patterns, for order, for meaning in experience; as moral beings, we can be satisfied only by discovering in the realm of good and evil the special kind of pattern or order which we call justice. Tragedy reconciles us to evil by showing us that it is not a single, separate phenomenon but one side of change of fortune, and makes us feel that the change of fortune of a representative man is just.[10]

**Euripides' *The Trojan Women*
dramatizes the sorrow and suffering
that followed the fall of Troy. The
devastation of Queen Hecuba and
the other grieving women elicits
feelings of pity and fear.** *(Aleka
Katseli as Hecuba, Epidaurus
Festival)*

From these opposing statements, it is clear that what constitutes the tragic
effect is capable of many interpretations. The effect is complex and highly
personalized, arrived at through one's own experiences in life.

In any discussion of the tragic effect, we must keep Aristotle's words *fear* and
pity before us. What did he mean by them? Pity is not simply pathos, a soft
sentiment of sorrow for one who is weak or unworthy, even though it arises from
"undeserved misfortune." Pity is not contemptuous or patronizing. Tragic pity
implies a sharing of grief. We enter into the experience of another through our
sympathy and our fellow feeling. Our pity for the tragic hero is an act of compassion.

Aristotle's concept of fear extends beyond sheer fright or terror to include
anxious concern, solicitude, awe, reverence, and apprehension. In tragedy, fear
is not merely a hair-raising, spine-tingling reaction of the nervous system; it is an
emotion that warms the heart and illuminates the mind. Fear carries a sense of
wonder that may include admiration for an individual whose spirit remains intact
despite all that the world can do to it. In tragedy, then, the purging of fear and
pity must be universalized into a general concern for others rather than a private
and personal identification with disaster.

The catharsis is not the automatic result of following a dramatic formula.
We have the capacity for compassion for many kinds of people, good and bad, in
many kinds of situations, provided that we have understanding. Our sympathies
can go out to foolish and evil characters like Lear and Macbeth. What really
counts is our ability to enter into the suffering of the characters as they are tested,
and to find within ourselves an echo of their frailty and their flaws.

This emotional response to tragedy is a complex one. It must be broad enough to encompass a variety of experiences and extensive enough to include shades of feeling, such as the heartbreak at the end of *King Lear, Phèdre, Romeo and Juliet,* and *Oedipus Rex;* the sense of triumph at the end of *Hamlet, The Crucible,* and *Antigone;* and the appalling sense of waste at the end of *The Trojan Women, Ghosts,* and *Othello.* Catharsis is a purging of the spectator's fear and pity, resulting in a sense of release and tranquility. We are cleansed and exhilarated when we are liberated from our own emotional entanglements, our disturbing passions. Fear gives way to certainty, even though that certainty is death. Pity goes beyond feeling and becomes understanding. The spectator leaves the theater "in calm of mind, all passion spent." The end result, as Frye suggests, is that the audience experiences a "kind of buoyancy." Or again, in Edith Hamilton's words, "the great soul in pain and death transforms and exalts pain and death." Myers universalizes the meaning more explicitly:

> These are the main features of the tragic spirit. It lifts us above self-pity and reconciles us to suffering by showing that evil is a necessary part of the intelligible and just order of our experience. It lifts us above the divisive spirit of melodrama by showing that men are neither naturally good nor inherently evil. It saves us all from the pitfalls of utopianism and fatalism. It teaches moderation by showing that the way of the extremist is short, but that at the same time it shows the man of principle that an uncompromising stand is not without its just compensations. And most important, it teaches us that all men are united in the kinship of a common fate, that all are destined to suffer and enjoy, each according to his capacity.[11]

The eminent Shakespearean scholar A. C. Bradley makes an interesting and valid contribution to the idea of tragedy by suggesting that catharsis results when pity and fear unite with a profound sense of mystery and sadness because of the impression of waste.[12] In the catastrophe, something of value is destroyed. Important and worthwhile connections are broken. This is perhaps one of the reasons the layperson speaks of the "tragedy" that occurs through some accident to a person of promise who had a bright future.

A POSITIVE STATEMENT

Although tragedy involves suffering, evil, and death, many critics feel it is a positive statement about life. As Allardyce Nicoll says, "Death never really matters in tragedy. . . . Tragedy assumes that death is inevitable and that its time of coming is of no importance compared with what a man does before his death."[13]

Death may overtake the protagonists, but they are spiritually victorious. They are not abject, craven victims of fate who go cowering to their doom. The principles for which they lived and died survive their passing. The hero dies; heroism lives on. We admire the audacity of those who disregard human frailty, revealing an astonishing capacity for suffering in matters of the spirit. Their action is an affirmation of life. They sustain our faith in humanity.

HONESTY

The writers of tragedy are unflinchingly honest. They show life as it is, not as one wishes it might be. They have the courage to confront the terrors and perplexities of life; they acknowledge human frailty. Their plots are not manipulated to spare the protagonist; the hero or heroine goes relentlessly to catastrophe. Nor does tragedy demonstrate poetic justice in which the virtuous are rewarded and the wicked punished. Instead, the dramatist shows the clash between our desire for justice and what really happens. The evil is presented along with the good. In the treatment of character, the protagonists are not the idealized heroes of romanticism or the unmitigated villains of melodrama. They are a mixture of clay and stardust; they are admirable characters, but they usually possess a flaw, and their imperfection links them to us. Tragedy rests on a solid basis of integrity, making no concessions to the wishes of the audience. In Jean Anouilh's modern version of *Antigone,* the chorus makes this cogent statement about tragedy:

> Tragedy is clean, it is firm, it is flawless. It has nothing to do with melodrama—with wicked villains, persecuted maidens, avengers, gleams of hope and eleventh-hour repentances. Death, in melodrama, is really horrible because it is never inevitable. The dear old father might so easily have been saved; the honest young man might so easily have brought in the police five minutes earlier. In a tragedy, nothing is in doubt and everyone's destiny is known. That makes for tranquility. Tragedy is restful; and the reason is that *hope,* that foul, deceitful thing, has no part in it. There isn't any hope. You're trapped. The whole sky has fallen on you, and all you can do about it is to shout. Now don't mistake me: I said "shout": I did not say groan, whimper, complain. *That,* you cannot do. But you can *shout* aloud; you can get all those things said that you never thought you'd be able to say—or never knew you had it in you to say. And you don't say these things because it will do any good to say them; you know better than that. You say them for their own sake; you say them because you learn a lot from them. In melodrama, you argue and struggle in the hope of escape. That is vulgar; it's practical. But in tragedy, where there is no temptation to try to escape, argument is gratuitous: it's kingly.[14]

SIGNIFICANT CONTENT

Tragedy achieves significance because it is concerned with the deep and abiding questions and problems that have perplexed humanity throughout the ages. As Nicoll says, tragedy puts us in "contact with infinity. If we are religious, we shall say it is in contact with forces divine; if we are aesthetic, we shall say it is in contact with the vast illimitable forces of the universe. Everywhere in tragedy there is this sense of being raised to loftier heights."

Myers asserts that "tragedy best expresses its conceptions of the orderly and absolute nature of values," and Fergusson observes that tragedy "celebrates the mystery of human nature and destiny with the health of the soul in view." Tragedy confronts suffering and evil with honesty in such a way as to reveal both the weakness and nobility of human beings, their strength of will, and their

In Shakespeare's *King Lear*, the protagonist experiences terrible suffering when he loses his throne and sees his kingdom torn by strife. It is a play of great magnitude that ends with release and reconciliation. *(Morris Carnovsky as Lear, American Shakespeare Festival, Connecticut)*

capacity for suffering without breaking in the face of inevitable doom. Tragedy is not the drama of small souls bedeviled by the minor irritations of humdrum life. It does not concentrate on the physical environment or welfare, on getting and spending, or on collecting things. On the contrary, tragedy lifts our vision beyond petty cares and mundane anxieties by focusing on the great issues that affect our spiritual welfare. Clytemnestra is caught between avenging the death of her daughter and her duty to her husband; Lear, between sympathy and pride; Macbeth, between ambition and conscience. Tragedy deals with matters of great consequence.

The significant content of tragedy gives this form of drama a sense of *universality*. The effect of the play goes beyond the particular characters and the immediate circumstances to achieve an atmosphere of broad application. If even kings may suffer, how vulnerable are we? To the Greeks and Elizabethans the fate of the rulers was connected directly with that of their subjects. There is implicit in genuine tragedy not only an elevation of life but also an acute awareness of our common frailty and humanity. Tragic characters face problems not of a particular group or society but of all people, ones that we all must face. The problems are not temporary, external ones that can be overcome once and for all. Tragedy is rooted in the nature of our humanity, in the clash between good and evil that

Although Mother Courage is a lowly creature, her grief over the dead body of her son gives a sense of universality to her suffering. *(Munich Kammerspiele)*

confronts all of us. Thus, the suffering and struggles of the tragic hero become a part of the universal experience of those who share the play.

MODERN TRAGEDY

Our modern temper, with its anxieties and doubts, is often regarded as inhospitable ground for the nurture of the tragic spirit. The political practice of raising the common man to a dominant position has changed our fashion in heroes from highborn and romantic characters to ordinary, contemporary individuals, certainly not those of magnitude and grandeur. But even more important, it is alleged, our cultural condition, which results from a shifting sense of values, and our exaggerated concern with the material world have crippled our spiritual vision, and we now find ourselves in a world of despair, anguish, and absurdity. In place of the "eternal verities," we have situational morality, adapting our ethics to the needs of the moment. Without a firm foundation to stand on, the modern playwright shows us the individual's desperate need for illusion—and what happens when illusions disappear.

As a result of the contemporary climate, tragedy is difficult or impossible to write, some critics claim, because the genre depends on characters of a heroic mold who spiritually transcend their sufferings to attain nobility, giving the spectator a sense of exaltation. Joseph Wood Krutch laments the "enfeeblement of the spirit" in our society and indicates why he thinks Ibsen could not write dramas of the heroic stature of Shakespeare's:

> The materials out of which the latter created his works—his conception of human dignity, his sense of the importance of human passions, his vision of the amplitude of human life—simply did not and could not exist for Ibsen, as they did not and could not exist for his contemporaries. God and Man and Nature had all somehow dwindled in the course of the intervening centuries, not because the realistic creed of modern art led us to seek out mean people, but because this meanness of human life was somehow thrust upon us.[15]

George Lukács, another critic, supports Krutch's view:

> The thematic material of bourgeois drama is trivial, because it is all too near us; the natural pathos of its living men is undramatic and its most subtle values are lost when heightened into drama; the fable is wilfully invented and so cannot retain the natural and poetic resonance of an ancient tradition.[16]

On the other hand, it is argued that expecting the modern playwright to imitate antiquity is a mistaken notion. John Gassner voices this point of view:

> A fundamental premise has been the opinion that a great deal of the tragic art of the past, while excellent as far as it went, belongs to the past. The pagan beliefs that served Attic tragedy twenty-five centuries ago are no longer acceptable to modern man. Neither are the beliefs of the Elizabethan period and the age of Louis XIV. There is simply no single time philosophy of tragedy any more than there is a single inviolable tragic form. Tragic art is subject to the evolutionary processes, and tragedy created in modern times must be modern. The fact that it will be different from tragedy written three, five, or twenty-five centuries ago does not mean that it will no longer be tragedy; it will merely be different. . . . We may also arrive at the conclusion that there is really no compelling reason for the modern stage to *strain* toward tragedy. There are other ways of responding to the human condition. . . . The creative spirit of an age should be allowed, and indeed expected, to engender its own dramatic forms or to modify existent ones.[17]

Gassner's point is well taken. After all, great tragedy is rare in theater history, and we should not castigate modern dramatists because they do not recapture the ancient grandeur. Since we are so much a product of the conditioning forces of our times, it is legitimate that the theater should express the concerns of our society—the identity crisis; the clash between generations and cultures; the loss of freedom, faith, and security; the disparity between illusion and reality; the cost of integrity; and the difficulty of finding meaning in a world of shifting values.

Two outstanding examples of our modern theater are Ibsen's *Ghosts* (1881) and Miller's *Death of a Salesman* (1949). *Ghosts*, one of the most violently protested plays in the history of the theater, tells the story of Mrs. Alving's unsuccessful

Arthur Miller's *All My Sons* deals with a powerful conflict between an unscrupulous manufacturer of airplane parts and his son. *(Directed by Philip Killian, Oregon Shakespeare Festival)*

attempts to escape from the conventional strictures of a sterile Victorian society. She married Captain Alving because he was regarded as socially acceptable, but she discovers that he is dissolute and has contracted syphilis. She sends her son, Oswald, abroad to study art and to shield him from his father's corruption. When the captain dies, Mrs. Alving uses his legacy to build an orphanage in his honor, thus concealing her husband's true character and preventing Oswald from inheriting a tainted fortune. As the play opens, Mrs. Alving is confident that she has successfully laid to rest the ghosts of the past. However, Oswald becomes involved with the maid, Regina, who is actually his illegitimate half-sister. Pastor Manders, who at one time rejected Mrs. Alving when she fled to him to escape from her dissolute husband, visits the house to inquire about the efficacy of insuring the new orphanage. Oswald reveals to his mother that he is fatally ill with the venereal disease he inherited from his father. He makes her promise to give him a deadly drug when he loses his mind. Regina refuses to have anything more to do with Oswald and goes off to work in a tavern as the orphanage burns down. Under the strain of learning about his father's degeneracy and of Regina's parentage, Oswald's mind gives way and he begs his mother to give him the drug that will release him from his miserable life. As the curtain comes down, Mrs. Alving stands over her babbling son, the poison in her hand, unable to act.

Mrs Alving and Oswald in the final scene of *Ghosts* in the first European production of Ibsen's controversial play.

Death of a Salesman (1949) shows Willy Loman, a traveling salesman, return-ing to his Brooklyn home after an aborted trip. At sixty-five, Willy has come to the end of his strength. Through flashbacks, we are taken back to earlier, happier times, when he pampered his sons, Biff and Happy, and sold them on his view of popularity and financial success based on a back-slapping personality and a snappy appearance. Willy is convinced that Biff, a high school football star, will make a name for himself in the world. But Biff has a crisis with his academic work and visits his father in Boston, where he discovers Willy in a hotel with a woman. Happy has become a self-indulgent womanizer. Willy struggles to pull himself together, but his young, callous employer fires him. Linda, the devoted wife and mother, defends Willy against his disrespectful sons. Biff accuses Willy of being a failure and of selling his sons a phony dream. As a final gesture, Willy commits suicide and leaves his paid-up insurance as a legacy. Miller ends with a requiem at Willy's grave, where Biff comments, "He had the wrong dreams. All, all wrong."

Both *Ghosts* and *Death of a Salesman* are serious, complete, and honest. The actions seem necessary and probable. There is a kind of universality in both plays because the characters and their environments were, in their time, common enough to be creditable to their contemporaries. Certainly, the narrow strictures of Victorian conventions were familiar enough to late nineteenth-century society, and Willy's empty, materialistic illusions are close enough to us for recognition

In *Death of a Salesman,* **Arthur Miller created a moving portrait of the common man as tragic protagonist in Willy Loman, who unfortunately "didn't know who he was."** *(Directed by Don Blakely, Wayne State University)*

and identification; but there is no sense of elevation, no enlightenment, no catharsis. Mrs. Alving and Willy are not positive characters striving to assert ethical values. On the other hand, Ibsen and Miller dramatize characters in scenes of intense suffering, and although the exhilaration of spiritual triumph is missing, we are caught up in the strong and vivid theatrical experiences with which we can identify.

In *The Crucible,* Arthur Miller dramatizes the seventeenth-century witch hunts in Salem, Massachusetts, as he explores the roots of intolerance and mass hysteria. The play reflects the irrational fears of the 1950s, when Senator Joseph McCarthy intimidated our national capital with his investigations in search of spies and "reds." Some Puritan girls, frustrated by their society's rigid moral code, find an outlet in dancing naked in the woods. When their escapades are discovered, they declare themselves victims of the Devil and accuse innocent citizens of witchcraft. Their accusations create an atmosphere of frenzy, greed, and hate. Deputy Governor Danforth dogmatically conducts hearings, which promote hysterical reactions and lead to the condemnation of innocent women. John Procter and his wife, Elizabeth, are drawn into the action when Abigail, who had once had an affair with Procter, accuses Elizabeth of witchcraft. Procter implicates himself in his attempt to rescue Elizabeth. When he is threatened with hanging, Procter agrees to confess to witchcraft. His wife is spared execution because she is now pregnant. When it comes time to sign the confession, Procter cannot accept the terms:

Danforth: Mr. Procter, I must have good and legal proof that you . . .

Procter: You are the high court, your word is good enough! Tell them I confessed myself; say Procter broke his knees and wept like a woman; say what you will, but my name cannot—

Danforth: *(With suspicion)* It is the same, is it not? If I report or you sign it?

Procter: *(he knows it is insane.)* No, it is not the same! What others say and what I sign to is not the same!

Danforth: Why? Do you mean to deny this confession when you are free?

Procter: I mean to deny nothing!

Danforth: Then explain to me, Mr. Procter, why you will not let—

Procter: *(With a cry of his whole soul)* Because it is my name! Because I cannot have another in my life! Because I lie and sign myself to lies! Because I am not worth the dust on the feet of them that hang! How may I live without my name? I have given you my soul; leave me my name!

Elizabeth pleads with him to relent, but Procter's mind is made up. They lead him out to the gallows, and as the drums roll, his wife makes a final judgment:

Elizabeth: He has his goodness now. God forbid I take it from him![18]

Some critics rejected *The Crucible* as a tragedy, because it did not deal with a man of high rank. They cited the classical tradition of Shakespearean and Greek tragedy, in which only royalty were fit subjects.

Other modern playwrights who have created compelling serious plays are Strindberg, Chekhov, O'Neill, Pirandello, O'Casey, Shaw, Williams, Anouilh, Beckett, Shepard, Osborne, Pinter, and Peter Shaffer. You will recall Bradley's view of tragedy, which includes the sense of waste. This feeling is aroused by contemporary playwrights, who often dramatize characters and conditions in which something of great value is lost—a potential not realized, a promising life destroyed, a dream unfulfilled. Although the fall is not from a high place, there is a stark urgency and immediacy in our response, because these people are familiar and their actions are close to our own experience.

Miller may be close to the mark when he says:

As a general rule to which there may be exceptions unknown to me, I think tragic feeling is evoked in us when we are in the presence of a character who is ready to lay down his life, if need be, to secure one thing—his sense of personal dignity. From Orestes to Hamlet, Medea to Macbeth, the underlying struggle is that of the individual attempting to gain his "rightful position in his society."[19]

When a broken-spirited Blanche is led away to an asylum at the end of Tennessee Williams's *A Streetcare Named Desire,* there is a tragic sense of waste.

The theater began with tragedy in the sixth century B.C. in Greece. Critical assessment generally regards tragedy as the highest form of dramatic art. The small collection of tragic plays is considered one of the most important aesthetic achievements of Western culture. However, although tragedy has attracted more critical attention than any other form of drama, it is the least produced. Tragedy confronts the individual with the most profound issues of life, with the complexities of human nature, with the forces of good and evil. It makes no concession to wish fulfillment, sugary optimism, or happy endings.

Although it is fashionable to indict our age for its doubt and skepticism, in our own serious drama there are echoes of the grandeur of tragedy. We are still able to respond to the great landmarks of the past, and, despite our vulnerability, we are aware of the capacity of the human spirit to survive suffering and defeat. Heroism is not dead. We all know among our contemporaries those individuals who put themselves at risk in making unselfish commitments of their lives. There are those who preserve their integrity in the face of great loss; those who take positive stands against overwhelming opposition; those who illuminate the darkness. Tragedy celebrates the greatness of the human spirit and, in that celebration, exalts us all.

PLAYS TO READ AND SEE

F = Film available; V = Videotape available.

		Sophocles, *Antigone, Oedipus Rex*
F	V	Arthur Miller, *Death of a Salesman*
		Henrik Ibsen, *Ghosts*

F	V	William Shakespeare, *Hamlet,* Olivier's *Hamlet,* Olivier's *King Lear,*
		Macbeth, Romeo and Juliet
F	V	Eugene O'Neill, *Long Day's Journey into Night*
F	V	*Shakespearean Tragedy*
F	V	Euripides, *The Trojan Women*
F		*What Happens in Hamlet*

BIBLIOGRAPHY

BRADLEY, A. C. *Shakespearean Tragedy.* London: Macmillan, 1957.

FRYE, NORTHROP. *The Anatomy of Criticism.* Princeton, N.J.: Princeton University Press, 1957.

HEILMAN, ROBERT BECHTOLD. *The Iceman, the Arsonist, and the Troubled Agent: Tragedy and Melodrama on the Modern Stage.* Seattle: University of Washington Press, 1973.

KERR, WALTER. *Tragedy and Comedy.* New York: Simon & Schuster, 1967.

KITTO, H. D. F. *Greek Tragedy.* London: Methuen, 1950.

LANGER, SUZANNE. *Feeling and Form.* New York: Charles Scribner's & Sons, 1953.

MULLER, HERBERT. *The Spirit of Tragedy.* New York: Knopf, 1976.

MYERS, HENRY ALONZO. *Tragedy: A View of Life.* Ithaca, N.Y.: Cornell University Press, 1956.

OLSON, ELDER. *Tragedy and the Theory of Drama.* Detroit: Wayne State University Press, 1961.

NOTES

1. Ingram Bywater, trans., *Aristotle on the Art of Poetry* (Oxford: Clarendon Press, 1920).

2. William Shakespeare, *Hamlet,* Act V, Scene 2.

3. Suzanne K. Langer, *Feeling and Form* (New York: Charles Scribner's & Sons, 1953).

4. Northrop Frye, *The Anatomy of Criticism* (Princeton, N.J.: Princeton University Press, 1957).

5. Robert F. Goheen, *The Imagery of Sophocles' Antigone* (Princeton, N.J.: Princeton University Press, 1951).

6. Sophocles, *Antigone,* trans. R. C. Jebb (Cambridge: Cambridge University Press, 1902).

7. Caroline Spurgeon, *Shakespeare's Imagery and What It Tells Us* (Cambridge: Cambridge University Press, 1935).

8. *Hamlet,* Act I, Scene 2.

9. Gilbert Murray, "Hamlet and Orestes," in *The Classical Tradition in Poetry* (Cambridge, Mass.: Harvard University Press, 1927).

10. Henry Alonzo Myers, *Tragedy: A View of Life* (Ithaca, N.Y.: Cornell University Press, 1956).

11. Ibid.

12. A. C. Bradley, *Shakespearean Tragedy* (London: Macmillan, 1957).

13. Allardyce Nicoll, *The Theory of Drama* (New York: Thomas Y. Crowell, 1931).

14. Jean Anouilh, *Antigone,* trans. Lewis Galantiere (London: Van Loewen, 1946).

15. Joseph Wood Krutch, *"Modernism" in Modern Drama* (Ithaca, N.Y.: Cornell University Press, 1953).

16. George Lukács, "The Sociology of Modern Drama," trans. Lee Baxandall, *Tulane Drama Review, 9* (Summer 1965).

17. John Gassner, "The Possibilities and Perils of Modern Tragedy," *Tulane Drama Review, 1*, No. 3 (June 1957).

18. Arthur Miller, *The Crucible*. Copyright 1952, 1953, 1954; renewed © 1980 by Arthur Miller. Used by permission of Viking Penguin, a division of Penguin Books USA, Inc.

19. Arthur Miller, "Tragedy and the Common Man," *New York Times*, February 27, 1949.

four
Melodrama

In the nineteenth-century melodrama *The Count of Monte Cristo,* Eugene O'Neill's father, James O'Neill, made a fortune playing the swashbuckling hero in almost six thousand performances. He appears here in a famous duel scene in a forest of painted trees.

Melodrama conjures up images of old-fashioned cliffhangers in which stalwart heroes rescue maidens in distress from the clutches of wicked villains just in the nick of time. We think of such bygone thrillers as *Under the Gaslight, Ten Nights in a Bar Room,* and *The Drunkard.* Although the outward trappings have changed, melodrama is very much in evidence today. It continues to dominate our motion picture and television fare in such hits as *The Hunt for Red October, Star Wars, Dick Tracy,* and *Batman.* A glance at a television guide lists these melodramas: *Destry Rides Again, Stagecoach, 20,000 Leagues Under the Sea,* and *Dracula.* The video guide has these "classics": *The Hunchback of Notre Dame, Raiders of the Lost Ark,* and *The Maltese Falcon.* In the live theater, melodrama has made its impact, especially in musicals such as *Phantom of the Opera, Les Misérables,* and *Sweeney Todd.*

The reason for the enormous popularity of melodrama is that something happens. People just don't sit around and talk or suffer. They do something. They become involved in strong conflicts. In Chapter 1, we talked about the importance of "empathy" in connection with audience response. You will recall that *empathy* means "feeling into," and it evokes a motor response. It explains the popularity of active sports. Fans get involved in the action. In the theater, the audience responds to the struggles of the hero and heroine to attain their goals. Eric Bentley suggests that one of the reasons that melodrama has such a wide appeal is that the spectators can "have a good cry"—the poor man's catharsis. Melodrama is a way of releasing frustrations and aggressions and of fulfilling one's wishes.

Eric Bentley has this evaluation of melodrama:

> It is the spontaneous, uninhibited way of seeing things. . . . The dramatic sense is the melodramatic sense, as one can see from the play acting of any child. Melodrama is not a special and marginal kind of drama, let alone an eccentric or decadent one; it is drama in its elemental form; it is the quintessence of drama.[1]

Outwardly, melodrama tries to create the illusion of real people in genuine jeopardy, but actually the plot is manipulated toward reprieve, rescue, or reform. It exploits physical and material difficulties. Escape from danger is a basic plot framework. Melodrama generates excitement, suspense, and thrills *for their own sake.* Melodrama is a *game;* although it builds tension, suspense, and surprise, it is transitory and without substance or significance. One leaves the theater with a sense of relief at the outcome, but untroubled by the conditions that caused the suffering and conflicts. The most convenient way to get rid of evil is to eliminate the evildoer.

We may define melodrama as that form of drama that is primarily concerned with exciting conflicts and plots that employ stock characters, notably a suffering hero and/or heroine, a persecuting villain, and lower-class comics. It is sentimental and optimistic in viewpoint and believes in a moral order. Characteristically, it has a happy ending, with virtue rewarded and evil punished. Melodrama depends on action and scenery. Music is often an important element to underscore the dramatic mood. Spectacular settings are important for astonishing effects and for giving the performers an environment for vigorous and violent action.

In the previous chapter we considered tragedy, the loftiest and rarest form of drama. How does it differ from melodrama, which on the surface seems to deal, like tragedy, with characters involved in serious and critical situations? Fundamentally, the distinction lies in the point of view. Tragedy confronts good and evil with unblinking honesty; melodrama escapes from life. Tragedy considers eternal spiritual problems; melodrama deals with the transitory, the material, the physical. Tragedy evokes fear and pity; melodrama arouses suspense, pathos, terror, and sometimes hate. However, melodrama is not mere ineffectual tragedy. As a matter of fact, a well-written melodrama may be superior to an inept tragedy. The point is that the two forms of drama are different. They are similar only in that they both *seem* serious, but in melodrama the seriousness is only a pretense for the sake of the theatrical game.

Melodramatic scenes and situations have been a part of the history of the theater almost from the beginning. Euripides, in striving for effect, was sometimes very close to melodrama, and Seneca exploited sensational and horrible material to the hilt. The Elizabethan "tragedies of blood" employed much of the machinery of melodrama, with scenes of horror and violence. Jacobean playwrights delighted in grisly scenes of exciting action. The early-eighteenth-century "she-tragedies" of Nicholas Rowe, with their sentimentalism and overwrought emotions, were in the melodramatic vein. Johann Schiller's romantic *The Robbers* (1781) capitalized on the fugitive situation so dear to writers of melodrama.

The term *melodrama* combines two Greek words meaning "music" and "drama." At one time the word was literally synonymous with opera. Melodrama was first allied with music in Italy and France. In Germany the term referred to dialogue passages spoken to orchestral accompaniment. The modern connotation of the word, however, stems from the late eighteenth-century French theater and its subsequent development, especially in England and America.

Until 1791, the Comédie Française and the Italian Comedians enjoyed monopolistic control over the legitimate theaters of Paris. Ingenious managers circumvented governmental restrictions by contriving a kind of entertainment based on pantomime accompanied by dance, song, and dialogue, which elicited a popular following because of its sensational qualities. When freedom of production was granted to all theaters, the word *melodrama* was attached to the pantomime with dialogue and music.

The French playwright Guilbert de Pixérécourt at the beginning of the nineteenth century became the foremost playwright of the new form, which exactly fit the taste of the lower classes. He made a careful study of his audiences until he perfected the machinery that was to dominate melodrama from that time to this and was to make him one of the most popular playwrights who ever lived. He wrote nearly sixty melodramas, which played more than thirty thousand performances in France alone. His plots were based on exciting action, surprise,

In 1802, Thomas Holcroft gave British audiences a taste for melodrama with *A Tale of Mystery*, featuring violent action in a gothic atmosphere.

and suspense—the sharp contrasts of vice against virtue, the comic versus the pathetic—and he thrilled his audiences with spectacular scenes such as fires, floods, and collisions. Although he wrote his plays rapidly, he worked with them in the theater personally, taking great pains to have them produced exactly as he intended. The success of his efforts caused him to be known as "the Napoleon of the Boulevard."

Before Thomas Holcroft returned to London from France with his popular melodrama, *A Tale of Mystery* (1802), the taste for its mood and action had already been set by the sentimentalized, long-suffering heroines of gothic novels and by the theater's spectacular scenery. "Monk" Lewis's *Castle Spectre* (1797) employed much of the machinery of melodrama in the dramatization of an orphan girl, Lady Angela, ensnared by the wicked Lord Osmond, who has slain her father and taken over his property. The setting is a castle haunted by the ghost of the girl's mother. Thanks to the efforts of Earl Percy, disguised as a farmer, the villain is foiled and a happy ending ensues. *Castle Spectre* was a smashing success, and its basic ingredients were endlessly copied.

In the late eighteenth century in Germany, August von Kotzebue wrote more than two hundred plays combining sensational scenes with heavy sentimentality. He was not only commercially successful but also very influential on playwriting for years to come. In England, Richard Sheridan translated and presented Kotzebue's *The Spaniard in Peru* as *Pizarro* in 1799; and in 1798 William Dunlap adapted Kotzebue's *The Stranger,* one of the first melodramas to be presented in the United States in the nineteenth century, although most plays were imported from France and England rather than from Germany. Later American playwrights learned to exploit the native scene for plays of big-city life, rural stories with local color, plays about firemen, and dramas of the wild West.

At first melodrama owed its popularity to its story line. Its pattern was a series of strong actions performed by clear-cut characters demonstrating the triumph of simple virtues and the ultimate defeat of villainy. To satisfy the tremendous demand for new material, playwrights ground out new plays as do today's television writers; and like their modern counterparts, most writers followed well-established formulas.

As the nineteenth century progressed, efforts were made to create more realistic melodramas. The easiest way to suggest reality was through the external aspects of production—especially the stage scenery. Toward the end of the century, the theater technician ran away with the show. New and spectacular effects became a primary source of appeal. The stage mechanic was called on not only to represent accurate replicas of familiar landscapes, buildings, and monuments but also to reproduce all manner of sensational effects. Melodrama tended to become simply a scenario for exciting actions. As a result of its elaboration of the visual aspects of production and its demand for strong stories and movements, nineteenth-century melodrama led directly to the development of the motion picture industry.

By the end of the nineteenth century the old-fashioned melodrama had run its course because of the increasing sophistication of the audience and the changes in the world outside. As drama moved toward realism, the old formulas and characters of melodrama gave way. Even when the theater aimed at the popular audience, it was necessary to make plots more credible, to include more kinds of characters and to give them more depth, and to capture the impression of more normal speech. As for one of the major appeals of melodrama—the sensational scenes—the new film medium offered spectacle far beyond the capacities of the limited stage.

PLOT

Melodrama in the nineteenth century relied heavily on stories that had colorful characters, opportunities for strong "sensation" scenes, and outlets for powerful emotions. Audiences preferred dramatic situations that showed characters struggling against fearful odds, trapped or marooned, but holding out until help comes—the last bullet, the last drop of water, the last bite of food, the last cent.

A scene from Dion Boucicault's melodrama *The Colleen Bawn,* when the villain, Danny, tries to drown the heroine, Eily. The scene was staged with every effort to make it as realistic and exciting as possible.

The art of playwriting, therefore, became the art of devising scenes of excitement. Melodrama exaggerated climaxes and crises so that the structure of the play was a series of peaks of action rather than a well-knit steady progression of logically related events. A typical scene of climax from Dion Boucicault's great favorite, *The Colleen Bawn* (1860), illustrates not only the kind of situation but also the emphasis on action:

> (*Music, low storm music. . . . Myles sings without, then appears U. E. R. on rock. . . . Swings across stage by rope. Exit U. E. I. H. Music, boat floats on R. H. with Eily and Danny. Eily steps on to Rock C. (Danny) stepping onto the rock the boat floats away unseen. . . . Music. Throws her into water, L. C. She disappears for an instant then reappears clinging to Rock C. . . . Thrusts her down. She disappears. . . . Shot heard U. E. L. H. Danny falls into water behind C. Rock. Myles sings without. . . . Swings across by rope to R. H., fastens it up, then fishes up Double of Eily—lets her fall. Strips, then dives after her. Eily appears for an instant in front. Then double for Myles appears at back and dives over drum. Myles and Eily appear in front of Center Rock. Tableau. Curtain.*)[2]

This kind of physical action is, of course, the standard material of melodrama, made appealing to nineteenth-century audiences by novel effects. It is interesting to note the use of character "doubles" in order to keep the scene moving. Other elements of special interest in this scene are the music for reinforc-

A famous Daumier print showing a sensational moment in a French melodrama. Notice the empathetic response of the audience.

ing the atmosphere and the tableau at the end of the act. The writer of melodrama depended on all kinds of *coups de théâtre* for releasing strong feelings, often utilizing climactic curtains, such as in this scene, literally as "clap traps."

To create continuity of the narrative, the dramatist tied the scenes together by a variety of techniques. Changes of scenery were covered by music or special lighting effects. Often, the scenes were changed in view of the audience. Sets were devised for the use of simultaneous or parallel action. Still another practice was that of shifting the locale from one place to another while the action continued. The following example from *A Race for Life* indicates this device, which anticipates cinematic practice:

> (*Officers fire. Convicts rush on, struggle with officers. Shots outside; Gaspard seizes Jacques—is thrown off. Officer seizes Jacques, he throws him off when Holmes struggles off with Brady R. H. Men and officers struggle off R. and L. when all clear. Sound Change Bell.*
>   *Rocks drawn off R. and L. Prison double set center revolves to old Light House and comes down stage. Jacques and Brady come on in boat. Men work sea cloth. Patty throws rope from light house window. Brady catches it. Picture. Slow curtain.*)[3]

Good writers of melodrama were skilled craftspeople with a shrewd sense of pace, rhythm, and a feeling for climactic action. They were adept storytellers and showmen. They not only knew the possibilities of the stage but also understood their audience. Logic did not interest them as long as their plays gave the impression of credibility, which they achieved by keeping the narratives moving and by creating the illusion of actuality through realistic backgrounds, appropriate costumes, and good casting.

CHARACTER

Robert B. Heilman suggests that the contrast between melodrama and tragedy is a matter of character treatment:

> The identifying mark of the melodramatic structure is not the particular outcome of the plot, but the conception of character and the alignment of forces. . . . In melodrama, man is seen in his strength or in his weakness; in tragedy in both his strength and weakness at once. In melodrama, he is victorious or he is defeated; in tragedy, he experiences defeat in victory, or victory in defeat. In melodrama, man is simply innocent; in tragedy, his guilt and his innocence coexist. In melodrama, man's will is broken, or it conquers; in tragedy, it is tempered in the suffering that comes with, or brings about, new knowledge.[4]

Heilman's concept, then, of the melodramatic hero is of a whole character, not one torn by internal stress, whereas the tragic hero is a divided human being confronted by basic conflicts, perhaps not soluble, of obligations and passions.

Nineteenth-century melodrama and our motion picture and television fare testify to the validity of Heilman's observation. Characters are generally one-dimensional figures, good or bad, who pursue their objectives in a straight line. The opposition comes from without rather than from within. Characters do not think—they act, and as a result they often become involved in entanglements a judicious person might avoid, such as being caught on a train trestle at midnight without a lantern, lost in a snowstorm without food or shelter, or duped by the villain's traps and schemes because of their own gullibility and ignorance. The writer of melodrama was not concerned with delineating characters as complex individuals who were conditioned by their backgrounds. They were people who were simple in heart and mind. As nineteenth-century melodrama developed, however, some playwrights made efforts to create more credible characters with more complex motivations. Indeed, the waywardness of the villain might be explained at some length as the result of an unfortunate conditioning experience in early life when he was abused or unjustly treated, and as a result he might make some claim on the audience's sympathy and understanding.

Most characters in melodrama were types. This was important in performance so that the spectator could readily recognize them, and it was also essential for the acting company in the distribution of the roles. Owen Davis, one of the most successful writers of melodrama in the early part of the twentieth century, used stock characters in such hits as *The Lighthouse by the Sea* and *The Chinatown Trunk Mystery*. He describes the typical personnel required for his plays:

> There were eight essential characters: the hero, who can be either very poor, which is preferable, or else very young and very drunk (if sober and wealthy he becomes

automatically a villain); the heroine, by preference a working girl (cloak model, "typewriter," factory girl, shop girl, etc.) and practically indestructible; the comic—Irish, Jewish, or German—played usually by the highest paid member of the company; the soubrette, "a working girl with bad manners and a good heart," devoted to the heroine; the heavy man, identified by a moustache, silk hat, and white gloves; the heavy woman, a haughty society dame or an "unfortunate"; the light comedy boy; and the second heavy, "just a bum," a tool of the villain; it was usual to kill him along toward the middle of the second act.[5]

The pivotal character of old-time melodrama was the villain, who was the motivating force of much of the plot. Just as it was essential to show the goodness of the hero and the heroine to enlist the sympathy of the audience, it was mandatory to demonstrate the wickedness of the villain to generate the audience's hostility. One of the pleasures of melodrama was loathing the evildoers and seeing them get the punishment they so richly deserved. Hence the playwright was careful to build up the iniquitous villains with their sinful desires, their smoldering grudges and passions, and their inexhaustible supply of devilish schemes.

Melodrama was the entertainment of the masses, and since maximum identification was the playwrights' aim, they often used characters from the ordinary walks of life. Heroes were not the elevated figures of the past; they were firefighters, cowboys, soldiers, sailors, farmhands. Although they were stock types, the bare outlines of the text were fleshed out by the imaginations and personalities of the actors who brought them to life. Leading roles in melodrama provided exceptional opportunities for some actors, who spent most of their careers identified with a single part. James O'Neill played in *Monte Cristo* for 5,817 performances, and Denman Thompson appeared in *The Old Homestead* more than 7,000 times.

THOUGHT

Most writers of melodrama were primarily concerned with entertaining an audience rather than delivering a message. But because of the genre's broad appeal, melodrama often reflected a vague humanitarianism in its sympathetic treatment of the downtrodden and its condemnation of arrogant authority, the overprivileged, and the avaricious manipulators in big business. Although there was frequently an implied suggestion to take action and throw off the tormentors so everyone could be free, the implication was not a direct call for rebellion. Instead, melodrama commonly expressed a staunch loyalty to orthodox morality, backed by an optimistic faith in the future. The root of the social evils that oppressed those who suffered was generally lodged in the evil nature of the villains rather than in the political or economic system.

It was customary to end melodramas with arbitrary scenes of poetic justice, in which couples were paired off, and rewards and punishments were parceled out according to the actions of the characters. As the final curtain descended, the audience was reassured that virtue will triumph, murder will out, and the wages of sin is death. But melodrama, with its sharp conflicts between good and evil, did not altogether neglect the opportunity for propaganda. The evil of drink was a favorite target, as were usury, heavy taxes, and the sinful nature of the big city. One of the most popular hits of all time was George L. Aiken's dramatization of Harriet Beecher Stowe's novel *Uncle Tom's Cabin* (1852), which held the stage for eighty years. Its depiction of slavery was one of the strongest pieces of propaganda of the nineteenth century.

Duty and self-sacrifice were pictured as the ennobling virtues of the lower classes. Whatever the misfortunes, the honorable person performed his or her duty, confident that in the end justice would be meted out—in the next world, if not here and now. Dozens of heroines declaimed such sentiments, as seen in the following passage from Augustan Daly's highly successful *Under the Gaslight:*

Laura: Let the woman you look upon be wise or vain, beautiful or homely, rich or poor, she has but one thing she can really give or refuse—her heart! Her beauty, her wit, her accomplishments, she may sell to you—but her love is the treasure without money and without price. She only asks in return, that when you look upon her, your eyes shall speak a mute devotion; that when you address her, your voice shall be gentle, loving, and kind. That you shall not despise her because she cannot understand all at once, your vigorous thoughts, and ambitious designs; for when misfortune and evil have defeated your greatest purposes—her love remains to console you. You look to the trees for strength and grandeur —do not despise the flowers, because their fragrance is all they have to give. Remember—love is all a woman has to give; but it is the only earthly thing which God permits us to carry beyond the grave.[6]

DICTION

The language of melodrama was often singularly undistinguished. Since common characters carried the burden of the plot, playwrights attempted to suggest onstage the everyday idiom. This effort performed some service in undermining the bombast and extravagance of romantic diction, although the writer of melodrama was not entirely immune from flowery language. In moments of strong emotion, characters spouted purple passages like the one cited from *Under the Gaslight.* But by and large, the playwright's emphasis on common characters involved in scenes of violent action led to dialogue that suggested the texture of ordinary speech. As a result of this attempt to imitate the language of life, some playwrights endeavored to copy the dialects and provincialism of specific locales, which was a move toward increased realism.

Writers of melodrama made free use of such technical devices as asides and soliloquies, which not only aided them in the difficult problems of exposition imposed by episodic structure but also gave them the opportunity to reveal character and motivation.

A climactic moment in *Under the Gaslight,* when the heroine escapes from the tool shed in the nick of time to rescue Snorky from the onrushing locomotive.

MUSIC

Melodrama, originally linked with music, continued that association. As the excerpt from *The Colleen Bawn* indicated, music was an important accompaniment to the action. When the motion pictures took over melodrama, music was soon found to be extremely useful for eliciting emotional response. Silent films were accompanied by appropriate scores for piano or pipe organ. For more ambitious productions such as *The Birth of a Nation,* a complete orchestral accompaniment was written and played. In our present films and television dramas, music continues to be an indispensable element of production to establish atmosphere, bridge the action, or generate excitement.

Nineteenth-century melodrama made another interesting use of music. The entrances and exits of leading characters were accompanied by special musical themes suitable for their roles. Actors often performed to music that not only helped them establish the emotional atmosphere of the scene but also influenced their timing and movement.

Sound effects were sometimes an important adjunct of productions, especially in climactic scenes—in "turf" dramas, when the horses thundered down the straightaway toward the finish line; or when in *Under the Gaslight* the rumbling, whistling train approached with its headlights picking up Snorky tied to the tracks while the heroine, Laura, frantically attempted to shatter the walls of the toolshed in time to save him; or when, in the fire plays, the firefighters raced to the scene of a spectacular blaze amid the crackle of flames, the cries for help, and the sound of the equipment.

SPECTACLE

In the first half of the century almost all theaters used two-dimensional stock pieces consisting of backdrops and wings on which were painted a variety of backgrounds, such as a kitchen, palace, prison, grotto, or woodland glade. This system possessed two virtues—it was economical and it made shifting rapid and easy. To change to a new setting, the backdrop was raised to reveal another one behind it, while wings slid along the grooves to uncover the new ones for the following scene. Throughout the country, theaters were equipped with stock sets, so that a touring company needed to bring only its special effects and costumes. But as the taste for sensational novelties grew, productions became increasingly elaborate and expensive. Metropolitan stages became more complicated, with bridges, traps, elevators, moving platforms, and paraphernalia for producing fires, floods, explosions, and all manner of astounding displays. The two-dimensional scenery was replaced by built-up solid pieces, making the sets substantial and difficult to move. Playwrights built their plays around sensational scenic displays. The following scene from *Pauvrette: or Under the Snow* shows the kind of effects required.

> *(The summit of the Alps. Rocks and precipices occupy the stage. A rude hut on one side in front. A bridge formed by a felled tree across the chasm at the back. The stone-clad peaks stretch away in the distance. Night . . . storm, wind. She (Pauvrette) throws her scarf around her, and hastily ascends the rock—utters a long wailing cry—listens. . . . Descends to her hut. Maurice cries for help. Takes her alpenstock and a coil of rope, and reascends the rock. The wind increases—the snow begins to fall. She crosses the bridge and disappears off left. Bernard appears below on the rocks, L. He climbs up the path. . . . Pauvrette appears on the bridge, leading Maurice. . . . They cross the bridge. . . . They descend and enter the hut. . . . Large blocks of hardened snow and masses of rock fall, rolling into the abyss. Pauvrette falls on her knees. . . . Pauvrette enters the hut. The avalanche begins to fall—the bridge is broken and hurled into the abyss—the paths have been filled with snow—and now an immense sheet rushing down from the R. entirely buries the whole scene to the height of twelve or fifteen feet, swallowing up the cabin and leaving above a clear level of snow—the storm passes away—silence and peace return—the figure of the virgin (in window) is unharmed—the light before it still burns.)*[7]

During the third quarter of the nineteenth century, Boucicault was the acknowledged master of melodrama, both in writing and in staging his plays. He catered to the taste of the public with his sensational scenes, to which he gave the

In such plays as Boucicault's *Pauvrette,* the stage effects were often more interesting than the characters. Staging a credible avalanche challenged the theater technician's skill to the utmost.

utmost care. *The Octaroon* (1859) featured a fire aboard a river boat; in *Arrah-na-Pogue,* Shaun's prison escape begins inside the cell, then turns inside out to reveal him coming out the window and over the wall.

At the turn of the century, "Drury Lane melodramas" were famous for their stage effects. *The Prince of Peace* (1900) presented Parliament in session, a wedding in Westminster Abbey, and a collision at sea in which a yacht is smashed by a steamer. *The Sins of Society* (1907) thrilled the spectators with a huge transport ship that slowly sank beneath the waves on a fog-shrouded stage, while a wireless crackled and sparked and a steam siren sounded the alarm.

David Belasco set a new standard for Broadway with the ultrarealistic staging of his melodramas celebrating the American heritage: *The Heart of Maryland* (1895), *Under Two Flags* (1901), and *The Girl of the Golden West* (1905). He toned down much of the violence and blatant sentimentality and made the plot and dialogue more credible, even though he depended a great deal on startling scenes carefully produced. He also had the advantage of working with electricity, which he used with imagination and taste. Typical of Belasco's theatricality was the staging of the prologue to *The Girl of the Golden West*. Frank Rahill describes it in some detail:

> . . . a painted canvas scene, rolled vertically on drums, presented a moving map-like panorama of the whole picturesque area where the action unfolds; first, the heights of cloudy mountain in the moonlight, then the girl's cabin perched aloft and a steep footpath winding down the walls of the canyon to the settlement below; and next, the little camp itself, shown at the foot of the path, the miners' cabins huddled about the Polka Saloon, through the windows of which drifts the muted din of rough revelry— the rattle of poker chips, the strains of banjo, and concertina, and masculine voices raised in a chorus of "Camptown Races." This is erased suddenly in a blackout, and a moment later the lights come on full to reveal the interior of the saloon, where a shindig is in full swing—the music continuing meanwhile and serving to bind the two scenes together.[8]

It should be remembered that although sensational scenery called attention to itself, it was also used for more than pictorial representation. The setting was functional in that it served the actors' needs in a particular scene. A waterfall was not simply shown as an enlarged calendar picture for its visual appeal. It became a factor in the action when the hero struggled to save the heroine from plunging to her death. A railroad trestle was set onstage not merely for the novelty of showing a train but also as a weapon of the villain, who tied the hero to the tracks as the train's light and whistle approached. The setting was an essential part of the action. Hence, a considerable amount of ingenuity was required by the stage mechanic to devise effects that were not only visually credible but also utilitarian enough to be used in chases, fights, and escapes. Incidentally, the actor had to be something of an athlete to dive from burning buildings, scale steep cliffs, and chase or be chased through a canvas jungle—while reciting lines. (It is no wonder that doubles were often used to keep the action continuous.)

One device by which melodrama sought to create an illusion of reality was the use of actual and authentic properties. Belasco actually bought pieces of buildings and moved them onstage. Some playwrights and producers cluttered their sets with endless detail to make the stage picture seem real. Often a real property, such as a rowboat, made an incongruous contrast with the obviously painted backdrop of the sea. On the other hand, the use of genuine and homely objects onstage enhanced the realism of the acting by giving the actors an opportunity to create business and pantomime. James A. Herne, a successful writer of melodrama who attempted to emulate the new realism, was very fond of filling his scenes with the everyday objects and actions of life. In some of his plays he brought on dogs, chickens, a horse, geese, and live babies. He showed a shipyard in operation, during which a boat was painted each evening.

As the elaboration of scenery progressed, it became increasingly difficult for a road company to tour because many of the outlying theaters could not accommodate the special scenery because of lack of room or equipment, not to mention the increased cost of the touring production. The solidity and complexity of scenery also affected playwriting. Scenes could not be shifted as rapidly as previously, and the cost of production mounted. The result was to reduce the number of scenes, so that there were fewer locales and episodes. Under these conditions, the dramatist was forced to use less physical action, the narrative lost some of its fluency, and there was a tendency toward fuller development of character and dialogue.

In summary, the characteristics of nineteenth-century melodrama are:

1. The plots are action stories with strong conflicts and exciting climaxes.
2. Stock characterization is used—romantic heroines (often in distress), wicked villains, strong heroes, low comics.
3. Poetic justice reigns. The good are rewarded, the evil punished. Love conquers all.
4. Dialogue is functional and relatively unimportant. The point is action, not talk.
5. Music and sound are very important in establishing and reinforcing atmosphere and feelings.
6. There is strong appeal to the eye through spectacular scenery and effects.

MELODRAMA AND FILM

As you glance at this list, you should be aware that these are the characteristics of many of our motion pictures as well. Early in the development of film, it became evident that it was the ideal medium for melodrama. Edwin S. Porter's short films, *The Life of an American Fireman* (1903) and *The Great Train Robbery,* taught moviemakers that the key to the industry was in showing action. Melodramas that relied on violent and vigorous conflicts were hard to handle onstage, but with film there was no problem. The action could use all of the outdoors—mountains, rivers, waterfalls, the ocean, deserts, cityscapes, landscapes, and seascapes, plus the sky above and the depths of the sea. It could realistically show volcanoes, floods, earthquakes, storms, fires, battles, and imaginary fantasies of animal and insect life. It could go freewheeling out in space, or instantly take the viewer from the Stone Age far into the future.

Characterization was of little importance because the emphasis was on external appearance and action, not on psychological probing. It was more important to establish the personality of the actor and actress, who could spend their careers playing themselves. The villain, likewise, was a two-dimensional character, whose outward appearance and behavior changed to fit the fashion of our public and political enemies.

Because the emphasis was on what the actor *did* rather than said, dialogue supported the action. It was commonplace, frank, and perhaps colorful, but without any literary concern. Conflicts were devised to suit the needs of the plot, rather than to explore meaning or motivation. Good usually triumphed in the end, and wishes were fulfilled. The audience had to be given the satisfaction of seeing the villain punished or eliminated, often in a violent way. Music was a

Recent musicals have gained popular approval with lavish sets and special effects, but the tradition goes back to the nineteenth century, when Henry Irving staged the storming of the Bastille in his London production of *The Dead Heart* in 1889.

necessary accompaniment to the action and was often far more effective than the acting.

The camera filled the eye with exciting, picturesque, exotic, and sensual images, and had a marvelous facility for taking the viewer into the action. Hence, to this day the basic product of film and television remains action stories, because that is what the mass audience wants to see.

In the current theater, melodrama is largely confined to murder mysteries and psychological thrillers—*Gaslight, Dial "M" for Murder, Angel Street, The Woman in Black,*—and plays about the adventures of Dracula or Sherlock Holmes. Two contemporary thrillers that were Broadway box office hits are Anthony Shaffer's *Sleuth* (1,222 performances) and Ira Levin's *Deathtrap* (1,793 performances). Both of these melodramas were built on the machinations of two mystery story writers who are familiar with the ways of setting diabolical traps that challenge audiences to follow the surprising twists and turns of the plot.

MELODRAMATIC MUSICALS

Recently, melodrama has made an enormous impact through three musicals: *The Phantom of the Opera, Les Misérables,* and *Sweeney Todd.*

One of the most successful musical spectacles in recent years was *Les Misérables*, a dramatization of Victor Hugo's novel.

The Phantom is based on a nineteenth-century melodramatic novel by Gaston Leroux. Several versions of it appeared in play form, and Lon Chaney made a popular film version of it in 1927. The present-day musical covers over its melodramatic base with Andrew Lloyd Webber's sensuous music, Marie Björnson's spectacular scenery and costumes, and the superlative performances of the stars. Underneath, however, are the old-fashioned formulas of the grotesque outcast and his ill-fated obsession for the charming young singer, Christine. When the Phantom kidnaps her, there is a sensational chase from the roof of the Paris Opera House to the lake in the sub-basement, where the couple are seen gliding in a boat across a candle-lit mist. Meanwhile, the audience is thrilled by the falling chandelier. These actions are played out against opulent settings with dazzling stage effects, to the accompaniment of a Webber score. The melodramatic machinery is well concealed, but underneath, *The Phantom* is part of the old tradition.

Likewise, *Les Misérables* was not far removed from melodrama in its use of such stock material as the outcast fugitive, the suffering orphan, the distressed, ill-treated woman, and the relentless arm of the law; in use of chases, fights, beatings, robberies, and the battle at the barricade. Hugo's language and the motivation of his characters go deeper than melodrama, however, and the music raises the level of the production.

Sweeney Todd, the Demon Barber of Fleet Street, which featured Stephen

Sweeney Todd is a musical based on the fascinating career of a nineteenth-century character known as "the demon barber of Fleet Street," whose objective was to gain revenge on the judge who sent him to prison. In this scene Sweeney has the judge in his barber chair. Despite such sensational scenes, *Sweeney Todd* escapes being melodrama by virtue of Stephen Sondheim's music.

Sondheim's music, created a sensation in 1979 with its melodramatic story of a man who returns from prison, determined to get revenge on the unscrupulous judge who framed him. The macabre events of the story rise above the blood and thunder, like the libretti of many operas, because of the elevated quality of the music.

Most serious plays are neither melodrama nor tragedy. They are, rather, middle-class plays for a middle-class audience, dealing with contemporary humankind in commonplace circumstances. Plays that have the objective of telling the truth about life are remarkably varied in style and content; but they do have a common denominator in attempting to examine values and to create a sense of awareness about the place of the individual in present-day society.

DRAME

This vast body of dramatic literature defies definition because of its great diversity, its experimentation in structure and production, and its mixtures of several

Drame includes plays like C. P. Taylor's *And a Nightingale Sang,* which saw World War II through the eyes of the Stott family. This production by the Hartford Stage Company offered a combination of light moments and dark.

forms and modes of writing at once—for example, realism with expressionism or comedy with tragic material. Some critics simply use the term *drama,* but I prefer, as a lesser evil, the French term *drame,* by which is meant those plays of serious intent usually dealing with contemporary life. Just as realism has been the dominant mode of modern drama, so drame has been the preponderant form.

Drame is allied to melodrama in that the playwright involves the spectator in the action through identification with familiar characters and the creation of suspense and tension through conflicts. Drame differs from melodrama in that it is concerned with the realm of ideas, with sociological and philosophical issues at stake, whereas melodrama deals with escape. In drame, characters participate in genuinely significant action that provokes discussion and reflection after the curtain has gone down. Melodrama, by contrast, is played at the game level. There is no residue of meaning.

Drame is allied to tragedy in its seriousness of purpose, in its relentless honesty of treatment, in its concern with the meaning of human conduct. Drame differs from tragedy in its narrowness of vision—its frequent emphasis on material, temporary, or local conditions that deny universality; its mechanistic or nihilistic sense of values; its general lack of elevation. Frequently, the writer of drames is fascinated by the psychological complexities of character. The dramatis personae are not the stock characters of melodrama; they are individuals with subtle and complicated motivations. Nor are they the tragic heroes of great stature who fall from high places; they are ordinary people painfully searching for meaning and security in a baffling world of shifting values. Drame often combines comic and serious material and, instead of offering solutions, raises questions.

PLAYS TO SEE

Melodramas available on videocassettes:

Deathtrap
Dial "M" for Murder
Dracula
Gaslight
Goldfinger
The Great Train Robbery—The Cinema Begins
The Hunt for Red October
The Phantom of the Opera
Raiders of the Lost Ark
Sherlock Holmes
Sleuth
Star Wars
Top Gun

Drames available on videocassettes:

Henrik Ibsen, *A Doll's House*
Robert Bolt, *A Man for All Seasons*
Charles Fuller, *A Soldier's Play*
Tennessee Williams, *A Streetcar Named Desire*
Herman Wouk, *The Caine Mutiny Court Martial*
Tennessee Williams, *Cat on a Hot Tin Roof*
John Osborne, *Look Back in Anger*
Edward Albee, *Who's Afraid of Virginia Woolf?*

BIBLIOGRAPHY

BENTLEY, ERIC. *The Life of the Drama.* New York: Atheneum, 1964.
BOOTH, MICHAEL. *English Melodrama.* London: Herbert Jenkins, 1965.
DISHER, MAURICE. *Blood and Thunder: Mid-Victorian Melodrama and Its Origin.* London: Muller, 1949.
HEILMAN, ROBERT BECHTHOLD. *The Iceman, the Arsonist, and the Troubled Agent: Tragedy and Melodrama on the Modern Stage.* Seattle: University of Washington Press, 1973.
LACEY, ALEXANDER. *Pixérécourt and the French Romantic Drama.* Toronto: University of Toronto Press, 1928.
MOSES, MONTROSE JONES. *American Dramatist.* New York: Benjamin Blom, 1964.
NICOLL, ALLARDYCE. *A History of the Late Nineteenth Century Drama, 1850–1900.* Cambridge: Cambridge University Press, 1946.
RAHILL, FRANK. *The World of Melodrama.* University Park: Pennsylvania State University Press, 1967.
VARDAC, NICHOLAS. *Stage to Screen.* Cambridge, Mass.: Harvard University Press, 1949.

NOTES

1. Eric Bentley, *The Life of the Drama*. Reprinted by permission of the publisher, Applause Theater Books. p. 216.

2. Dion Boucicault, *The Colleen Bawn* (New York: Samuel French, n.d.).

3. Dion Boucicault, *A Race for Life* (New York: Samuel French, n.d.).

4. Robert B. Heilman, "Tragedy and Melodrama," *Texas Quarterly*, Summer 1960.

5. Owen Davis, *I'd Like to Do It Again* (New York: Farrar, 1931).

6. Augustan Daly, *Under the Gaslight* (New York: Samuel French, n.d.).

7. Dion Boucicault, *Pauvrette* (New York: Samuel French, n.d.).

8. Frank Rahill, *The World of Melodrama* (University Park and London: The Pennsylvania State University Press, 1967). Copyright 1967 by the Pennsylvania State University. Reproduced by permission of the publisher.

five
Comedy

The comic spirit has a long tradition. One of the most popular comedies in the English language is Oscar Wilde's delightful *The Importance of Being Earnest.* Shown here is the production at the Pacific Conservatory of Performing Arts, directed by Jonathon Gillard Daly.

(Scene: Morning-room in Algernon's flat in Half-Moon Street. The room is luxuriously and artistically furnished. The sound of a piano is heard in the adjoining room. Lane is arranging afternoon tea on the table, and after the music has ceased, Algernon enters.)

Algernon: Did you hear what I was playing, Lane?

Lane: I didn't think it polite to listen, sir.

Algernon: I'm sorry for that, for your sake. I don't play accurately—anyone can play accurately—but I play with wonderful expression. As far as the piano is concerned, sentiment is my forte. I keep science for Life.

Lane: Yes, sir.

Algernon: And speaking of the science of Life, have you got the cucumber sandwiches cut for Lady Bracknell?

Lane: Yes, sir. *(Hands them on a salver.)*

Algernon: *(Inspects them, takes two, and sits down on the sofa.)* Oh! by the way, Lane, I see from your book that on Thursday night, when Lord Shoreman and Mr. Worthing were dining with me, eight bottles of champagne are entered as having been consumed.

Lane: Yes, sir, eight bottles and a pint.

Algernon: Why is it that at a bachelor's establishment the servants invariably drink the champagne? I ask merely for information.

Lane: I attribute it to superior quality of the wine, sir. I have often observed that in married households the champagne is rarely of a first-rate brand.

Algernon: Good heavens! Is marriage so demoralizing as that!

Lane: I believe it is a very pleasant state, sir. I have had very little experience of it myself up to the present. I have only been married once. That was in consequence of a misunderstanding between myself and a young person.

Algernon: *(Languidly)* I don't know that I am much interested in your family life, Lane.

Lane: No, sir; it is not a very interesting subject. I never think of it myself.

Algernon: Very natural, I am sure. That will do, Lane. Thank you.

Lane: Thank you, sir. *(Lane goes out.)*

Algernon: Lane's views on marriage seem somewhat lax. Really, if the lower orders don't set a good example, what on earth is the use of them? They seem, as a class, to have absolutely no sense of moral responsibility.[1]

This opening scene from Oscar Wilde's *Importance of Being Earnest* (1895) tells us immediately that we are in the field of comedy. Wilde takes us into an artificial world of bright talk, filled with comic incongruity. He sets up a conta-

The **Restoration** was a period of high comedy that exposed the follies of the upper classes. In William Wycherly's *The Country Wife*, a middle-aged husband brings his young bride to London and tries unsuccessfully to protect her from the wolves. *(Directed by Richard Spear, Wayne State University)*

gious sense of fun that invites us to join in the game of following the nimble repartee.

One of the most popular pleasures of life is the enjoyment of laughter, and we seek its solace and release in all manner of activities. Not content with laughter arising spontaneously out of personal experience, we are avid customers of comedy in the theater and on the screen. Making people laugh is a big business, and there is an eager audience waiting for the skilled comedian and the hit play or musical.

THE NATURE OF COMEDY

Comedy's purpose is to delight and entertain an audience through characters in action in the spirit of fun. There is also a form of comedy, sometimes called black or dark comedy, that uses contrast to evoke a kind of grim humor. Ridiculous and serious materials are combined to generate harsh laughter that is sardonic or savage. The gravediggers in *Hamlet* crack jokes while they prepare Ophelia's grave. Sir Thomas Moore, too weak to ascend the steps to the gallows where he is about to be hanged, says, "If you'll help me up, I'll see to the coming down." But in general, comedy works best in a light, congenial environment. Tragedy achieves its catharsis through fear and pity; comedy purges through laughter to help us retain our balance and sanity and to remind us of our human frailties.

High comedy—that is, social comedy or comedy of manners—is intellectual in appeal, catering to the tastes of a sophisticated audience with a commonly accepted code of behavior that is a matter of manners, not morals. The Restoration period in the late seventeenth century in England is generally acknowledged to be the apex of high comedy. William Congreve, William Wycherly, Sir George Etherege, and Sir John Vanbrugh ridiculed the gauche, the outsiders, the pretenders whose awkward conduct caused them to lose their sense of control. In other periods of theater history, writers have used the wit of high comedy to direct criticism at more universal targets. Aristophanes scorned the militarists, sophists, and politicians; Molière attacked hypocrisy and pretense; Shaw delighted in exposing the sham behind the sentimental and rigid precepts of Victorian society. High comedy is, therefore, a social weapon armed with critical laughter.

At the other end of the comic scale is farce, or low comedy, whose main purpose is to amuse. The response to farce is immediate and direct. The language barriers are apt to be slight, since comedians express themselves in the universal vocabulary of action. Along with melodrama, farce is our most popular kind of theater.

Farce may be presented as a complete play, such as Shakespeare's *The Comedy of Errors; No Sex Please, We're British;* or *Noises Off,* or as such film and television fare as that of "Fawlty Towers," *Ghostbusters,* and *Crocodile Dundee.*

In between the extremes of high comedy and low is a vast area, which for want of a better term, can simply be referred to as "comedy" to distinguish plays that rely heavily on neither intellectual appeal nor exaggerated physicality. These plays attend more to character and the significance of the action. Molière's farces, such as *Sganarelle* and *The Doctor in Spite of Himself,* are based on extravagant situations calculated to elicit easy laughter, but when he was more concerned with character and ideas, as in *Tartuffe* and *The Miser,* Molière wrote plays in the general area of comedy.

THE COMIC ATTITUDE

The question of pain and pleasure arises in comedy as well as in tragedy, for laughter and ridicule can be dangerous weapons. Molière, who was frequently in hot water for satirizing the law, medicine, and the church, observed that people do not mind being portrayed as wicked, but "they object to being made ridiculous." As Freud pointed out, comedy becomes aggressive and easily leads to abuse and to the destruction of its essential lightness of spirit. Teasing turns into torment, mischief into vandalism.

In tragedy, there is a good deal of suffering when the integrity of the characters is tested. In comedy, there is apt to be discomfiture. The butts of the jokes, usually the unsympathetic characters who arouse our hostility because of their antisocial behavior or self-ignorance, are put in situations that release our aggression or sense of superiority. The objects of our derision are embarrassed, rejected, defeated, deflated, unmasked, or deprived of their status or possessions. Even sympathetic characters may be laughed at, especially if they deserve it. In any case, the discomfiture must not become genuinely painful or the comic atmosphere is destroyed.

KINDS OF COMEDY

Comedy wears many masks and appears in many guises—the ill-fitting tattered rags of the drunken hobo, the elegant evening clothes of the sophisticated

The program cover of *Noises Off* at the Ahmanson Theater in Los Angeles makes it clear that the play is a farce.

aristocrat, the overdressed finery of the fop. Comedy evokes many responses—the belly laugh, warm and sympathetic general laughter, a well-concealed smile, or derisive ridicule. Its armor includes such a variety of weapons as the rapier, the slapstick, the barbed shaft, and the custard pie. Comedy speaks many languages—epigrams, conceits, puns, obscenities, bon mots, wisecracks, insults, double entendres, hard and ruthless mockery—ranging from high to low.

Most comic playwrights are aware of the need to establish a light atmosphere at the outset. You know you are in for comedy when the program cover of *Noises Off* features Mrs. Clackett, a rattlebrained housekeeper, staring cross-eyed at a sardine. When the curtain rises, Mrs. Clackett appears, carrying a plate of sardines. She is stopped by the voice of the director, Lloyd Dallas, from the rear of the auditorium:

Lloyd: You leave the sardines, and you put the receiver back.

Dotty: Oh, yes, I put the receiver back.

(*She puts the receiver back and moves off again with the sardines.*)

Lloyd: And you leave the sardines.

Dotty: And I *leave* the sardines?

Lloyd: You *leave* the sardines.

Dotty: I put the receiver back and I leave the sardines.

Lloyd: Right.

Dotty: We've changed that, have we, love?

Lloyd: No, love.

Dotty: That's what I've always been doing?

Lloyd: I shouldn't say that, Dotty, my precious.

Dotty: How about the words, love? Am I getting some of them right?

Lloyd: Some of them have a very familiar ring.

Dotty: Only it's like a fruit machine in there.

Lloyd: I know that, Dotty.

Dotty: I open my mouth, and I never know if it's going to come out oranges or two lemons and a banana.

Lloyd: Anyway, it's not midnight yet. We don't open till tomorrow.[2]

Playwright Michael Frayn immediately catapults his audience into the daffy atmosphere of *Noises Off.*

In Arthur Kopit's play, the title, *Oh Dad, Poor Dad, Momma's Hung You in the Closet and I'm Feeling So Sad,* indicates the bizarre nature of his comedy, but you are not quite sure of the comic climate when two bellboys enter a hotel room

In Arthur Kopit's offbeat play *Oh Dad, Poor Dad, Mamma's Hung You in the Closet and I'm Feeling So Sad,* **a guileless boy is no match for the flirtatious baby sitter.** *(Directed by Kirk Willis, Cleveland Play House)*

carrying a coffin. The handles come off and the coffin crashes to the floor. You soon learn through other objects and stage business that you are in for an off-beat experience.

Max Eastman analyzed the conditions essential for the "enjoyment of laughter" in his book of the same title. He observed that humor depends on the existence of a favorable circumstance, and he concludes that "the condition in which joyful laughter most continually occurs is that of play."[3] As part of his evidence, Eastman cites the naive response of a child who may welcome shock and disappointment as a pleasurable experience provided that an atmosphere of play has been established. But if the child is teased when tired or hungry, the fun is over; the spirit of play has been destroyed.

In Shakespeare's romantic comedies, in the plays of Sheridan and Oliver Goldsmith in the eighteenth century, and in many of our contemporary works, the spectator is invited to enter into the emotions of the characters. We become concerned about the fortunes of the protagonist; our sympathies and hostilities are aroused by the playwright's treatment of the characters, so that we take pleasure in seeing the hero and heroine achieve their objectives, usually accompanied by the jingle of money and the ringing of wedding bells. The characters may be laughable, may at times appear foolish and weak, but the playwright treats them with tolerance and indulgence. Examples of comedies that involve our sympathies are *As You Like It, The Rivals, She Stoops to Conquer, Born Yesterday, The Odd Couple, My Fair Lady, Lettice and Lovage, Shirley Valentine, Steel Magnolias, Driving Miss Daisy, Talley's Folly,* and *Fiddler on the Roof.* We usually sympathize with the characters in their struggles. For example, in *Fiddler* there is no malice in

Another favorite character from musical comedy is Tevye in *Fiddler on the Roof*. *(Directed by Carol Blitgen, Clarke College)*

our laughter when we respond to Tevye, the Jewish dairyman in a small Russian village, as he seeks help from above:

Tevye: Today I am a horse. Dear God, did you have to make my poor old horse lose his shoe just before the Sabbath? That wasn't nice. It's enough you pick on me, Tevye, bless me with five daughters, a life of poverty. What have you got against my horse? Sometimes, I think when things are too quiet up there, You say to Yourself: Let's see what kind of mischief I can play on my friend, Tevye? . . . As the Good Book says, "Heal us, O Lord, and we shall be healed." In other words, send us the cure, we've got the sickness already . . . I'm not really complaining—after all, with your help, I'm starving to death. I realize, of course, that it's no shame to be poor, but it's no great honor, either. So what would have been so terrible if I had a small fortune?[4]

Driving Miss Daisy has a gentle, warm atmosphere, designed to evoke sympathetic laughter, as in this exchange between Daisy and her chauffeur Hoke in the cemetery, where she is looking for a tombstone of a departed relative. She asks Hoke to help her, but he confesses he can't read.

Daisy: You know your letters, don't you?

Hoke: My ABC's? Yassum, pretty good. I jes' cain' read.

Daisy: Stop saying that. It's making me mad. If you know your letters, then you can read. You just don't know you can read. I taught some of the stupidest children God ever put on the face of this earth, and all of them could read enough to find a name on a tombstone. The name is Bauer. Buh buh buh buh Bauer. What does that buh letter sound like?

Hoke: Sound like B.

Daisy: Of course. Buh Bauer. Er er er er. Bauer. That's the last part. What sounds like er?

Hoke: R?

Daisy: So the first letter is a—

Hoke: B.

Daisy: And the last letter is an—

Hoke: R.

Daisy: B-R, B-R, B-R, Brr. Brr. It even sounds like Bauer, doesn't it?

Hoke: Sho' do Miz Daisy. Thass it?

Daisy: That's it. Now go over there like I told you in the first place and look for a headstone with a B at the beginning and an R at the end and that will be Bauer.

Hoke: We ain' gon' worry 'bout what come in the middle?

Daisy: Not right now. This will be enough for you to find it. Go on now.

Hoke: Yassum.

Daisy: And don't come back here telling me you can't do it. You can.[5]

Henri Bergson argues that "laughter has no greater foe than emotion. . . . Its appeal is to the intelligence, pure and simple." Alonzo Myers supports Bergson in this view: "Without detachment, we cannot realize the effect of comedy, which transforms the frustrations of reason into laughter." This point of view is well taken, especially at the extremes of the comic scale—low comedy and high. In most farce, enjoyment stems from the action itself, the momentary laugh, the sudden release. We recognize that it is a form of playing; we do not take the

Duerrenmatt's The Visit *at the University of California, Santa Barbara (set design by L. Vychodil; directed by Theodore Hatlen).*

Set design by Ladislav Vychodil for a production of Dostoevski's Crime and Punishment *at the Stockholm State Theater.*

Pacific Overtures, *as performed at Santa Barbara City College (directed by Adrianne Maloney Harrop; set by Tom Geary).*

Two captivating characters from the musical The Roar of the Greasepaint, the Smell of the Crowd *at the Paper Mill Playhouse, Millburn, New Jersey.*

In Ibsen's play Peer Gynt, *the madcap hero, after wandering throughout the world, finally returns to his dying mother, Aase, and in a tender scene, drives her through St. Peter's gate to her eternal reward (Oregon Shakespeare Festival; directed by Jerry Turner).*

The Phantom rows Christine across the underground lake in The Phantom of the Opera *(directed by Hal Prince; sets and costumes by Maria Bjornson).*

The final scene of Ibsen's Ghosts *at the Pacific Conservatory of Performing Arts Theaterfest.*

Peter Brook's Mahabharata, *with its exotic visual elements and theatricalized actions.*

characters' sufferings seriously. No one feels genuine pain; the emotions do not penetrate the grease paint. Thus the spectators are detached from reality and are conscious of the artificial world before them.

Dark Comedy

There is, however, a kind of drama, sometimes called black or dark comedy, in which a "gallows humor" creates an emotional jarring—a harsh contrast. Comedy and serious material are combined to generate an uneasy or bitter laughter that is apt to be sardonic or even savage. In the film *M*A*S*H*, for example, the characters at a Mobile Army Surgical Hospital in Korea relieve the tension and horror of their situation through laughter that is often harsh and mordant.

The practice of introducing comic relief into a serious situation to heighten the effect by contrast is an old one. We think of the porter in *Macbeth* and the gravediggers in *Hamlet*. With the coming of realism and its emphasis on objective observation, it was apparent to some playwrights that in life, the incongruous was often side by side with the beautiful, the comic with the tragic—like grotesque gargoyles on the façade of a beautiful cathedral. Many of the outstanding playwrights of the last century have united the dark and the light. We think of Chekhov, Pirandello, and Shaw, and of present-day playwrights Sam Shepard, David Mamet, Edward Albee, Beth Henley, Lanford Wilson, John Guare, and August Wilson. Even though plays like *Amadeus* and *The Dresser* end in death, they contain considerable comic material, arising mostly from the characters themselves.

Following World War II, the absurdists, among them Beckett and Ionesco, expressed their feelings of alienation and spiritual dislocation in plays filled with bizarre and bleak humor—*Waiting for Godot* and *Rhinoceros*. Ionesco's *Rhinoceros*, like other absurdist plays (see pp. 227–233), may be considered as a protest against the dehumanization of society. His work has the idiocy of a nightmare, as the playwright gradually reveals that human beings are being turned into rhinoceroses. At first, their thundering feet and trumpeting are heard off in the distance. Eyewitnesses describe seeing them. A woman comes in with a dead cat that has been trampled. Finally, Berenger visits his friend Jean and sees him transformed into a rhinoceros on stage, in a scene made memorable by the performance of Zero Mostel. Jean appears earlier in his pajamas; his skin is turning green and the bump on his forehead gets larger and larger. He paces, and pants, and dashes in and out of the bathroom before his bewildered friend, Berenger.

Jean: *(From the bathroom, in a very hoarse voice, difficult to understand)* Utter rubbish.

Berenger: I'm amazed to hear you say that, Jean, really! You must be out of your mind! You wouldn't like to be a rhinoceros yourself, now would you?

Jean: Why not? I'm not a victim of prejudice, like you.

Berenger: Can you speak more clearly? I didn't catch what you said. You swallowed the words.

Ionesco's *Rhinoceros* is an absurdist play based on the transformation of human beings into rhinoceroses. Berenger is aghast when his friend Jean begins to change before his eyes. *(Directed by Theodore Hatlen, University of California, Santa Barbara)*

Jean: *(Still in the bathroom)* Then keep your ears open.

Berenger: What?

Jean: Keep your ears open. I said what's wrong with being a rhinoceros? I'm all for the change.

Berenger: It's not like you to say a thing like that.

Berenger stops short, for Jean's appearance is truly alarming. Jean has become, in fact, completely green. The bump on his forehead is practically a rhinoceros horn. Oh! You really must be out of your mind!

(Jean dashes to his bed, throws the covers on the floor, talking in a fast and furious gabble, and making very weird sounds.)

You mustn't get into such a state—calm down! I hardly recognize you any more.

Jean: *(Hardly distinguishable)* Hot . . . far too hot! Demolish the lot, clothes itch, they itch! *(He drops his pyjama trousers.)*

Berenger: What are you doing? You're not yourself! You're generally so modest!

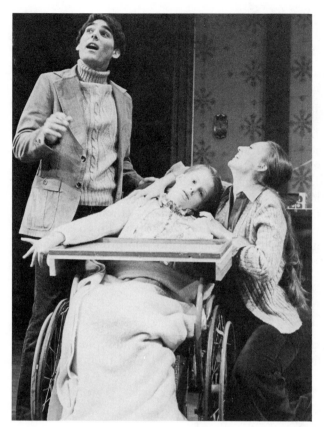

In *A Day in the Death of Joe Egg* by Peter Nichols, the parents of a handicapped child try to lighten their somber situation by forcing themselves to play games. The resultant laughter has the bitter quality of black comedy. *(Purdue University)*

Jean: The swamps! The swamps!

Berenger: Look at me! Can't you see me any longer? Can't you hear me?

Jean: I can hear you perfectly well! *(He lunges toward Berenger, head down. Berenger gets out of the way.)*

Berenger: Watch out!

Jean: *(Puffing noisily)* Sorry! *(He darts at great speed into the bathroom.)*

Berenger: *(Makes as if to escape by the door left, then comes back and goes into the bathroom after Jean, saying)* I really can't leave him like that—after all he is a friend. *(From the bathroom)* I'm going to get a doctor! It's absolutely necessary, believe me!

Jean: *(From the bathroom)* No!!

Berenger: *(From the bathroom)* Calm down, Jean, you're being ridiculous! Oh, your horn's getting longer and longer—you're a rhinoceros!

Jean: *(From the bathroom)* I'll trample you, I'll trample you down!

(A lot of noise comes from the bathroom, trumpeting, objects falling, the sound of a shattered mirror; then Berenger reappears, very frightened; he closes the bathroom door with difficulty against the resistance that is being made from the inside.)

Berenger: *(Pushing against the door)* He's a rhinoceros, he's a rhinoceros! *(Berenger manages to close the door. As he does so, his coat is pierced by a rhinoceros horn.)*[6]

In postwar England, black comedy, with its bitterly satiric overtones, made an enormous impact on the theater. Simon Gray in *Butley* mocks the academic world through the protagonist, a university professor who is transformed from a promising scholar into a detestable bureaucrat. Joe Orton's wildly imaginative dark farces, such as *Loot* and *What the Butler Saw*, are scathing satirical assaults on the establishment, particularly the police, the Roman Catholic Church, and psychiatry. Peter Nichols, in *A Day in the Death of Joe Egg*, shows how a couple with a severely retarded child attempt to retain their sanity and preserve their marriage through jocular banter and improvised games.

SOURCES OF LAUGHTER

The sources of comic effect have given scholars, critics, philosophers, and psychologists endless stimulation for speculation, and although their efforts have

In Aristophanes' *Peace* (421 B.C.), the comic hero flies to Olympus on a dung beetle to ask Zeus for peace. During his trip, he criticizes the audience. *(Greek National Theater)*

resulted in no universally accepted conclusions, we may find some substance in their ideas. Let us briefly examine three theories cited by Nicoll in *The Theory of Drama* as the most prominent, realizing that a good deal of their validity depends on personal interpretation and careful selection of examples. The three theories are *derision, incongruity,* and *automatism.* You will recognize immediately the tendency of the theories to overlap because of the mercurial nature of comedy.

Derision

Aristotle's observation that comedy deals with men as "worse than they are" implies a comic theory of *derision* or degradation. Derision is ordinarily used as a form of criticism to combat pretentiousness or ignorance. Its objective is to keep people humble, balanced, and human. The legitimate targets of derision are stupidity, hypocrisy, and sanctimoniousness. As in life, laughter is used to keep people in line, to ensure conformity to a socially acceptable code of behavior. Certainly, Aristophanes was fully aware of the possibilities of derision when he ranged far and wide in his jibes against his contemporaries. Not even the audience was safe from his wit. In Aristophanes' *Peace* (421 B.C.) the protagonist, Trygaeus, rears a huge dung-beetle on which he attempts to fly to Olympus to beg peace from Zeus. As he flies aloft on the back of the beetle, Trygaeus looks down at the spectators and jeers at them:

> Ah! it's a tough job getting to the gods! My legs are as good as broken through it. *(To the audience)* How small you were to be sure, when seen from heaven! You all had the appearance too of being great rascals, but seen close, you look even worse.[7]

Greek comedy ridiculed physical deformities as well as conduct. Comic characters were intentionally distorted and misshapen in appearance through the use of masks, phallic symbols, and padded costumes. Ambitious individuals' attempts to rise above themselves were often counteracted by the reminder of their biological needs. Aristophanes delighted in mocking men and gods alike by exhibiting them in all kinds of embarrassing physical situations. He was ruthless in aiming his shafts of wit at all levels of life. The satirist exploits situations in which characters are debased and reduced to objects of scorn by such formula devices as physical beatings and bodily functions, situations in which an individual is caught off balance, red-handed, under the bed, in the closet, in underwear—in any of the circumstances of life in which people are exposed, their dignity punctured, their flaws revealed, reminding everyone of their kinship with the animal world.

Degradation of character often involves a reversal of status. The deviates from normal social behavior or inflated persons are brought down off their pedestals. Such stock offenders against common sense and decent humanity as fools, fops, hypocrites, bumpkins, louts, misers, philanderers, braggarts, bores, and battleaxes are ridiculed because of their deformed behavior; lack of wit; or excess of ambition, greed, lust, or stupidity. The satirist uses barbs of derisive laughter to prick the inflated reputation of entrenched authority, often a popular form of comic appeal since the common people find release and enjoyment in the discomfiture of those above them.

Sigmund Freud described this process of degradation:

> The methods that serve to make people comic are: putting them in a comic situation, mimicry, disguise, unmasking, caricature, parody, travesty and so on. It is obvious that these techniques can be used to serve hostile and aggressive purposes. One can make a person comic in order to make him become contemptible, to deprive him of his claim to dignity and authority.[8]

Although physical degradation and insulting language are confined mostly to farce, the satirist bent on attacking ideas also makes use of ridicule. Ben Jonson used his wit as an instrument of mockery against his fellow Elizabethans, as he indicated when he stated the purpose of his comedy: "to strip the ragged follies of the time." Molière likewise brought low those who were guilty of excess, deriding people who were too ambitious in *Le Bourgeois Gentilhomme,* too clever in *Les Precieuses Ridicules,* too exacting in *Le Misanthrope,* and too gullible in *Tartuffe.* As we noted earlier, comedy since World War II has been notable for its vigorous

A good deal of the comedy in *I'm Not Rappaport* comes from the incongruity of two mismatched characters, Judd Hirsch (left) and Cleavon Little (right).

aggression and, in the 1960s, for its radicalization, so that today there is no target immune from the satirists' slings and arrows. Derision is an effective weapon, and it often antagonizes those who are laughed at and may arouse bitter retaliation.

Charles Ludlum's Theater of the Ridiculous has been lampooning cultural and political institutions since 1966 with its clowning style that tends toward kitsch, camp, and parody. *Hamlet* becomes *Stage Blood*, a backstage burlesque of a Shakespearean-style whodunit. The Lady Godiva fable becomes, in the playwright's words, a preposterous "hysterical adventure of Coventry Convent." *Le Bourgeois Avant-Garde* uses Molière's seventeenth-century comedy as a point of departure for ridiculing the modern penchant for artistic novelty and for the avant garde.

El Teatro Campesino, founded by Luis Valdez in 1965, uses comedy as a weapon in the battle of the Chicano migrant workers against Anglo growers in California. Its short, dramatic pieces, called *actos*, though filled with burlesque and caricature, had the serious purpose of inspiring the audience to social action.

In the 1960s the San Francisco Mime Troupe began with an improvised commedia dell'arte technique in its productions but later developed its own style of broad comic playing that includes circus techniques. Its comic arsenal has been used to promote its political concerns in mobilizing its audiences against war, racism, industrialism, and social conformity.

Such groups as the Ridiculous Theater Company and the San Francisco Mime Troupe use comedy in much the same way as political cartoonists satirize the contemporary scene.

Incongruity

Perhaps because it is the most elastic and extensive theory of comedy, the idea of *incongruity* has the widest application. Incongruity is the result of the tension or dissonance set up by the juxtaposition of two objects or people that creates a laughable contrast, such as a large, fat woman mated with a small, skinny man, or a person out of place in the surroundings—in a bathing suit at the opera or in formal clothes at the beach. The contrast usually depends on the establishment of some kind of norm so that the discrepancy is emphasized. The gap between the expected and the unexpected, between the intention and the realization, between the normal and the abnormal results in comic discord.

Incongruity may take several forms—situation, character, and dialogue. The comic situation based on incongruity presents a contrast between the usual or accepted behavior and the unusual or unacceptable. A typical pattern is to place a character in an environment that reveals that person's social incongruity, such as a country bumpkin in polite society, a member of the social elite in bucolic surroundings, an intellectual among barbarians, a clown or an inebriate in a dignified gathering, a sailor in a harem, a tramp in the mayor's bed. Shaw built *Pygmalion* on the incongruous stunt of transforming Eliza, a cockney flowerseller, into a lady who circulates in high society. In *A Midsummer Night's Dream* the fairy queen, Titania, falls in love with Bottom, the weaver, who has been burdened with an ass's head. In the Joseph Papp production of *The Pirates of Pen-zance*, the swashbuckling Pirate King stabs himself in the foot. Juxtaposition of contrasting characters is the basic comedic idea behind Neil Simon's *The Odd Couple*, when two men, separated from their wives, try to live together. One is sloppy and the other is fastidious; the result is comic conflict.

Incongruity of character involves a contrast between expectation and reality. For example, most of us came to *Amadeus* with a preconceived impression that Mozart, because of his elevated music, must have been a man of exemplary social conduct. But in the play, he makes his first entrance in quite an unexpected manner, as already seen (p. 64).

Incongruity of language occurs when the language has the opposite effect from that intended by the speaker. Mrs. Malaprop, in Sheridan's *The Rivals*, gave her name to this kind of incongruity, as when she spoke of "the allegories on the banks of the Nile." Another kind of incongruous diction occurs when the language is in sharp contrast to the social or emotional situation. For example, in Beth Henley's Pulitzer Prize–winning play, *Crimes of the Heart*, the three McGrath sisters in Hazlehurst, Mississippi, await the news of their grandfather's fate in the hospital. Here is their incongruous reaction:

Babe: Ah, Meg—

Meg: What—

Babe: Well, it's just—It's . . .

Lenny: It's about Old Granddaddy—

Meg: Oh, I know; I know. I told him all those stupid lies. Well, I'm gonna go right over there this morning and tell him the truth. I mean every horrible thing. I don't care if he wants to hear it or not. He's just gonna have to take me like I am. And if he can't take it, if it sends him into a coma, that's just too damn bad!

(Babe and Lenny look at each other. Babe cracks a smile. Lenny cracks a smile.)

Babe: You're too late—Ha, ha, ha!

(They both break up laughing.)

Lenny: Oh, stop! Please! Ha, ha, ha!

Meg: What is it? What's so funny?

Babe: *(Still laughing)* It's not—It's not funny!

Lenny: *(Still laughing)* No, it's not! It's not a bit funny!

Meg: Well, what is it, then? What?

Babe: *(Trying to calm down)* Well, it's just—it's just—

Meg: What?

Babe: Well, Old Granddaddy—he—he's in a coma!

(Babe and Lenny break up again.)

Meg: He's what?

Babe: *(Shrieking)* In a coma!

Meg: My God! That's not funny!

Babe: *(Calming down)* I know. I know. For some reason, it just struck us as funny.

Lenny: I'm sorry. It's—it's not funny. It's sad. It's very sad. We've been up all night long.

Babe: We're really tired.

Meg: Well, my God. How is he? Is he gonna live—

(Babe and Lenny look at each other.)

Babe: They don't think so!

(They both break up again.)

Lenny: Oh, I don't know why we're laughing like this. We're just sick! We're just awful!

Babe: We are—we're awful!

Beth Henley's wacky small-town sisters in *Crimes of the Heart* **call for a special kind of relaxed realism.** *(Directed by Jane Ridley, University of California, Santa Barbara)*

Lenny: (*As she collects herself*) Oh, good, now I feel bad. Now I feel like crying. I do; I feel like crying.

Babe: Me, too. Me, too.

Meg: Well, you've gotten me depressed!

Lenny: I'm sorry. I'm sorry. It, ah, happened last night. He had another stroke.[9]

Another example of incongruous dialogue is found in Robert Harling's *Steel Magnolias.* In a multiple-station hairdressing salon in a small town in Louisiana, six desperate women gather for their ritual of exchanging views on various aspects of their lives. Over a two-year period they sustain one another through a range of good times and bad. The playwright's sharply drawn figures are an interesting and entertaining mix, as revealed in the women's colorful dialogues. They are obviously old hands at exchanging jibes, many of them directed at Ouiser, a good-natured but sharp-tongued gorgon, a role performed effectively in the film version of the play by Shirley Maclaine.

Clairee: Ouiser, you're almost chipper today. Why are you in such a good mood? Did you run over a small child or something?

Ouiser: Do you or do you not want tomatoes?

Clairee: Don't give me all of them.

In Robert Harling's *Steel Magnolias,* a colorful assortment of small-town characters is brought together in the local beauty salon.

Ouiser: Somebody's got to take them. I hate 'em. I try not to eat healthy food if I can help it. The sooner this body wears out the better off I'll be. I have trouble getting enough grease into my diet.

Annelle: Then why do you grow them?

Ouiser: I'm an old Southern woman. We're supposed to put on funny looking hats and ugly old dresses and grow vegetables in the dirt. Don't ask me why. I don't make the rules.

Clairee: You should get some gloves. Your hands look like a couple of T-bone steaks.

Shelby: Health is the most important thing, Miss Ouiser. Trust me on this.

Ouiser: And. While I have everybody's attention . . . this morning I went to my mailbox and found that someone . . . *(Directed at Annelle)* . . . has put me on the mailing list for the Riverview Baptist Church. Lucky me. I am now receiving chain letters for Christ.

Annelle: They aren't chain letters. They're part of my prayer group's "reach out and touch" project. We are supposed to write somebody in the community that we thought might be in spiritual trouble and invite them to worship. *(Ouiser plops down a big wad of mail.)* I guess you were on everybody's list.

Ouiser: I think it's in the worst possible taste to pray for perfect strangers.

Clairee: "Reach out" to Ouiser and you'll pull back a bloody stump.[10]

Automatism

One of the most imaginative and provocative theories of comedy is that advanced by Henri Bergson in his book *Laughter,* in which he contends that the essence of the laughable is *automatism*—"something mechanical is encrusted on the living." Automatism of character occurs when individuals lose their human flexibility and their behavior becomes mechanical in its repetition, or when people become puppets, no longer in control of their actions. The gist of Bergson's thinking is indicated by these representative statements about comedy and character: "We laugh every time a person gives us the impression of being a thing." "Any individual is comic who automatically goes his own way without troubling himself about getting in touch with the rest of his fellow beings." "Rigidity, automatism, absentmindedness, and unsociability are all inextricably entwined, and all serve as ingredients to the making up of the comic in character."[11]

Bergson's point of view on one-sided characters is similar to that of Jonson's comedy of "humours," in which he ridiculed those characters who were guilty of some imbalance, some excess:

> As when some one peculiar quality
> Doth so possess a man, that it doth draw
> All his effects, his spirits, and his powers

> In their confluctions, all to run one way
> This may be truly said to be a humour.[12]

In Jonson's *Epicoene, or the Silent Woman,* old Morose, obsessed with silence, is tricked into marrying Epicoene, the silent woman, who turns out to be a boy. *Volpone, or the Fox* shows a group of characters who have lost their humanity because of their greed. Molière used comic targets who were out of balance because of some fixation—Orgon in *Tartuffe* for his gullibility, Harpagon in *The Miser* for his avarice, and Alceste in *The Misanthrope* for his intolerance of human frailty.

Automatism of situation is often based on repetition. Characters are caught in the grip of circumstances and subjected to mechanical domination. Chaplin used this device in his famous mechanized corn-on-the-cob eating sequence and his hilarious shaving pantomime to the accompaniment of a Brahms Hungarian Dance. Repeated patterns of behavior have been used very often as the framework for comedy, as in D. L. Coburn's *Gin Game,* in which the central action of the play is a series of gin rummy games played by two senior citizens. Fonsia, an apparently prim woman, is inexperienced in card playing, but she wins every hand against Weller, who considers himself an expert. Coburn skillfully devises ways to use repetition not only for comic effect but also to reveal the meanness of the characters. Simon's *The Last of the Red Hot Lovers* exploits repetition in the story of Barney Cashman, a middle-aged proprietor of a fish restaurant, who makes three unsuccessful attempts at seduction. Vsevolod Meyerhold, in directing his interpretation of Chekhov's farce *The Proposal,* found thirty-eight references to fainting, which he exploited as a recurrent leitmotif in production.

Automatism of dialogue takes several forms. For example, Bergson says, "Inadvertently to say or do what we have no intention of saying or doing, as a result of inelasticity or momentum is, as we are aware, one of the sources of the comic."[13] Inelasticity, of course, implies repetition, a standard form of comedy. To mock the monotonous dullness of ordinary social conversation, Ionesco, in *The Bald Soprano,* uses the phrases "that is curious," "how bizarre," "what a coincidence," in various forms more than two dozen times in four pages of dialogue.

One of the most successful uses of automatism of language occurs in Molière's *The Imaginary Invalid,* when Toinette, a pert maidservant, is pretending to be a physician examining her hypochondriac master, Argan:

Toinette: Let me feel your pulse. Come, come, beat properly, please. Ah! I will soon make you beat as you should. This pulse is trifling with me. I see that it does not know me yet. Who is your doctor?

Argan: Mr. Purgon.

Toinette: That man is not noted in my books among the great doctors. What does he say you are ill of?

Argan: He says it is the liver, and others say it is the spleen.

Toinette: They are a pack of ignorant blockheads; you are suffering from the lungs.

Argan: The lungs?

Toinette: Yes; what do you feel?

Argan: From time to time great pains in my head.

Toinette: Just so, the lungs.

Argan: At times it seems as if I had a mist before my eyes.

Toinette: The lungs.

Argan: I feel sick now and then.

Toinette: The lungs.

Argan: And I feel sometimes a weariness in all my limbs.

Toinette: The lungs.

Argan: And sometimes I have sharp pains in the stomach, as if I had the colic.

Toinette: The lungs. Do you eat your food with appetite?

Argan: Yes, Sir.

Toinette: The lungs. You feel sleepy after your meals, and willingly enjoy a nap?

Argan: Yes, Sir.

Toinette: The lungs, the lungs, I tell you. What does your doctor order you for food?

Argan: He orders me soup.

Toinette: Ignoramus!

Argan: Fowl.

Toinette: Ignoramus!

Argan: Veal.

Toinette: Ignoramus!

Argan: Broth.

Toinette: Ignoramus!

Argan: New-laid eggs.

Toinette: Ignoramus!

Argan: And at night a few prunes to relax the bowels.

Toinette: Ignoramus!

Molière's *The Imaginary Invalid.* (Texas Christian University)

Argan: And, above all, to drink my wine well diluted with water.

Toinette: Ignorantus, ignoranta, ignorantum.[14]

Bergson's theory is, of course, an interesting extension of the idea of incongruity, the jostling together of the human and the mechanical. By his ingenuity and persuasiveness, Bergson makes quite a plausible argument for automatism, especially for the comedies of Molière. But like other comic theories, automatism does not explain all the sources of laughter, nor is it appropriate to all kinds of comic effects.

From the preceding discussion, it is apparent that a case can be made for derision, incongruity, and automatism. It should also be obvious that it is impossible to fix comedy in a single rigid mold, although recurrent patterns and mechanisms show through the diverse forms. This will be increasingly evident as we consider the structure and content of comedy.

PLOT

Comedy requires skillful plotting. A comedy is not simply a loosely knit accumulation of gags. Laughs must be carefully timed and built, in context with the complete structure of the play. The jokes are important as they relate to the total effect, not as isolated laughs. On the other hand, the writer of comedy has more freedom in developing the play's structure than in any other form of drama, since the audience cares more about entertainment than it does about logic.

Laughter is the result of the mechanism of tension and release. On the printed page, a joke takes this form:

She: --------

He: --------

She: --------

He: --------

She: --(Punch line)---!

A comic strip often assumes this pattern:

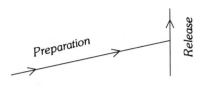

			!

         Preparation   *Release*

The mechanism for inducing laughter has this structure:

Preparation → *Release*

The punch line releases the tension. A surprise occurs. Expectancy is tricked. There is a sudden change in direction. The light bulb goes on.

In making or telling a joke, the structure is important. It cannot be too long or wordy; the punch line must be concise and on cue. The preparation must build expectancy. Without this tension, there is no release. Laughter depends on the structure as well as on the idea or the language.

A comedy playscript is a score for playing; just as the composer must be cognizant of the possibilities of the music in the hands of musicians, the writer of comedy must be fully aware of the techniques and resources of the actor that will animate the material.

The comic writer is acutely concerned with the individual in a social environment. Basic patterns of comedy depict a character who deviates from the norm or who is out of place with the surroundings. The implicit contrasts and conflicts require adroit delineation of the social milieu in order to expose the laughable elements of conduct. Tragic writers may concentrate on heroic figures isolated from other characters, from the human scene, from the group situation, and from the interrelationships of characters. Comedy emphasizes the here and now, not the long perspective. The playwright frequently develops timely allusions, local references, and contemporaneous characters. Comic material must have a sense of crispness and spontaneity. It must not smell of the museum or the dead past. Hence, it is difficult for comedy to survive its time and place of origin because many of its most telling referents are gone.

The earliest extant comedies are those of Aristophanes from the fifth century B.C. His typical plots were based on "a happy idea." The women in *Lysistrata* hope to bring about peace by a sex strike; in *The Acharnians* a private citizen negotiates his own personal peace treaty with Sparta. In *The Frogs,* Dionysus decides to take a trip to Hades to visit the tragic poets Aeschylus and Euripides. In each play, the merits of the idea are debated, and, despite opposition, the happy idea is put into practice and the results demonstrated. The plays end in revelry.

In the subsequent development of comedy, the original pattern persists. Characters strive for objectives and are thwarted by obstacles and opposition, but their problems are solved when misunderstandings are cleared up and the truth emerges and/or the opponents are reconciled. The play ends happily, often with the lovers united in an embrace, a reminder of the orgiastic celebration of the end of most old comedies.

Jan Kott sees the basic comic plot in these terms: "The oldest and most enduring kind of comic action, from ancient comedy to commedia dell'arte, from popular farce to Molière, is a clash between two houses."[15] One house represents authority and appearances; in the second house are bachelors, easy girls, thieves, and crooks. Kott suggests that the fundamental plot is the aggression on the house of virtue by the house of ill repute. Although Kott's theory is not universally applicable, his analysis is basically sound in that the comic plot usually involves an imbalance caused by the presence of some ridiculous element through error, ignorance, or ambition. The resulting conflicts and contrasts create comic tension, which is released in laughter.

The plots of most comedies are made up of sharp conflicts that require careful craftsmanship in the use of exposition, climaxes, crises, discoveries, and the donouement. The tangled threads of action must remain clear to the audience, which is tricky business in plays of rapid action, mishaps, and misunderstandings. The climaxes and crises of comedy demand technical mastery because the high points of the action often involve a social situation in which a number of people are caught in the same net, obliging the playwright to deal with complex materials. Frequently, the emotional peaks are those of action and discovery, which require the playwright to have a strong sense of visual humor. Climaxes must be built and sustained without being prolonged beyond the limits of the material. The playwright's touch must be deft and sure to keep the pace rapid and to create the special climate of comedy that will ensure laughter.

The structure of farce is a framework for vigorous, rapid, and exaggerated action in which the characters move, rather than think, and where laughter justifies nearly any means. Once the engine has been cranked up and set in motion, the speed is accelerated; by expected blowouts, backfirings, and explosions, the mechanism careens crazily, gathering momentum, until it finally lurches to an awkward but happy end in a cloud of steam with all the parts still spinning. Although there has been a whirlwind of activity, the machine has not really moved an inch in any direction.

The skill of plotting farce is determined by the dramatist's ingenuity in inventing a variety of entanglements that will give the comedian a chance to play for laughs. The playwright usually exploits a basic situation that is highly improbable and atypical: a woodcutter reluctantly consents to become a court physician to cure the king's daughter of a feigned illness; two long-lost twin brothers, whose servants are another pair of twins, strive for reunion; two young Communists, sharing a one-room apartment, fall in love with each other's newlywed wives; a shy greeting-card writer becomes involved with a gang of racetrack touts because of his skill in predicting winners; a taxicab driver is married to two women, and his secret is disclosed because of an automobile crash; an inexperienced amateur replaces a famous tenor.

Low comedy exploits the physical aspects of humanity. The body, its desires and functions, is a primary source of comic material. To a large extent, farcical situations depend on visual humor. Not only sex but also any drive or appetite that causes one to lose one's balance or control is a target for ridicule. Farcical characters move in an active physical world; they are out of place in an intellectual atmosphere.

In the days of the silent motion picture, farce was exceedingly popular in the slapstick comedies created by Mack Sennett, Charlie Chaplin, and Buster Keaton. The basic requirement for silent pictures was action; hence it was a medium ideally suited for farce. Comedians tumbled their way through crazy situations, full of violence set off by the slightest provocation, and usually ending in a chase that annihilated all the restrictions of time and space. For example, Harold Lloyd, playing a book salesman, approaches a tough customer and is thrown out. He returns a dozen times, accelerating the pace. On another occasion, he serves as a practice tackling dummy for a football squad. He makes a speech at a dance with a kitten crawling inside his sweater. Keaton chases butterflies in the countryside, completely oblivious of a band of wild Indians who pursue him. In another picture, he sits on a hot stove, then on a cake of ice, which melts rapidly. Ben Turpin, a cross-eyed explorer, surrenders to a stuffed lion.

These familiar farcical patterns are still in use today. Consult the television listings or a movie guide and you will find such farcical situations as these:

> Arnold and Lisa are trapped in the boiler room while working on a school photograph project.
>
> Harvey and Tim go to the Hollywood bus terminal as a place to pick up starlets.
>
> Natalie is eager to cover an inside story on an ROTC parachute group, only to learn she is expected to jump along with the troops.
>
> The surgeons become impromptu bartenders at Rosie's.
>
> Love-struck Vanessa tries to hide a poor report card.

The materials from which comedies are made are venerable ones, as old as the theater itself. The sources of comic effect, which the ancient playwrights Aristophanes, Plautus, and Terence used to delight audiences of Athens and Rome, can still be seen on your television or motion picture screen tonight.

Similarly, the *devices* of comedy that the playwright uses are well established. Let us consider three representative examples of common mechanisms for evoking laughter.

COMIC MECHANISMS

Teasing

One of the most reliable comic mechanisms is that of *teasing*, which may take a variety of forms, for example, the delay of news when the Nurse withholds Romeo's message from Juliet. In *Lysistrata*, Myrrhina, having joined the women in a sex strike to make peace, teases her amorous husband, Cinesias, by a series of delaying tactics. Another form of teasing occurs when characters are intentionally placed in embarrassing or awkward situations. Tony Lumpkin, in *She Stoops to Conquer*, teases his mother by driving her around her own garden in a carriage at night, pretending that they are beset by robbers.

> *(Enter Mrs. Hardcastle.)*

Mrs. Hardcastle: Oh, Tony, I'm killed. Shook. Battered to death. I shall never survive it. That last jolt that laid us against the quickset hedge has done my business.

Tony: Alack, mama, it was all your own fault. You would be for running away by night, without knowing one inch of the way.

Mrs. Hardcastle: I wish we were at home again. I never met so many accidents in so short a journey. Drench'd in the mud, overturn'd in a ditch, stuck fast

In Aristophanes' fifth-century B.C. comedy *Lysistrata,* the women strive for peace by holding a sex strike. In this teasing scene, Myrrhina finds ways to keep away from her husband. *(Greek National Theater)*

                    in a slough, jolted to a jelly, and at last to lose our way. Whereabouts do you think we are, Tony?

Tony: By my guess we should be upon Crackskull Common, about forty miles from home.

Mrs. Hardcastle: O lud! O lud! the most notorious spot in all the country. We only want a robbery to make a complete night on't.

Tony: Don't be afraid, mama, don't be afraid. Two of the five that kept here are hanged, and the other three may not find us. Don't be afraid. Is that a man that's galloping behind us? No; it's only a tree. Don't be afraid.

Mrs. Hardcastle: The fright will certainly kill me.

Tony: Do you see any thing like a black hat moving behind the thicket?

Mrs. Hardcastle: O death!

Tony: No, it's only a cow. Don't be afraid, mama; don't be afraid.

Mrs. Hardcastle: As I'm alive, Tony, I see a man coming towards us. Ah! I'm sure on't. If he perceives us, we are undone.

Tony: *(Aside)* Father-in-law, by all that's unlucky, come to take one of his night walks. *(To her)* Ah, it's a highwayman, with pistils as long as my arm. A damn'd ill-looking fellow.

Mrs. Hardcastle: Good heaven defend us! He approaches.

Tony: Do you hide yourself in that thicket, and leave me to manage him. If there be any danger, I'll cough, and cry hem. When I cough be sure to keep close.

(Mrs. Hardcastle hides behind a tree in the back scene.) (Enter Hardcastle.)

Hardcastle: I'm mistaken, or I heard voices of people in want of help. Oh, Tony, is that you? I did not expect you so soon back. Are your mother and her charge in safety?

Tony: Very safe, Sir, at my Aunt Pedigree's. Hem.

Mrs. Hardcastle: *(From behind)* Ah death! I find there's danger.

Hardcastle: Forty miles in three hours; sure, that's too much, my youngster.

Tony: Stout horses and willing minds make short journies, as they say. Hem.

Mrs. Hardcastle: *(From behind)* Sure he'll do the dear boy no harm.

Hardcastle: But I heard a voice here; I should be glad to know from whence it came?

Charley's Aunt by Brandon Thomas has delighted audiences for nearly a century with the exploits of Lord Fancourt, who is coerced into disguising himself as a middle-aged aunt. *(Repertory Theater of St. Louis)*

Tony: It was I, Sir, talking to myself, Sir. I was saying that forty miles in four hours was very good going. Hem. As to be sure it was. Hem. I have got a sort of cold by being out in the air. We'll go in, if you please. Hem.

Hardcastle: But if you talk'd to yourself, you did not answer yourself. I am certain I heard two voices, and am resolved *(raising his voice)* to find the other out.

Mrs. Hardcastle: *(From behind)* Oh! he's coming to find me out. Oh!

Tony: What need you go, Sir, if I tell you? Hem. I'll lay down my life for the truth—hem—I'll tell you all, Sir. *(Detaining him)*

Hardcastle: I tell you, I will not be detained. I insist on seeing. It's vain to expect I'll believe you.

Mrs. Hardcastle: *(Running forward from behind)* O lud, he'll murder my poor boy, my darling. Here, good gentleman, whet your rage upon me. Take my money, my life, but spare that young gentleman, spare my child, if you have any mercy!

Hardcastle: My wife! as I'm a Christian. From whence can she come, or what does she mean?

Mrs. Hardcastle: *(Kneeling)* Take compassion on us, good Mr. Highwayman. Take our money, our watches, all we have, but spare our lives. We will never bring you to justice, indeed we won't, good Mr. Highwayman.[16]

The highwayman turns out to be her husband, and Tony's ruse is discovered.

Reversal

Another familiar plot mechanism is *reversal,* or inversion. The entire play may be based on the turnabout of a downtrodden character who ultimately achieves a dominant position, as in such plays as *The Solid Gold Cadillac* and *Born Yesterday.* The reversal may be one in which the characters are temporarily thrown out of their usual milieu, only to return to their customary status; for example, in *Jeppe of the Hills,* the drunken ne'er-do-well is placed in the mayor's bed, pampered for a day, and then returned insensible to the gutter where he was found. In Brecht's *Caucasian Chalk Circle,* an outcast suddenly becomes a judge and rules over the district. Nikolai Gogol's play *The Government Inspector* tells the story of a disreputable, down-and-out clerk, who, being mistaken for the inspector general, makes use of the opportunity; he is wined and dined as if he were an aristocrat, and the mayor's wife and daughter make a play for him. At the end, the real inspector arrives and the circle is about to begin again.

Another well-worn comic device that frequently includes inversion is the unfamiliar. A character or group of characters are placed in strange surroundings, or they are engaged in unaccustomed activities. One form this device takes is that of teaching something to an inexperienced and often inept person, such as the English lesson in *Henry V,* the fencing lesson in *Everyman in His Humour,* and the dancing lesson in *Le Bourgeois Gentilhomme*. The humor may be heightened by the additional twist of having the instructor as ignorant as the pupil. The awkward, embarrassed, or shy person, making an adjustment to a new experience or surroundings, is used again and again for comic effect.

One of the favorite reversal devices is the sex switch—men playing female roles. Dustin Hoffman, in the film *Tootsie*, disguises himself as a woman and gets involved in a series of awkward comic situations, such as being the object of his girlfriend's father's romantic advances. This same sex switch was employed by Aristophanes twenty-five centuries ago in *Thesmophoriazusae*, in which a male dons female attire and spies on the women's assembly. Brandon Thomas has delighted theatergoers since 1892 with *Charley's Aunt*, which has the same device of putting a man disguised as a woman in unfamiliar situations, even a marriage proposal.

These comic devices—teasing, reversal, and the unfamiliar—are three of the venerable mechanisms that have been repeated endlessly ever since the origin of theatrical performances. Other familiar devices are mistaken identity, pretense or deception, jeopardy, violence, and fancy footwork or skillful recovery. This is not an exhaustive list, nor do the devices occur separately; rather, they mix freely with one another. It is interesting to note that the mechanism by itself will not create a comic effect. Indeed, many of these patterns also appear in tragedy—for example, the reversal formula: a highborn character in an elevated position at the beginning of the play falls to catastrophe, as in *Hamlet* and *Antigone*. In comedy the reversal often goes in the other direction. The little person, ignored and beaten down, emerges at the end of the play in a dominant position, as in the musical *How to Succeed in Business without Really Trying,* in which a window washer manipulates his way to becoming the president of a large corporation.

CHARACTER

Comedy wears many guises. Characters may be comical because of their eccentric behavior; their lack of wit or judgment; their delightful facility with language, engaging vivacity, or animal spirits; their charming manners; their buoyant attitude toward life; or their extraordinary appearance, speech, or life-style. Comic characters are often associated with a performer who plays the same role again and again, such as Charlie Chaplin, Woody Allen, and Bill Cosby.

Comic characters tend to be stock types. Playwrights frequently are more concerned about developing the intricacies of plot than about revealing depth of character. Hence they sketch their figures lightly or resort to readily recognizable types. Comic dramatists may deliberately create one-sided, exaggerated characters who show their inhumanity by their fixations and inflexibility. Or dramatists may purposely create stock figures to prevent excessive emotional attachment that might destroy the light atmosphere of comedy. As character becomes more genuine and complex, drama moves away from comedy. As an example of how a type character may evolve into a sympathetic and complex human being, thus altering the flavor of the play, we may consider the case of the braggart soldier. As

Some of Shakespeare's most memorable characters are in *Much Ado About Nothing*. (*Oregon Shakespeare Festival*)

Lamachus in Aristophanes' *Acharnians*, Miles Gloriosus in Plautine comedy, and the Capitano in commedia dell'arte, he is an elementary source of comic effect because of the disparity between his pretended bravery and his cowardice in the face of danger. As Shakespeare's Falstaff, the character is vastly enriched as he rollicks his way throught *The Merry Wives of Windsor* and then is developed into a complete personality in *Henry IV*.

Comic characters and their eccentric behavior have been the prime movers in many of the successful plays throughout the history of the theater: *Lysistrata*, *Two Gentlemen of Verona*, *The Rivals*, *The Miser*, *The Imaginary Invalid*, *The Country Wife*, *The Man of Mode*, *The Playboy of the Western World*, *The Odd Couple*, *Volpone*, *The Importance of Being Earnest*, *Pygmalion*, and *Driving Miss Daisy*.

THOUGHT

Most comedy does not bear a heavy burden of thought. The comic playwright usually is concerned more with the interaction of characters in a social situation than with a serious treatment of emotionally loaded problems.

Georges Feydeau, a nineteenth-century farceur, is noted for complicated action played at breakneck speed. This typical scene from *Hotel Paradiso* was directed by Tom Moore at the American Conservatory Theater in San Francisco.

In the high comedy of Restoration England, the plays demonstrated who won and lost in the social games that everyone played. The winners were witty, self-assured, sophisticated individuals who were always in control. The losers were out-of-place, awkward pretenders, unaware people, flawed in their manners. The comic dramatists wrote plays about this artificial world as part of the game, and there was no genuine concern for humanity under the polished surface.

Goldsmith and Sheridan, in the eighteenth century, used much of the same comic machinery in their sentimental comedies *The Rivals* and *She Stoops to Conquer,* but they stressed the good side of most of their comic characters rather than emphasizing their foibles and frivolities.

Shaw stands virtually alone in the twentieth century as a satirist who attacked conventional ideas of morality and manners with keen intelligence and incisive wit. His comedies of ideas were written to produce what George Meredith called "thoughtful laughter," notable in *Candida, Major Barbara, Pygmalion, Man and Superman,* and *Heartbreak House.*

The modern writer of popular comedy is much more concerned with amusing those who come to the theater—who wish to avoid facing someone else's problems and who have no immediate interest in intellectual stimulation. They want to have a good time, to laugh and to forget themselves. This attitude is evident when one looks at the list of the most popular plays on Broadway. The twenty-five longest running productions have been comedies, mostly musicals. The only serious play that ran for over one thousand performances was *Equus.*

Although such entertainment may imply an accepted code of behavior and a system of values, the emphasis is not on weighing the merits of social conduct, except insofar as it serves as a frame of reference for displaying incongruity. The comic playwright does not question values, but rather exposes ridiculous behavior or characters. The action is more important than the meaning of the action. As Gary Trudeau said in a TV interview, "True satire—that is, satire guided by a moral purpose—is more difficult to take, and people at this point want comedy that is mindless. . . . Today, the joke's the thing. . . . The gag is more important than any sustained point of view."

Yet, as suggested earlier, recent writers of dark farce frequently use broad comic plots and characters to attack their political and cultural adversaries. Likewise, the protest theater often resorts to a blatant style of low comedy for maximum shock value. An outstanding example was the "tribal love-rock musical" *Hair* of the 1960s, which boasted such show-stopping numbers as a song-and-dance sequence when the flower children break up a high-society party.

Such comedy is not without significance because it releases a good deal of aggression by permitting the gratification of repressed tendencies through laughter. In the darkened auditorium we feel free to laugh at authority and conventional restrictions of speech and behavior. For a moment we are superior to the characters who are ridiculed onstage. In the nineteenth-century French "bedroom farces" of Feydeau and Labiche, there is implicit criticism of society and its mores—particularly of hypocrisy and pretension—but this is a by-product of the farcical action, not its main reason for existence.

DICTION

Comedy employs a wide variety of language devices for its effect, from cleverly turned conceits and one-liners to crude puns, insults, vulgarisms, and deformed words. We have already observed some of the comic uses of language in derision, automatism, and incongruity. Most successful comic writers have an excellent ear for dialogue and take apparent delight in their verbal skill. The Elizabethans were fond of exploiting language for comic effect.

The writer of high comedy, of course, is especially concerned with dialogue, since wit and repartee are the drama's chief appeal; the animated language and nimbleness in playing with ideas replace physical action. The English Restoration playwrights of the late seventeenth century, such as Congreve, Wycherly, Vanbrugh, and Etherege, wrote for a select, sophisticated audience, mostly about amorous adventuring—depicting true wit in contrast to the unconscious incongruities of the inept pretenders. The polished dialogue of this comedy of manners appeared again briefly in the late eighteenth century in the dramas of Goldsmith and Sheridan.

Among modern playwrights, no one was more skilled in making his characters articulate than Shaw. In *Major Barbara* he contrasts Barbara, who is devoted to the Salvation Army, with her father, Undershaft, a munitions manufacturer who considers poverty the greatest evil.

Undershaft: I save their souls just as I saved yours.

Barbara: *(Revolted)* You saved my soul! What do you mean?

Undershaft: I fed you and clothed you and housed you. I took care that you should have enough to live handsomely—more than enough; so that you could be wasteful, careless, generous. That saved your soul from the seven deadly sins.

Barbara: *(Bewildered)* The seven deadly sins!

Undershaft: Yes, the deadly seven. *(Counting on his fingers)* Food, clothing, firing, rent, taxes, respectability, and children. Nothing can lift those seven millstones from Man's neck but money; and the spirit cannot soar until the millstones are lifted. I lifted them from your spirit. I enabled Barbara to become Major Barbara; and I saved her from the crime of poverty.

Cusins: Do you call poverty a crime?

Undershaft: The worst of crimes. All the other crimes are virtues beside it, all the other dishonors are chivalry itself by comparison. Poverty blights whole cities; spreads horrible pestilences; strikes dead the very souls of all who come within sight, sound or smell of it. What you call crime is nothing; a murder here and a theft there, a blow now and a curse then; what do they matter? They are only the accidents and illnesses of life; there are not fifty genuine professional criminals in London. But there are millions of poor people, abject people, dirty people, ill-fed, ill-clothed people. They poison us morally and physically; they kill the happiness of society; they force us to do away with our own liberties and to organize unnatural cruelties for fear they should rise against us and drag us down into their abyss. Only fools fear crime: we all fear poverty.[17]

Among present-day comic playwrights, Tom Stoppard is noted for his flair with comic language. In *Travesties* he shows off his verbal dexterity with parodies, puns, alliterations, double entendres, literary allusions, and music hall patter. In this play, Stoppard brings together in Zurich in 1919 a marvelous assortment of characters—Lenin, James Joyce, Tristan Tzara (one of the founders of Dadaism), and Carr, a minor official in the English ministry who remembers imperfectly the events that occurred. The odd combination of characters gives Stoppard the chance to play with words and ideas in a dazzling manner.

Carr: It is the duty of the artist to beautify existence.

Tzara: *(Articulately)* Dada dada dada dada dada dada dada dada dada dada dada dada dada dada dada dada dada dada dada dada dada dada dada dada dada dada dada dada dada dada dada dada dada dada dada dada.

Carr: *(Slight pause):* Oh, what nonsense you talk!

Tzara: It may be nonsense, but at least it's not clever nonsense. Cleverness has been exploded, along with so much else, by the war.

Carr: You forget that I was there, in the mud and blood of a foreign field, unmatched by anything in the whole history of human carnage. Ruined several pairs of trousers. Nobody who has not been in the trenches can have the faintest conception of the horror of it. I had hardly set feet in France before I sank in up to the knees in a pair of twill jodphurs with pigskin straps handstitched by Ramidge and Hawkes. And so it went on—the sixteen ounce serge, the heavy worsteds, the silk flannel mixture—until I was invalided out with a bullet through the calf of an irreplaceable lambswool dyed khaki in the yarn to my own specification. I tell you, there is nothing in Switzerland to compare with it.[18]

Diction in farce, on the other hand, is not distinguished by literary pretensions. Only in rare instances has a playwright like Wilde combined the framework of farce and the repartee of social comedy, because wit depends on an intellectual frame of reference. A critical ear is incompatible with farce. The linguistic devices of low comedy are puns, repetitions, tag lines, wisecracks, insults, vulgarisms, and deformed language. The playwright needs an excellent sense of theater to pace the dialogue, build for laughs, and realize the comic possibilities in the contrast of words and phrases—the incongruities of human speech.

MUSIC

In most comedies, music is incidental, but the books for many musicals have been based on comedies, such as *Oklahoma (Green Grow the Lilacs)*, *Kiss Me Kate (The Taming of the Shrew)*, *Where's Charley? (Charley's Aunt)*, *The Boys from Syracuse (Comedy of Errors)*, and *My Fair Lady (Pygmalion)*.

COMEDY IN PERFORMANCE

More than other forms of drama, comedy depends on performance for its full effect. The timing of the actors, their ability to play pieces of business, to project laugh lines, to bring out the ridiculous in situation and character without de-

Music adds another dimension to *She Stoops to Couquer* in this imaginative version of Goldsmith's eighteenth-century comedy at the Cincinnati Playhouse in the Park.

stroying the light atmosphere—these are special requisites for the complete realization of comedy.

Comedy often appeals to the eye, so that scenery, properties, and costuming play essential parts. Some comedies rely heavily on "comic business"—the actions of the characters in the play, such as fights, flirtations, chases, and all kinds of pretense. Peter Shaffer's *Lettice and Lovage* offers many such examples in a play that contrasts two strong female characters. Lettice, a born romantic, daughter of an actress, has an irrepressible flair for the theatrical, which causes her to distort her commentary as a tourist guide through the Grand Hall of Fustian House. As a result, she is discharged by Lotte, who is a staunch conservative, an undemonstrative woman, until Lettice manages to loosen her up. On one occasion, when the pair get carried away while reenacting the execution of Mary, Queen of Scots, Lotte is accidentally wounded by a falling sword. Bardolph, a middle-aged soliciter, comes to investigate the accident and is promptly and reluctantly lured into playing the drums for the execution scene:

Peter Shaffer's *Lettice and Lovage* gave the performers an exceptional chance for comic business, and Maggie Smith made full use of the opportunity!

Lettice: You're going to be the drums. I had to do them myself last time and it didn't work at all. Now you can fill in while I dress.

Bardolph: I couldn't.

Lettice: Of course you can. It's just a sound.

Bardolph: No, I really couldn't.

Lettice: You *must*, or we'll lose all the tension! Imagine them—beating all down Whitehall, hundreds of drums, without remorse of voice! . . . Pam-tititi-pam! . . . Pam-tititi-pam! . . . *(Pleading)* Try it, Mr. Bardolph. It can really be thrilling if you do it properly . . . Won't you—*please?* . . . *(Showing him, with solemn hand gestures)* Pam-tititi-pam! . . . Pam-tititi-pam!

Bardolph: *(Imitating reluctantly and off the beat)* Pam-tititi-pam . . . Pam tititi-pam . . .

(Lettice shakes her head.)

Lettice: More menace. It has to have more menace. . . . Remember these were the most dreadful drums in England. They were announcing the end of everything.

Bardolph: What do you mean?

Lettice: All the color! The age of color! The painted churches! The painted statues! The painted language! They're all about to go forever—at one stroke of an axe! In their place will come gray! The great English gray! The gray of Cromwell's clothes! The gray of Prose and Puritanism, falling on us like a blight forever! *(Pause)* Play your role, Mr. Bardolph! It is a great one! The honest yeoman wearing the helmet and breast-plate against his will—beating out on his drum the end of old England! . . . Let them hear it now! Fill the snowy streets of London with it! *(Louder)* Pam-tititi-pam! . . . Pam-tititi-pam! . . . Come on now, Mr. Bardolph—steady and terrible! Pam-tititi-pam! . . . Pam-tititi-pam!

(Seduced, Bardolph joins in.)

Bardolph: Pam-tititi-pam! Pam-tititi-pam!

Lettice: That's it! Excellent! . . . Steady and terrible, that's the secret . . . steady and terrible!

Bardolph: *(Growing more and more committed)* Pam-tititi-pam! . . . Pam-tititi-pam!

Lettice: *Bravo!*

(Suddenly he begins to march around the room to his own beat. Lotte, on her knees, stares at him dumbfounded.)

(Clapping; delighted) Bravo, Mr. Bardolph! Well done . . . Keep it up! . . . Let all England hear you!

(She watches for a second—then slips into the bedroom as the lawyer, transported, moves uninhibitedly around the room at a slow and menacing march, banging his invisible drum and calling out his pam-tititi-pams with increasing excitement. Lotte watches in amazement. Suddenly from the bedroom we hear Lettice's voice join his in wild soprano doubling. Their noise rises in a crescendo.)

Bardolph and Lettice: Pam-tititi-pam! . . . Pam-tititi-pam! . . . Pam-tititi-pam! . . . Pam-tititi-pam!!!!

(Abruptly the duet breaks off. Lettice has reappeared. She stands before the astonished lawyer in her disguise, holding the sword at attention with both hands. She wears her black Mary Queen of Scots cloak, only back to front; over her eyes is a black executioner's mask; over her chin is a false ginger beard; over her head, completing an appearance of the utmost grotesqueness, is Lotte's discarded and of course ill-fitting wig. Bardolph stares at her, open-mouthed. Lotte turns away, refusing to look. A pause.)

Lettice: Never forget—the most brilliant period in English history was brought to an end by a man looking like this. *(She advances into the room.)* The rest is quick to tell. I raised the axe—*(Demonstrating with the sword)* and *she* came in! . . . I'd forgotten, you see, to close this door.

Bardolph: *(Bewildered)* Who? . . . Who came in?

Lettice: Felina, Queen of Sorrows.

Bardolph: *Who?*

Lettice: My cat. Lotte is terrified of cats. And of course Felina, the wicked thing, knew it. She bounded in—saw Lotte there on the floor—and simply jumped with all claws—right on top of her. Like this—*MEOW!*

   (Lettice jumps on Lotte with claws extended. Lotte jumps up in shock.)

Lotte: *Get off!* . . .

   (Lettice drops the sword.)[19]

Since disguises, concealments, discoveries, fights, chases, and entrapments are standard comic fare, the physical aspects of production are apt to be very important in devising "sight gags." In high comedy, in which much of the laughter stems from the wit or awkward social behavior, less emphasis is placed on visual humor, but farce is apt to tax the physical facilities of production to the utmost.

PLAYS TO READ AND SEE

F = Film available; V = Videotape available.

F	V	Neil Simon, *Barefoot in the Park*
F	V	Leonard Gershe, *Butterflies Are Free*
F	V	Alfred Uhry, *Driving Miss Daisy*
F	V	Joe Orton, *The Entertaining Mr. Sloan*
F	V	Harold Brighouse, *Hobson's Choice*
F	V	Oscar Wilde, *The Importance of Being Earnest*
F	V	Nikolai Gogol, *The Inspector General*
F	V	Neil Simon, *I Ought to Be in Pictures*
F		Molière, *The Misanthrope*
F	V	Neil Simon, *Odd Couple*
F	V	Willy Russell, *Shirley Valentine*
F	V	Robert Harling, *Steel Magnolias*

BIBLIOGRAPHY

BENTLEY, ERIC. *Let's Get a Divorce and Other Plays.* New York: Hill and Wang, 1958.

BERGSON, HENRI. *Laughter,* trans. Cloudesley Brereton and Frank Rothwell. London: Macmillan, 1917.

BERMEL, ALBERT. *Farce: A History from Aristophanes to Woody Allen*. New York: Simon & Schuster, 1982.

EASTMAN, MAX. *Enjoyment of Laughter*. New York: Simon & Schuster, 1942.

FELHEIM, MARVIN. *Comedy, Plays, Theory and Criticism*. New York: Harcourt Brace Jovanovich, 1962.

KERR, WALTER. *Tragedy and Comedy*. New York: Simon & Schuster, 1967.

KRONENBERGER, LOUIS, ed. *Cavalcade of Comedy*. New York: Simon & Schuster, 1953.

LAUTER, PAUL. *Theories of Comedy*. New York: Doubleday, 1964.

NICOLL, ALLARDYCE. *The Theory of Drama*. New York: Barnes & Noble, 1962.

STYAN, J. L. *The Dark Comedy: The Development of Modern Comic Tragedy*. Cambridge: Cambridge University Press, 1962.

NOTES

1. Oscar Wilde, *The Importance of Being Earnest*, 1985.

2. Michael Frayn, *Noises Off* (London: Methuen, 1982). Copyright © 1982 by Methuen London, Ltd.

3. Max Eastman, *Enjoyment of Laughter* (New York: Simon & Schuster, 1942).

4. Joseph Stein, *Fiddler on the Roof* (New York: Crown Publishers, 1964). Copyright © 1964 by Joseph Stein. Used by permission of Crown Publishers, Inc.

5. Alfred Uhry, *Driving Miss Daisy* (New York: Flora Roberts, 1987).

6. Eugene Ionesco, *Rhinoceros* (London: John Calder, 1960).

7. Aristophanes, *Peace.*, trans. anonymous.

8. Sigmund Freud, *Jokes and Their Relation to the Unconscious*, trans. James Strachey (New York: W. W. Norton, Inc., 1960).

9. Beth Henley, *Crimes of the Heart*. Copyright © 1981, 1982 by Beth Henley. Used by permission of New American Library, a division of Viking Penguin USA, Inc.

10. Robert Harling, *Steel Magnolias* (New York: Dramatists Play Service, 1987). Copyright 1988 by Robert Harling.

11. Henri Bergson, *Laughter*, trans. Cloudesley Breretorn and Frank Rothwell (London: Macmillan, 1917).

12. Ben Jonson, Introduction to *Every Man out of His Humour*, 1600.

13. Bergson, *Laughter*.

14. Molière, *The Imaginary Invalid*, in *The Dramatic Works of Molière*, trans. C. H. Wall (London: George Bell & Sons, 1900).

15. Jan Kott, "The Eating of 'The Government Inspector'," *Theatre Quarterly*, 5, no. 17 (1975).

16. R. B. Sheridan, *She Stoops to Conquer*.

17. George Bernard Shaw, *Major Barbara* (New York: Dodd, Mead & Company, 1941). Copyright © 1941 by Dodd, Mead & Company. Reprinted by permission of the Society of Authors on behalf of the Bernard Shaw Estate.

18. Tom Stoppard, *Travesties*. Copyright © 1975 by Tom Stoppard. Used by permission of Grove Press, Inc.

19. Peter Shaffer, *Lettice and Lovage* (New York: Harper & Row, 1987).

six
Traditional Modes

The tradition of the theater as a cultural institution began with the Greeks in the sixth century B.C. The earliest dramas were associated with celebrations in honor of Dionysus, god of wine and fertility, and patron of drama depicted here in a fragment of Corinthian sculpture.

CLASSICISM

One of the most astonishing periods in the history of civilization was the fifth century B.C., when the small city of Athens (population approximately 100,000) gave the world a magnificent outpouring of creative energy that expressed itself in architecture, sculpture, philosophy, and the theater. Politics were a factor. Democratic in spirit if not always in practice, Athens produced a citizenry with exuberant pride, independence, and curiosity. Religion was probably another ingredient, because the Greeks developed a personal relationship with their colorful collection of gods, who placed the emphasis on the here and now—not the hereafter—an attitude that encouraged free expression in the arts as well as in daily living. In part, their animated spirit may have been due to their recent triumphs at Marathon, Thermopylae, and Salamis, where the Greeks, against formidable odds, proved themselves triumphant in warfare. Seldom have the quest for knowledge and the desire to enjoy the privilege of being alive ever been more exciting. The Greeks gave the world a totally new idea of what human life was all about and showed, for the first time, what the human mind was capable of doing.

The Greeks had a strong sense of wholeness. Life was unified, not fragmented nor splintered. Their concern with the mind was balanced by their interest in the body. As Professor Kitto points out, it was as natural for them to have gymnasia as it was to have theaters, a public assembly, and warships.[1]

Their sense of unity, so evident in the symmetry of their architecture, is also characteristic of their drama. Simplicity of form, so apparent in their sculpture and pottery, marks the plot structure of plays like *Oedipus Rex, Antigone,* and *Medea.* The Greeks did not decorate their temples with complex ornamentation like that of Gothic cathedrals, nor did their plays crowd the stage with complex actions of kings and clowns, mixing comedy and tragedy.

Classicism also embraced the idea of the "golden mean"—nothing too much—moderation in all things. The Greeks aspired to a sense of control and balance, not because their dramas were blighted and chill but because they realized the consequences of extravagance and excessive emotional display.

Reason, control, unity, simplicity—these attributes are evident in all aspects of the Greeks' aesthetic life. In drama, the plots were unified and whole. They were built around clear ideas, presented in simple terms.

The religion that the Athenian playwrights explored was quite different from the Judaeo-Christian concept, because the Greeks did not have a single all-powerful deity or an established code of good and evil. Instead, they had a full panoply of gods with conflicting desires and powers. Gods were like human beings in shape and emotions, but they were separate from humankind.

The theater in Athens, where the classic tragedies and comedies were first performed, was a part of the sacred precinct of Dionysus, god of wine, vegetation, and fertility. Greek drama grew out of religious ritual and was presented as part of a communal celebration. The sources of Greek tragedies were the traditional myths, which might contain only a slender outline or synopsis of a story. Tragic writers of the fifth century then amplified the stories and fleshed out the characters. Because the audience was familiar with these myths, the playwright was relieved of the burden of exposition. Spectators were, therefore, not primarily interested in the outcome of the story, because they already knew the ending. Their interest was centered on how well the dramatist handled the plot.

Plays were presented as a celebration in honor of Dionysus in the form of a prize contest under the sponsorship and jurisdiction of a state official. Each playwright submitted four plays—three tragedies and a satyr play (a ribald afterpiece). The cost and responsibility for presenting each tetralogy was assigned to a wealthy citizen. Judges were selected by lot. Each of the poets supervised his own production.

The Chorus was the first element in the Dionysian celebrations, and in early plays, such as *The Suppliants* by Aeschylus, it had a dominant role. But as the second and third actors were added, the part of the Chorus diminished. Some of the finest lines in Greek drama were written for the Chorus. It is a mistake to think of it as a limiting device. When properly trained in singing and dancing, the Chorus is a highly important element of the performance. Although it is constantly present, the very large orchestra, some eighty feet across, gives ample room to get the Chorus out of the way, because the spectator can see over them to the actors. This large acting area also allows the Chorus ample room for making great sweeping entrances and exits, as well as an area for lively dancing.

In Greek tragedy, the playwrights were limited to three actors and a Chorus of twelve or fifteen. Actors could play several parts by changing masks and costumes, but there were never more than three speaking characters before the audience at one time. In *Oedipus Rex,* there were seven speaking characters; in *Antigone,* nine. All of the actors were men who were assigned to the playwright by the magistrate. This convention was not as restrictive as it first sounds; many modern productions call for the actors to play multiple roles, as in *The Grapes of Wrath, Nicholas Nickleby,* and the *Mahabharata.*

Death and bloodshed did not occur before the eyes of the audience. If Medea is to slay her children, or Clytemnestra is to murder Agamemnon, the violence must take place behind the stagehouse. The cries of the victims could be heard, and dead bodies could be wheeled in on a platform or carried into the orchestra. The results of violence could be displayed, but the actual acts of destruction were supposed to happen in interior scenes. There were several reasons for this convention. One was that it is awkward to deal with a corpse out in the open in the daylight, when there is no curtain and no other way of blocking out the scene. Also, the simulation of murder would be improper on ground sacred to Dionysus, especially since his statue and temple were in close proximity.

Three terms that crop up from time to time in dramatic literature are the so-called *unities* of *time, place,* and *action.* The Greek writers were not obliged to follow them, but they are important because later on, especially in Renaissance France and Italy, they came to be regarded as laws.

By convention, unity of place was observed in most tragedies, which meant that all the action occurred in one locale. Because there was no attempt at scenic background in the Greek theater, unity of place was a preferred way of handling a plot. In most plays it was not a hindrance. When the playwright wanted to bring the audience's attention to time or place outside of the action, he made use of narration by the chorus or messenger, and some of the finest poetry in Greek drama served this purpose.

Greek tragedy, according to Aristotle, endeavors as far as possible to keep within "a single revolution of the sun." He is describing a convention observed by the tragic writers, not a rigid rule imposed by authority. Plots were simple and unified, and required only a few characters. The interest was in the matrix of the story, not in its background or ramification in other actions.

Unity of action meant that Greek plays, in almost all cases, dealt with a single line of action. There were no subplots or scenes with comic relief. Greek tragedy was spare and compact.

These unities of time, place, and action were never meant to be rules. They were merely the conventional practice of playwrights observed by Aristotle.

Greek dramatic production grew out of choric odes with dancing and music. *(Attic frieze)*

Aeschylus

Aeschylus (525–456 B.C.) wrote between seventy and ninety plays, only seven of which are extant. He won the first prize in the City of Dionysus competition fourteen times. *The Suppliants,* his earliest surviving play, features the pageantry of a Chorus of fifty maidens who had fled from Egypt to avoid an enforced marriage. Aeschylus made an important contribution to drama by introducing a second actor, thus making it possible to have a more complicated plot, as well as to strengthen the dramatic intensity by having two characters in sharp conflict with one another. His greatest creation was the *Oresteia,* a trilogy which includes *Agamemnon, The Libation Bearers,* and *The Eumenides.* It is a powerful portrayal of guilt and retribution. Aeschylus is also credited with improving the production of his plays through costuming and scene painting.

Sophocles

Sophocles (497–406 B.C.) wrote at least 110 plays and won first prize eighteen times. Seven of his plays have survived, most notably *Electra, Antigone,* and his masterpiece, *Oedipus Rex.* He was twice elected general. His chief contribution to dramatic structure was in introducing a third actor, which gave him more latitude in developing the plot and its complications. He also made the language more human. Sophocles had a special aptitude for showing his characters under stress. He also used dramatic irony in a powerful way.

Euripides

Euripides (485–406 B.C.) is credited with nearly a hundred plays, but only five won first prize. His characters were more human, and sometimes there were happy endings and touches of ordinary domestic life that made him fair game for the satirical thrusts of Aristophanes' comedies. His best known works are *Medea, Hippolytus, The Trojan Women, Orestes,* and *The Bacchae.* Euripides imitated life more closely than did his fellow tragic writers, and he widened the scope of characterization to include psychological complications that anticipate some of our modern drama.

CLASSIC COMEDY: ARISTOPHANES

Classic comedy in Greek theater, like tragedy, grew out of Dionysian worship, but it developed independently and was never intermingled. Comedy had its origin in fertility rites and the mumming of rustics during harvest and spring festivals. These were occasions of special license, and comedians felt free to ridicule everything. Beneath the jibes and laughter, however, there was often a serious purpose. Aristophanes, for example, took great delight in poking fun at Socrates and Euripides because of their "advanced ideas."

In the Aristophanic comedy *The Birds,* two Athenians, disenchanted with Athenian life, attempt to find a new haven in Cloud-Cuckooland among the birds. The American Conservatory Theater adapted the ancient comedy and called it *Feathers. (Directed by John C. Fletcher)*

The Aristophanic pattern for a comedy consisted of setting forth "a happy idea" in the prologue and then showing what happens when it is put into practice. The Chorus of twenty-four consisted of human characters as well as clouds, wasps, birds, and frogs, and gave free rein to imaginative performance in costume and choreography. At one point in the play, the *parabasis* occurs, during which Aristophanes felt free to express his personal opinions. The plays customarily ended in revelry with a happy ending—a trademark of comedy ever since.

A surprising quality of Aristophanes' comedy was his exquisite lyricism, which was combined with broad farce. It was a strange mixture. As Brander Matthews says of Greek old comedy: "It was a medley of boisterous comic-opera and of lofty lyric poetry, or vulgar ballet and of patriotic oratory, of indecent farce and of pungent satire, of acrobatic pantomime and of brilliant literary criticism, of cheap burlesque and of daringly imaginative fantasy."

Aristophanes (ca. 445–c.388 B.C.) is the only representative of old comedy whose works survive. Eleven of his plays are extant. Although he was completely fearless in attacking everyone—political figures, tragic poets, and even Dionysus himself—Aristophanes was essentially a conservative, clinging to the "good old days" in the face of new ideas in education, philosophy, and music, and especially in all political measures favoring a welfare state. It is a tribute to the freedom of speech of his day that Aristophanes felt free to ridicule Athenian leaders for their militarism in the midst of the Peloponnesian War, and even to express sympathy for the views of the enemy.

One of the most striking aspects of Aristophanes' comedies was his fantastic comic imagination. Is life unsatisfactory in Athens? Build a Utopia in the sky (*The Birds*). Are modern playwrights inept? Bring the old ones back from Hell (*The Frogs*). Is the war getting on your nerves? Make your own personal peace treaty with the enemy (*The Acharnians*), or confront the warriors with a sex strike (*Lysistrata*).

In *The Frogs* (406 B.C.), the god Dionysus, lonesome for the poets of the past with their lofty themes and styles, decides to go to Hades in an effort to see Euripides. He disguises himself as Hercules, and, accompanied by his servant Xanthias, sets out on his journey, ferried in a boat across the lake of the dead. During the trip, Dionysus changes disguises with his servant in order to avoid the threats along the way. He promptly gets a beating. When Dionysus arrives in Hades, he finds Euripides in a dispute with Aeschylus. He calls for a trial to settle the argument between the two playwrights. Each dramatist criticizes the other's works in a debate that is full of satirical literary criticism. Finally, scales are brought in to weigh their work, and Aeschylus is declared the winner because his poetry is more substantial than that of Euripides.

During the parabasis, Aristophanes takes the opportunity to get in a few serious words in favor of recalling her exiles, victims of the war. Along with this combination of political and literary material, Aristophanes manages to cut loose with comic fantasy, such as an encounter with dancing girls and the picturesque Chorus of Frogs. Throughout the centuries, Aristophanes stands as one of the most inventive comic talents to write for the theater.

ROMAN DRAMA

Roman drama is relatively unimportant in the history of the theater, except for its influence on French and English plays, because the Elizabethans had easier access in Latin to the plays of Plautus, Terence, and Seneca than they did to those of the Greeks. Roman playwrights wrote in imitation of the Greeks, but they had a far different audience from those of Athens. The Roman public theaters aimed at a public with little taste for thought or aesthetic values, and the most successful playwrights wrote comedy.

Plautus

Plautus (254–184 B.C.) has twenty-one extant plays, the best of which are *The Menaechmi, The Pot of Gold*, and *Amphitrion*. The latter two were adapted by

Molière, and the first play was the basis for Shakespeare's *Comedy of Errors*. All of Plautus' plays were based on Greek originals. He had a flair for vigorous farce that pleased the motley Roman crowds.

Plautus' basic plot centers around the adventures of a young lover who is accompanied by a tricky servant. A favorite comic device was mistaken identity, as in *The Menaechmi,* when a long-lost twin from Syracuse comes to Epidamnus to look for his brother. He is mistaken for his twin by his brother's mistress, cook, servant, wife, and father-in-law. These mix-ups are played at a pace that never lets up. Plautus had an excellent sense of rowdy comedy. *The Menaechmi* was adapted by Shakespeare, who further complicated the plot by adding twin servants to the twin brothers!

Terence

Terence (c. 195–159 B.C.) was less successful in pleasing the public, but his superior taste made him a more important writer from a literary standpoint. Like Plautus, he relied on Greek sources, but Terence developed a far more polished style. His dialogue was more refined and his characters were truer to the Greek original, although they included the same types as those used by Menander in Greek New Comedy: the sad lover and his unscrupulous slave, the scheming courtesan, the jealous wife, and the maiden in distress. His best play was *Phormio* (161 B.C.).

Seneca

The most important serious writer among the Romans was Seneca (3 B.C.–65 A.D.), who wrote ten tragedies. They were imitations of Greek plays but were probably not meant for performance. Seneca was a rhetorician, so it was natural that his plays should be full of ponderous dialogue in stilted language, which he combined with ghosts, deeds of violence, and bloody passages. Although Seneca's plays were not good theater pieces, Renaissance critics and playwrights venerated him and found to their liking his use of the five-act form, his blood and thunder, and his use of supernatural forces.

The theater in Rome never achieved the social status of the Greek theater, nor did the plays begin to reflect the glory and majesty of the Athenian masterpieces.

FRENCH NEOCLASSICISM

In medieval France, popular Biblical plays were performed in marketplaces, in courtyards, and before cathedrals. Each element of the story was played in a different area with an appropriate setting, such as a temple, a grotto, or a manger. When the French Parliament decided in 1548 that the material was becoming too vulgar and secular, it forbade the production of such plays. A year later, the

Pleiade was organized by a handful of intellectuals who wanted French drama to follow the example of the ancients in creating plays that conformed to the alleged rules of Aristotle and Horace.

Jodelle, in 1552, wrote the first French tragedy, *Cléopatre*, which had unity of time, place, and action, but it was a failure because it was all dull talk. Writers of comedy had a freer hand and were more successful in borrowing their materials from Plautus and Terence.

In spite of the lackluster production of *Cléopatre*, the classic rules became firmly set and dominated the French theater's serious dramas for two centuries. The basis for the rules was *verisimilitude*—the appearance of reality. The action of a play was supposed to be one story without comic relief, taking place in one setting in the space of twenty-four hours. These classic rules supposedly were attributed to Aristotle, but, of course, he did not lay down any rules; he merely reported on practices of Greek tragic writers before him, who wrote with no rules at all.

The Academy was organized in 1629 to govern public taste in French language and literature. Under Richelieu, the powerful chief minister of the Court, the Academy was given a royal charter, and it has been the overseer of French literary style ever since.

In Paris, acting companies increased in popularity in the 1620s, and by 1629 there were two public theaters—the Hôtel de Bourgogne and the Théâtre du Marais. All major troupes began to receive royal financial backing.

Corneille

The most successful writer of French serious drama in the seventeenth century was Pierre Corneille (1606–1684). He brought out *Le Cid* (1636), which was popular with the public but set off a storm of abuse from the critics. It was based on a Spanish six-act play that moved around in space and time and had a complex plot. Corneille concentrated the action into a simple plot in five acts, with four settings in the same town over a twenty-four-hour period.

In *Le Cid*, the hero, Rodrigue, is in love with Chimène, the daughter of Don Gomez, a proud nobleman, who is embittered because the king has appointed Rodrigue's elderly father, Don Diegue, to an important post. A quarrel ensues in which Don Gomez insults Don Diegue, but since he is too feeble to fight, Rodrigue takes over his duty to save the family honor. Despite his love for Chimène, Rodrigue challenges and kills her father in a duel. He is called away to war, where his heroic fighting drives the Moors away. But Chimène is obligated to avenge the death of her father by killing Rodrigue. A compromise is reached by arranging a duel between Le Cid and Chimène's representative. Rodrigue wins again, and the king decrees that Chimène will be free to marry Le Cid after a year of mourning.

Although Corneille was aware of the "classified rules," *Le Cid* is actually his answer to Cardinal Richelieu's attempt to dominate the theatrical and literary life of the time. Corneille got away with his rebellion because the play was received enthusiastically by theatergoers, and because the king praised the play and it was presented three times at Court. *Le Cid* was a successful theater piece because Corneille developed strong conflicts between colorful and powerful characters who were given rich language to convey their passions.

Racine

French neoclassical tragedy reached its peak through the plays of Jean Racine (1639–1699). He was a well-educated man, acquainted with the classics, whose style and structure he found compatible with his own. His greatest work was *Phèdre* (1666–1667). Racine dramatized the internal conflicts of his leading characters in compelling language and action. His protagonists were torn between conflicting emotions—often involving honor, duty, and passion. Because he developed inner tensions and conflicts, Racine did not need changeable scenery, violent actions, or a loose plot. He was right at home within the classical framework.

Racine employed lofty personages and his choice of historical and legendary subjects provided him with familiar characters for his plays. Racine's elegant simplicity was ideal for the classical style based on reason, form, and unity.

One of the most popular of Molière's comedies is *The Miser*. In it, the miserly Harpagon is ridiculed for his avarice. Here Harpagon ogles a prospective bride. *(Directed by Douglas Campbell, Guthrie Theater)*

Molière

Molière (Jean-Baptiste Poquelin, 1622–1673) is regarded as one of the outstanding playwrights of all time. Like Shakespeare, Molière gained his early experience in the theater as an actor. He knew at first hand the problems of dealing with an audience, especially since he had become the leader of a troupe of actors that went through the rigors of trying to make a living by playing in the provinces for twelve difficult years. When he returned to Paris and came to the attention of the king, the tide turned, and he and his actors became an established company.

As we have seen, writers of comedy in Greece and Rome had far more freedom than their serious contemporaries in both form and subject matter. While the French Academy was firm in its advocacy of regularizing the French neoclassical tragedies of Corneille and Racine, Molière's pressures came from other directions. Clarity and logic are regarded as characteristics of the French mind. In Molière's opinion, the function of comedy was the correct portrayal of his society. But as a practical man of the theater, Molière realized that his first obligation was to entertain his audience. As a consequence, his plays are full of humorous situations that reveal character. But the comedy is a weapon. His plays imply a moral lesson. In keeping with the neoclassical ideal of the golden mean, Molière teaches that excess results in disaster. His plays expose human foibles— in *Tartuffe*, hypocrisy; in *The Miser*, avarice; in *The Learned Young Ladies*, pretentious affectation. Molière followed the neoclassical ideal of using drama to delight and teach; but in ridiculing hypocrisy, avarice, and pretentiousness, he alienated many of his contemporaries.

ENGLISH NEOCLASSICISM

In Elizabethan England, there was no Academy to dictate taste. There were critics like Sir Philip Sidney, who pleaded the case for classical rules and restraints; but except for Ben Jonson, the playwrights were deaf to scholarly criticism and wrote to please the popular taste for conglomerate plays. Jonson's attempt to write two "regular tragedies" met with failure, but he was far more successful with his comedies.

During the Restoration, the English stage came under the influence of the French theater, because of Charles II's taste for Molière. Sporadic efforts were made to write in a more classical style, following the example of Continental playwrights. For a time, "heroic tragedies" were in vogue, with their florid speeches and rhymned couplets. They dealt with idealized heroes and heroines in such plays as Dryden's *Conquest of Granada,* but their inflated style was punctured by the Duke of Buckingham's spoof, *The Rehearsal* (1671).

Another attempt was made to regularize serious drama through the use of blank verse. John Dryden's *All for Love,* based on Shakespeare's *Anthony and Cleopatra,* was a noteworthy attempt. But the most successful serious playwright of the period was Thomas Otway, whose plays *The Orphans* and *Venice Preserv'd* are two of the best acting vehicles since Shakespeare. Although Otway was not a rigorous neoclassicist, he came as close as any English playwright to working in that mode and still produce highly effective theater. Two other factors had stronger influences on the theater than did critical theory: the first appearance of actresses on the English stage and the coming of the proscenium arch with its changeable scenery.

The Elizabethans

Before Shakespeare's birth in 1564, students at all levels of learning were exposed to the classics, especially in Latin. Instructors attempted to enliven their teaching by performing and writing plays in the classical style. The most important play before Shakespeare was *Gorboduc* (1560), written by two young lawyers, Sackville and Norton. They followed the classic unities, preserved decorum, and kept the violent action offstage. Since the plot involves one brother slaying another and the mother murdering the surviving son, after which the people revolt and kill the king and queen, much of the play is taken up by messengers' speeches. The result was a dull play. On the other hand, *Gorboduc* had an immediate appeal because it was written in English. Perhaps more important, the playwrights introduced the use of blank verse on the English stage.

When the Renaissance came to Elizabethan England, it produced a remarkable intellectual ferment, with great interest in literature, language, and politics. The spirit of the times was positive, dynamic, tumultuous, which made for a lively audience that regarded the theater as its way of keeping up to date, much as we rely on newspapers, television, and radio. Following the English defeat of the Spanish Armada in 1588, patriotism was high. Londoners delighted in "chronicle" plays rooted in English history. There was a lively sense of expansion and discovery in nearly all aspects of culture, and the theater was an ideal institution to reflect this exuberance.

Shakespeare's early life gave no clue to the preeminent playwright who was to emerge in London. He was born in the small town of Stratford-on-Avon and given an ordinary education. His childhood and early youth, spent in rustic and natural surroundings, are reflected in his imagery later on.

Shakespeare apparently came to London about 1588 and immediately became attached to the Globe Theater as an actor and play-doctor. While there is no accounting for genius, there were at least three important influences on Shakespeare as a playwright: (1) the medieval tradition, (2) the theatrical conditions under which he worked, and (3) the influences of his contemporaries.

The *medieval tradition* for producing plays grew out of the church's attempt to make Biblical stories more graphic for their faithful flocks. After seeing the discovery of the empty tomb for themselves in *Quem Quaeritis* (p. 17), congregations wanted to see more. The clergy obliged by adding more and more visual material to the liturgy, until it became too secular and too complicated for the Church. It was then taken over by the guilds and performed out of doors. The loose structure of episodes mixed serious material with comic and high characters with low. The practice was to show as much of the action as possible. This medieval tradition of dealing with a complex story, told in segments of action and blending together all kinds of material and characters, had its impact on the Elizabethan playwrights, who also wrote complex plots that moved around freely in time and space.

This visual tradition carried over into dramaturgy because playwrights wanted to tell a complete story, with all of the important incidents included. In performance, especially with traveling companies that now emerged, it became impossible to back each scene with a stage setting. Specific locale was established by dialogue, costume, and properties.

When players began playing in inn yards, the custom of using a bare stage was continued, so that when the first professional theater, The Theater (1576) was built, the practice of using an empty platform was well established. As the professional theaters developed, the stage was far more than boards on a trestle. The Fortune Theater (1600) contract calls for a stage twenty-seven and a half feet deep by forty-three feet wide—a very large playing area—backed by two big doors and a multilevel façade of the stage house. Hence, the acting area could accommodate a great many people and a lot of action. The stage could also hold a variety of properties that could be brought on, and there were no doubt trapdoors and equipment for flying in some properties and even characters. But by and large this enormous playing area was nonillusionistic. There was no way to set or change movable scenery for each locale, nor would the sight lines permit it. This practice meant that the Elizabethans had a remarkably flexible theater that was ideally suited for a plot that put most of the action of a complicated plot before an audience. *Anthony and Cleopatra* has forty-three different changes in locale, more than a dozen in a single act. This versatile bare platform gave Shakespeare and his contemporaries an ideal playing space for the lively and varied kind of performances their plays required.

The *theatrical conditions* refer to Shakespeare's connection with the professional company at the Globe. We have already mentioned the highly demonstrative audience, which was capable of responding to everything from broad farce and tragedies of blood, to childlike story plays full of fantasy, as well as to somber tragedies with majestic characters and some of the finest language ever heard in the theater. This was not an audience that cared about strict classical rules and decorum. The Elizabethans wanted to see the action—all of it. And they wanted surprise and spectacle, pomp and circumstance, and all the aspects of war.

Shakespeare soon occupied a unique position in the theater as a resident playwright and part owner of an established company of actors. With this kind of leverage, no doubt Shakespeare had a good deal to say about how his plays were to be performed. He was singularly blessed in having as his leading actor Richard Burbage, who must have been one of the most versatile and talented actors in theater history, judging by the range of roles that he played: Hamlet, Othello, Macbeth, Romeo, King Lear, Prospero, and Henry V, to mention just a few.

One of the difficult conventions that Shakespeare had to contend with was that of using boys in the female roles. This was especially trying when he wrote romantic comedies and was compelled to avoid ardent love scenes. Shakespeare's ingenuity in handling this convention is evident in the variety of ways he managed to keep the lovers apart. One of his ways of dealing with his young heroines was to put them in disguise in men's clothing.

Another important influence on Shakespeare was that of his contemporaries. Consider the conditions under which they were working. Here were six professional companies competing with one another for the thirty thousand or so who came to the theater every week, demanding fresh, exciting new plays. As soon as one hit on a popular idea—when Thomas Kyd (1558–1594) scored a hit with *The Spanish Tragedy* (c. 1587), a "tragedy of blood"—it was immediately followed by a dozen plays by his rivals that made use of many of the same ingredients, such as a revenge story, insanity, ghosts, a play within a play, and considerable violence. Shakespeare followed the general practice of borrowing plot material for almost all of his plays, as well as themes, lines, and characters, from classic literature and his fellow playwrights. He was fortunate to be surrounded by so many other talented and exciting writers, who were almost always working either in competition or in collaboration with one another. Thomas Kyd's *Spanish Tragedy*, in fact, had an obvious impact on Shakespeare's *Titus Andronicus* and *Hamlet*.

Shakespeare's Contemporaries

Christopher Marlowe (1564–1593) was one of the most promising talents to appear at the end of the sixteenth century. When he died at the age of twenty-nine, he had already written four extraordinary plays: *Tamburlaine* (1587), *The Jew of Malta* (1589), *Dr. Faustus* (1589), and *Edward II* (c. 1590). His two most important influences on Shakespeare were the examples of tragic heroes of great magnitude and intensity, and his superlative use of blank verse in drama, such as these famous lines:

> Was this the face that launched a thousand ships,
> And burnt the topless towers of Ilium?[2]

John Lyly (1554–1606), who wrote mostly for troupes of boy actors and chapel choirs, was famous for his pastoral comedies of classical mythology and English life. Lyly's work is noted for his elegant style and refined characters, especially in *Endymion* (c. 1588). We find echoes of Lyly in *As You Like It* and *A Midsummer Night's Dream*.

George Peele (c. 1558–1598), a better poet than a playwright, also wrote pastoral dramas in a poetic style. He was noted for his charming heroines, who resembled those found in Shakespeare's romantic comedies—*Love's Labour's Lost* and *All's Well That Ends Well*.

Ben Jonson (1563–1637), the most learned of the Elizabethan playwrights, was well acquainted with classical rules and wrote some of the best dramatic criticism of his time. He even attempted to write two "regular tragedies" following the ancient style, *Sejanus* (1603) and *Catiline* (1611), but neither play met with popular approval. His reputation was made in his comedies, where Jonson was freer to pursue his natural instincts for bitter satire and his flair for recording contemporary London life. His *Everyman in His Humour* (1598) is noteworthy for illustrating Jonson's theory of comedy, in which he held up to ridicule characters who were dominated by one drive or passion, as in *Volpone* (1605), *The Silent Woman* (1609), and *Bartholomew Fair* (1614). Jonson's comedies made him very popular at the box office, and many regarded him as the best playwright of his time.

Shakespeare's Plays

Shakespeare's reputation as the outstanding playwright of all time is due to a rare blend of talent and imagination, coupled with the practical know-how to bring his creations to life on stage before an audience. His universality of thought, magnificent use of language, and vividness of characterization were combined with his sense of humanity, which shows how well he knew and loved human beings and wrote about them with insight and compassion.

Scholars often group Shakespeare's plays into four periods. The first, from 1590 to 1594, was a period of experimentation that showed his remarkable diversity, ranging from the Marlowesque tragedy of *Richard III*, to romantic

Shakespeare's comedies are often filled with romance, such as *Two Gentlemen of Verona* at the Oregon Shakespeare Festival.

comedies that echoed Lyly in *Two Gentlemen of Verona* and *Love's Labour's Lost,* to the "chronicle" style of the *Henry VI* plays.

The period from 1595 to 1600 established Shakespeare as a mature playwright fully in charge of his materials. Again, there is a wide diversity of style, from *Richard II* and *Henry V* to the delightful pastoral comedies *As You Like It, Twelfth Night,* and *Much Ado about Nothing.*

Between 1601 and 1608 Shakespeare wrote three comedies that resembled Jonson's in their occasional gloomy atmosphere, but his major achievement was a staggering outpouring of creative energy in producing *Hamlet, Othello, King Lear,* and possibly *Anthony and Cleopatra.* Although these tragedies include some of the melodramatic machinery of his contemporaries, such as the use of ghosts, insanity, and the revenge theme, Shakespeare transcends these devices through his powerful characterization and soaring poetic language.

The final period, 1609 to 1611, marks the decline of Shakespeare's interest in themes of great magnitude. He returned to writing comedies, sometimes dark, sometimes romantic, but always with his special touch of humanity and fantasy.

Hamlet

Hamlet is regarded as Shakespeare's most important play. It is full of rich imagery and exciting action, and its central character has challenged scholars and actors

One of Shakespeare's most successful history plays is *Henry V,* with its appealing hero and vigorous action. *(Directed by James Edmondson, Oregon Shakespeare Festival)*

for five centuries. There are memorable soliloquies and poetic passages, as well as some of the most striking scenes in the theater. *Hamlet* has been endlessly discussed and has been performed under all kinds of conditions with a wide spectrum of interpretations. It remains the most controversial and stimulating play ever written.

Although Shakespeare was a highly successful and popular playwright in his time, Elizabethans did not regard him as a towering genius, as we do today. During the Restoration and the eighteenth century, he was often criticized for his loose structure and disregard of classical rules. He was also at a disadvantage when the proscenium arch was introduced, with changeable, pictorial scenery, which destroyed the flexibility Shakespearean productions demand. During the nineteenth century, several ingenious managers staged Shakespeare in lavish productions oftentimes by drastically cutting the text, blending scenes together or changing their order, or giving very long performances. It was not until the advent of the modern stage, when changes in theater architecture, machinery, and lighting could restore flexibility, that Shakespeare's full power was realized.

GERMAN ROMANTICISM

German romanticism is associated with the *Sturm und Drang* ("storm and stress") movement, from 1767 to 1787. This was a period of experimentation by rebellious young playwrights who rejected the attempt to establish French neoclassical rules on the German stage. They demanded the freedom to write about shocking and exciting characters and to deal with subject matter that gave free play to their emotions. They took a liking to Shakespeare's style of playwriting, although they wrote their plays in prose, not poetry. Shakespeare has been a part of the German theater tradition ever since.

Goethe

When he was twenty-four, Johann Wolfgang von Goethe captured the attention and adulation of his revolutionary contemporaries with *Goetz von Berlichingen* (1773), an episodic play with fifty-four scenes. It was received with wild enthusiasm. Goethe was dubbed the "German Shakespeare," and he became the leader of the romantic rebellion.

In *Goetz von Berlichingen*, Goethe included three basic ideas of the Sturm und Drang movement: an impetus to return to nature, a rejection of French taste and its neoclassicism, and an enthusiastic acceptance of Shakespeare. Goetz was a picturesque hero from the Peasants' War of 1316. He was involved in a complicated plot, full of intrigue and treachery, that dramatized the conflict of a free spirit against the strictures of law and order. He was finally killed in battle.

Goetz was important in the history of the German theater because it broke away from neoclassicism with an exuberant, episodic play, full of action and feeling, and helped to establish the Shakespearean free approach to plotting. The

1774 production of Goethe's play in Berlin was noteworthy because, for the first time, the stage abandoned the dress of the French court in favor of authentic period costuming. It also set the fashion for playwrights to take their plots and characters from German history.

Schiller

Johann Christoph Schiller's *The Robbers* was written by the nineteen-year-old German playwright in 1773 out of his hatred for the severe discipline at his regimental school. *The Robbers,* in the spirit of romanticism, dramatizes the exploits of Karl von Moer, who flees from his father's corrupt court to become a kind of German Robin Hood in the forests of Bohemia. Karl is pitted against his villainous brother, Franz, who holds power over Karl's beloved Amelia. The play was full of passion, action, and patriotic fervor. In the end, Karl ends Amelia's suffering.

Schiller's *Wilhelm Tell* (1804) deals with the citizens of a Swiss canton in 1308 who rebelled against their crushing mistreatment at the hands of the Austrian governor. Driven by their vigorous desire for independence, they were determined to set up the first democratic government in Europe. Caught up in this

Daniel Chodowiecki's engraving of a performance of *Hamlet* at the Royal Theater in Berlin. Shakespeare was a great favorite of German audiences.

protest, the nobles, who were conservatively aligned with the emperor because of the privileges they enjoyed, were impelled to take a stand for freedom, so they joined with the common people and burghers to demand their rights. These elements were bound together with the legendary tale of Wilhelm Tell, the skilled archer, who was ordered by the tyrant Gessler to shoot an apple from his son's head. His aim was true and he succeeded, but Gessler discovered that Tell had a second arrow intended for him if he had failed. Tell was arrested, but he killed Gessler and led in the struggle to set Switzerland free from Austria. The play was not only a rich historical pageant but also Schiller's dramatic plea for freedom.

ENGLISH ROMANTICISM

In England, romanticism is most closely associated with poetry and the novel, especially the novels of Sir Walter Scott, whose works were adapted to the stage. James Sheridan Knowles's *Virginians* (1820), a pseudo-Shakespearean attempt in the romantic spirit, was widely played. By and large, the audience found its taste

Shakespeare's tragedies were often given "romantic" treatment with elaborate scenery and costumes, as in Henry Irving's late nineteenth-century version of the final scene from *Romeo and Juliet*.

for romanticism most satisfactorily expressed in sensational melodramas. Those who preferred a more literate drama found their leanings toward romanticism reflected in the staging of the plays of Shakespeare and Otway, often cut and altered, staged with picturesque and sensational scenery, and emphasizing a bombastic acting style.

As we have seen, romanticism began as a revolt against the rigid rules of neoclassicism, because playwrights insisted on dealing freely with the imaginative aspects of nature and humanity. The romanticists delighted in giving full rein to their emotions. They insisted on freedom for a wide scope of action celebrating the individual as a child of nature, and they contrasted beauty and the grotesque, the lowly and the elevated. Such plays as *Wilhelm Tell, Goetz von Berlichingen,* and *Cyrano de Bergerac* expressed a sense of wonder and mystery of life; the action was often remote, exotic, and astonishing.

Although romanticism was effective in clearing the stage of the austere rigidity of the past, its built-in tendency toward excess made it susceptible to such

Hugo's *Hernani* caused a pitched battle for forty-three nights at the Comedie Française before romanticism was accepted on the French stage.

abuses as straining too much for effect, and superficiality in character and motivation. When the theater turned more and more to escape, romanticism lost its contact with the real world and everyday life. The new way of looking at the world brought with it the development of realism. Nevertheless, the spirit of romanticism is always with us when we wistfully compare our present-day mechanized, regimented world with the idealized notion of the individual as a child of nature.

FRENCH ROMANTICISM

Rostand

Edmond Rostand's *Cyrano de Bergerac* (1897) was the high point of French romanticism, which began with Victor Hugo's *Hernani* in 1830. Rostand's masterpiece is regarded as the most successful example of romanticism in the theater.

Cyrano establishes his swashbuckling character with his first entrance. The scene is set in the theater—the Hôtel de Bourgogne in Paris in the early seventeenth century. On stage, the rotund, florid actor-manager, Montefleury, is trying to perform before a crowd of gallants and aristocrats. Suddenly, a voice is heard denouncing the actor. An arm is seen above the crowd, shaking a cane—and then Cyrano mounts a chair, captures everyone's attention, and orders Montfleury to leave the stage amid the clamor of the audience.

A Voice: *(In the middle of the audience)* Rascal, didn't I forbid you for a month?

> *(Astonishment. Everyone turns around. Murmurs.)*

Various Voices: What . . . ? What is it?

> *(They get up in the boxes, to see.)*

Cuigy: It is he!

Le Bret: *(Terrified)* Cyrano!

The Voice: King of Clowns, off the stage immediately!

All the House: *(Indignantly)* Oh!

Montfleury: But . . .

The Voice: You resist?

Various Voices: *(From the audience and boxes)* Hush!—Enough!—Montfleury, play! Do not fear anything . . .

Montfleury: *(In an uncertain voice)* "Happy is he who, far from the busy stream, in a solitary place . . ."

The Voice: *(More menacing)* Well? Is it necessary that I plant, O Monarch of Clowns, a forest of wood about your shoulders? *(A cane at the end of an arm bursts out above the heads of the crowd.)*

Montfleury: *(In a voice more and more feeble)* "Happy is he . . ."

> *(The cane is waved.)*

The Voice: Leave!

The Audience: Oh!

Montfleury: *(Choking)* "Happy is he who, far from the stream . . ."

Cyrano: *(Surging from the audience, stands on a chair, arms crossed, felt hat in battle-array, mustache bristling, nose terrible)* Ah! I am getting angry! *(There is a sensation at his appearance.)*

Montfleury: *(To the Marquises)* Come to my aid, Gentlemen!

A Marquis: *(Indifferently)* Well, play then!

Cyrano: Fat man, if you play, I will be obliged to thrash you!

The Marquis: Enough!

Cyrano: The Marquises will keep silent on their benches, or I will prod their service ribbons with my cane!

All the Marquises: *(Standing)* This is too much! . . . Montfleury . . .

Cyrano: Montfleury will leave or I will clip his ears and unravel him!

A scene from the original 1897 production of *Cyrano de Bergerac* at the Theatre Porte Saint-Martin. Cyrano, on the chair, is taunting Montfleury.

A Voice: But . . .

Cyrano: He must go!

Another Voice: However . . .

Cyrano: It is still not done? *(With a gesture of turning up his sleeves)* Good! I am going onto the stage, which is like a refreshment table, to slice to pieces this Bologna sausage from Italy!

Montfleury: *(Mustering all his dignity)* In insulting me, Sir, you insult Thalia!

Cyrano: *(Very politely)* If this Muse, Sir, to whom you are nothing, had the honor to make your acquaintance, believe me that on seeing you so fat and stupid like an urn, she would fling you down with her leather boots.

Audience: Montfleury! Montfleury!—Baro's play!

Cyrano: *(To those who are shouting around him)* I beg of you, have pity on my scabbard; if you continue, it is going to give up its sword! *(The circle around him widens out.)*

The Crowd: *(Drawing back)* Say! There!

Cyrano: *(To Montfleury)* Leave the stage!

The Crowd: *(Coming closer and grumbling)* Oh! Oh!

Cyrano: *(Turning around quickly)* Does someone protest? *(A new retreat)*

A Voice: *(Singing in the rear)* Monsieur de Cyrano
  Truly oppresses us.
  In spite of this tyrannical dynamo
  "La Clorise" will still be played!

All the Hall: *(Singing)* "La Clorise, la Clorise!" . . .

Cyrano: If I hear this song one more time, I will slay you all.

A Citizen: You are not Samson!

Cyrano: Are you willing to lend me, Sir, your blockhead?

A Lady: *(In the boxes)* This is unheard of!

A Gentleman: It is scandalous!

A Citizen: It is disgraceful!

A Page: This is amusing!

The Audience: Hiss!—Montfleury!—Cyrano!

Cyrano: Silence!

The Audience: *(In a frenzy)* Hi han! Bee! Ouah! Ouah! Cocorico!

Cyrano: I . . .

A Page: Miauo!

Cyrano: I order you to keep quiet!—and I address a challenge to all the audience! I will write down the names! Approach, young heroes! Each one in
his turn! I am going to give out numbers! Come, who is the one who
wishes to start the list? You, Sir? No! You? No! The first duellist to offer
will be given all the burial honors due him! All those who wish to die, raise
your hands. *(Silence)* Does modesty prevent you from seeing my naked
blade? Not a name? Not a hand?—All right. I will continue. *(Turning back
towards the stage, where Montfleury waits, in anxiety)* Now then, I want to see
the theater cured of this inflammation. If not . . . *(His hand on his sword)*
the surgical knife!

Montfleury: I . . .

Cyrano: *(Gets down from the chair, sits in the middle of the circle that has formed, and
installs himself as if he were at home)* My hands are going to strike three times,
full moon! At the third time, you will be eclipsed . . .

The Audience: *(Amused)* Ah?

Cyrano: *(Clapping his hands)* One!

Montfleury: I . . .

A Voice: *(From the boxes)* Stay!

The Audience: He will stay . . . he will not stay . . .

Montfleury: I believe, Sirs . . .

Cyrano: Two!

Montfleury: I am sure it would be better . . .

Cyrano: Three!

> *(Montfleury disappears as if through a trap door. A storm of laughter, whistles,
> and hoots.)*[3]

Rostand's masterpiece tells the story of a romantic poet who is also a skilled
swordsman and swaggering soldier, but he has one flaw—an enormous nose.
Cyrano is in love with the beautiful Roxane, but he is too self-conscious of his
physical deformity to attempt courtship. Instead, he comes to the aid of his
friend, Christian, who is too inarticulate to be an effective lover. Cyrano composes
Christian's love letters and, in a memorable balcony scene, he prompts Christian
by giving him romantic passages that touch Roxane's heart. In the war, Christian
is wounded and dies. Fifteen years pass, and Roxane, who has entered a convent,
awaits Cyrano's periodic visit. He has suffered a serious head wound but manages
to keep his appointment with her. Roxane discovers that Cyrano was the author
of the letters sent by Christian and that it was the poet's spirit she really loved all
the time. He dies content.

Rostand wrote *Cyrano de Bergerac* for Coquelin, one of the most famous and
talented actors in France. Seldom has a play received such a tumultuous recep-

The battle scene from the Pioneer Theater Company of the University of Utah's staging of *Cyrano de Bergerac.*

tion. On opening night, after every act, the audience was on its feet, wildly applauding. *Cyrano de Bergerac* was immediately brought on stage all over Europe and America, where it was hailed as a masterpiece. In 1946 a José Ferrer production brought this comment from the Broadway critic Robert Coleman: "For our money, *Cyrano de Bergerac* is the greatest theater piece ever penned."[4]

Rostand's play came at the end of the nineteenth century and represents a culmination of the romantic movement in France, which had begun a century earlier when a new audience made up of the middle classes and young rebels demanded a new kind of drama that brought on stage the "natural man"—a highly volatile individual, unfettered by the shackles of organized society, a hero whose conduct was guided by his heart.

Hugo

The answer to their demands grew out of another play that was accorded one of the wildest receptions in the history of the theater, when Victor Hugo attempted to stage his *Hernani* (1830) at the Comédie Française. Three years earlier, in the preface to his *Cromwell,* Hugo called for a new spirit in the theater that "will set about doing as nature does, mingling in its creations—but without compounding them—darkness and light, the grotesque and the sublime." He determined to put

In *Hernani* the setting and costumes reinforce the plot and its melodramatic machinery.

his theories into practice by producing a play that broke the rules that had hamstrung French playwrights for two centuries.

When *Hernani* went into rehearsal, members of the French Academy, an organization of critics and scholars appointed to preserve high standards in language and literature, vainly petitioned the king to prohibit the play from reaching the public. The battle was joined between young rebels who sided with Hugo and arch conservatives who vowed to keep the Comédie Française clear of such "barbarous material." *Hernani* opened in February 1830, amid such a clamor between the two factions that not a line of dialogue could be heard. The furor lasted for forty-three nights before things quieted down and *Hernani* was finally accepted by the public. The stranglehold of the Academy's neoclassicism was broken.

Hernani has a complicated plot involving the exploits of an outlaw hero in his attempts to win his love, Dona Sal, against the opposition of two rivals—her elderly guardian, Don Ruy Gomez, and Don Carlos (King Charles V of Spain).

The conflicts of honor reflect its Spanish origin. The play is filled with action in palaces and castles and even in the tomb of Charlemagne at Aix-la-Chapelle. The play ends when Hernani and Dona Sal take poison and die on what was to have been their wedding night.

The reason for such a stormy protest was that the conservatives predicted that if *Hernani* succeeded, it would change the traditions of the French theater—traditions that had been kept for two centuries. In particular, they objected to the mixture of humorous and serious material, the disregard of the unities of time and place, and especially the distortion of the language and the alexandrine verse form. The conservatives felt that Hugo had deliberately set out to break the traditional rules. They were right. Hugo triumphed, and the French theater was never the same again.

PLAYS TO READ AND SEE

F = Film available; V = Videotape available.

		Aeschylus, *Agamemnon*
		John Dryden, *All for Love*
		Pierre Corneille, *Le Cid*
F	V	Edmond Rostand, *Cyrano de Bergerac*
		Christopher Marlowe, *Dr. Faustus*
		Aristophanes, *The Frogs*
F	V	William Shakespeare, *Hamlet*
		Victor Hugo, *Hernani*
		Euripides, *Hippolytus*
		William Shakespeare, *King Lear*
F	V	William Shakespeare, *Macbeth*
		Plautus, *The Menaechmi*
F	V	William Shakespeare, *A Midsummer Night's Dream*
F	V	Sophocles, *Oedipus Rex*
		Jean Racine, *Phèdre*
F	V	William Shakespeare, *Romeo and Juliet*
		Molière, *Tartuffe*
		William Shakespeare, *Twelfth Night*
		Ben Jonson, *Volpone*
		Johann Christoph Schiller, *Wilhelm Tell*

BIBLIOGRAPHY

Arnott, Peter. *The Theater in its Time*. Boston: Little, Brown, 1981.
Brockett, Oscar G. *The Essential Theater*. New York: Holt, Rinehart & Winston, 1980.
Corrigan, Robert, ed. *Tragedy: Vision and Form*. San Francisco: Chandler, 1964.
Langer, Suzanne K. *Feeling and Form*. New York: Charles Scribner's Sons, 1953.
Muller, Herbert. *The Spirit of Tragedy*. New York: Knopf, 1976.
Myers, Henry Alonzo. *Tragedy: A View of Life*. Ithaca, N.Y.: Cornell University Press, 1956.

NICOLL, ALLARDYCE. *The Theater and Dramatic Theory.* New York: Barnes and Noble, 1962.
STYAN, J. I. *Elements of Drama.* Cambridge: Cambridge University Press, 1965.

NOTES

1. H. D. F. Kitto, *The Greeks* (Baltimore, Maryland: Penguin Books, 1951).

2. Christopher Marlowe, *Dr. Faustus,* Scene XIII.

3. Edmond Rostand, *Cyrano de Bergerac,* trans. Dorcas Hatlen.

4. Robert Coleman, quoted in Joseph T. Shipley, *Guide to Great Plays* (Washington, D.C.: Public Affairs Press, 1956).

seven
Realism

Henrik Ibsen's play *A Doll's House* is often credited with the emergence of realism at the end of the nineteenth century. The play features a domestic conflict between Nora and Torvald, shown here in a production at Toledo University directed by George Beck.

The chapter opening photograph is from the Toledo University production of Ibsen's *Doll's House* (1880), one of the pivotal plays in all dramatic literature. It was important for several reasons:

1. The basic conflict was built around Nora's battle for her personal integrity against the narrow conventions of Victorian society.

2. It set off a storm of controversy that made the play a significant subject of public discussion.

3. *A Doll's House* brought in a new style of drama: realism. William Archer (1906), a foremost critic, observed that "When Nora and Helmer faced each other and set to work to ravel out the skein of their illusions, then one felt oneself face to face with a new thing in drama—an order of experience, at once intellectual and emotional, not hitherto attained in the theater."

Before the play begins, Nora, who was brought up in a "sheltered doll's house" atmosphere by a doting father, has forged a signature on a note in order to save the life of her ill husband, Helmer.

The Doll's House has a single setting—the Helmers' living-room in Christiania. As the curtain opens, Nora is seen returning home from Christmas shopping.

> *(Nora enters humming gayly. She is in outdoor dress, and carries several parcels, which she lays on the right-hand table. She leaves the door into the hall open, and a Porter is seen outside, carrying a Christmas tree and a basket, which he gives to the Maidservant who has opened the door.)*

Nora: Hide the Christmas tree carefully, Ellen; the children must on no account see it before this evening, when it's lighted up. *(To the Porter, taking out her purse)* How much?

Porter: Fifty ore.

Nora: There is a crown. No, keep the change.

> *(The Porter thanks her and goes. Nora shuts the door. She continues smiling in quiet glee as she takes off her outdoor things. Taking from her pocket a bag of macaroons, she eats one or two. Then she goes on tiptoe to her husband's door and listens.)* Yes, he's at home. *(She begins humming again, crossing to the table on the right.)*

Helmer: *(In his room)* Is that my lark twittering there?

Nora: *(Busy opening some of her parcels)* Yes, it is.

Helmer: Is the squirrel frisking around?

Nora: Yes!

Helmer: When did the squirrel get home?

Nora: Just this minute. *(Hides the bag of macaroons in her pocket and wipes her mouth)* Come here, Torvald, and see what I've been buying.

Helmer: Don't interrupt me. *(A little later he opens the door and looks in, pen in hand.)* Buying, did you say? What! All that? Has my little spendthrift been making money fly again?

Nora: Why, Torvald, surely we can afford to launch out a little now. It's the first Christmas we haven't had to pinch.

Helmer: Come, come, we can't afford to squander money.

Nora: Oh, yes, Torvald, do let us squander a little now—just the least little bit! You know you'll soon be earning heaps of money.

Helmer: Yes, from New Year's Day. But there's a whole quarter before my first salary is due.

Nora: Never mind; we can borrow in the meantime.

Helmer: Nora! *(He goes up to her and takes her playfully by the ear.)*[1]

Into this peaceful environment, Ibsen introduces a conflict. Krogstad, a former clerk in Helmer's bank, discovers the forgery and attempts to blackmail Nora so that he can regain his job. She spurns his threat, because she believes her husband will come to her defense, since her crime was committed out of her

In this scene from *A Doll's House*, Nora attempts to divert her husband's attention by dancing the tarantella. Note the realistic set in this 1879 production at the Royal Theater in Copenhagen.

devotion to him. At this point, Krogstad returns the forged note, and the audience expects the traditional happy ending and reconciliation. They are astonished when Nora and Helmer, instead of rushing into each other's arms, sit down at Nora's insistence and have their first serious conversation in eight years of married life. When her husband berates her for her unlawful act, Nora realizes her status as a mere doll. She decides that the only way to preserve her own integrity and self-respect is to leave her husband and children. She hands back her wedding ring and goes out the door.

The slamming of that door was heard around the world. Ibsen's play became the subject of controversy wherever it was printed. When it appeared in London, it aroused a great critical clamor that found George Bernard Shaw coming to Ibsen's support in a rancorous controversy. In order to get *A Doll's House* produced in Germany, Ibsen was forced to write a happy ending, in which Nora changes her mind and decides to stay. When the play appeared in New York, not only did the production include the happy ending, but a comic maid was introduced in order to give the play an even lighter touch.

A Doll's House was one of the most influential plays ever written—and it set the pattern for realism. It is a play about ordinary, contemporary people, in ordinary, domestic surroundings, speaking in everyday language about commonplace things. Yet notice what Ibsen has accomplished in just a few lines. The relationship between the husband and wife is shown in Helmer's reference to her as a "twittering lark" and a "frisking squirrel." His preoccupation with money is revealed in his chiding her about squandering money and in his reference to her as a "little spendthrift." Notice also Ibsen's stage directions, which *show in action*, through stage business, revealing aspects of character. Nora hides the macaroons and tries to keep her husband from knowing about them. This is preparation, because later in the play we learn that she has been secretly sewing in order to cover the note she forged. Nora has some skill in deception. At the outset, Nora's business with taking off her wraps, humming to herself, handling the Christmas packages, and tiptoeing to her husband's door create a lively sense of ordinary domesticity. It is by these details, drawn from ordinary life, that realism established a new kind of theater.

The term *realism* in the arts is an arbitrary one. An easel painting on a framed flat piece of canvas may be an aesthetic representation of an actual landscape, but viewers know that they are not looking through a window at genuine trees, water, and sky. Likewise, the spectator in the theater knows that the stage setting is not a real room and that the characters in it are performers. What is meant by realism is the suggestion of actuality—the impression of truth—by the depiction of characters whose speech and actions convey the effect of reality. Realism deals with the here and now; it is "concerned essentially with detail"; it is a "copying of actual facts"; it is "a deliberate choice of the commonplace"; it is "a factual interpretation of life"; it is, in short, *truth*.

Despite the enormous changes of life in the century since Ibsen, realism has remained remarkably persistent. Commonplace characters in domestic surroundings, facing personal problems, are very much in evidence in today's theater. For example, here is the opening of Beth Henley's Pulitzer Prize–winning *Crimes of the Heart,* written a century after *A Doll's House.*

> *(The lights go up on an empty kitchen. It is late afternoon. Lenny McGrath, a thirty-year-old woman with a round figure and face, enters from the back door, carrying a white suitcase, a saxophone case, and a brown paper sack. She sets the sax case down and takes the brown sack to the kitchen table. After glancing quickly at the door, she gets the cookie jar from the kitchen counter, a box of matches from the stove, and then brings both objects to the kitchen table. Excitedly, she reaches into the brown sack and pulls out a package of birthday candles.)*[2]

Clearly, Henley's intention is to communicate the impression of reality. Realism has been the dominant mode of theater for over a century. By *mode* I mean the temper or spirit that affects the creator's point of view. The mode reflects the cultural climate in which a work of art was created.

THE REALIST MOVEMENT

From the change in speculative thought arising from the works of such men as Charles Darwin, Sigmund Freud, and Karl Marx, three implications are of particular significance to drama and the theater. The first is the dynamic notion of change. In place of the older, static concept of a perfect creation a few thousand years ago, the scientist presented the idea that all life is in a constant process of alteration, and, as a part of nature, humankind, too, is subject to change.

A second implication is that a person is a biochemical entity. There seems to be nothing about human life or behavior that is not susceptible to explanation according to naturalistic laws and principles. The individual is a product of a callous nature, rather than a child of special providence whose life is subject to divine intervention and revelation. We act mechanistically. Physiology is as important as intellect in determining our conduct. The human being is merely the leading member of the simian group and, for the time being, the dominant species of the animal kingdom on this planet.

A third implication of the new thought is that humanity is subject to scientific inquiry. A person can be a case study, capable of being examined and investigated.

These changes in the intellectual climate have been variously interpreted. At one extreme, Émile Zola, the nineteenth-century French firebrand, and his fellow naturalists emphasized the sordid and mechanistic aspects of life to the exclusion of all else. Their thinking was shadowed by a somber view of life, which threw a blighting chill of determinism on all human conduct. At the opposite extreme, many realists saw in science a buoyantly optimistic assurance of the ultimate perfectability of humanity. They extended the doctrine of evolution to a view of the entire universe as fulfilling the promise of one glorious purpose—the elevation of humankind.

The realistic movement had its origin in nineteenth-century French fiction.

Honoré de Balzac, Gustave Flaubert, and the brothers Edmond and Jules Goncourt created conspicuous examples of the new attitude. The nature of that realism and its guiding principles is summed up by Bernard Weinberg:

> Realism aims to attain truth. Now truth is attainable only by the observation (scientific and impersonal) of reality—and hence of contemporary life—and by the unadulterated representation of that reality in the work of art. Therefore, in his observations, the artist must be sincere, unprejudiced, encyclopedic. Whatever is real, whatever exists is a proper subject for art; this means that the beautiful and ugly, the physical and spiritual, are susceptible of artistic treatment; it does not imply that the artist refrains from choosing his subject and his detail, for choice is fundamental in art. The principal object of imitation is always man; description of the material world, construction of plot, are thus subsidiary and contributory to character portrayal.[3]

In French drama, the theory of realism was rooted in the teaching of Denis Diderot, who in the eighteenth century called for "middle-class tragedy." In the early nineteenth century when Pixérécourt popularized romantic melodrama, he required realistic scenery with usable steps, bridges, and boats for the exciting action of his bourgeois plays. Eugene Scribe's technical dexterity in manipulating plots and his portrayal of types found in contemporary society gave his plays an air of superficial probability. His skill as a craftsman resulted in the writing of what became known as "well-made plays," whose techniques were so popular in the theater that his structural pattern was widely imitated.

In a well-made play the author attempts to deal naturally with current society, constructing a play with careful craftsmanship so that all parts are interconnected in a plausible way. Climaxes are carefully built up by cause-and-effect progression. The well-crafted play is a controlled environment influencing the characters that inhabit it. Scribe was followed by Émile Augier, an enormously successful playwright whose impartiality of treatment, careful depiction of background based on minute observation of objects and incidents, and competence in characterization took drama a step nearer to realism. Alexandre Dumas *fils* continued the advance by his concern with the decadence of the social scene in such plays as *Le Demi-Monde* (1855) and *La Question d'Argent* (1857). His treatment of men and women who were not heroic, but weak, sensuous, and selfish, added new roles to the theater. Together with Augier, Dumas made a critical assault on the corruption of middle- and upper-class society.

Elsewhere in Europe, the intellectual revolution taking place found expression in the new playwrights—Ibsen, Tolstoi, Chekhov, Strindberg, and Gerhart Hauptman. They were interested in telling the truth about the common person in everyday circumstances; but because their dramas were so outspoken and their subject matter so bold, they found it difficult to get a hearing until the Independent Theater movement, a group of subscription theaters, was organized for the specific purpose of opening up the theater to the new drama. Under the leadership of Andre Antoine in Paris, Otto Brahm in Berlin, Stanislavski in Moscow,

In 1877 Andre Antoine inaugurated the Théâtre Libre to give a chance to realistic playwrights. The natural style of performance is apparent in this old photograph of Métenier's *En Famille.*

and John Grein in London, this movement broke the shackles of tradition and introduced an exuberant new spirit into the drama, linking the stage once more with literature and life.

Ibsen's *Ghosts* (1881) was an especially important work because of its sensational impact wherever it was produced. In this play, which was partially a response to the bitter criticism of *A Doll's House,* Ibsen shows what happens to a woman who is faithful to her dissolute husband. Her life is devoted to protecting her son, Oswald, from the sins of the father; but in the end Oswald loses his mind because of his inherited venereal disease. The curtain goes down when he demands "the sun, the sun," while his agonized mother stands over him with morphine powder in her hand.

Because of its bold subject matter *Ghosts* stirred up some of the most vituperative critical abuse in the history of the theater. In Berlin (1889) when the censor banned the play in the public theaters, it played to a subscription audience at the

Freie Bühne. English reaction to *Ghosts* (1891) was especially virulent. One London critic, Clement Scott, compared Ibsen's play to "an open drain, a loathsome sore unbandaged, a dirty act done publicly, a lazar house with all its doors and windows open."

In America in the 1890s, James Herne and a number of disciples of the new realism in fiction attempted to introduce the new spirit through productions of Herne's *Margaret Fleming* in Boston and New York. This play, the first sociological play in the American theater, recalled Ibsen's boldness in its theme of a wayward husband whose affair with a maid results in her death and the birth of an illegitimate child. But the play ends on an upbeat note because Margaret Fleming forgives her husband and accepts the child as her own. Herne's effort appealed to a limited audience; American theatergoers were not hospitable to such advanced subjects.

In addition to the development of realism as literary theory during the latter part of the nineteenth century, there was also considerable change taking place in the techniques of writing and producing farces and melodramas, which made up most of the popular stage fare. Characters of humble origin became more and more prominent, local color was exploited, native speech and costuming were more accurately reproduced, and the stage scenery and effects became increasingly more substantial and convincing. Although much of the plot and character motivation were artificial, realism made its influence felt, especially in the external aspects of production.

Realistic playing is essential in performing Chekhov's plays, which, like this production of *Three Sisters* at the Oregon Shakespeare Festival, are rich in characterization.

The ultimate result of the revolution in the late-nineteenth-century theater was to win the twentieth century over to realism. Although realism as a complete aesthetic theory soon lost its impetus, its techniques and attitudes have nevertheless continued to dominate our modern stage, even in the face of a great deal of experimentation with new forms and despite a rather general dissatisfaction with its restrictive outlook.

Observation and Objectivity

Having received their inspiration from the scientists, the realists turned to science for their techniques as well, attempting to follow basic concepts drawn from the scientific method. The realist, therefore, came to rely on meticulous and precise observation, analysis, and recording of specific details. Minutiae that previous writers passed by were accumulated a bit at a time to build up character or locale in much the same manner that Georges Seurat used to apply his paint in tiny spots of broken color. And like Gustave Courbet and Edouard Manet, who took their easels out of their studio to paint commonplace subjects from direct observation, rather than saints and miracles from their inspiration and imagination, realistic writers looked hard at life at first hand and jotted down in their notebooks the texture of their responses. It was their mission to see, hear, and report everything.

Such an emphasis on observation affected not only the realist's choice of subject but also the method of handling it. The plot must be allowed to develop where an honest treatment of the characters takes it; the environment and its atmosphere must be depicted with scrupulous fidelity; emotion must be employed without artificiality or sentimentalism; the writer must be faithful to the facts as observed.

Against this general background of a literary theory stemming from the intellectual revolution of the nineteenth century, let us now consider the application of realism to specific dramatic problems.

Plot

The dramatic structure of the early realists resembles classical drama in its concentration on characters caught in moments of crisis. Thus the realist generally uses a late point of attack, employs a few incidents, and deals with a small group of characters over a short space of time. The result of this dramaturgy is a gain in intensity and dramatic tension because the action is continuous and concentrated, free from the extraneous diversions of constantly changing locales and complicated plots and subplots. The writer of popular nineteenth-century melodrama dramatized simple people in a complicated plot based on a pattern of physical conflicts. The realist reversed this approach by showing complex characters in a simple plot involving psychological action. The result was realistic *drame*.

Realistic plays are not full of arbitrary climaxes, building up to "big scenes" of violent action. Even in moments of great stress, emotional expression is often deliberately restrained, underplayed, suggested rather than exploited. Playwrights learned that the most telling moments of their plays might be the quiet closing of a door, the distant sound of an axe on a tree. There is an absence of sensational and "stagey" devices, but not an absence of emotional effect.

To secure the semblance of reality, the realists were obligated to make their work seem logical and plausible, with no clanking machinery or whirr of motors. They avoided all manner of contrivances that might destroy illusion. They did not interrupt the action to make explanations, preferring to integrate exposition by gradual revelation throughout the course of the play.

The realist's method of handling plot was responsible for clearing away much of the trickery of popular drama. Plays became much more credible, closer to actual experience and the observed facts of life. Because they based their dramas on problems and ideas rather than on external action, and because they were concerned with character revelation, the realists achieved an intensity of effect. On the other hand, their method of working narrowed the scope of action, slowed down the pace, and sometimes became downright sedentary. Critics were quick to point out that in their attempts to condense the action and frame it in a logical, tight mold, amid a welter of concrete details, the realists sacrificed the chance to stimulate the imagination and to give free play to fancy. They had trapped themselves in the stuffy atmosphere of a middle-class living-room.

As realism has developed in the past half century, the validity of this criticism has been acknowledged, and the contemporary playwright breaks through the conventional realist's methods and has enormous freedom while working within the realistic mode. For example, in Taylor's *And a Nightingale Sang*, Helen Stott serves both as narrator and as the leading character in the play. In the middle of a dialogue with another character, she pauses to talk directly to the audience. Meanwhile, her father, George, is at the piano, picking out pieces throughout the play that are appropriate to the action. Although most of the play takes place in the Stotts' drab home in an interior setting, the downstage area, used as an unlocalized area, becomes a park and a hotel. Charles Fuller begins his Pulitzer Prize–winning *Soldier's Play* with a flashback showing the murder of a black soldier who is drunk. The rest of the play is an investigation of the crime through a series of scenes played in fragmentary set pieces in a horseshoe set of several platforms at varying levels. The staging is open theater in technique, but essentially the play is realistic. For want of a better term to describe this freer use of the theater, *selective realism* can be used, which simply means that complete sets with three walls and a ceiling and a room full of furniture and props have been replaced by a few selected pieces that convey the impression of the environment.

Character

The realists' attempt to achieve objectivity and their reliance on observation brought into the theater an entirely new gallery of characters who were delineated in a new way. In the past, playwrights used lower-class people mostly for minor or comic roles. Now attention was focused on humble, downtrodden, and ordinary people. This concern with common people, begun by Ibsen, Hauptmann, and Chekhov, continues today, as indicated by three recent Pulitzer Prize winners.

Marsha Norman, in *'night, Mother* (1983), shows the intimate details of two individual, ordinary women, as the daughter moves relentlessly toward suicide in the face of her mother's ineffectual protest. In *Crimes of the Heart* (1981), Beth Henley lights up the stage with her account of three McGrath sisters in Hazelhurst, Mississippi, after the youngest of them shoots her pompous husband in the stomach. Fuller's *Soldier's Play* involves a dozen segregated black enlisted men (and one white captain) in the investigation of the death of a black sergeant in Fort Neal, Louisiana.

Dramatists became concerned about psychological forces that conditioned behavior, and they brought into the theater characters whose pathology was explained in terms of repression, subconscious desire, and early childhood conditioning. The playwright dramatized these people at critical moments of their lives, not those of violent physical action so much as times of inner crisis, thus penetrating the surface and giving insight into their desires, aspirations, and frustrations. Realists seemed especially concerned with presenting women on the stage, and they created such memorable feminine characters as Strindberg's Laura and Julie; Chekhov's Madame Ranevsky and Nina; Shaw's Candida and Eliza; and Ibsen's Nora, Hedda, Rebecca West, and Mrs. Alving.

In shifting the attention to people from the common walks of life, realists lost the elevation and magnitude of classic tragedy with its heroic figures. The naturalists, as we shall see later in the chapter, carried the mechanistic and bestial aspects of people to an extreme in their overemphasis on the sordid and the bizarre. The realists, however, found it possible to show both sides of humankind, and they dealt with many characters who had redeeming qualities—characters who were close to the norm in behavior and outlook.

Significant contributions to drama were made by the realists in the integrity of their characterization, their concern with sound psychological motivation, their cumulative technique of character revelation, and their treatment of protagonists drawn from the common walks of life. Although many playwrights today remain deeply concerned with the problems stressed by early realists, they now have greater flexibility in treating characters. Because of a freer approach to playwriting and staging, characters can be revealed more deeply by more exposure. Flashbacks, monologues, and direct communication with the audience provide for more extensive commentary than the simulated conversation of many parlor-talk plays. A character may now begin a speech as a young person and shift to old age within a few lines simply by modifying the voice. People mix with animals that may be shown as complex creatures with human traits—without destroying theatrical credulity. Although realism gave up much of the grandeur associated with classic drama and the dynamic, imaginative protagonists of romanticism, realists peopled the stage with a remarkable gathering of fascinating creatures, whom we have come to know as authentic human beings.

August Wilson, who in the late 1980s suddenly became one of the outstand-

In August Wilson's *Fences,* Troy brings home his illegitimate baby, hoping his will wife will take care of it. *(Directed by Lloyd Richards, Yale Repertory Theater)*

ing playwrights in the world with his studies of blacks in big-city environments, writes in a realistic style. He is not preoccupied with plot structure, but his gift for creating credible characters and graphic language have the stamp of authenticity in plays like *Ma Rainey's Black Bottom, Fences, Joe Turner's Come and Gone, The Piano Lesson,* and *Two Trains Running.* Wilson's persistent theme is: To have a future, blacks in the United States must first define who they are by reclaiming their past. Wilson is fond of giving some of his characters extended monologues that testify to his talent of storytelling, and he often works music into the action. Essentially, Wilson writes in the realistic mode, with small casts in a single domestic setting. Here is a scene from his play *Fences.*

From his sharecropper father, Troy Maxson learned the violence begot by poverty and frustration. But he also learned to respect hard work and that a man must take responsibility for his family. In the following excerpt, we learn that Troy has had an affair with another woman, who died, leaving their child motherless. He brings it home, wrapped in a blanket, and confronts his wife, Rose.

(*There is a long, awkward silence, the weight of which grows heavier with every passing second.*)

Troy: Rose . . . I'm standing here with my daughter in my arms. She ain't but a wee bittie little old thing. She don't know nothing about grownups' business. She innocent . . . and she ain't got no mama.

Rose: What are you telling me for, Troy?

(She turns and exits into the house.)

Troy: Well . . . I guess we'll just sit out here on the porch. *(He sits down on the porch. There is an awkward indelicateness about the way he handles the baby. His largeness engulfs and seems to swallow it. He speaks loud enough for Rose to hear.)* A man's got to do what's right for him. I ain't sorry for nothing I done. It felt right in my heart. *(To the baby)* What you smiling at? Your daddy's a big man. Got these great big old hands. But sometimes he's scared. And right now your daddy's scared cause we sitting out here and ain't got no home. Oh, I been homeless before. I ain't had no baby with me. But I been homeless . . .

(Rose enters from the house. Troy, hearing her step behind him, stands and faces her.)

She's my daughter, Rose. My own flesh and blood. I can't deny her no more than I can deny my boys. *(Pause)* You and them boys is my family. You and them and this child is all I got in the world. So I guess what I'm saying is . . . I'd appreciate it if you'd help me take care of her.

Rose: Okay, Troy . . . you're right . . . I'll help you take care of your baby . . . 'cause like you say . . . she's innocent . . . and you can't visit the sins of the father upon the child. A motherless child has got a hard time. *(She takes the baby from him.)* From right now . . . this child's got a mother. But you a womanless man. *(Rose turns and exits into the house with the baby.)*[4]

Thought

The realists dealt boldly with new themes, many of them growing out of their awakened interest in the social sciences—economic conflicts, sex problems, domestic difficulties, and social strife. Emulating the ways of science, playwrights attempted to record life objectively, so they pulled no punches, honored no taboos, found no material too commonplace or sordid for their probing. They became absorbed in the facts of human existence here and now—commonplace facts about contemporary, commonplace people. They tried to discard everything that smacked of the artificial, the contrived, the sentimental. The result was to open the doors of the theater to the dramatization of day-to-day existence. In insisting on complete freedom in the treatment of character, dialogue, and subject matter, the realist brought about a franker, freer stage, so that today there are almost no holds barred.

Diction

The realists' interest in accurate observation and reporting prompted them to suggest the speech of everyday life. Dialogue frequently was ungrammatical, fragmentary, and blatantly frank. Realists abandoned the theatrical devices of unmotivated "purple passages" and the inflated bombast of "paper speeches." Even in scenes of strong emotional climax, the dramatist avoided rhetorical display, having learned the eloquence of a broken phrase, a small gesture, and silence. Stage dialogue became more utilitarian, serving to advance or delineate character rather than to call attention to itself.

As Shaw demonstrated, another benefit that resulted from realism was the opportunity to exploit discussion in drama. Playwrights were concerned with ideas, and they took pains to stimulate the audience's thinking about their ideas by expressing them onstage. Ibsen's and Shaw's characters not only act, they also think—and they discuss their thoughts. Their dialogue becomes action—an investigation, an adventure, a verbal tug-of-war.

Critics of realism lament that the speech of the new drama drove poetry out of the theater. It is true that playwrights turned their ear in another direction and sacrificed poetic speech, but it is also true that much of the embellished dialogue of nineteenth-century romantic writers of melodrama was poor stuff—sentimental and pretentious. Moreover, in the hands of skillful playwrights, realistic speech has a clarity and intensity that goes directly to the heart of the matter:

> How true and unconventional his style. We hardly realize how false and stilted current stage conversation is, till we hear the real word spoken there. His words come to us at times like the thrusts of the naked fist. They shake the hearer with their weight of real passion. In one sense it is astoundingly direct, and then again it is subtly indirect—as in life.[5]

A good example of the eloquence of small talk is in Lanford Wilson's *Talley's Folly,* in which Matt Friedman, a St. Louis accountant, woos Sally, a shy spinster of thirty-one, in a dilapidated boathouse on the river bank in Lebanon, Missouri. He strives to break through her protective shell and wants her to come away with him.

Matt: . . . Oh, my gosh! I do not know how to begin! I am walking into an unfriendly church in my underdrawers here.

Sally: What are you talking about?

Matt: You don't have a dream? I congratulate you. That is a terrible dream. I mean, I am at such a disadvantage here. *(With an energy born from frustration)* None of my skills is appropriate to the situation I find myself in. And I have amazing skills. I could be an attraction in a sideshow. Give me a list of three, six, up to fifteen numbers, five digits each, I'll tell you the sum immediately. In my head, Mr. Adding Machine. Everybody gapes. How does he do that? He's got it all written down. I know the multiplication table up to seventy-five times seventy-five. Truly. It's something I know. What is sixty-seven times sixty-eight? Four thousand five hundred fifty-six. I have amazing skills. Only I feel like Houdini in the iron box under

Lanford Wilson's *Talley's Folly*, involves two characters in an off-beat romance that depends on amusing dialogue and comic business. *(Circle Repertory Company production featuring Judd Hirsch and Trish Hawkins)*

the ice at the bottom of the river. I forgot where I put the key to the handcuffs. Such a frustrating dream.

Sally: One of the boys at the hospital is an artist. He's developed a facility for when a dream starts to go bad. It starts to get scary. He, in the dream, changes it all into a drawing, wads it up, and throws it away.

Matt: Freud wouldn't like it.

Sally: Oh, drive him crazy.

Matt: I am foolish to insinuate myself down here and try to feel like one of the hillbillies. Who ever heard of this Friedman—I don't blame you. I won't be Matt Friedman any more. I'll join the throng. Call myself . . . August Hedgepeth. Sip moonshine over the back of my elbow. Wheat straw in the gap of my teeth. I'm not cleaning my glasses, I'm fishing for crappie. Bass.

Sally: Sun perch.

Matt: Oh, heck yes. Only I'm not. I can't even take off my shoes without feeling absurd.

Sally: People don't walk around with their shoes off here, sipping moonshine. It isn't really the Hatfields and the McCoys. The ones who go barefoot only do it because they can't afford shoes.[6]

Matt persists in his romancing, and in the end Sally goes with him.

Spectacle

Although realistic scenery had been employed in the theater in the past, its appeal was based on novelty and picturesqueness. The realist had quite a different purpose. It became important to show the environment in order to understand the character. Thus, realistic scenery is not a mere accompaniment of the action; it is a causal force of the action. It shapes and molds the characters. In such plays as *American Buffalo, Look Back in Anger, Fences,* and *The Effect of Gamma Rays on Man-in-the-Moon Marigolds,* the setting is an obvious source of character motivation, with its sociological implication that to improve the person it is necessary to improve the circumstances.

The early realists' observation of actuality and concern with the commonplace prompted them to locate the action in a setting crammed with the domestic details of everyday life. The stage and action of their plays were filled with properties, but in the hands of the genuine realist these were not mere clutter for verisimilitude; they were selected because of their organic and symbolic relationship to the characters—Hedda's pistols, Nora's macaroons, and Oswald's pipe. The use of such props illustrated the notion of the significant trifle. Incidentally, the props were an enormous help to the actors in achieving naturalness in performance.

Just as the realists rejected the cardboard cutout figures of the past, they also discarded the "painty" two-dimensional wing-and-groove and backdrop setting. The box set (with three continuous walls, often capped with a ceiling), which had been introduced earlier in the nineteenth century, became a standard requirement for realistic drama. Practical doors and windows, appropriate furniture, and genuine props were added to further the illusion of actuality. The actor was now surrounded by scenery and played *within* a locale rather than in front of it. As a logical accompaniment of the new scenery came the convention of the "fourth wall"—a tacit agreement with the audience that the opening framed by the proscenium arch was the fourth wall of the set, thus giving the illusion of a solid room instead of a platform. The fourth wall defined the downstage limit of the acting area and confined the actors to the setting; they pretended not to see or communicate with the audience. Realism is no longer restricted to box sets and rigid time limitations. The playwright is free to move around to suit the needs of

Ming-Cho Lee's design using a few simple elements creates a realistic atmosphere for the bums who frequent the bar in *The Iceman Cometh*. *(Circle-in-the-Square Theater)*

the plot. Many productions these days are performed in arena theaters with little or no scenery; locale of the action is established by furniture, props, and dialogue.

NATURALISM

The term *naturalism,* sometimes used interchangeably with *realism,* is historically an independent movement that began in France in the 1870s under the messianic leadership of Zola. It differed from realism in its concentration on the squalid side of life, its atmosphere of despair, and it was structurally different in avoiding theatrically motivated situations, climaxes, and curtains. Like the realist, the naturalist responded to the influence of science—especially to the notion of environmental conditioning of contemporary humankind. It was Zola who wrote the first naturalistic play and bombarded the senses of his contemporaries as he clamored for a dramatic style that would reflect the method of science:

I am waiting for them to rid us of fictitious characters, of conventional symbols of vice and virtue which possess no value as human data. I am waiting for the surroundings to determine the characters, and for the characters to act according to the logic of the facts. . . . I am waiting until there is no more jugglery of any kind, no more strokes of the magical wand, changing in one minute persons and things. I am waiting, finally, until this evolution takes place on the stage; until they return the source of science to the study of nature, to the anatomy of man, to the painting of life in an exact reproduction, more original and powerful than anyone has so far dared to place upon the boards.[7]

Zola's play *Thérèse Raquin* (1873) dramatizes the story of Thérèse and her lover, who drown her unwanted husband but are unable to live down their crime under the accusing eyes of the dumb and paralyzed mother of the victim. Zola's play was not a popular success, but his example led to similar attempts by others. Henri Becque, in *The Vultures* (1882), depicts the destruction of a family and its fortune as a result of the sudden demise of the father and the predatory activities of the dead man's business associates. Hauptmann, in *Before Sunrise* (1889), a story of misery and death, gave Berlin's independent stage, the Freie Bühne, a graphic view of the degradation of a Silesian coal-mining family suddenly grown rich. His *Weavers* (1892) has a rioting mob as the protagonist in one of the earliest and best plays of social conflict. Tolstoi, in *The Power of Darkness* (1886), tells a grim story of illicit love, drunkenness, and murder, although he tempers the gloom with spiritual overtones. Strindberg's *Miss Julie* (1888) is a story of lust and suicide. Shaw, who wrote two plays in naturalistic style, *Widower's Houses* (1892) and *Mrs. Warren's Profession* (1898), indicates his motivation for writing as he did: "I felt the need for mentioning the forbidden subjects, not only because of their own importance, but for the sake of destroying taboo by giving it the most violent shocks."

The naturalists introduced a new collection of characters to the stage—the dregs of society, the wayward and twisted victims of the lower depths. Their characters are bedeviled by doubts and frustrations, torn by inner conflicts, ridden by passions. As Strindberg says, "They are conglomerates made up of past and present stages of civilization, scraps of humanity, torn-off pieces of Sunday clothing turned into rags—all patched together as is the human soul itself."[8]

Naturalists attempted to translate into concrete images what they had gained from changing thought. The hard shell that protected the traditional views of love, authority, duty, honor, and morality was shattered when the playwright probed beneath the surfaces to investigate the innermost desires and passion of individuals in their relations with their mates, their families, and their society.

Although the rigid realism and naturalism of the first part of the twentieth century has given way to much more freedom and experimentation, many playwrights today aim at presenting the illusion of authentic daily life, especially in characterization, dialogue, and thought. The realists' and naturalists' penchant for forbidden or controversial material characterizes the theater of shock and cruelty that has emerged since World War II.

The naturalist's dialogue had a new texture and frankness as it reflected the speech of the lowborn and humble. Themes that had hitherto been considered too controversial or salacious for the theatergoing public became the accepted norm. Although the new boldness aroused shocked protest in many places, the

The naturalistic setting and characters in Gorki's *The Lower Depths* showed life in the slums of Moscow. *(Moscow Art Theater, 1902)*

naturalists performed an important service in ridding the stage of bombast and sentimentality. They also made painstaking efforts to show the locale of their action as accurately as possible in order to emphasize how physical conditions may deform character. Sometimes the result was an excess of clutter and an obsession with the solidity and authenticity of material objects, which at its extreme led Antoine of the Théâtre Libre to hang sides of beef on the stage.

As a literary style, naturalism gave way to the more moderate realism, which found ways of relieving the steady diet of misery, crime, and disintegration; but the naturalist did succeed in bringing to the stage new characters and themes with honesty and forthrightness. Although naturalism as a movement lost its impetus, echoes of its quality are seen in the present theater in such plays as Jack Gelber's *The Connection* (1959), a brutal portrait of drug addicts waiting for a fix; Kenneth H. Brown's *The Brig* (1963), an attack on the inhumane conditions in a Marine Corps prison; in LeRoi Jones's plays of racial discrimination, *The Dutchman* and *The Toilet* (1964); Rabe's plays of the Vietnam War, *The Basic Training of Pavlo Hummel* (1972) and *Sticks and Bones* (1972).

Sam Shepard is a maverick contemporary playwright who defies classification because of his unique way of making theater. In some respects his plays

Sam Shepard's special view of the American scene was captured in the Cornell University production of Buried Child. *(Directed by Stephen Cole)*

relate to naturalism, because they often deal with misfits and outcasts, rock stars and cowboys, gangsters and short-order cooks, against backgrounds that are grotesque and sordid. His characters usually speak in the appropriate vernacular, but they may take off in extended monologues or pieces of astonishing business that lift the plays out of the moment and can stir an audience with their sheer explosiveness. He has little use for linear plots or sequential action. Shepard's objective seems to present a fractured view of the decaying American dream in a compelling way. "I have American scars on my brain," says the playwright, who shares these scars with his audience in such actions as this fragment from *Fool for Love*, which depicts the ill-fated attachment of May for her half-brother, Eddie. She is a short-order cook and he is a rodeo cowboy.

> . . . *Eddie enters fast from stage-left door carrying two steer ropes. He slams door. Door booms. He completely ignores May. She completely ignores him and keeps staring at the bottle. He crosses upstage of bed, throws one of the ropes on bed and starts building a loop in the other rope, feeding it with the left hand so that it makes a snakelike zipping sound as it passes through the honda. Now he begins to pay attention to May as he continues fooling with the rope. She remains staring at the bottle of tequila.)*

Eddie: Decided to jump off the wagon, huh?

Mike avenges the brutal beating his sister suffered from her husband in Shepard's *A Lie of the Mind.* *(Directed by Albert Takazaukas, American Conservatory Theater)*

(He spins the rope above his head in a flat horn-loop, then ropes one of the bedposts, taking up the slack with a sharp snap of the right hand. He takes the loop off the bedpost, rebuilds it, swings and ropes another bedpost. He continues this right around the bed, roping every post and never missing. May takes another drink and sets the bottle down quietly.)

May: *(Still not looking at him)* What're you doing?

Eddie: Little practice. Gotta' stay in practice these days. There's kids out there ropin' calves in six seconds dead. Can you believe that? Six and no change. Flyin' off the saddle on the right hand side like a bunch a' Spider Monkeys. I'm tellin' ya', they got it down to a science.

(He continues roping bedposts, making his way around the bed in a circle.)

May: *(Flatly, staring at bottle)* I thought you were leaving. Didn't you say you were leaving?

Eddie: *(As he ropes)* Well, yeah, I was gonna'. But then it suddenly occurred to me in the middle of the parking lot out there that there probably isn't any man comin' over here at all. There probably isn't any "guy" or any "man" or anybody comin' over here. You just made all that up.

May: Why would I do that?

Eddie: Just to get even.

> *(She turns to him slowly in chair, takes a drink, stares at him, then sets bottle on table.)*

May: I'll never get even with you.

> *(He laughs, crosses to table, takes a deep drink from bottle, cocks his head back, gargles, swallows, then does a backflip across the stage and crashes into stage-right wall.)*[9]

David Mamet's *American Buffalo* (1977) is in the naturalistic tradition in its sleazy skid row characters, its squalid junk shop setting cluttered with the nondescript debris of our urban society, and its amoral view of characters who feel "the only way to teach these people a lesson is to kill them." The meager plot is based on their incompetent scheme to pull off a robbery, which never occurs. The play ends with a scene in which they trash all the junk in the store. Mamet was attempting to criticize the American business ethic, but the play's inhumanity never really took hold. Mamet has continued his savage attack on greed in his Pulitzer Prize–winning play *Glengarry Glen Ross* (1984) and *Speed-the-Plow* (1989). The absence of humanism is a recurring motif in Mamet.

EXPRESSIONISM

Another mode of modern drama that was a reaction to realism is *expressionism*. The expressionist is actually a superrealist, insisting that reality is not to be judged by external appearance. Truth is within. Beneath the social façade of behavior is a vast jungle of secret and often unconscious desires, aspirations, conflicts, frustrations, and hallucinations. It is this strange and confusing subjective reality that the expressionist explores. Although this perspective never became dominant, it attracted some remarkable talent and had an important impact in production techniques, especially in musical comedies and motion pictures.

Strindberg was the first to state the expressionist's approach to drama: "Anything may happen; everything is possible and probable. Time and space do not exist. On an insignificant background of reality, imagination designs and embroiders novel patterns; a medley of memories, experiences, free fantasies, absurdities, and improvisations." A drama, he said, may have the "disconnected but seemingly logical form of a dream." He demonstrated his theory in two remarkable plays, *The Dream Play* (1902) and *The Ghost Sonata* (1907). For a time, Strindberg was an isolated innovator, but from 1912 to 1925 expressionism became an important theatrical style, especially in Germany for those who knew the traumatic experiences of World War I and its aftermath.

Expressionists rejected the ordered structure of the realist, since they wished to center their attention on specific instances without being obliged to provide a chain of causes and effects. They presented the essential action—the

In Elmer Rice's *The Adding Machine*, diagonal lines express Mr. Zero's mental state.
(Setting by Lee Simonson, New York Theater Guild)

high points of an experience—without being bogged down by small talk or the machinery of plotting. The critical moments of a career were shown in a jagged series of explosive scenes. In Elmer Rice's play *The Adding Machine* (1923), Mr. Zero's crime and punishment were shown in seven fragmentary scenes; O'Neill's *Hairy Ape* (1922) dramatized the important steps in Yank's quest for status; Georg Kaiser's *From Morn to Midnight* (1916) was a disconnected series of events that showed a bank clerk's theft, spending orgy, and death; in Ernst Toller's *Transfiguration* (1918), a kaleidoscope of dream pictures illustrated the horrors of war. Arthur Miller in *Death of a Salesman* (1948) effectively used expressionistic scenes combined with realistic ones to define Willy Loman's mental state. Expressionists flung open the windows of the mind and allowed the spectator to look in on the private, disordered, associative processes of their characters. They rejected the carefully shaped, logically organized structure of the realist and used a fragmentary system of actions because it created the effect they desired—a view of the chaotic inner reality.

Characters in expressionistic plays are often depersonalized. They are not individuals but types, who are given such names as the Gentleman in Black, the Billionaire, the Young Woman in Taffeta, Mr. Zero, the Blues and the Yellows. They are not psychologically complex except perhaps for the protagonist, through whose eyes all the action may be seen. To reveal the inner state of the character, playwrights revived the technique of the soliloquy so that the characters could externalize their private thoughts. In witnessing the distortion that characterized the protagonist's subjective point of view, the spectator was often confused by bewildering symbols and actions, especially when the distortion was that of an abnormal psychic condition. Character itself was often handled symbolically and with great freedom, as Strindberg indicates in *The Dream Play:* "The characters split, double, multiply, evaporate, solidify, diffuse, clarify. But one consciousness reigns above them all—that of the dreamer; it knows no secrets, no incongruities, no scruples, no law." Sometimes, the protagonist is the voice of the author, as in Toller's *Transfiguration,* in which the hero, Friedrich, is the playwright protesting against militarism and nationalism. Friedrich is something of an individual with a specific background, but he is also an abstract symbol of humanity, appearing in many guises—soldier, professor, sculptor, judge, priest, and laborer.

Peter Shaffer, who is extraordinarily innovative in his theatricalism, confesses that he struggled for a year to create an effective way of beginning *Amadeus.* He finally hit on an approach that is expressionistic in style.

Act One, Scene 1, Vienna

(Darkness
Savage whispers fill the theater. We can distinguish nothing at first from this snake-like hissing save the word Salieri! repeated here, there and everywhere around the theater. Also, the barely distinguishable word Assassin!

The whispers overlap and increase in volume, slashing the air with wicked intensity. Then the light grows Upstage to reveal the silhouettes of men and women dressed in the top hats and skirts of the nineteenth century—citizens of Vienna, all crowded together in the Light Box, and uttering their scandal.)

Whisperers: Salieri! . . . Salieri! . . . Salieri! *(Upstage, in a wheelchair, with his back to us, sits an old man. We can see, as the light grows a little brighter, the top of his head, encased in an old red cap, and perhaps the shawl wrapped around his shoulders.)*

Salieri! . . . Salieri! . . . Salieri!

(Two middle-aged gentlemen hurry in from either side, also wearing the long cloaks and tall hats of the period. These are the two venticelli: purveyors of fact, rumor and gossip throughout the play. They speak rapidly—in this first appearance extremely rapidly—so that the scene has the air of a fast and dreadful overture. Sometimes they speak to each other, sometimes to us—but always with the urgency of men who have ever been first with the news.)

Venticello 1:   I don't believe it.

Venticello 2:   I don't believe it.

V. 1:   I don't believe it.

V. 2:   I don't believe it.

Whisperers: *Salieri!*[10]

In general, expressionists have had an axe to grind. Their plays have been linked to social causes, for example, in Germany, where the frustrations and yearnings of a people tormented by guilt and despair found in expressionism not merely a theatrical style but also a desperate and agonized plea for some kind of salvation. In Kaiser's *Coral* (1917) the Billionaire's son revolts against the injustice of capitalism: "We are rich, and these others who stifle in torment and misery are men like us." Again, in *From Morn to Midnight,* Kaiser directly attacks materialism: "Not with all the money from all the banks of the world can one buy anything of value. . . . Money is the crowning deceit of all."

The expressionists' free use of language anticipated most of the "innovations" of the absurdists and the present workers in the new theater. They also expanded the theatricalism so that playwrights who were writing in another mode used expressionistic techniques, for example, to depict distorted mental images in emotionally loaded situations.

In another Peter Shaffer play, *Equus,* about a seventeen-year-old mental patient, the psychiatrist explores the boy's tortured psyche and finally exposes the jealousy that drove him to blind seven horses with a spike. The technique of revealing an emotionally disturbed character's state of mind through expressionistic techniques is clearly evident in this scene, in which the psychiatrist Dysart confronts the boy with his jealousy:

> *(The boy turns round, hugging himself in pain. From the sides two more horses converge with Nugget on the rails. Their hooves stamp angrily. The Equus noise is heard more terribly.)*

Dysart: The Lord thy God is a Jealous God. He sees you. He sees you forever and ever, Alan. He sees you! . . . *He sees you!*

Alan: *(In terror)* Eyes! . . . White eyes—never closed! Eyes like flames—coming—coming! . . . God seest! God seest! . . . NO! . . .

> *(Pause. He steadies himself. The stage begins to blacken.)*

> *(Quieter)* No more. No more, Equus.

> *(He gets up. He goes to the bench. He takes up the invisible pick. He moves slowly upstage towards Nugget, concealing the weapon behind his naked back, in the growing darkness. He stretches out his hand and fondles Nugget's mask.) (Gently)* Equus . . . Noble Equus . . . Faithful and True . . . Godslave . . . Thou—God—Seest—NOTHING!

> *(He stabs out Nugget's eyes. The horse stamps in agony. A great screaming begins to fill the theatre, growing ever louder. Alan dashes at the other two horses and blinds them too, stabbing over the rails. Their metal hooves join in the stamping. Relentlessly, as this happens, three more horses appear in cones of light; not naturalistic animals like the first three, but dreadful creatures out of nightmare. Their eyes flare—their nostrils flare—their mouths flare. They are archetypal images—judging, punishing, pitiless. They do not halt at the rail, but invade the square. As they trample at him, the boy leaps desperately at them, jumping high and*

naked in the dark, slashing at their heads with arms upraised. The screams increase. The other horses follow into the square. The whole place is filled with cannoning, blinded horses—and the boy dodging among them, avoiding their slashing hooves as best he can. Finally they plunge off into darkness and away out of sight. The noise dies abruptly, and all we hear is Alan yelling in hysteria as he collapses on the ground—stabbing at his own eyes with the invisible pick.)

Alan: Find me! . . . Find me! . . . Find me! . . . KILL ME! . . . KILL ME! . . .[11]

American expressionists worked over familiar social themes in a much milder vein. O'Neill's *Hairy Ape* is a criticism of human disorientation in a materialistic society. His *Emperor Jones* dramatizes man's inability to escape from his primitive past. Rice's *Adding Machine* is a merciless satire on the plight of the little man trapped in a mechanistic world; and George Kaufman and Marc Connelly's *Beggar on Horseback* (1924) lampoons philistinism in the United States. The expressionists were not so notable for their advanced thinking as for their theatrical ability to give new shape and expression to familiar ideas.

One of these ways was a theatrical treatment of language to create effects and atmosphere. An interesting device was the use of short, rhythmic bursts of staccato speech with a sharply marked tempo. The effect was to remove the speaker one step from reality, reinforcing the offbeat atmosphere and the dehumanized characterization. A typical example occurs in Kaiser's *Gas* (1918), Part One:

(The door to left is flung open. A Workman—naked—stained by the explosion totters in.)

Workman: Report from Shed Eight—Central—white cat burst—red eyes torn open—yellow mouth gaping—humps up crackling back—grows round—snaps away girders—lifts up roof—bursts—sparks!—sparks! *(Sitting down in the middle of the floor and striking about him)* Chase away the cat—Shoo! Shoo!—smash her jaws—Shoo! Shoo! bury her eyes—they flame—hammer down her back—hammer it down—thousands of fists! It's swelling, swelling—growing fat—fatter—Gas out of every crack—the tube![12]

Where the realists stressed the outward appearance of actuality in solid-looking stage settings, the expressionists used fragmentary, distorted images, skeletal pieces, and odd lighting effects to reveal a disordered world. In so doing, they created a frankly theatrical world. The phantasmagoria of weird landscapes, of the dream world where images and symbols are projected in baffling and exaggerated shapes, colors, and patterns, made expressionism a challenge to the designer's imagination and ingenuity. In Kaiser's *From Morn to Midnight*, a guilty fugitive suddenly sees a tree trunk transformed into a pursuing skeleton; in Strindberg's *Dream Play*, eerie landscapes appear, merge, and alter like disconnected fragments of a nightmare.

In Georg Kaiser's *From Morn to Midnight,* the protagonist's guilty state of mind is shown in Cesar Klein's scene design, when a tree turns into a skeleton. *(Berlin, 1923)*

The expressionists' bold theatricalism demonstrated new and effective uses of the medium; it cleared the stage of the rigid three walls and replaced the clutter with a few imaginative fragments, picked out by light on a relatively bare stage, which gave the actors the appropriate psychological setting for their performance. The creative influence of the expressionists was apparent in ballet, musical comedies, motion pictures, and the simple settings of realistic plays. Every experimental venture in the twentieth century is in debt to the expressionists for their innovative theatricalism.

As literary movements, naturalism and expressionism are passé, and a revolt against realism is now going on. Actually, a revolt has gone on within the mode itself, so that present-day realism bears little resemblance to Ibsen's. Our increased technical skills and facilities, the use of light, film, and sound, the arena and thrust stages give the playwright a previously unknown freedom. Moreover, today's audience, in its willingness to participate imaginatively in all kinds of new theatrical practices, has encouraged more creative and flexible playwriting and production.

The case against realism is couched in such terms as *narrow, commonplace, superficial, contrived, passive,* and *illusionary.* It is criticized as being a device for avoiding life rather than facing it—a process of hypnosis and delusion, deficient in spirit. In its selection of character and incident it is said to be too artificial. It is charged with being too narrowly confined to a few unimportant people partitioned off from the real world, too much involved with psychological case studies rather than with the more significant issues of society. It is said to make a fetish of external appearance and factual data and to be theatrically pedestrian and trivial in its restrictions of setting, vocabulary, plot situations, and style of performance.

Supporters of realism and its derivatives point out that historically it accomplished its initial objective of ridding the theater of much that was meretricious and false. Realistic playwrights turned the theater to a serious purpose and dealt with its fundamental theme—the dignity and integrity of the individual and the vital interests of the common person. In their emphasis on the conditioning power of heredity and environment, the realists made the public aware of an important concept of human behavior. They created a respect for the objective observation of facts, but they went beyond them to a concern with humanity's spiritual destiny in a changing and perplexing world.

The realists replaced inflated and artificial rhetoric with new means of communication in speech, action, and setting that encouraged more direct interaction. They were concerned with the problems that engage our foremost experimentalists today—self-realization and freedom from bourgeois conventionality. In their efforts to imitate real people's action, the realists turned the theater in a new direction by their emphasis on the careful observation of human behavior. They sought to give pleasure through learning by means of their fresh perceptions of contemporary people and their world.

PLAYS TO READ AND SEE

F = Film available; V = Videotape available.

Realism

F	V	Eugene O'Neill, *Anna Christie* (Greta Garbo)
F	V	Tennessee Williams, *Cat on a Hot Tin Roof*
F		Anton Chekhov, *The Cherry Orchard, The Three Sisters*
F	V	Beth Henley, *Crimes of the Heart*
F	V	Henrik Ibsen, *A Doll's House, Hedda Gabler*
F	V	Charles Fuller, *A Soldier's Play (A Soldier's Story)*
F		David Rabe, *Streamers*
F	V	Tennessee Williams, *A Streetcar Named Desire*

Naturalism

David Mamet, *American Buffalo*
Sam Shepard, *Buried Child, Fool for Love*
Jack Gelber, *The Connection*
Maxim Gorki, *The Lower Depths*
August Strindberg, *Miss Julie*

Expressionism

Elmer Rice, *The Adding Machine*
George S. Kaufman and Marc Connelly, *Beggar on Horseback*

Eugene O'Neill, *The Emperor Jones*
F   Arthur Miller, *Death of a Salesman*

Film: *The Cabinet of Dr. Caligari* (1919)

BIBLIOGRAPHY

ANTOINE, ANDRÉ. *Memories of the Théâtre-Libre*. Coral Gables, Fla.: University of Miami Press, 1964.

BENTLEY, ERIC. *The Playwright as Thinker*. New York: Meridian Books, 1957.

BIGSBY, C. W. E. *Confrontation and Commitment: A Study of Contemporary American Drama, 1959–1966*. London: MacGibbon & Kee, 1967.

BOGARD, TRAVIS, and WILLIAM I. OLIVER. *Modern Drama: Essays in Criticism*. New York: Oxford University Press, 1965.

BROCKETT, OSCAR G., and ROBERT R. FINDLAY. *Century of Innovation*. Englewood Cliffs, N.J.: Prentice-Hall, 1973.

BRUSTEIN, ROBERT. *The Cultural Watch: Essays on Theater and Society*. New York: Knopf, 1975.

BRUSTEIN, ROBERT. *The Theater in Revolt*. Boston: Little, Brown, 1962.

CLARK, BARRETT H., and GEORGE FREEDLEY. *A History of Modern Drama*. New York: Appleton-Century-Crofts, 1947.

CLURMAN, HAROLD. *The Fervent Years*. New York: Hill and Wang, 1957.

MILLER, ANNA IRENE. *The Independent Theater in Europe, 1887*. New York: Ray Long and Richard R. Smith, 1931.

SOKEL, WALTER. *The Writer in Extremis: Expressionism in Twentieth-Century German Literature*. Stanford, Calif.: Stanford University Press, 1959.

WAXMAN, S. M. *Antoine and the Théâtre Libre*. Cambridge, Mass.: Harvard University Press, 1926.

NOTES

1. Henrik Ibsen, *A Doll's House*, trans. William Archer (New York: Charles Scribner's Sons, 1911).

2. Beth Henley, *Crimes of the Heart*. Copyright © 1981, 1982 by Beth Henley. Used by permission of New American Library, a division of Viking Penguin USA, Inc.

3. Bernard Weinberg, *French Realism: The Critical Reaction, 1830–1870* (New York: Oxford University Press, 1937).

4. August Wilson, *Fences*. Copyright 1986 by August Wilson. Used by permission of New American Library, a division of Penguin Books USA, Inc.

5. Hamlin Garland, "Ibsen as a Dramatist," *Arena, 2,* June 1890.

6. Lanford Wilson, *Talley's Folly* (New York: Hill and Wang, 1983). Copyright © 1979 by Lanford Wilson. Reprinted by permission of Hill and Wang, a division of Farrar, Straus and Giroux, Inc.

7. Émile Zola, *The Experimental Novel* (New York: Cassell, 1893).

8. August Strindberg, Preface to *Miss Julie*, in *Plays of Strindberg*, Vol. I, trans. Edith and Warner Oland (New York: Bruce Humphries, 1912).

9. Shepard, *Fool for Love* from *Fool for Love and Other Plays*. Copyright © 1983 by Sam Shepard. Used by permission of Bantam Books, a division of Bantam Doubleday, Dell Publishing Group.

10. Peter Shaffer, *Amadeus* (New York: New American Library, 1984).

11. Peter Shaffer, *Equus* (New York: Avon Books, 1974).

12. George Kaiser, *Gas I* (Cologne: Verlag Kiepenheuer & Witsch, 1918). Reprinted by permission of the publisher.

eight
Theatricalism and the New Theater

Beckett's *Waiting for Godot* dramatized the plight of two vagabonds, Estragon and Vladimir, who wait for someone who never comes—or may not even exist. This absurdist play epitomized the revolution that took place in the theater in the aftermath of World War II. (Directed by Frederick Thon, University of California, Santa Barbara)

When the curtain went up at the Theâtre de Babylone in Paris in 1952, there was little to show that Samual Beckett's *Waiting for Godot* was destined to become one of the most provocative plays in the postwar world. Two vagrants, on a small mound with only a skimpy little tree, seem to be the survivors in an empty universe. They ask questions without answers and wait for someone who never comes. But their unanswered questions set up shock waves that precisely echoed the temper of disillusion and doubt that followed the catastrophe of World War II.

Beckett's forthright theatricalism without a story line, with no beginning, middle, or end, and no concession to the public's taste for spectacle, was symbolic enough in its spare outline to make an unforgettable impact wherever it was performed (including a performance before inmates in a California state prison who knew all about waiting). *Waiting for Godot* symbolized the revolution against traditional theater values. Escape was replaced by confrontation. This was the beginning of *absurdism,* one of the new weapons in the arsenal of theatricalism.

The twentieth century has seen a motley parade of rebels, visionaries, and avant garde experimentalists marching to the beat of varied drummers. They follow an odd assortment of leaders or strike out in broken ranks; some they follow are soon obscure, some frenzied and vulgar, but always defiant and confident that they are the voices of truth. There is a glint in their eyes and a sense of urgent dedication that often belies their incongruous manner. Their destinations may not be clear, but they are on the march—a march of protest, a boisterous, scathing protest. The world must change, and the theater with it. The linking of these two objectives is important, for the avant garde is alienated from the total human condition. Out of this rebellion came a rejection of the traditional, illusionistic dramatic performance and a new interest and stress on theatricalism.

THEATRICALISM

Theatricalism is a catchall term for all types of nonrealistic stylization, free from any effort to create the illusion of actuality. Theatricalism accepts the premise that performer and spectator share an experience that is frankly a *theater piece.* The actor suggests or assumes a role, rather than creating a psychological character. The performer may step in and out of character, go from youth to old age in a single speech, play several roles, go in and out of emotional states, address the audience directly, comment on the action, or simply tell a story. The performers may lead the audience as the high priests of a celebration.

In staging, theatricalism may employ scenery, lighting, costuming, and sound effects for their own sakes, not as accessories for creating atmosphere or eliciting emotional responses appropriate to the play. The total effect of the production may come from a series of signals in spurts, juxtaposed or simultaneous, projected in incongruous ways without obvious continuity or significance. In traditional theater, all elements are synthesized in support of the text; in the new theater, all aspects celebrate a theatrical occasion.

Pablo Picasso's "Guernica" (1937) projected the anguish and terror of senseless warfare through the distorted shapes of people, animals, and objects. Guernica, an ancient Basque city, was bombed during the Spanish Civil War.

This contemporary age of anxiety had its roots in the scientific and technological revolutions of the nineteenth century. We have already seen how that disruption touched off a rebellion in the theater under the label of realism and its derivatives, as people tried to orient themselves to a materialistic and mechanical world. But this quest for meaning and identity was subverted by the holocaust of World War I. The old faith in political institutions and the beneficence of scientific progress was shaken by the spectacle of toppling regimes, the barbarism of mechanized warfare, and the dehumanization of the individual. Those closest to the flames were infected by a deep sense of frustration, which broke out in the savage distortions of the expressionists and in the Dadaists' brash assault on everything. The Great Depression, World War II, the uneasy peace under an ominous bomb, the Vietnam disaster, the exposure of sordid political corruption, and the ruthless struggle for power turned pessimism and doubt into a general malaise instead of a localized infection confined to the defeated or the have-nots. The result has been a universal sense of concern, a gnawing doubt about the ability of the race to survive, and a search for something solid to hold on to.

Beginning with realistic playwrights, questions have been raised about humanity's place in the universe, but drama has not been overly concerned with social and economic conditions. Moreover, theater, a social institution, usually tied by its purse strings to the status quo, has often lagged behind the others in revolutionary fervor. Dissidents have had a difficult time in attracting sympathetic audiences with the ability to pay. To many, the popular function of the commercial theater is to provide relaxation, not friction or serious investigation of the problems of society. Some questions one does not ask in public. The audience might listen to the voice of protest if it were as witty as Shaw's, or tolerate

Tom O'Horgan's *Hair,* an entertaining protest musical, was a huge box-office hit in the 1960s. Its exhuberant spirit and rock music captured the public's fancy.

political didacticism if it were as theatrical as Brecht's, but the main course of the drama was not marked by militant dispute. As the outside world became more precarious, however, the protest grew louder and the walls could no longer keep out the clamor. Indeed, because those within began to bring their doubts with them, the theater could not remain aloof. The rebels found their way into song, film, and the visual arts. They turned coffeehouses into theaters, found audiences on the sidewalks and in the streets, and staged their own brand of events with such impressive numbers and raucous insistence that their message came through: The world must change and the theater with it.

The rebels opposed both form and content in drama. They would relegate the traditional, carefully structured system of action to the scrapheap, for to them system and order are suspect. Human experience, they said, is not tidily organized into a beginning, middle, and end. Life comes at us in spurts—without clear causes or predictable effects. People are not rational, logical creatures. The protesters found support for this view in such statements as Freud's description of the id: "a chaos, a cauldron of seething excitement with no organization and no unified will, only an impulsion to obtain satisfaction for the instinctual needs, in accordance with the pleasure principle." The form of art, the rebels insist, reflects the form of our lives—bewildering, confusing, illogical, incomprehensible.

As for the content of drama, it must deal forthrightly with the larger issues of the human condition. It is not enough to dwell on the petty squabbles of little lives or to probe into the personality problems of insignificant individuals. The visionaries ask for a theater that will rise up against all powers and institutions that belittle the individual, a theater that expands our levels of awareness—that challenges, stimulates, offends, and shocks.

Dadaism

Just as the cultural turbulence following World War II was mirrored by an assault on the conventional forms of the theater, the upheaval of World War I was reflected in the arts. The poet Tristan Tzara led a group of European artists, writers, and thinkers in a nihilistic onslaught against nearly everything, including the standards of conventional aesthetics. During a five-year period, Tzara and the Dadaists expressed their disgust with social and artistic traditions as they "spat in the eye of the world." Their attack against the façade of the bourgeois ethic was motivated by a desire to clear the way for a better society. They rejected "art-art" in favor of anti-art. Instead of pure painting, they "engineered" new works. The Dadaists exploited the "gratuitous act," the spontaneous, chance gesture, which, by its rejection of preplanning, could convey the irrational and subconscious. Improvisation was at the center of their activities. Individual words on slips of paper were drawn out of a hat in a random fashion to become poems. Their often chaotic and accidental pranks and displays anticipated the "happenings" of the 1960s and the "performance art" of the 1980s and 1990s. (Tom Stoppard's *Travesties*, 1975, deals with Tzara and some of the Dadaists' activities in Zurich.)

Schwitters and Collage

In any discussion of theatricalism and the new theater, the term *collage* occurs frequently. The man who pioneered much of the work with collage, around the year 1920, produced over 2,000 pieces in this area as well as experiments in poetry and theater with what he called his "Merz" creations. Kurt Schwitters, one of the most prominent Dadaists, disdained traditional painting and the galleries that displayed them. Instead of working like the usual easel painter with oil or watercolors, Schwitters gathered together "found" materials such as old papers, photographs, worn fabrics, and burlap, which he pasted on a background. He was interested in juxtaposing objects so that they played against one another—a torn piece of a letter next to an old, faded photograph; a column of figures against a label; a fragment of yellowed newspaper against a railroad ticket. Although his compositions were abstract, there were recognizable words, numbers, headlines, and scraps of handwriting or printed papers.

Schwitters describes his approach to art:

> Art is a primordial concept, exalted as the godhead, inexplicable as life, indefinable and without purpose. . . . The medium is unimportant. I take any material what-

Collage has become an influential art form in the twentieth century. Kurt Schwitters, a pioneer collage maker, created his compositions out of scraps of paper and other materials, as in this "Merz: Santa Claus" (1922).

soever if the picture demands it. When I adjust materials of different kinds to one another, I have taken a step in advance of mere oil painting, for in addition to playing off color against color, line against line, form against form, etc., I play off material against material.[1]

When writing poetry, which Schwitters read publicly, his collage approach to the use of language parallels his work with visual material. His poem "Green Child," written about 1918, deals with a child's nightmare flight from imprisonment.

[. . .]
Blood —
Fear —
Chase —
Fly —
Scream —
Blood grins yellow-bright-yellow

Yellow green —
Brightyellowgreen —
Brimstoneyellowgreen —
Brightbrimstoneyellowgreen —
Blood grimaces brightbrimyellowstoneyellowgreen.
Could I but wash the green blood![2]

Schwitters's creative work illustrates two important principles that characterize much of the avant garde of the twentieth century: first, the rejection of traditional forms and techniques and, second, the fragmentation of disparate objects and images, instead of a unified design built around a center of interest. A collage is a key symbol of our aesthetic landscape.

Another group of rebels were the surrealists, who, like the Dadaists, took the view that "man must escape from the control of reason" and that the artist should "surrender to the dark forces of the unconscious." They were interested in exploring the world of dreams and the imagination. They improvised games of automatic writing and drawing—creations entirely free from rational control, made up of strange and distorted images. André Breton, their chief spokesman, said that the surrealist "took pleasure in reuniting the sewing machine and the umbrella on the dissecting table." Their purpose was to bring about a kind of super or absolute reality—*surrealité*.

Sorg Zimmermann's set design for Duerrenmatt's *The Meteor* at the Munich Kammerspiele recalls Kurt Schwitter's approach to collage in juxtaposing various shapes, textures, and objects.

   The works of art growing out of Dadaism and surrealism are characterized by incongruous combinations of objects and figures, simultaneous action, fragmentation, and the distorted and seemingly irrational atmosphere of a dream. These characteristics of visual art are similar to those of much of avant garde drama, for they are rooted in a rejection of the strictures of conventional theater and an insistence on the need to be liberated and spontaneous.

Vakhtangov and Meyerhold

Following the Russian Revolution (1917), the Soviet theater showed its dissatisfaction with the old regime by its rejection of Stanislavski's realism and illusionistic production. To show their hostility to the old order, the constructivists devised scenery that was deliberately antidecorative, emphasizing instead the stage as a machine, with playing areas of steps, ramps, and platforms to serve the actors' functions.

Meyerhold's highly energized theatricalism was received enthusiastically by Moscow audiences in the 1920s, as in this celebrated performance of Gogol's *The Government Inspector*.

Two examples from the Russian theater of 1920s show the nature of the theatricalism espoused by Eugene Vakhtangov and Vsevolod Meyerhold. In 1922, Vakhtangov staged a highly theatricalized production of Carlo Gozzi's *Turandot* in Moscow. He told his cast, "Our work is senseless if there is no holiday mood, if there is nothing to carry the spectators away. Let us carry them away with our youth, laughter, and improvisation." When the spectators came into the theater, the actors were already onstage, wearing street clothes. They talked to the audience about the play and what they would see. As a waltz played, the actors improvised costumes from pieces of cloth and fabric, turning rags into riches. Stagehands moved furniture and properties into place, while scenery appeared like magic from the flies and wings—window frames, doors, and pillars. It was in this playful atmosphere that the play continued and became one of the notable Russian productions of the decade.

Our second example of theatricalism occurred in 1926 in Meyerhold's last great production—Gogol's nineteenth-century satire on greed and hypocrisy, *The Government Inspector*. The director transferred the locale from the provinces to Moscow and updated the text to make the comedy more relevant and biting. Gogol's plot deals with civic officials who learn of an impending visit of the government inspector. They mistake a ne'er-do-well young man, Kheslakov, and his companion for the inspector and his valet. Kheslakov, an opportunist, exploits the situation to the limit, accepting the officials' bribes and favors and pretending a romantic interest in the mayor's daughter. Before being exposed as an impos-

Meyerhold drew these characters from *The Inspector General* to show the actors how he wanted them to freeze for the final curtain, when they have been duped by an imposter.

tor, Kheslakov manages to escape with the loot just when the real inspector is about to arrive.

Meyerhold's theatricalism in this production made an enormous impression. In the bribery scene, the setting is made up of fifteen highly polished mahogany doors. Following a public reception, Kheslakov returns to his quarters, where he is besieged by fifteen petty officials who offer him bribes. Two guards stand at attention before the central doorway. Kheslakov staggers in through the wrong door, almost falls but regains his feet with acrobatic dexterity, and drops into a chair. He confides to the audience that he is dead drunk. One of the officials hurries in to notify Kheslakov that others are coming to grease his palm. Suddenly, all fifteen doors open at once, and the politicians enter with the mechanical movements of robots, chanting their lines in unison. Kheslakov responds in the same rhythmical manner, accepting each of the proffered gifts with clockwork precision. The image is of an immense bribe machine.

Meyerhold, originally associated with Stanislavski, became dissatisfied with conventional techniques and freely experimented with those borrowed from the oriental theater, carnival, music hall, and circus. He devised an acting style known as *biomechanics,* in which actors perform as gymnasts or machines to convey their feelings through physical gestures. For example, to express joy an actor might turn a handspring or slide down a pole. Meyerhold's theory was that behavior is

Meyerhold rejected Stanislavski's realism and developed his own lively style of performance. This is his famous constructivist setting of wood and metal, a bare framework for the actors to exploit, for the 1922 production of *The Magnificent Cuckold*.

best expressed through theatricalism—not by words but by carefully controlled poses, movements, and gestures. Meyerhold's theories and methods were demonstrated in several remarkable productions, especially *The Magnificent Cuckold*, in which he erected on a bare stage the skeletal suggestion of a hill, reached by stairs and ramps, with a bridge, trapeze, and other mechanical devices. The actors, dressed as workers, gave an acrobatic performance accompanied by a jazz orchestra.

Meyerhold's essential contribution was in his attitude toward the theater as a total vehicle to be exploited in all possible ways. By word and especially by example, he was the epitome of the theatricalism of the twentieth century.

Brecht

Bertolt Brecht (1898–1956) was one of the most influential playwrights and theoreticians of the twentieth century. Fleeing Germany in 1933, he wrote most of his major plays while living abroad. In 1947 he returned to Berlin, where he founded The Berliner Ensemble, which specializes in producing Brecht's plays and is one of the most remarkable acting companies of our time. He was influenced by Dadaism and expressionism, as well as by his association with Erwin Piscator and Max Reinhardt in Berlin. His first popular success occurred in 1928 with *The Threepenny Opera*.

Brecht links himself with theatricalism through his rejection of the illusionistic stage. "How long," he asked, "are our souls going to have to leave our gross bodies under cover of darkness to penetrate into those dream figures up there on the rostrum in order to share their transports that would otherwise be denied us?" Brecht was a rebellious spirit, who mixed his theatricalism with political propaganda, who explored, with incredible verve and gusto, his "ugly, brutal, dangerous" man in the seamy side of his existence. He was a brilliant inventor and a notorious borrower whose proclivity for criticism of humankind and all its institutions naturally included overthrow of the conventional theater and led him to create his own imaginative "epic theater."

Traditionally, the epic form was sharply separated from drama, the latter being characterized by compact action that could be presented by living performers. The epic, because of its freedom of time, place, and action, was confined to the written word. But Brecht did not see these two forms as irreconcilable because technical advances enabled the modern theater to exploit the narrative through projections, films, lighting, and machinery for changing scenery more rapidly. Furthermore, Brecht felt that the most important human experiences were no longer personal stories of individuals but, rather, significant social events and the forces that caused them.

Since he was dealing with social content rather than emotions, Brecht sometimes described his stage as a "tribunal," in which he wanted "to teach the spectators to reach a verdict." The analogy is an apt one. Instead of presenting a tightly knit plot, Brecht used the stage to present evidence piece by piece, as in a trial, to introduce witnesses with conflicting testimony who are interrupted and

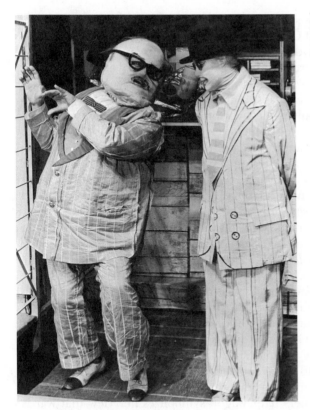

The acting in the Volksbuhne Theater, Berlin, production of Bertolt Brecht's *Good Woman of Setzuan* required a stylized kind of performance.

cross-questioned. They testify by giving facts or by relating events rather than by impersonating characters. Evidence is presented in a variety of exhibits—weapons, drawings or photographs of where the action occurred, documents, letters, tape recordings, slides, models, and films. The intention is to put the event itself on trial.

Brecht's plots often startled and shocked the audiences, thus counteracting the tendency toward illusion. He deliberately broke the mood of a scene by interrupting action with music, by playing irony against sentiment and comedy against seriousness, and by the constant use of inversion and reversal.

As a young man coming out of a bitter experience in the military as a medical orderly and acutely aware of the social and economic calamities of postwar Germany, Brecht wrote savagely from his view that "the meanest thing alive, and the weakest, is man." His early plays are filled with depravity and crime and illustrate his cynical theme that virtue brings no reward; indeed, ethical behavior is really a sign of stupidity. He looked at all men with suspicion, for the poor are as cruel as the rich. As for justice—it is a delusion.

After he accepted Marxism, Brecht came to believe that the evils of the world could be cured by revolution, and to that premise he devoted a number of his *Lehrstücke,* or learning pieces. In 1928 Brecht, along with Kurt Weill, who wrote the music, staged his most commercially successful work, *The Threepenny Opera.* He borrowed the plot of Gay's *Beggar's Opera,* a fashionable London hit of 1728. But where the original had been a lighthearted lampoon of the aristocracy, Brecht's play was a scathing satire of the bourgeoisie. He created a vivid collection of depraved characters, thieves, swindlers, prostitutes, and crooks who infest a human jungle—a jungle whose code is summed up in the pawnbroker Peachum's words: "What keeps a man alive—he lives on others by grinding, sweating, defeating, beating, cheating, eating some other man." But Brecht relieved the sting of the characters and situation through his considerable gifts as an entertainer, which he was never quite able to suppress despite his political purpose. He was fond of slapstick, vaudeville, sporting events, clowns, and beerhall entertainers, and his theatricalism stems in part from the direct and earthy quality of these kinds of performers and performances.

Brecht's mature years are notable for his three "parables," which constitute his major contribution: *The Good Woman of Setzuan, Mother Courage and Her Children,* and *The Caucasian Chalk Circle.*

Mother Courage, which Brecht wrote just before the outbreaks of World War II, is a bitter attack on militarism as an aspect of capitalism. To Brecht, heroism invariably comes from human error and brutality. His attention is not focused on the military action, which is narrated with legends and slogans, but on Mother Courage, a camp peddler in Germany during the Thirty Years' War (1618–1648). She is a scheming, salty character who will use any means to serve her purpose. And her purpose is to survive, by buying and selling life's necessaries, and to protect her children from harm amid the shifting fortunes of princes and their marauding bands of soldiers. Her wagon symbolizes her view that war is "just the same as trading" and "you must get in with people. If you scratch my back, I'll scratch yours. Don't stick your neck out." It is while she is involved in bargaining that each of her children dies. In a magnificently theatrical scene, Courage's good-hearted, mute daughter, Kattrin, climbs up on a rooftop and drums a tattoo to warn the villagers of the invading soldiers, until she is shot down. Like Miller's Willy Loman, Courage's absorption with profits causes her destruction, but she must go on—and at the end, having learned nothing, but with her spirit apparently unquenched, she finds it possible to continue dragging her load of misery behind her.

In his last work, *The Caucasian Chalk Circle,* written in 1944–1945, Brecht's tone mellowed and the political message was incidental. The story concerns a young girl, Grusha, who saves the despotic governor's infant son during a rebellion. She makes her escape with the child, submits to a marriage of convenience and is ultimately brought to trial; thanks to an eccentric judge, she is allowed to keep the child because she had demonstrated true motherly spirit.

The "epic" qualities of this play are seen in the prologue and epilogue, which frame the main story; in the sharp break between Grusha's adventures and the trial scene; in the extension of the social environment to include the military uprising and the comic marriage; and in the use of song and dance.

As we look at Brecht's plays, we are struck by the contradiction between his theory and practice. He speaks of scientific objectivity, whereas one of the sources of his power is the towering indignation that gives his work such force and texture. His didactic purpose is deadly serious, but his lyrical gifts, his flair for the comic, and his talent for showmanship burst through the seams of his intent. He repudiates realism and the Stanislavski method of acting because they are based on emotional involvement, and he speaks of his wish to keep the audience "cool" and estranged. Ironically, his plays offer some of the most irresistible acting roles in the theater, which, time and time again in performance, arouse the emotions of the audiences profoundly. This contradiction brings us back to the playwright's problem of relating action and its effect.

Let us examine two widely quoted statements of Brechtian theory and attempt to reconcile them with his practice. In the following chart, Brecht compares the traditional stage and his own:

The Dramatic Theater	*The Epic Theater*
the stage embodies a sequence of events	the stage narrates the sequence
involves the spectator in an action and	makes him an observer but
uses up his energy, his will to action	awakes his energy
plot	narrative
implicates the spectator in a stage situation	turns the spectator into an observer, but arouses his capacity for action
wears down his capacity for action	forces him to take decisions
provides him with sensations experience	picture of the world
the spectator is involved in something	he is made to face something
suggestion	argument
instinctive feelings are preserved	brought to the point of recognition
the spectator is in the thick of it, shares the experience	the spectator stands outside, studies
the human being is taken for granted	the human being is the object of the inquiry
he is unalterable	he is alterable and able to alter
eyes on the finish	eyes on the course
one scene makes another	each scene for itself
growth	montage
linear development	in curves
evolutionary determinism	jumps
man as a fixed point	man as a process
thought determines being	social being determines thought
feeling	reason[3]

A second important statement, which Brecht included in "Little Organum" in 1948 after his plays were written, reads,

> Since the public is not invited to throw itself into the fable as though into a river, in order to let itself be tossed indeterminately back and forth, the individual events must be tied together in such a way that the knots are strikingly noticeable; the events must not follow upon one another imperceptibly, but rather one must be able to pass judgment in the midst of them. . . . The parts of the fable, therefore, are to be carefully set off against one another by giving them their own structure, that of a play within a play.[4]

Brecht is describing here his technique of alienating the audience by breaking up the structure into separate events so that the spectator can "pass judgment in the midst of them"; the knots must be "strikingly noticeable." What is the basis for this theory of structured action? To encourage the spectator to think rather than to feel. But action has a way of speaking more strongly than words.

In Brecht's three parables, *The Good Woman of Setzuan* (1938–1940), *Mother Courage* (1937), and *The Caucasian Chalk Circle* (1944–1945), the action follows the most surefire melodramatic device of all: Women in distress try valiantly to protect their children against overwhelming forces of evil. In spite of Brecht's avowed purpose of interrupting the sequence to avoid empathic response, an audience has a way of holding on to the emotional momentum, just as an exciting football game on television keeps the audience in suspense through the interruptions by commercials. Despite the "noticeable knots" and Brecht's theory of keeping each event separate, his practice suggests that, step by step, his structure in these three parables intensifies the emotional response. We do care about the outcome. In a tribunal, the evidence and testimony form a structure leading suspensefully to a verdict that completes the action. If you put a woman on stage—even a sharp-tongued, grasping one—show her attachment and devotion to her children, place them in jeopardy, and give the audience concrete signs of her suffering, the effect is to gain sympathy. This engagement is especially true if the dramatist creates generous, well-intentioned characters like Shen Te, Grusha, and Kattrin. Show a woman trying to save a child by crossing an abyss over a rickety bridge pursued by brutal soldiers, and the audience will root for her. Show a mother the bullet-riddled body of her child and force her to conceal her agony for fear of losing her own life, and the audience will be stirred.

Brecht was aware of the emotional consequences of the actions he placed onstage, and he took great pains to divert the normal response in another direction. Furthermore, the plays are not melodramas, because at the end reward and punishment are not parceled out according to individual merits. Even in the case of Grusha, the ending is not personal but social. Nor is there an orderly world of good and evil. By showing with abrasive humor the futility of heroism and virtue, Brecht combats sentiment for justice. Instead of conceding to the audience's eagerness for wish fulfillment, he tramples on it. His frankly theatrical way of showing an action is intended to dilute the emotional content. In performance, however, what counts more than the degree of realism is the audience's *willingness to believe*. And an audience is quite capable of believing in actions in all kinds of styles, including the "epic."

Brecht is a significant force in the contemporary theater not only because of his theories of a new kind of theater but also because of the theatricalism of his productions and plays. He gave the experimental theater of this century what it needed most—a first-rate playwright. He gave us a fresh insight into the uses of the theater and enlarged its scope, although the breath of fresh air was tinged with a chill that could cut to the bone.

Artaud

One of the most imaginative and influential figures between the great wars was Antonin Artaud (1896–1948). A tormented iconoclast, with scant success in actual production, he was, nevertheless, the fountainhead of much of the experimental theatricalism on the contemporary stage. He began working in the theater in Paris in 1921 and in 1927 opened his Théâtre Alfred Jarry (named in honor of another French innovator, who wrote *Ubu Roi* in 1896 and is sometimes credited as the first absurdist because of his mockery of traditional values and conventional drama). Artaud spent two seasons with this theater, dedicated to the production of nonrealistic plays. Artaud's importance is not for his practical work in the theater but for his astonishingly prolific imagination and his vision of theatricalism. His book *The Theater and Its Double* (1938) advanced many ideas that are the basis for the contemporary revolt in acting, playwrighting, design, directing, and architecture.

Artaud's criticism springs basically from his dissatisfaction with the shape of the world about him. In *The Theater and Its Double,* he said, "I believe that our present social system is iniquitous and should be destroyed." And again, "There are too many signs that everything that used to sustain our lives no longer does so, that we are all mad, desperate and sick." The existing theater outraged Artaud because it failed to deal seriously with man's social and moral systems. The theater had lost its feeling for seriousness and laughter. It had "broken away from the spirit of profound anarchy which is the root of all poetry."[5] Artaud called for a rejection of the idolatry of fixed masterpieces reserved for the self-styled elite and not understood by or appealing to the public. He raged against the falsehood and illusion of popular distractions that serve as an outlet for our worst instincts. These descriptive and narrative distractions provide stories that satisfy only Peeping Toms—a theater to decorate our leisure with intimate scenes from the lives of a few puppets. He repudiated well-made plots, which serve only to exploit the psychological aspects of human interest. He was enraged to see the theater offering stories about money, social careerism, the pangs of love, and sugar-coated sexuality—stories that fail to touch the public interest, stories that leave no scars.

Artaud was not merely an anarchist determined on a course of destruction; he was a true revolutionary, dedicated to change. Although his criticism of the modern theater was scathing, he was even more vehement about suggesting a cure. Extraordinarily creative about all aspects of the stage, technical as well as theoretical, he envisioned a radically different kind of drama and production techniques to implement it. Although he was never able to thoroughly realize his ideas in his own Théâtre Alfred Jarry, the audacity and sweep of his imagination can scarcely be ignored by anyone involved in the contemporary theater.

Artaud emphasized the creation of a theater that "stages events, not men," that deals with the metaphysical concerns of ancient rites—"an exorcism to make our demons flow." The theater must give us "crime, love, war, or madness, if it wants to cover its necessity." It must deal with "atrocious crimes" and "super-human devotions" as the ancient myths do. His notion of a "theater of cruelty" stems from the mystical, magical forces of a "theater in which violent physical images crush and hypnotize the sensibility of the spectator seized by the theater as by a whirlwind of higher forces." His intention was to free the repressed uncon-scious in dramatic performance, which resembles a plague because "it is the relevation, the bringing forth, the exteriorization of a depth of the latent cruelty by means of which all perverse possibilities of the mind . . . are localized."

The cruelty that Artaud called for is not physical, nor is the violence for its own sake. Rather it is a process of purification, which "causes the mask to fall, reveals the lie, the slackness, baseness, and hypocrisy of our world." The theater is a means of ridding society of its institutionalized violence. For after experiencing the cruelty that he envisioned in the theater, Artaud said, "I defy the spectator to give himself up once outside the theater to ideas of war, riot and blatant murder."

Artaud conceived of theater as total spectacle that must have the "ceremonial quality of a religious rite." Made up of violent and concentrated action "pushed beyond all limits," it is addressed to the senses and to the theatricality of the unconscious.

Artaud rebelled against the conventional use of language in the theater. To understand his attack, one must remember his background. The French, more than any other people, have placed a high value on polished diction, and the tradition of their theater is rich in rhetoric. Artaud found the language of the theater "dead and fixed in forms that no longer respond to the needs of the time." He objected to the "tyranny of the word" and the dictatorship of the writer. Actually, his rebellion was against the conventionalized nature and form of drama, and in his call for a new theatricalism, language was his first target. He wanted to get away from mere words addressed to the mind. He proposed to use language in a "new, exceptional and unaccustomed fashion." He wanted to replace the utilitarian spoken word with an active language "beyond customary feelings and words," to create a "subterranean current of impressions, correspondences and analogies." Communication in his theater was not merely from actors making speeches; rather the stage was to be a place filled with its own language to include sounds used for their "vibratory quality," onomatopoeia, cries, and into-nations. He wanted words to have about the same importance "as they have in dreams." Indeed, Artaud urged an extension of theatricalism so that everything that occupied the stage would create an effect on the senses, even to the point of physical shock.

Too much criticism of Artaud has been directed at his vivid rhetoric rather than at the spirit of his ideas. He was not a pessimistic, destructive sensationalist. At the core, his views were serious, humane, and positive. He invited us to take the theater seriously, to cut through the sham and hypocrisy of society, to face ourselves honestly, and to trap our deep, latent powers that will enable us to take a "superior and heroic attitude." The process involves the cruel practice of expos-ing society and *oneself* with complete honesty.

Samuel Beckett's *Waiting for Godot* had an enormous influence on modern drama because of its philosophical perspective and its style of writing and performance. *(Directed by Beckett at the Schiller Theater, West Berlin)*

THE ABSURDISTS

Beckett's *Waiting for Godot* in 1952 focused attention on a new dramatist and subsequently a new theatrical movement known as the *theater of the absurd*. When the curtain opened the first night, the audience saw two bedraggled bums, Estragon and Vladimir, waiting in a deserted place for a mysterious Godot. His identity is not clear and their relationship to him is never made explicit. A master driving a heavily burdened slave appears briefly, and later a boy enters to inform the tramps that Godot will not arrive tonight. The play ends as it began, with the two waiting. While they wait, they talk, and the conversation explores such themes as death and salvation, the need for affection, the perplexed state of humankind, their personal biological problems, and the recurrent motif—waiting for Godot. The dialogue is interlocked with a wealth of seriocomic business, and the lines as well as the action provide an effective vehicle for the performers.

    The audience greeted the play with mixed reactions. Some found it bewildering and dull; others, provocative and fascinating. In any case, the play made a remarkable impression throughout the theater world, and *Waiting for Godot* became the prime example of absurdist theater. In addition to Beckett, the most prominent absurdists are Ionesco, Arthur Adamov, Harold Pinter, and Edward Albee. These absurdists are not neatly compartmentalized, and each of them works in a variety of ways. What brings them together is the absurdist point of view, foreshadowed by Albert Camus in his celebrated statement in *The Myth of Sisyphus:*

> A world that can be explained by reasoning, however faulty, is a familiar world. But in a universe that is suddenly deprived of illusions and of light, man feels a stranger. His is an irremediable exile, because he is deprived of memories of a lost homeland as much as he lacks the hope of a promised land to come. This divorce between man and his life, the actor and his setting, truly constitutes the feeling of Absurdity.[6]

Another dramatist who was spiritually related to the absurdists was Alfred Jarry, whose *Ubu Roi* caused a sensation when first produced in Paris in 1896 because of its blatant presentation of human grossness and sensuality. Jarry's intentions were clear:

> When the curtain rose, I wanted the stage to be before the audience like a mirror . . . in which the vicious one would see himself with the horns of a bull and the body of a dragon, according to the exaggeration of his vices; and it is not surprising that the public was stupefied at the sight of its ignoble reflection which had not yet been completely presented to it.[7]

Jarry's play dramatizes the career of King Ubu, whose wife, like Lady Macbeth, drives him to murder the King of Poland in order to gain the crown for himself. His evil ways force him to hide in a cave, where he is haunted by the specters of his victims. The content of the play is not as important as Jarry's prophetic view of the world and his way of handling theatrical materials. The sacrilegious spirit of his attack, the naive directness of his characters and their speech, his sense of raillery—these are seeds that found root later on.

Jarry used the theater in a new way to produce a new effect. This was precisely the case with the absurdists, who viewed the conventional drama with contempt. They wanted to put it to new uses. To understand their point of view, we must take into account the fact that those who led the movement and gave it stature shared a similar experience: Beckett (born in Ireland), Ionesco (born in Rumania), and Adamov (born in Russia) all lived in Paris during World War II. At first hand they witnessed the military defeat of France and suffered through the occupation by the German forces. The defeat meant the destruction of the political and social fabric and the ruin of civilian morale, and the occupation resulted in an agonizing sense of frustration in the face of overwhelming power. The existentialists—Jean-Paul Sartre, Jean Anouilh, and Albert Camus—responded to this experience by using conventional literary forms to probe into such philosophical questions as the role of humankind in the universe and the effect of materialism on the human spirit. Their answers suggested that one is utterly alone and must create one's own world, one's own set of values.

Alfred Jarry's *Ubu Roi* as performed at the Royal Court Theater in London.

The absurdists, who lived through the same era, asked the same questions but did not arrive at the same answers. They generalized from their experience. They felt that there were no answers—life was absurd—and it was this attitude that they put into action in the theater. They were dramatizing a simple but terrifying idea: Humanity is lost.

Waiting for Godot begins with Estragon's line: "Nothing to be done." And the play ends,

Vladimir: Well, shall we go?

Estragon: Yes, let's go.

(They do not move. Curtain.)[8]

Harold Clurman calls our attention to a parallel passage in Pinter's play *The Birthday Party:*

Stanley: How would you like to go away with me?

Lulu: Where?

Stanley: Nowhere. Still we could go.

Lulu: But where would we go?

Stanley: Nowhere. There's nowhere to go. So we could just go. It wouldn't matter.

Lulu: We might as well stay here.

Stanley: No. It's no good here.

Lulu: Well, where else is there?

Stanley: Nowhere.[9]

One doesn't go, because there is no purpose to going. As Camus said, we have no homeland to return to and no promised land before us. We have lost our identity in a dehumanized world; we have lost our perspective in a world without God or a fixed scale of values, and we have lost our reason for going because there is really no place where we can make a meaningful connection. From bitter experience, we are wary of hollow ideas and of each other. We are trapped in the frustrations of an enigmatic universe.

An elderly couple on a lonely island await the arrival of distinguished guests to hear the orator's important message. As the invisible guests arrive, the couple greet them and fill the stage with chairs. When the orator comes, the couple throw themselves out the window and his message is gibberish (Ionesco, *The Chairs*). A lonely, guilt-ridden pianist seeks sanctuary in a seaside rooming house. It is revealed that in the past he has offended someone with considerable power. Two sinister strangers appear, and the fear-wracked Stanley realizes they are after him. A mock birthday party, staged in his honor, turns out to be a grotesque ritual at which Stanley goes berserk. At the end, the two men take the crushed Stanley away in a long black car (Pinter, *The Birthday Party*). A family replaces an adopted child with a handsome physical specimen of American manhood, who turns out to be hollow inside (Albee, *The American Dream*).

In such plays as these, the playwright abandons the notion of depicting psychologically complex characters. They are more apt to resemble puppets or marionettes because they are not personally responsible for their actions. They have been set in motion by an outside force. They cannot act rationally because there is no longer such a thing as logical behavior. They have no means for creating a complete identity, and since communication is virtually impossible, they are not able to relate to one another with understanding and affection.

In a world devoid of meaning, language loses its value, Ionesco wrote his first play, *The Bald Soprano*, as the result of his efforts to learn a foreign language by memorizing standardized phrases. The play parodies the spoken word by exposing its banal vacuity. Here is its opening:

> (Scene: A middle class English interior, with English armchairs. Mr. Smith, an Englishman seated in his English armchair and wearing English slippers, is

The crowd in Ionesco's *The Leader* anticipates the arrival of the leader, but when he arrives, he has no head. *(Buffalo Festival of the Arts)*

smoking his English pipe and reading an English newspaper, near an English fire. He is wearing English spectacles and a small gray English mustache. Beside him, in another English armchair, Mrs. Smith, an Englishwoman, is darning some English socks. A long moment of English silence. The English clock strikes seventeen English strokes.)

Mrs. Smith: There it's nine o'clock. We've drunk the soup and eaten the fish and chips and the English salad. The children have drunk English water. We've eaten well this evening. That's because we live in the suburbs of London and because our name is Smith. *(Mr. Smith reads and clicks his tongue.)*

Mrs. Smith: Potatoes are very good fried in fat, the salad oil was not rancid. The oil from the grocer at the corner is better quality than the oil from the grocer across the street. It is even better than the oil from the grocer at the bottom of the street. However, I prefer not to tell them that their oil is bad.

(Mr. Smith continues to read, clicks his tongue.)

Mrs. Smith: However, the oil from the grocer at the corner is still the best.[10]

Ionesco has a special flair for satirizing language with gibberish, nonsense words, and broken speech. On the other hand, Beckett and Pinter have a gift for common language that in its diction and rhythm has almost the evocative power of poetry in its ability to suggest meanings beneath the surface. Albee has a good ear for the flavor of the American idiom plus an aptitude for parodying our colloquial speech. The dialogue in an absurdist's play is open to many interpretations and is remarkable for what it leaves to the imagination.

    In an attempt to produce their desired effects, the absurdists have created their own arsenal of weapons: the use of shock effects by inverting behavior, by contemptuous mockery of sacrosanct ideas and institutions, by their candor and sometimes their bold frankness. Their comedy, often used ironically, crops out in unexpected places. They present the bizarre, the grotesque, and the unusual. They startle and astonish the audience by their wild flights of fancy and their sometimes incredible inventions. They keep an audience off balance by concealing their hands, making sudden shifts in direction. They bewilder the spectators, and then lead them to a startling discovery. They use the theatrical tricks of the circus clown, the slapstick comedian, and the music hall entertainer, as this comic routine from *Waiting for Godot* indicates:

    (Lucky has left his hat behind. Vladimir finds it.)

Vladimir: Must have been a very fine hat. *(He puts it on his head. Estragon puts on Vladimir's hat in place of his own which he hands to Vladimir. Vladimir takes Estragon's hat. Estragon adjusts Vladimir's hat on his head. Vladimir puts on Estragon's hat in place of Lucky's which he hands to Estragon. Estragon takes Lucky's hat. Vladimir adjusts Estragon's hat on his head. Estragon puts on Lucky's hat in place of Vladimir's which he hands to Vladimir. Vladimir takes his hat. Estragon adjusts Lucky's hat on his head. Vladimir puts on his hat in place of Estragon's which he hands to Estragon. Estragon takes his hat. Vladimir adjusts his hat on his head. Estragon puts his hat in place of Lucky's which he hands to Vladimir. Vladimir takes Lucky's hat. Estragon adjusts his hat on his head. Vladimir puts on Lucky's hat in place of his own which he hands to Estragon. Estragon takes Vladimir's hat. Vladimir adjusts Lucky's hat on his head. Estragon hands Vladimir's hat back to Vladimir who takes it and hands it back to Estragon who takes it and hands it back to Vladimir who takes it and throws it down.)* How does it fit?

Estragon: How would I know?

Vladimir: No, but how do I look in it?

    (He turns his head coquettishly to and fro, minces like a mannequin.)

Estragon: Hideous.

Vladimir: Yes, but not more so than usual?

Estragon: Neither more nor less.

Vladimir: Then I can keep it. Mine irked me. *(Pause)* How shall I say? *(Pause)* It itched me.[11]

The absurdist, antitheater in the approach to plot, makes no pretense of interesting the audience in story or character. The difference in the outcome from the traditional play is that the ending does not answer the questions raised, or else the ending is contrary to the expectations of the characters or the audience. The great leader has no head, the orator can only babble, the gorgeous young man is a hollow shell, the intellectual is really a barbarian, and Godot never comes. The playwright gives you a set of figures to add up, but your total is zero. An absurd play is characterized by an absurd ending because that is how the playwright feels about the world. In some plays the playwright doesn't give us an answer at all but brings the action back to the beginning of the circle, which is another way of saying that life is absurd because there are no answers.

Absurdists do not offer a neatly organized, carefully selected set of signs, nor do they lead you by the hand so that you will know where you are all the time. You may get lost and return to your starting place. You may be the victim of a sudden ambush or a strange trap; you will be baffled by directional signs pointing every which way or straight down. You may find yourself in a completely foreign place among strangers speaking in unknown tongues, behaving in odd ways. But the playwrights have a map of the territory and they know what they are about, although their method may baffle you. They may ask you to look at the stars and then pour a bucket of water over your head; they may invite you to climb a tree to find your way and then chop it down from under you. Absurdists offer an absurd experience because they want you to be aware that the world is absurd.

If the absurdists reject a carefully organized chain of action, have no interest in story values, make little effort to reveal the psychological aspects of characters, are uninterested in emotional involvement, refrain from specific identification of locale or character, what effects do their works achieve as theater?

Some spectators are bewildered and irritated because the action in an absurdist play seems nonsensical. Others enjoy it as a kind of intellectual game by trying to piece together the bits of experience offered to them. Their critical faculties are involved, and they enjoy the learning process of seeking a fresh perception imaginatively presented. They may delight in the playwright's skill of execution or in that of the performers. At a more profound level, the theatergoer becomes acutely aware of the universality suggested by the specific stimulus of the play, and from this awareness may come a strong sense of personal involvement in the playwright's statement.

Jean Genet

A direct spiritual descendant of Artaud was another Frenchman, Jean Genet (1910–1986), who conceived of the theater in terms of symbol and ritual. Just as the existentialists found it necessary to reorient themselves philosophically to a shattered world by creating their individual sets of values, so Genet shaped his own existential view of the world from his strange, tormented childhood and early adult life. An illegitimate child, an unwanted orphan, he found out at age ten that he had no connection with the world, and from that discovery he developed his own inverted hierarchy of values. "I rejected a world which rejected me." A homosexual who had no identity and no status, he turned to a life of crime. He attempted to find his life by losing it. While serving a prison sentence, he began to write and showed so much artistic promise that some leading French intellectuals secured his release. In his plays *The Balcony, The Blacks, The Maids,* and *The Screens,* he gained recognition as one of the most provocative playwrights of our day, and in his works some of Artaud's ideas of a theater of cruelty have been most successfully realized.

Out of his personal anguish, he visualized dramatic works of myth and ceremony, but in a world of reversed values. Instead of climbing the heights and seeking salvation, humanity finds its spiritual identity by plunging into the depths of darkness and evil. The soul is redeemed only by death, and only the criminal with the dedication of a saint can attain grace. Murder is the highest crime, and the act of betrayal is a sacrament.

A metaphor that Genet finds appropriate to his purpose is a series of mirrors, some of them placed at odd angles, some that invert or distort the image, and some that, like Alice's looking-glass, allow us to see into an oddly perverted wonderland. His metaphor suits his purpose well, for Genet is concerned with the varied facets and layers of reality: the discrepancy between the genuine and the illusionary, and the loss or disguise of identity through assumed appearances and roles. In his plays, the spectators are often bewildered by the dazzling surfaces and strange perspectives, so that they are not sure if they are seeing an actual character in a genuine event or a pretender in a masquerade.

Like Artaud, Genet admires primitive rituals and the oriental theater. He is enamored of the masks, the rich use of spectacle, and the communal act of participation in an event of primary significance enacted in mystery and symbols. He sees the playwright's purpose fulfilled as, in Artaud's phrase, "a master of sacred ceremonies." Ritual provides the opportunity for gaining status by assuming roles and participating in significant acts. In Genet, these become reflections of the dark areas of the unconscious, where primitive rites and sadomasochistic fantasies hold their strange spell—a many-faceted view through the myths of cruelty whose cathartic powers celebrate a collective ecstasy.

Peter Brook

Peter Brook (b. 1925) has earned a reputation as one of the most daring and innovative directors in the last two decades. He came out of the traditional theater, serving as an associate director at the Royal Shakespeare Company at Stratford and the Aldwych, where he staged several notable Shakespearean productions, such as *King Lear* (1962) with Paul Scofield. He achieved international fame because of his bold theatricalism. Although he was not at first associated with experimental groups, he prepared the way for much of the avant garde. He introduced Jerzy Grotowski to London, and in 1964 his production of *Marat/Sade* was based on Artaud and his concept of the theater of cruelty. Indeed, the staging of the play grew out of an experimental workshop that explored Artaudian principles.

In 1969 Brook published his influential book *The Empty Space,* which attacks current theater practice and points the way to the theatricalism that Brook envisions for the future.

He categorizes four kinds of theater:

1. The *deadly theater* is the sterile, conventional one that acts as a museum for the "classics," particularly Shakespeare, Molière, and opera.

2. The *rough theater* is close to the people; down-to-earth; natural and joyous; without style; antiauthority; and filled with noise, vulgarity, and boisterous action. Examples are the Elizabethans and Meyerhold's productions.

3. The *holy theater* is one of revelation and ceremony. Its rituals are the genuine ones that affect people's lives, not the pseudorituals injected in much of the contemporary theater. Artaud is the prophet of the holy theater and Grotowski its chief disciple for such productions as *The Constant Prince.*

4. The *immediate theater* is an eclectic one, vigorous, restless, full of joy—a combination of the rough and the holy. It is dynamic, not rigid. Brook's productions demonstrate his commitment to the immediate theater.[12]

A lively battle scene from Peter Brook's highly theatrical *Mahabharata.*

Brook's ambitious project, the *Mahabharata* (1987), emphasized again the director's imaginative use of the theater. It was a condensation of a very long (fifteen times the length of the Bible) Sanskrit epic that was cut and adapted for the stage by Jean Claude Carriere and was translated by Brook, the director. Originally played at Avignon and in Paris, the *Mahabharata* was the centerpiece of the Los Angeles Film Festival in 1987 and has since been made into a three-hour film.

The complex plot, with its numerous characters played by two dozen actors from many different countries, was too diverse and scattered to have a cohesive impact, but the magnitude of the production achieved a kind of universality. The production was kept alive by its theatricalism, stemming from many kinds of stimuli—aural and visual. There were echoes of Brecht, Artaud, Grotowski, and Meyerhold—but mostly there was Brook. The battle scenes were particularly effective, using a variety of weaponry, sounds, smoke, and action, played out on a dirt floor, against a crude wall. Throughout the performance, there were lavish costumes, archaic instruments, and memorable images that Brook combined in vivid theatricalism.

Jerzy Grotowski

One of the most vital forces in the contemporary theater was the Polish Laboratory Theater and its moving spirit, Jerzy Grotowski (b. 1933), whose seriousness of purpose and ability to create dramatic experiences with the authenticity of myth linked him with Artaud and Genet. His emphasis was on the actors, who are called on to use all their mental and physical powers—mime, gesture, intonation, association of ideas—to bring about a fusion of movement and meaning. Rejecting the "wealth" of the traditional theater with its technical facilities. Grotowski called for a "poor theater," stripped of nonessentials, in order to concentrate on the performer. Grotowski's book *Towards a Poor Theater* and his wide-ranging tours to England, Europe, and America made him one of the most influential theatrical forces in the 1970s. More recently, Grotowski migrated to California, where he teaches.

Two of his best known works, *The Constant Prince* and *Apocalypsis cum Figuris*, conveyed the quality of an authentic ritual. *The Constant Prince* was a free adaptation of Pedro Calderón's seventeenth-century Spanish play, in which five characters acted out the hypocrisy and corruption of the world and caused the humiliation, anguish, and death of the Prince in an emotionally charged atmosphere that suggested the crucifixion. The *Apocalypsis cum Figuris* was a work assembled out of the experiments of the actors and directors, in which the verbal aspects were improvised in rehearsal as needed. When the production took shape, quotations were substituted from well-known sources: Feodor Dostoevski, the Book of Job, the New Testament, T. S. Eliot, and the Song of Solomon. Although the Bible was often a verbal source, and the characters were named after Biblical characters, the work did not make a precise religious statement; however, the impact of the production is described as an exploration of the sources of myth—a fusion of religion and drama. The effect that Grotowski's theater achieved was chiefly the result of the shattering quality of the acting. His performers were remarkably trained in all aspects of their craft—speech, mime, and gesture—but in addition they conveyed the impression of a monastic zeal, as if the body were the outward manifestation of the secrets of the soul.

THE NEW THEATER

In the United States, the social upheaval stemming from the Cold War and the disastrous entanglement in Vietnam were reflected in a "new theater" movement through which protesters vociferously expressed their discontent with nearly every facet of the establishment—including the theater itself. Just as many European artists and writers were dissatisfied with the political and social conditions that followed World War I, the American dissidents of the 1960s regarded the conventional commercial theater as a shallow and outdated institution. They were antitext, antiillusionistic production, and antitheater as a place for performing. On the creative side, they were for new kinds of theatrical material—a mixture of action, words, sound, music, and theatrical effects.

Even plays written to be performed in a proscenium arch theater were now conceived of in terms of their theatrically. In *Amadeus*, a single unit set serves for thirty-one scenes over a span of forty-two years. In one scene, Salieri begins as an old man in a wheelchair and ends by transforming himself before the audience into a young man in the prime of life. Throughout the play, he confides to the audience, discusses his motives and feelings of guilt, and provides necessary exposition.

One of the chief targets of the new theater was the tyranny of the word—the sanctity of the text. Traditionally, the script was the core of the production, and those who brought it to life onstage attempted to be faithful to the playwright's words and purpose. Now the script is often regarded as just one element of the performance, no more important than the acting or setting or music. Fragments of several plays may be pieced together in nearly haphazard fashion, or the language and images may be probed for a subtext to make the meaning relevant to the contemporary world.

The new theater was not an organized, widespread, sharply defined movement but the result of the efforts of several highly visible groups and individuals who demonstrated their talent for theatricalism. These efforts came mostly from outside the commercial theater, from coffeehouses and off-off-Broadway groups or from actors' and dancers' workshops such as Ellen Stewart's La Mama Experimental Theater Club and Joe Cino's Café Cino, which provided opportunities for an enormous outpouring of theatrical energy. In the early years, most of the participants received no pay, and productions were put together on shoestring budgets. The productions were notable for their forthright theatricalism, which put on stage many of the ideas offered by innovative predecessors, such as Meyerhold, Artaud, and Brecht, and contemporary theater practitioners—Grotowski, Brook, and the absurdists.

The Living Theater

One of the most visible groups in the new theater was the Living Theater, founded by Judith Malina and Julian Beck. The company first attracted attention with its performance of Jack Gelber's play *The Connection* in 1959. As a metaphor for everybody's compulsion or obsession, the plot deals with a number of drug addicts awaiting the arrival of Cowboy and his supply of drugs. The performance was two-edged, so that the audience was not quite sure what was real and what was pretense, even to the cast members who circulated among the audience during the intermission demanding a handout. The next production to achieve notoriety was Kenneth Brown's *The Brig* (1963), a violent, brutal depiction of the rigors of existence in a marine camp. The play was performed with searing directness, underscoring the naked brutality of the situation.

The Living Theater used its plays for Marxist political persuasion, played with frenetic fervor. It was the aim of the actors to tear down the wall that separated them from the spectators. When asked, "Why do we go to the theater?" Beck replied, "To crack your head open and let in oxygen. . . ."

The Open Theater

The Open Theater began in 1963 as a workshop primarily interested in exploring acting skills. Joseph Chaikin indicates the purpose of the Workshop: "My intention is to make images into theater events, beginning simply with those which have meaning for myself and my collaborators; and at the same time renouncing the theater of critics, box office, real estate, and the conditioned public."

The Open Theater was originally rooted in a series of exercises aimed at developing a nonrealistic style of acting that emphasized ensemble play. It finally staged productions of one-act plays, then Megan Terry's *Viet Rock* at the Sheridan Square and La Mama theaters. The Open Theater's leading writer, Jean-Claude van Itallie, wrote *America Hurrah!,* one of the most provocative plays of the 1966–1967 season. When Chaikin declared the Open Theater closed, he could look back on one of the most interesting experimental ensembles of the new theater.

The Performance Group

The Performance Group in New York City was spawned by Richard Schechner's contact with Grotowski's Workshop. The Group's aim was to purge the sentimentalism of the traditional American theatrical experience by shattering the boundary between audience and performer and by involving all elements in a communal celebration. Working with exercises derived from Grotowski that

The Performance Group fashioned a theater out of a garage and placed the spectators on scaffolding. The workshop quality of their performances is evident in this shot from *Commune,* **a collective creation.**

subsequently became a part of the performance, Schechner's Group produced *Dionyus in 69,* based on *The Bacchae* of Euripides and on rituals that grew out of exercises and rehearsals. Language was distorted, fragmented, and amplified, and the chorus chanted and wailed in projecting the impression of ritualistic fervor. Schechner's vociferous theatricalism, which exploited sound, movement and nudity, made an impact, although his aesthetic objectives were not clearly apparent from the performance.

OTHER NEW THEATER GROUPS

Another innovative group that has demonstrated its staying power is Charles Ludlam's Ridiculous Theatrical Company, founded in 1967. Ludlam borrowed freely from the commedia dell'arte and anything else that suited his slam-bang, comic-strip style for ridiculing everything in sight. One of the company's productions was its freewheeling *Le Bourgeois Avant-Garde* (1983), a scathing satire on various "isms" to champion a new one.

Peter Schumann's Bread and Puppet Theater is a unique kind of folk theater that plays in streets and open public places. Its brand of theatricalism stems from the use of puppets, some as tall as eighteen feet. Schumann's background as a sculptor and choreographer is evident in the remarkable puppets and their actions. The Theater seems to be motivated by a strong Christian drive, aimed at spiritual renewal. It uses simply fairy stories or tales from the Bible, sometimes treated ironically. The puppets go through the movements; their dialogue is taped or narrated. A blend of "poor" and "total" theater, Schumann's Bread and Puppet Theater has established a solid reputation for its humanistic concerns and its extraordinary manner of expression in gestures and ceremony.

The San Francisco Mime Troupe

The politically activist San Francisco Mime Troupe began performing outdoors in 1962—playing in parks, in marketplaces, and on the streets. Using the broad comic techniques of improvised Italian comedy and working under the motto "Engagement, Commitment, and Fresh Air," the Troupe satirizes the establishment. With its Marxist orientation ("a small theater collective, dedicated to the principle that all art is political"), the company regards spectators not as passive onlookers but as a human resource to activate and mobilize in its attack on war, racism, industrialism, and conformity.

El Teatro Campesino

Luis Valdez began his theatrical career with the San Francisco Mime Troupe, but he became involved in supporting a strike of migrant field workers in California. Recruiting his talent from field hands, Valdez formed El Teatro Campesino to play agit-prop *actos* before Chicano audiences as a way of inspiring political action. These sketches satirized those who exploited the poor in an entertaining way, which was very effective propaganda. Their theatricalism was characterized by an exuberant spirit and broad comic action. Valdez became interested in broadening the base of El Teatro Campesino, moving away from political action to a concern with the spiritual and literal spirit of the Chicano culture. In 1978 he produced a full-scale drama, *Zoot Suit*, which played successfully at the Mark Taper in Los Angeles, although it failed to attract a wide audience on Broadway. El Teatro Campesino continues as a virile cultural force, pursuing Valdez's call for "a teatro of ritual, of music, of beauty, and spiritual sensitivity. A teatro of legends and myths. A teatro of religious strength."

THE THEATER OF IMAGES

Despite the avowed protest against "the tyranny of the word," most theater productions revolve around a written script. There are, however, notable innovators who are interested in the presentation of images. Most prominent among these are Robert Wilson, Richard Foreman, and Lee Breuer's Mabou Mines Company.

Robert Wilson has an uncanny capacity for creating beguiling images, such as this one intended to be part of the mammoth production of *CIVIL warS*. *(Walker Art Center, Minneapolis)*

Robert Wilson

Robert Wilson is a highly regarded experimentalist whose theatricalism appeals primarily to the eye. He has been called a "seer genius" and a "feeler genius" because of his imaginative productions of striking visual displays in *The Life and Times of Sigmund Freud, Deafman Glance* (1971), *A Letter for Queen Victoria* (1975), *The Life and Times of Joseph Stalin, Einstein on the Beach* (1976), *I Was Sitting on My Patio This Guy Appeared I Thought I Was Hallucinating* (1977), and *Death, Destruction and Detroit* (1979). *Einstein on the Beach,* which was performed at the Metropolitan Opera House after highly successful productions in major European cities, combined all aspects of the theater, but the emphasis was on the sensual imagery loosely tied to musical motifs. Wilson's background as a painter explains his visual approach to theatrical production.

> I am always concerned with how the total stage picture looks at any given moment. The placement and content of film, paths and gestures of performers, and lighting were all major considerations, no less important than the dialogue or music.[13]

In *Death, Destruction and Detroit,* which premiered in West Berlin (1979), Wilson makes more extensive use of language than in his previous works. Some of it is fragmentary, oblique, precise, and lyrical, but there is an ordered verbal sequence. Like the other elements—music, dance, and spectacle—the language is a way of stirring the imagination and expanding the awareness rather than a means of conveying factual information.

Death, Destruction and Detroit concerns the Nazi leader Rudolf Hess, confined since 1945 in a prison in Berlin. One scene, particularly striking because of the evocative images that Wilson fashions, suggests Hess's prison cell. Dale Harris describes the action:

> . . . Hess, now an old man dressed in white tie and tails, dances by himself to the sound of a Keith Jarrett piano solo. He is preoccupied, self-absorbed, utterly content. Even when the stage begins to fill up—first with couples in evening dress, then with waiters carrying huge salvers and domed lids, all of them dancing with the same self-absorption and fixity of purpose—he stays in his own world, weaving in and out of the crowd as if they didn't exist. At the front of the stage, in the center, stands a little boy (who may or may not be Hess's son), wearing scarlet diplomat's dress, gleaming with gold frogging—a colorful note among the pervading shades of grey and black.
>
> Meanwhile, from one side of the stage a woman (who may or may not be Hess's wife) stares out at the audience during the course of the scene being transformed from a shabby looking *Hausfrau* with a cotton scarf knotted under chin to a *grande dame* in magnificent black evening dress, her head crowned with feathers, her wrists and neck encircled with diamonds. It is hard to imagine a more telling comment on the economic rise and gradual historical amnesia of West Germany between 1945 and the present.[14]

Wilson's "planetary opera" *CIVIL warS* was originally scheduled as part of the Los Angeles Arts Festival for the Olympic Games (1984) but had to be postponed because of financial and scheduling difficulties. It was finally produced at the American Repertory Theater in 1985. The opera, in five acts, with fifteen scenes and thirteen entr'actes ("knee plays"), ran for twelve hours. It was a collaborative effort involving an Argentine filmmaker, a German dramatist, an American composer, and a Japanese costume designer. Initially, it was intended to deal with the Civil War and the Industrial Revolution in the United States, but the idea was enlarged to include universal civil strife. Wilson produced striking, brutal images from the American Civil War and other graphic material to illustrate the theme of death and destruction. Other intriguing titles of Robert Wilson's works are *The Golden Windows* and *I Was Sitting on My Patio This Guy Appeared I Thought I Was Hallucinating.*

Wilson's work cannot be judged in the usual dramatic way, because it is unique in conception and lacking in the usual literary referents. However, it is clear that Robert Wilson has attained a highly personal and provocative theatricalism that depends on very special conditions for production.

Richard Foreman

Richard Foreman is another experimentalist who has received considerable attention through his Ontological-Hysteric Theater productions of *Dr. Selavy's*

Magic Circus, Elephant Steps, Angel Face, Hotel for Criminals, Penguin Touquet, and *Café Amerique.* Like Wilson, he is interested in the presentation of a series of theatrical, provocative images, without a story line or continuity. He delights in the "act of making the thing we are looking at," which he regards as constantly changing directions. When asked what he would like an audience to experience from his productions, Foreman replied, "I would like them to feel refreshed, you know, energized."

Foreman's own plays are a collection of tableaux joined to disruptive dialogue and arbitrary visual images and sound effects. Seeking to destroy the stage through delicate maneuvers, he deliberately distorts his materials to avoid linear and logical patterns. His plays are intended to reject the tyranny of meaning, although Foreman in his *Manifesto* and other writings explains at length his rejection of a clear rationale. In dealing with the unimaginable, he has created his own version of the absurd.

The Mabou Mines Company

Linked with Wilson and Foreman in its visual approach to theater is the Mabou Mines Company, an ensemble that since the early 1960s has written and produced its own plays. The group toured Europe for three years before becoming the resident company first at La Mama and then at the New York Festival Theater.

The company works as a collective under the guidance of Lee Breuer, who serves as director, writer, and actor. His early plays featured animals as their main characters, in what he calls "Animations": *The Red Horse* (1970), *B. Beaver* (1974), and *Shaggy Dog* (1978). They are satirical, highly imaginative fables that attack contemporary culture through pop music, films, television, and the high gloss of Madison Avenue commercialization. They aim at stripping away the veils that conceal romanticism and sentimentality. The *Shaggy Dog* animation presents the life and loves of a dog named Rose, who develops a fixation for her master and longs to take on human characteristics. Rose is played by a puppet about two-thirds human size, manipulated by from one to four of the actors. The dog's past and her thoughts and feelings are projected over a sound track and accompanied by strange and evocative actions and images.

Some of the members of Mabou Mines work both in and out of the group. Mabou Mines has experimented freely with high-tech production techniques, such as using holographs to project the illusion of three dimensions with laser beams. A notable example of new aspects of theatricalism was in Breuer's production of *Hajj* (1982) at Joseph Papp's Public Theater, which involved the use of mirrors, closed-circuit video cameras, and recorded tapes.

Sophocles' *Oedipus at Colonus* is a Greek classic that depicts the ancient, blinded Oedipus wandering about with his daughter seeking sanctuary. The original play ends with his death and transfiguration offstage, narrated by a Messenger. In Breuer's modern adaptation, the Messenger is a preacher who has been an eyewitness to the miracle, which he ecstatically describes onstage with the help of a gospel-style choir that performs with the ardor of a black Baptist church revival meeting.

PERFORMANCE ART

For a time, a good deal of experimentation came under the catchall term *happenings*. More recently, *performances* is the key word, with such ramifications as *auto-performances, activities,* and *performance workshops.* Sally Barnes describes performance art as "an anti-theatrical forum that displaces illusion with real time, character with personality, skill with spontaneity, artifice with the banal. It values idea over execution. . . . It is a kind of throw-away art." As Barnes says, "performance art" is actually antitheater in concept in that it reverses or negates traditional theater values.

You will recall Aristotle's hierarchy of plot, character, thought, diction, music, and spectacle. Performance art *reverses* the importance of these elements by placing top priority on spectacle and music. Plot, a sequential orderly structure of elements, organized on the basis of the "necessary and probable," is replaced by broken fragments that avoid complications and resolutions and are replaced by abstracted images without beginning, middle, and end.

The performers are not characters but agents of the action, without psychological complexity. Their humanity may be delimited by the use of masks or the substitution of puppets. Their speech and actions are flat and abstracted. There is no clear thought element, no didactic purpose. The meaning is the act itself, which is deliberately opaque or ambiguous, as if to warn the spectator against the danger of seeking a clear rationale.

Performance art is geared toward private responses; it is self-oriented. The diction is not dialogue to reveal character or to advance the plot. It takes the form of exposition or description, often lyric in feeling. The verbal material uses diaries and biographies, sometimes taped or shared by several performers. The sound element may include all kinds of music, generally electronically performed. Jazz and rock music and a variety of sound effects are played from tapes. The spectacle depends on the projection of images—slides and home movies arranged in conflicting or ambiguous patterns. And through it all, the performer remains remote, austere, and depersonalized.

Performance art is more at home in a gallery or studio than it is onstage because in many ways it is an extension of the painter's printmaker's art than it is of the theater. Titles of some of the pieces suggest the nature of the subject matter: *Are-Are, Here and Now, Vacuum, Car Dance II, Why What Is Is, Spectacle V,* and *Adjusting the Idle.* Like so many other innovations in the arts, performances emphasize the creative process rather than the final product, and technical skill often yields to improvised inspiration. The act is its own excuse for being.

The future of the new theater will no doubt depend on the social climate of the times. The valid gains it has made in promoting a varied brand of theatricalism will be reflected in the main current of the theater, while fresh attempts will be made to express the human experience. The door is wide open—never before has there been such a wide range of styles, technical facilities, or tastes. As always, with every form of theater, the future will depend mostly on the talent and imagination that is attracted to its service.

The new theater is no longer a strident voice of protest, but it continues in many forms to be a theater of experimentation that emphasizes theatricalism. However, the shock has worn off, and many of the freedoms that the experimentalists fought for have been won. The theatricalism that so short a time ago seemed novel has merged into the mainstream of the theater. Playwrights immediately exploited the new permissiveness in language, behavior, nudity, and subject matter. Writers now find far more latitude in shaping their material or in using the technical facilities of production. In short, those who boldly struck out to find new territory have broadened the horizons of us all.

PLAYS TO READ AND SEE

F = Film available; V = Videotape available.

F		Jerzy Grotowski, *Akropolis*
F	V	Peter Shaffer, *Amadeus, Equus*
F		Federico Garcia Lorca, *Blood Wedding*
		Bertolt Brecht, *Caucasian Chalk Circle*
F	V	Rad Ragni, *Hair*
F		Peter Weiss, *Marat/Sade*
F	V	Arthur Kopit, *Oh Dad, Poor Dad*
F	V	Thornton Wilder, *Our Town, Skin of Our Teeth*
F	V	Eugene Ionesco, *Rhinoceros*
F	V	Samuel Beckett, *Rockalby* (Alan Schneider)
F		Friedrich Duerrenmatt, *The Visit*

BIBLIOGRAPHY

ARTAUD, ANTONIN. *The Theater and Its Double*, trans. Mary C. Richards. New York: Grove Press, 1958.

BLAU, HERBERT. *Take Up the Bodies*. Urbana: University of Illinois Press, 1982.

BRAUN, EDWARD. *The Theater of Meyerhold: Revolution of the Modern Stage*. London: Drama Bk., 1979.

BROOK, PETER. *The Empty Space*. London: MacGibbon and Tree, 1968.

CHAIKIN, JOSEPH. *The Presence of the Actor*. New York: Atheneum, 1972.

ESSLIN, MARTIN. *The Theater of the Absurd*. New York: Doubleday, 1961.

EVANS-ROOSE, JAMES. *The Experimental Theater*. New York: Universe Books, 1970.

GROTOWSKI, JERZY. *Towards a Poor Theater*. New York: Simon & Schuster, 1968.

KIRBY, MICHAEL. *The New Theater Performance Documentation.* New York: New York University Press, 1978.

MALINA, JUDITH. *The Diaries of Judith Malina, 1947–1957.* New York: Grove Press, 1984.

MARRANCA, BONNIE. *The Theater of Images.* New York: Drama Book Specialists, 1977.

SCHECHNER, RICHARD. *Public Domain: Essays on the Contemporary Theater.* Indianapolis: Bobbs-Merrill, 1969.

SHANK, THEODORE. *American Alternative Theater.* New York: Grove Press, 1982.

WELLWARTH, GEORGE. *The Theater of Protest and Paradox.* New York: New York University Press, 1967.

NOTES

1. Kurt Schwitters, quoted in Robert Motherwell, *The Dada Painters and Poets* (New York: Wittenborn, Schultz, 1951).

2. Quoted in John Elderfield, *Kurt Schwitters.* Copyright © 1985 by Thames & Hudson, Ltd. Reprinted by permission of the publisher.

3. Brecht, *Brecht on Theatre,* trans. John Willett (London: Methuen, 1964).

4. Brecht, "Little Organum for the Theater," trans. Beatrice Gottlieb, *Accent, 11* (1951).

5. Antonin Artaud, *The Theater and Its Double,* trans. Mary C. Richards (New York: Grove Press, 1958).

6. Albert Camus, *The Myth of Sisyphus,* trans. Justin O'Brien (New York: Knopf, 1955). Copyright A. A. Knopf, Inc.

7. Alfred Jarry, cited in Leonard Cabell Pronko, *Avant-Garde: The Experimental Theater in France.* Copyright 1962 The Regents of the University of California.

8. Samuel Beckett, *Waiting for Godot.* Copyright 1954 by Grove Press, Inc.; copyright renewed © 1982 by Samuel Beckett. Used by permission of Grove Press, Inc.

9. Harold Pinter, *The Birthday Party.* Copyright © 1959, 1960 by Harold Pinter. Used by permission of Grove Press, Inc.

10. Eugene Ionesco, *The Bald Soprano,* from *Four Plays by Eugene Ionesco,* trans. Donald M. Allen. Copyright © 1958 by Grove Press, Inc. Used by permission of Grove Press, Inc.

11. Beckett, *Waiting for Godot.*

12. From the Introduction by Peter Brook to the play *The Persecution and Assassination of Jean-Paul Marat as Performed by the Inmates of the Asylum of Charenton under the Direction of the Marquis de Sade,* by Peter Weiss. Copyright © 1965 by John Calder Ltd. Reprinted by permission of Atheneum Publishers.

13. Robert Wilson, "I Thought I Was Hallucinating," *Drama Review, T76,* December 1977.

14. Dale Harris, "Berlin Report," *Performing Arts,* June 1979.

nine
The Director

Peter Brook has been one of the most influential directors and leaders in the modern theater. His books and his innovative productions have earned him international recognition. He is seen here, working with his cast in his highly theatrical *Mahabharata*.

The Suppliants (c. 492 B.C.) is generally regarded as the oldest extant play in western European literature. When the author, Aeschylus, won the right to present his play at the Festival of Dionysus, like other Greek dramatists, he was obliged to direct his own work. He must have learned that directing a play is a complex and tricky business. Since he was the author, he did not have the usual problem of interpreting the meaning of his text, but like all directors, he went through the intriguing and sometimes frustrating process of putting the words into action. Aeschylus had to make sure his lines were spoken or sung correctly; he had to work out all the movement and choreography of the actors and chorus members; and he supervised all aspects of production—costumes, casting, music, and dance.

Even a cursory glance at *The Suppliants* indicates the need for painstaking planning and rehearsal. Aeschylus dramatized the story of the fifty daughters of Danaus who flee to Argos, seeking sanctuary from the pursuing sons of Aegyptus. At the climax of the play, Herald and his attendants attempt to carry off the maidens by force, but they are saved by the King, who refuses to release them.

Perhaps the most difficult task Aeschylus faced in producing his play was that of training the chorus of fifty maidens, who recite and chant more than 600 lines of poetry, sometimes combining words with dance and sometimes engaging in vigorous action, as when they cling to the altar in terror, pleading for asylum.

Directing an ancient play in a Greek theater was no simple task, especially a play like *The Suppliants* by Aeschylus. The director had to organize the singing, dancing, action, and the arrangement of actors and a Chorus of fifty in an enormous acting area. *(Modern revival directed by A. Solomos at the theater in Epidaurus)*

In addition to the careful preparation of speech and choreography of the chorus, it was necessary to provide them with appropriate costumes—striking Egyptian robes and linen veils fastened to their heads with gold bands. In the action of the other performers, two entrances required special care. In the first, the King and his retinue make a dramatic entrance, probably with horses and chariots. The second complicated entrance occurs when the Herald and his coterie appear and threaten to tear the suppliant maidens away from the altar. Although this play has a simple plot, its implicit demands for the movement of a large group of performers must have required arduous rehearsal. We may be sure that Aeschylus was grateful for his military experience when he prepared *The Suppliants* for performance.

Throughout the history of the theater, the manifold tasks of production have been handled in a variety of ways. In the ancient Greek theater, the assigned officials and playwrights were in charge of the presentation of tragedies. In the medieval cycle plays, with their fragmented episodes, many of them requiring realistic staging, an enormous amount of organization was necessary, much of which was parceled out to various participating groups. In the Elizabethan theater, with its permanent professional companies of actors and playwrights, the theater manager selected the plays and assigned the casts. Undoubtedly, the playwrights took considerable interest in seeing that their works were performed as they intended them to be. And just as Hamlet found it expedient to advise the players about their style of acting in the play within the play, it requires little stretch of the imagination to believe that Shakespeare made a similar effort in the performance of his dramas at the Globe. Molière, in the seventeenth-century French theater, labored for twelve years with his troupe in the provinces, polishing and perfecting the performance of his plays before returning to Paris. That Molière not only set an example for his company but also took care to improve the quality of his productions is suggested by his wry comment that "actors are strange creatures to drive."

In the eighteenth and nineteenth centuries, such stars as David Garrick and William Macready attempted to make play production less haphazard, but in general many of the responsibilities of organization were delegated to underlings or ignored altogether. Often plays were patched together, with "typed" characters assigned to roles, little or no genuine rehearsal, and almost no concern for ensemble acting. Stock sets were refurbished on a makeshift basis, and little attention was paid to lighting. Costuming was mostly a matter of individual taste, and apparently no one worried about the resulting incongruities. There were, of course, a few notable exceptions to these practices. In the 1850s, Charles Kean staged remarkable productions of Shakespeare, for which special scenery was designed and painted with accurate geological and botanical detail. In his productions of *A Midsummer Night's Dream* and *Henry VIII*, Kean was praised for the harmony of effect that resulted from music, scenery, and choreography especially created for the occasion. A decade later, Squire Bancroft and Marie Wilton Bancroft introduced rehearsal reforms that were in the direction of greater unity.

THE MODERN DIRECTOR APPEARS

The Duke of Saxe-Meiningen in Germany performed an invaluable service for the theater through his exemplary staging of Shakespeare, Ibsen, and Schiller. All aspects of production were integrated into an artistic whole—acting, scenery, and costumes. His troupe emphasized ensemble playing, paying special attention to the use of crowds. The duke's company tour of the major theatrical centers of Europe (1874–1890) inspired theater workers elsewhere to emulate his synthesis of production and helped to establish the position of the director as the dominant force.

With the coming of naturalism and realism in the latter part of the nineteenth century, directors and actors became increasingly concerned with unifying all elements of the performance. The new plays, representing authentic views of daily life and based on firsthand observation, demanded a new kind of scenery and acting. Since the conventional commercial theaters were not hospitable to innovation, it became necessary to set up "independent theaters"—places where a subscription audience could see the new kind of drama appropriately played. Andre Antoine led the way with his Théâtre Libre in Paris (1887), in which he directed all phases of production. He made a hall into an improvised theater, selected the plays and the casts, set the style of acting by directing and performing himself, and devised the scenery. He even went out and rounded up an audience through hand-delivered letters and personal contacts. His efforts resulted in a unique integration of performance based on his ideal of achieving an honest representation of reality. In Berlin (1889), Otto Brahm followed Antoine's example at the Freie Bühne, another subscription theater that demonstrated realism, especially in the plays of Ibsen and Hauptmann. In Russia, the Moscow Art Theater (1898) did similar work with the plays of Chekhov under the direction of Stanislavski. The independent theater idea was also influential in England at the Independent Stage Society under J. T. Grein, and in the United States James Herne directed a production of his own *Margaret Fleming* (1890) in Boston. These efforts to achieve a style appropriate to the new playwriting were instrumental in defining the role of the director as the one responsible for aesthetic unity and the dominant one in the production hierarchy.

In addition to the independent theater pioneers, two visionaries championed the concept of unity in play production in a series of notable stage designs, as well as in their writings. These men were Gordon Craig and Adolphe Appia, whose contributions are discussed in Chapter Ten. Several forces were at work in the late-nineteenth-century theater that led to the guiding principle that all aspects of play production should grow from a central interpretation. The corollary of this idea was that to secure such unity, a single creative intelligence must be responsible for designing the whole production—namely, the director. This idea is widely accepted in the twentieth-century theater, and this dominating role has been assumed notably by Max Reinhardt, Alexander Tairov, Jacques Copeau,

Constantin Stanislavski, Vsevelod Meyerhold, Leopold Jessner, Tyrone Guthrie, Erwin Piscator, Elia Kazan, Jean-Louis Barrault, Peter Brook, Peter Stein, and Victor Garcia.

Directors work under rehearsal conditions that vary, depending on the type of theater they serve. A Broadway director may find it necessary to throw a play together in three weeks; in Russia, some plays have taken two years of rehearsal. Meyerhold, after two months of rehearsal, had not settled on the casting on any one of the three characters for a one-act play! Reinhardt preplanned his performances to the last detail, so that the rehearsal period was one of teaching the actors what he wished them to do. Arthur Hopkins simply turned his actors loose with occasional stimulation and encouragement, his idea of direction being to "put on a play without anyone realizing how it was done." Some directors find that the law of diminishing returns sets in for rehearsals lasting longer than three hours. Belasco was known to rehearse for twenty hours at a stretch; Meyerhold gave his actors every piece of business and read every line for them; Brecht sat and waited for his actors to show him the meaning of his own plays; Vakhtangov conducted round-table discussions with his casts, trying to arrive at a common interpretation; and Stein, through seminars and directed reading, led his company in researching the period of the play to comprehend its cultural roots.

THE FUNCTIONS OF THE DIRECTOR

As the unifying force in the production of a play, directors have a number of specific assignments. From the time the script is placed in their hands until the curtain rises on opening night, it is the director who initiates and controls all aspects of the presentation. Directors analyze the script; audition actors; cast the roles; set the basic floor plan for the sets; supervise the design of costumes, scenery, and lighting; instruct the cast in the meaning of the play; conduct rehearsals, during which they block out the action; assist the actors with interpretation of character and the reading of lines; and, finally, polish, time, and unify the play into a cohesive whole. Everything about the interpretation and performance of the play is the director's business.

The director's function may be indicated by quoting representative statements by outstanding men of the theater. John Mason Brown said that the "director is a critic in action." Tyrone Guthrie, well known for his highly personalized productions, said: "The director, then, is partly an artist presiding over a group of other artists, excitable, unruly, childlike and intermittently inspired. He is also the foreman of a factory, the abbot of a monastery, and a superintendent of an analytic laboratory. It will do no harm, if in addition to other weapons, he arms himself with the patience of a good nurse, together with the voice and vocabulary of an old-time sergeant-major."[1] Meyerhold describes his purpose in these terms: "A director builds a bridge from the spectator to the actor. Following the dictates

Hal Prince directs the leads in the original London production of *Phantom of the Opera*.

of the author, and introducing on the stage friends, enemies, or lovers, the director with movements and postures must present a certain image which will aid the spectator not only to hear the words, but to guess the inner, concealed feelings." The eminent French director Louis Jouvet described his task as follows: "He must organize that area where the active players on the stage and the passive players in the auditorium meet each other, where the spectators penetrate and identify themselves with the action on stage." Alan Schneider was one of the most energetic and imaginative directors who worked in a variety of theaters and plays, but he is remembered especially for the first American production of Beckett's *Waiting for Godot* and *End Game,* and of Albee's *American Dream.* He stated his view of the director's prime responsibility: "To me a play is a series of relationships. A dramatic action, to me, means a change in relationship."

THE DIRECTOR AT WORK

Although this text is not a manual of play production, nor is it our intent to discuss in detail every phase of the director's function, it may be helpful in understanding the director's contribution if we indicate the use of stage movement.

A play in the theater is dynamic. It is in a continual process of ebb and flow, action and reaction, adjustment and readjustment. Through its characters, changes take place: the frustrated boy finally gets the girl; a woman comes to understand herself through suffering; a hero falls from a high place to catastrophe; the downtrodden little man achieves status.

When Aristotle described the playwright's approach to writing a play, he suggested that the first step was to frame the central action. The director follows a similar process by searching first for the *main action* of the play, sometimes referred to by theater people as the *spine* or the *superobjective*. In Clurman's analysis of *The Member of the Wedding*, he found that the main action was to get "connected." Franco Zefferelli, in speaking of a production of *Hamlet*, saw the hero as "living in a hard world—with no elasticity about it—a closed world, with high walls, no windows, lots of storms. Like a prisoner in a tower." Brook found his approach to *Romeo and Juliet* in a single line: "These hot days is the mad blood stirring." Thus, the director works through the play, line by line and scene by scene, finding the most effective means of forming the action.

Sometimes, the director envisions almost all the action and gives it to the cast. Other directors set a general framework and then encourage the actor to work creatively within it. Joan Littlewood, the colorful English director, approaches the play through the actor, as she did in Brendan Behan's play *The Quare Fellow*, through improvisation to capture the feel of the play before tackling the script. The play is laid in a Dublin prison, so she had her cast begin by simulating aspects of prison life, such as the dull marches in the "yard" and the bleak confinement of cell living.

The director *blocks the movement* of all of the action of the play. He or she is responsible for the traffic pattern of the cast and the position of every performer. Many amateur directors regard blocking as their most important job. Although the script indicates much of the essential action, the total use of movement is, of course, a basic tool in interpreting the play, and a skillful director finds many creative ways to move and position the characters through the use of space, levels, areas, postures, tempo, light, and color to bring out the meaning of the text.

Consider for a moment the opening scene from *Hamlet*. This is a relatively uncomplicated "beat" (a *beat* is a short unit of the play for rehearsal purposes). It requires five characters who will be in close proximity. The director's objective is to establish the audience's acceptance of the ghost. Most likely, the ghost will be kept remote from the audience, played in a dim light and in deep shadow, in an elevated position, and separated from the others. The actor playing the ghost must be able to move freely, so that his exits and entrances create the illusion of an apparition in space. The attempt of Horatio and the soldiers to strike at it must not destroy the feeling of the majesty of the dead King. In blocking the three watchers, Horatio must occupy the dominant position, since the others look to him for counsel and he carries the burden of the dialogue. The audience needs to see him during his speeches. The director composes a constantly shifting pictorial arrangement of the actors in accordance with their emotional states and the relationship of one to another.

Throughout a play one of the functions of the director is to place the audience's attention where it belongs in order to show character relationships and to tell the story. Congenial people draw together; enemies keep their distance until there is a showdown, when they are brought face to face in open conflict. The blocking of the action shows the moment-by-moment interaction of the characters in physical terms. Performers must act out the playwright's scenario. Orgon must hide under the table while his wife, Elmire, baits the impostor, Tartuffe. At the end of *A Doll's House,* Nora must walk out on her husband. In *Amadeus,* Mozart must die in his wife's arms. These obligatory actions must be staged by the director to convey the playwright's meaning—and the staging requires the director to decide precisely how and where they are to take place. A dominating figure may be given an elevated position, facing front, emphasized by a bright light, a striking costume, visual focus, and movement; a subservient character may grovel on the floor in dim light in a drab costume, turned away from the audience. The director composes a constantly changing pictorial arrangement in accordance with the emotional states of the characters. The director is concerned with all aspects of movement—extent, speed, direction, length, style, position of the mover, manner of moving, and the relationship of the performer's action to other characters, scenery, and important props.

Another function of the director, closely allied to the blocking of movement, is that of inventing and assisting the actor in creating "stage business"—that is, the detailed actions of the individual characters, such as using a cane, opening a letter, pouring tea, smoking a pipe, and so on. Stage business is similar to movement in its uses. In general, it is the director's and actor's way of giving life and verisimilitude to the play. Like movement, business may be inherent in the playwright's script, such as Hedda burning Lövberg's manuscript, Juliet drinking the potion or Captain Boyle cooking his "sassige." However, much of the business that is not essential to the plot, but is necessary for enriching the performance, is imposed on the presentation by the inventiveness of the director and the actor. This is especially true in comedy, where one of the marks of the skilled performer is ingenuity in creating original business.

The following example records Stanislavski's preparation for a performance of *Othello* at the Moscow Art Theatre in 1929. This excerpt shows Stanislavski's interpretation of the first few lines of the scene in Act III, in which Othello, his suspicions aroused, comes to Desdemona's bedchamber. The first line is spoken by Emilia, Desdemona's nurse.

Emilia: Look, where he comes.

> (*In the last pause Emilia hears steps below. She rushes to the stairs, sees Othello coming and then hurries to Desdemona so as not to be compelled to call out. Her movement shows alarm and excitement.*)

Emilia thinks differently from Desdemona. She did not like Othello's behavior during the day. It does not seem the way to spend one's time during the first days of one's marriage.

Hearing that he is coming and thinking of last night's wonders, Desdemona wants to meet him suitably. She runs to the mirror to touch up her hair. Emilia waits respectfully at the stairs to disappear at the first opportune moment and not to disturb the husband and wife.

Desdemona: I will not leave him now till Cassio
       Be call'd to him.

She speaks these word while smartening herself up. Her hair done, she runs to the banisters to meet Othello.

   (Enter Othello)

Pause. Othello's entry should be delayed to underline its significance. He enters trying to seem cheerful and cordial at all costs and not make Desdemona see how he feels inside.

   How is't with you, my lord?

She speaks, leaning over the banisters. Thus their meeting takes place as follows: flirting lightly, Desdemona at the banisters, looking at him questioningly and trying to find out how he is, while Othello stops on the stairs, having had not time to come up yet. Their heads are on a level.

Othello: Well, my good lady. O, hardness to dissemble! *(Aside)*

He tries to sound cheerful. Desdemona suddenly puts her arms around him over the banisters, leaving his head uncovered. His face is turned to the audience, she is showing the back of her head.

   How do you, Desdemona?

Desdemona stops dead still in the embrace. He starts at it. The embrace is intolerable, but he restrains himself. One can see by his arms how he would like to, but he cannot make himself, put them around her. His face shows suffering. The embrace over, however, he will try again to seem, if not gay, at least calm.

By the way—it would be better were the actor to make it his task to be cheerful; should he not succeed in being sincere about it, even better: this failure will accentuate the artificiality which Othello requires at the moment.

Pause. This scene of meeting and embrace must be played right through to the end; do not be afraid of prolonging the pause.[2]

Many directors today do not work out the blocking and business in advance; these aspects are developed in the rehearsal process as a joint effort. The blocking may not be set until the final rehearsals, or it might even be changed after opening night. In any case, it is the director who ultimately must decide exactly what the audience will see.

THE DIRECTOR AS AN INTERPRETER

The most important function of the director is to interpret the play.

When such playwrights as Aeschylus, Shakespeare, and Molière produced their plays, they worked directly with the actors; the shape and meaning of the performance was undoubtedly determined by the dramatist. But when the playwright was not experienced in the practical aspects of the theater or not available, individual actors were left to their own devices. This usually meant that the leading actors were concerned only with being seen in a favorable light and considered their colleagues only when the latter affected their own performance. Only a century ago it was customary for star actors to join a local stock company to play the lead in a Shakespearean play without a single rehearsal. Supporting actors adjusted their traditional business and movements to accommodate the leading actors, which pretty much meant leaving the downstage center area open and keeping clear of the stars so that they had ample room to gesture. With the development of the contemporary theater, the director took over the responsibility for integrating the production—and the most important task of deciding on the interpretation of the play.

Max Reinhardt converted a Berlin circus building into a theater with a large playing area, like a Greek theater, for his 1910 production of *Oedipus Rex*.

This goes far beyond a mere acquaintance with the story line or even an intimate knowledge of the play's structure. Drama shows people in action—making decisions, reaching for objectives, attacking, withdrawing, resisting, yielding—and in the course of the action there is talk—argument, pleading, persuasion, discussion. All this action and talk is about something; that is, there is a residue of meaning beneath the surface—the *subtext*. Directors search the play for the essential core of meaning they choose to convey.

Norris Houghton, in *Moscow Rehearsals*, a fascinating account of his visit to Russia in the 1930s, describes Meyerhold's approach to directing. He read the play through a single time, trying to grasp the meaning of the author, noting his first impression of the script. When he produced a play, Meyerhold often changed the text to suit the interpretation he gained from his first reading. Once he determined the motivating idea, he visualized a tentative plan for the scenery and lighting. He came to the first rehearsal without any notes or promptbook but apparently with his head swarming with ideas, which he released spontaneously as he worked with the actors on their interpretation of the lines and their invention of movement and business. A staff of eight to twelve assistants recorded in detail every aspect of each rehearsal, so that by the time the play reached production there was a vast accumulation of material about the play and its performance.

Houghton describes Meyerhold's interpretation of Chekhov's *The Proposal*, which he gave to the actors at the first rehearsal: "Two things are essential for a play's production, as I have often told you," Meyerhold began.

> First, we must find the thought of the author: then we must reveal that thought in a theatrical form. This form I call a *jeu de théâtre*, and around it I shall build the performance. Molière was a master of *jeu de théâtre:* a central idea and the use of incidents, comments, mockery, jokes—anything to put it over. In this production I am going to use the technique of the traditional vaudeville as the *jeu*. Let me explain what it is to be. In these three plays of Chekhov I have found that there are thirty-eight times when characters either faint, say they are going to faint, turn pale, clutch their hearts, or call for a glass of water; so I am going to take this idea of fainting and use it as a sort of leit-motif for the performance. Everything will contribute to this *jeu*.[3]

After this introduction, Meyerhold read the script to the cast and dismissed the rehearsal.

The noted German director Reinhardt, famous for his theatricalism, like Meyerhold, dictated every detail of the production. However, he did not depend on the inspiration of the moment. Reinhardt's presentations were the result of months of careful preparation, during which time he developed a complete annotated account of the play. The purpose of his rehearsals was to teach his interpretation line by line to the actor. Raikin Ben-Ari, who worked with Reinhardt, describes his methods in this fashion:

> Reinhardt comes to work with his secretaries and his assistant directors all laden with books. They are volumes with interpretations and explanations, with various data, drawings and symbols relating to the production—the evidence of colossal artistic

and technical work which was done in preparing the manuscript for the stage. In these books the working out of every scene, every phrase, is recorded exactly and in detail—precisely when this or that player, when this or that group has to move to another part of the stage; how many musical intervals they have before they move; how much space they have to move in; the exact moment when the light is to go on.[4]

Two American directors who owe a good deal to Stanislavski in their approach are Harold Clurman and Elia Kazan. Both worked with the Group Theater, one of the most influential production companies of the 1930s that was associated with method acting. Clurman and Kazan make a careful study of the script, searching for a basic interpretation, their interest centering on the psychological backgrounds of the characters. They make detailed notes to guide their thinking during rehearsals.

Here are sample notes Clurman made when he was preparing for a production of *Long Day's Journey Into Night* by Eugene O'Neill, considered one of the most important plays of the American theater. The director made this breakdown of his "First Impressions":

Guilt—a keynote
Apprehension—suspense   The characters are
More guilt   sustained by no
Self-accusation   faith
The eyes of each character are on the other.
Foghorn—a desolate sound of aloneness.
Loneliness—everyone is alone with his or
    her own secret and guilt.
The spine of the play: to probe within oneself
    for the "lost something.

Chekhov's plays are noted for their rich characterization of frustrated individuals. When Clurman prepared to direct *Uncle Vanya*, these are some of his notations on the motivating forces of the leading roles:

> **Vanya:** *Spine:* to find some way—some positive way—to live through the suffocation of his life.
> **Astrov:** *Spine:* to do what he has to—despite everything.
> **Yelena:** *Spine:* to obey and to justify her obedience—as the only thing she can do.[5]

George Bernard Shaw's plays are sometimes criticized as lacking in characterization; they are simply the varied viewpoints of the same individual, the playwright. But when Clurman directed Shaw's *Heartbreak House,* he found interesting views of the characters. In his preliminary analysis, Clurman says:

> Everyone in the play wants somehow to escape his or her condition. All are dissatisfied with it . . . it's a crazy house, driving them crazy. All in a sense are "crazy," not true to themselves, not what they seem to pretend to be. So everyone is somehow odd, a *clown*—disguised, masked.

In this scene from *A Streetcar Named Desire*, Marlon Brando, as Stanley Kowalski, is about to break up the birthday celebration because of his resentment of Blanche's disruption of his married life. *(Directed by Elia Kazan)*

"In this house," says Hector, "everybody poses. The trick is to find the man under the pose."[6]

In a similar fashion, Elia Kazan, who also came from the Group Theater, analyzes the theme and characters for his famous production of *A Streetcar Named Desire*. Kazan describes the theme as "a bit of light" that "is snuffed out by the crude forces of violence, insensibility, and vulgarity . . ." He views the spine of the character Blanche as "to find *protection*."[7]

Clurman and Kazan worked from a close analysis of the text, probing into the psychological roots of the action. Their approach is a standard one for many directors working with modern plays written in a realistic vein or centered on revealing complex character motivation.

When the director Robert L. Benedetti was invited to direct *Hamlet* at the Oregon Shakespeare Festival, he made it an interesting project by keeping a production log that described the step-by-step progress of a production in rehearsal. Benedetti describes the steps of preparation: "Research," "Understanding the action," "The shape of drama," "Understanding character," and "Forming a production concept." His approach is broader than that used by Clurman and Kazan because he gives considerable thought to the social and political environment of the action and the structure of the play. Benedetti also works on "Focusing on a theme" of *Hamlet,* which he summarizes in this way:

1. The complex relationship which binds sons and mothers (the so-called Oedipal theme)

2. The way in which unchecked evil breeds ever more evil (as we see in the poison which flows from Claudius, both literally and figuratively, until it infects the entire court)

3. The conflict between the absolute ethic of the feudal world and the relative ethic of the humanist world, which tears Hamlet between his sense of duty to the Ghost's demand for vengeance and his "university" sense that "two wrongs do not necessarily make a right"

4. The need for the balancing of Will and Understanding ("Thus conscience doth make cowards of us all.")[8]

Other directors have turned away from the Stanislavski type of production. Guthrie, for example, who left the British theater to establish outstanding companies, first in Ontario, Canada, and then in Minneapolis at the theater that bears his name, was often criticized for "fooling around with Shakespeare." He explained his motives in these terms:

> . . . I should like to discuss what to me is the most interesting part of the job, the blending of intuition with technique. If I may elaborate those terms, by intuition, I mean the expression of a creative idea that comes straight from the subconscious, that is not arrived at by a process of ratiocination at all. It is my experience that all the best ideas in art just arrive, and it is absolutely no good concentrating on them hoping for the best. The great thing is to relax and just trust that the Holy Ghost will arrive and the idea will appear.[9]

Guthrie's view of an intuitive approach to directing is shared by many of the foremost directors today, who regard the text as a launching pad for their flights of fancy. These directors view established plays as complex, many-layered, wide-open works whose meanings vary from generation to generation. They are not content to accept the classics as immutable works, set in cement. They regard a play as an invitation to explore new ground, a challenge to find a fresh impact. For them, the theater is a medium for understanding and taming the world. A glance at several contemporary directors indicates the scope of their creative vision. They feel free to cut lines or even whole scenes, to change the sequence of action, to eliminate characters, to use the same actor for multiple roles, or to play the single role with several actors. They do not hesitate to shift the locale from Illyria to India, from the moors of Scotland to a tropical island, from ancient Greece to Nazi Germany.

This freewheeling attitude is partly the result of the avant garde protest against the sanctity of the text and the tyranny of the word, and partly it stems from the desire to make dramatic production more theatrical, more intense, more exciting.

It is quite easy to understand how the English and European theaters would be open to experimentation, since their classic repertoires have been played so frequently that they are worn out unless someone breathes new life into them. Moreover, state-supported resident companies, with whom box office appeal need not be the primary consideration, can afford to take risks that are impossible on the commercial U.S. stage. In addition, we do not have a classic repertoire of native plays. It is also noteworthy that when directors choose vehicles for innovative interpretations, they generally avoid contemporary, realistic plays in favor of those that give them a broader scope—Shakespeare, Carlo Goldoni, Gogol, Molière, and Beaumarchais. Among the contemporary writers, Chekhov is a favorite because of the challenge to the director to externalize the subtext. In any case, much of today's theater is a "director's theater."

Peter Brook, always an innovator, directed this production of Shakespeare's *The Tempest* at the Roundhouse Theater London. The setting of scaffolding and runways recalled the "biomechanical" style of Meyerhold.

Peter Brook

Peter Brook is one of the most imaginative and important directors today. He directed for years at the Royal Shakespeare Company before establishing his own International Centre for Theater Research in Paris, where he works with a company of actors from all over the world. He has directed some of the most striking productions in the modern theater, including *Marat/Sade*, *A Midsummer Night's Dream*, and *Mahabharata*. His two books, *The Empty Space* (1969) and *The Shifting Point, 1946–1987* (1988), are stimulating works on the theater.

When asked how he would define *directing*, Brook replied:

> I think one must split the word "direct" down the middle. Half of directing is, of course, being a director, which means taking charge, making decisions, saying "yes" or "no," having the final say. The other half is maintaining the right direction. Here, the director becomes guide, he's at the helm, he has to have studied the maps and he has to know whether he is heading north or south.[10]

Brook's productions are always based on a series of discoveries. He comes to them open and alert, looking for clues in the script, for some potential to develop.

> It's the sense of the potential that then guides him to finding the space, the actors, the forms of expression, a potential that is there and yet unknown, latent, only capable of being discovered, rediscovered, and deepened by the active work of the team.[11]

Brook is famous for his relationship to his cast in devising a variety of ways to inspire and encourage each of the players in a personal exploration of the character and the play.

Charles Marowitz, who was associated with Brook, especially in the preparation for a production of *Marat/Sade*, insists that the director's function is to reinterpret a play in terms of its present relevance. In his stimulating book, *Prospero's Staff*, Marowitz has this to say about the director's obligation to give a play a fresh interpretation:

> A director who does not proceed in this way, who chains himself to unwavering fidelity to the author and pursues his work in selfless devotion to the "meaning of the text," is unknowingly abdicating a director's responsibility. . . . The director who is committed to putting the play on stage as it is written is the equivalent of the cook who intends to make the omelette without cracking the eggs. The director is the master of the subtext, and his dominion includes every nuance and allusion transmitted in each moment of the performance.[12]

In his controversial production of Weiss's *Marat/Sade*, Brook fashioned a "total theater" out of a welter of sensory stimuli, which resulted in the "density" he was talking about and which links him to Artaud. His production offered an emotional impact that recalled primitive ritual in its use of incantation, ensemble

Brook's *A Midsummer Night's Dream* was one of the most interesting and controversial productions since World War II. Brook stripped the play of nonessentials and created an entirely fresh and stimulating interpretation.

miming, discordant music, and the force of the acting, which seemed to be on several levels at once. The action of the play was set in a madhouse, where the inmates acted out their fantasies, giving the director unique opportunities for theatricality and macabre business—such as the mass guillotining to the accompaniment of raucous sound effects, and the pouring of red paint down the drains as some of the inmates jumped into a cavity so that only their heads showed next to the guillotine.

Before the production of *Marat/Sade,* Brook and Charles Marowitz set up an acting workshop affiliated with the Royal Shakespeare Company. Its purpose was to experiment with new kinds of acting—not the Stanislavski approach, with its search for inner authenticity, but closer to Artaud's vision of shaping the image of communication from a sequence of movements and gestures—a theater of cruelty.

One of Brook's most celebrated theater offerings was his *Midsummer Night's Dream* (1970) by the Royal Shakespeare Company. The production became a famous one, playing for a total of 535 performances in thirty-six cities in England, Europe, Japan, Australia, and the United States. Although some critical ink was spilled because of Brook's "impertinent travesty" of Shakespeare, in general audiences were enraptured by the magical world invoked. Clive Barnes, the drama critic of the *New York Times,* commented:

> It is a magnificent production, the most important work yet of the world's most imaginative and inventive director. . . . Brook has approached the play with a radiant innocence. He has treated the script as if it had just been written and sent to him through the mail. He has staged it with no reference to the past, no reverence for tradition. He has stripped the play down, asked exactly what it is about. . . . He sees the play for what it is—an allegory of sensual love, and magic playground of lost innocence and hidden fears.[13]

David Selbourne, an English dramatist, was invited to make an "eyewitness" account of Brook's production over the eight-week rehearsal period at Stratford in the summer of 1970. His observations, *The Making of A Midsummer Night's Dream,* are a fascinating account of the rehearsal process, from the initial meeting of the company to opening night. They reveal the immense sensitivities and skills of an imaginative director, leading the cast in an exploration of the play. At the outset, Brook decided to double the roles of the four leading actors; to use a white-walled set that looked like a squash court or exercise room; and to use circus techniques in the playing, such as swinging from trapezes and ladders, tumbling, juggling, walking on stilts, and spinning metal discs at the ends of rods.

Brook began his rehearsal period by inviting the seventeen performers from the Royal Shakespeare Company to investigate and experiment with a "wide range of acting styles" in order to achieve "different kinds of illusion and presentation, and to discover which illusion is the most effective." At the first rehearsal, "the mechanicals," the low-comedy characters of a *Dream,* began with exercises accompanied by a drum beat, and the actors were told to "search for the experienced physical gesture of the experienced craftsman." Brook explained to the cast that "your task is to bring *A Midsummer Night's Dream* to life through your rehearsal of 'Pyramus and Thisby.' " This is a comic interlude to be performed by the artisans before the court. The plot resembles the fatal love affair of Romeo and Juliet with its tragic deaths.

As a part of the process of exploring the play, Brook conducted discussions about ways of discovering hidden meanings in the text, of finding rhythms deeper than words. The nonverbal area of performance is one of special interest to Brook, and in working the cast he often used exercises based solely on sounds, rhythms, and fragments of lines and words. Sometimes the actors were directed to repeat words and lines freely, speaking simultaneously and adding improvised sounds like a jazz combo.

The cast also began experiments and exercises to acquire new skills— spinning discs, swinging on ropes, and walking on stilts. At one rehearsal, the actors were invited to "walk like water." They experimented with gliding, wading, making rippling movements, and simulating a waterfall. A favorite rehearsal technique was for the cast to sit on the floor in a tight circle, while they recited lines from their parts and improvised language, rhythms, and dances.

Brook's rehearsals were intense sessions of exploration and are evidence of his astounding creativity in finding ways to, as he says, "create the circumstances for performers to do interesting work"; "work can only be done with a sense of the magical word. Then the whole world opens." It is the process of opening this world that Brook sees as his particular function.

Selbourne's rehearsal log is valuable in showing how one of the most creative directors of this generation works with his actors. He is not the dictator who has planned everything in advance, but rather he considers himself the leader of an exploration party who can find his destination only with the help of his companions. "I can know what is right, but I cannot discover the experiences for you," he said. What is surprising to the outsider in Selbourne's account is to learn of the doubts and anxieties that bedeviled the actors and Brook in putting the play together—especially in the first public performances before audiences of children and invited guests. It was not until a tryout performance at the Midland Art Center in Birmingham that the production finally reached the level Brook was striving for.

Selbourne's book provides remarkable insights into the ways that an outstanding director works with his cast, especially in investigating acting techniques rather than direct confrontation with the text.

Joan Littlewood

Joan Littlewood made a notable reputation as director and leader of the Theater Workshop. Working mostly with young people who were dissatisfied with the commercial theaters of London, Littlewood and her group toured England and Europe, and settled in a suburb so that they could appeal to a working-class audience. Her strong sense of social purpose resulted in productions that combined didacticism with earthy entertainment that was appealing to the audiences as music hall entertainment. Littlewood said that "Theater must be in the present tense." She was deeply committed to working on the actors so that they could play in a direct way, free from ostentation. Her ways of working borrowed from both Stanislavski and Brecht.

The most important new playwright to work with this group was Brendan Behan, whose plays *The Quare Fellow* and *The Hostage* were remarkable productions. Since *The Quare Fellow* was set in a prison and none of the actors had personal experience with prison life, Littlewood began conditioning her cast to that life in a series of games, even before they saw the scripts. Improvised situations were set up to simulate experience in confinement, such as living in and cleaning their cells, eating in the mess hall, and going into the exercise yard. By the time the actors received their scripts, they had already developed a feel for the play. As a result, the performances of Littlewood's productions are marked by a basic honesty and directness that had a powerful impact on the Theater Workshop's audiences.

Littlewood had little respect for the polished style of English acting, with its dignified poses, slick personalities, and modulated tones. Her greatest ability was to draw people out—and she was relentless in her approach. One actor attested to the experience of auditioning for a play directed by Littlewood, who had him read all the parts. Littlewood said, "You are either an actor, or you can't." It was a memorable experience for him and gave him a new perspective on his art. Littlewood made a strong impression on the English theater by emphasizing the human side.

Three Romanian Directors

Three Romanian directors who came to this country and gained attention by their use of extravagant and imaginative theatricalism were Andrei Serban, Liviu Ciulei, and Lucian Pintilie. Serban worked with Brook in Paris and then came to the United States, where he first directed three Greek plays at La Mama. Serban prefers to work with established texts. (Many contemporary playwrights consider him to be too idiosyncratic to deal with their plays.) Serban's association with Brook is evident in his concern with sounds in an attempt to catch the rhythms and emotions behind spoken language. When he directed the Greek plays, Serban experimented with his cast in finding the sounds and rhythms, not only in Greek and Elizabethan English, but in two esoteric African languages as well.

In his production of *Agamemnon,* at Lincoln Center, Serban rejected the traditional approach to the play. He set the action in a wire cage inside a pit at the front of the auditorium, and his performers were more concerned with evoking feelings by strong aural and visual signs of the subtext rather than with a faithful rendition of an ancient drama. Serban's interpretation of his role as a creative artist was not to show the audience a play but to involve the spectators in an experience that happened to be theatrical.

His most notable productions have been with Chekhov's plays. At the American Repertory Theater in Cambridge, Serban set the action in a mirrored floor, backed by large red curtains and with floodlights at the sides to suggest the theatricality of the event. Serban's version of *The Cherry Orchard* at Lincoln Center in 1977 aroused a good deal of comment because he departed from the conventional sad and bittersweet interpretations of Chekhov. Instead, he livened up the action with comic business, chases, and falls—adults playing at children's games. But the metaphor of disintegration was not neglected. Santo Loquasto's setting was remarkably effective with its white carpeting and no walls—only the cherry trees in the background. Against this light background, the actors' movements and groupings emphasized the alienation and separation taking place. At the end of the play, when all of the family have gone away in carriages, old Firs, a servant, totters in. He has been forgotten. Finding an old coat, he covers himself and lies down in a pool of light. There is the sound of a broken string, and then the chopping of an axe. This was a stunning theatrical image of separation and destruction.

A second Romanian director was Liviu Ciulei, who in the early 1970s was affiliated with a leading theater in Bucharest, where he attempted to "retheatri-

Director Lucian Pintilie staged highly theatricalized versions of *Tartuffe* at the Guthrie and Arena theaters. In this Minneapolis version, the King's messenger, who rescues the gullible Orgon from the clutches of Tartuffe, makes a spectacular entrance by driving a Dusenberg through the tiled wall. In the Arena version, he entered in a space ship.

calize" the conservative stage. His efforts alienated the Romanian authorities, so he came to the United States, where he worked at the Guthrie Theater and aroused a good deal of controversy by his daring version of Shakespeare's *Tempest*. Mike Steele, drama critic of the *Minneapolis Star*, describes the set, which gives us some clue to the fertility of Ciulei's imagination:

> The Guthrie's expansive thrust stage had become an island surrounded by a moat of gelatinous blood. Floating in the moat were some of the most familiar artifacts of western culture: a Mona Lisa, clocks without hands, a gleaming suit of arms. Amid the litter on shore was a Venetian horse head, ripped from San Marco, next to a stuffed chicken wrenched from a Robert Rauschenburg collage. Surprisingly beauti-

ful scientific equipment from Galileo's time rested atop a legless piano propped up by stacks of huge books. Double sets of stairs rose to a makeshift Captain's bridge in what looked like a large, mirrored industrial warehouse. A faceless factory window to the rear opened onto constantly changing Magritte landscapes.[14]

Another Ciulei production at the Guthrie was Ibsen's *Peer Gynt,* designed by Santo Loquasto, in a setting that featured a series of movable mirrors.

The third Romanian director was Lucian Pintilie, whose extraordinary theatricalism gained wide attention. Pintilie's first notable directing assignment in America was Chekhov's *Sea Gull* at the Guthrie in 1983. He revised the order of events by shifting the shooting sequence from the end of the play to the beginning. He pointedly rejected the Stanislavski style of playing Chekhov with subdued voices and gestures. Instead, Pintilie found ways to present metaphors in physical, overt terms. When characters became angry or frustrated, they flung books at one another or threw themselves on the floor.

Another startling Pintilie production was Molière's *Tartuffe,* first at the Guthrie and then at the Arena Stage in Washington, D.C. The director chose to set the play in a white-tiled room that suggested an asylum or a laboratory rather than a home. The production was full of sight gags, such as spilling a basket of red apples onto the white floor. Orgon's treasures were kept in a vault beneath the floor so that entrances to this area were highly theatricalized.

Pintilie went to great lengths to stage the arrival of the King's officer at the end of the play. Molière's text simply indicates that the officer makes an entrance through the door, presents the King's edict that revokes Tartuffe's claim to Orgon's estate, and takes the impostor off to prison. In Pintilie's Guthrie Theater version, the officer arrived by smashing through a brick wall in a Dusenburg.

In the Arena production, the Messenger and his Mafia-like thugs descend from the grid in a whirling helicopter. Tartuffe is captured in a tumultuous scene in which the tiled floor of the stage splits asunder, leaving a great yawning, smoking hole. The production is replete with Pintilie's inventions: pratfalls, sexual innuendo, and physical comedy, played with enormous energy. The effect was an exuberant and stimulating theatrical experience, but at the expense of the basic values of Molière's play—such as credible characters and their relationships and much of the original comic spirit.

Ariane Mnouchkine

Ariane Mnouchkine's Théâtre du Soleil in France gained an outstanding reputation for her productions. The company began in 1964 as a workers' collective and attracted attention with compelling performances of Maxim Gorki's *The Courageous One* and Arnold Wesker's *The Kitchen.* But the ensemble wanted to dramatize historical events from a popular point of view to show how "people might imagine, feel, live, and suffer during the Revolution." Its goal was achieved through a striking performance of *1789,* a collective creation growing out of months of workshops and rehearsals. The actors' performances were improvised to the extent that no one knew precisely what anyone would do or say, but they worked from a general outline that encouraged individual adaptation.

Mnouchkine's ensemble was invited to perform at the Olympic Arts Festival in Los Angeles in the summer of 1984. It made two remarkable contributions with performances of *Richard II* and *Twelfth Night.* They were played in a large, bare television studio in Hollywood, on a fourteen-meter-square platform before temporary bleachers.

The director chose to place the action of *Twelfth Night* in an illusory India, suggested by sumptuous costumes, properties, and decorative backdrops in vivid colors, and with harem pants, veils, masks, turbans, and huge parasols. Guy-Claude Francous' set design conveyed the feeling of a Japanese Noh stage because it was covered with hemp and marked off by seven thick black lines like a tatami mat. Four horizontal entrance ramps led to decorative paneled pavilions with oversized umbrellas. The exotic visual atmosphere was enhanced by music from an orchestra that accompanied the action with strange and interesting sounds from flutes, whistles, drums, gongs, and stringed instruments.

The acting style was likewise extremely stylized, sometimes suggesting commedia dell'arte, sometimes marionettes, and sometimes the dance movements of India. For example, Sir Toby Belch and Maria walked with a mincing, tipsy gait as

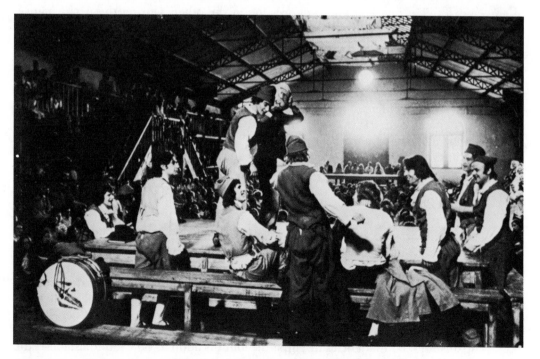

Ariane Mnouchkine's Théâtre du Soleil earned a reputation for forthright theatricalism, as in this production of *1789* in a theater that was formerly a factory.

they precariously avoided the black stripes or tried (vainly) to keep from falling off the edge of the stage.

Mnouchkine's *Twelfth Night* was a far cry from the Elizabethan stage, but Shakespeare's play served as a framework for a charming and exceptional theatrical experience.

Mnouchkine's production of *Indiad or The Indre of Their Dreams* (1987) was first played on the bare stage of their performance hall in Paris. The cast of sixty, who live and work together as a collective, made 44,000 thin bricks to cover the playing area. They also made wooden cots with hand-woven jute and covered them with mattresses. Overhead was a white canopy decorated with stars and bright saris.

For more than a quarter of a century now, Mnouchkine has been successfully pursuing her goal of demystifying the theater for her actors and audiences.

Peter Stein

Stein is another ingenious director, who has brought to the stage at the Hallenschen Schaubühne in West Berlin extraordinary productions of well-known plays. Instead of producing *Peer Gynt* in a theater, Stein elected to stage it in a large exhibition hall at the fairgrounds. Spectators sat in rows of seats at the side of a long rectangular playing area covered with a canvas and shaped so that there was a hill at one end and a depression at the other. During the performance, which lasted nearly seven hours over two consecutive evenings, props and set pieces were brought in for the eight phases of Peer's career. The leading role was divided among six actors, who played variations of a basic type—a bourgeois dreamer.

Stein's production rejected illusionary scenery and acting, avoided psychological involvement, focused on ideas rather than entertainment, and created excitement by its frank and imaginative theatricalism in a space outside the conventional playhouse. In this instance, because the Schaubühne was concerned with its social message as a people's theater, Stein's interpretation was a group effort.

Bertolt Brecht

When playwrights direct their own productions, they are not concerned with a new reading of their texts but, rather, with finding the most telling ways to project their words and actions to the audience.

Brecht, in directing his own plays at the Berliner Ensemble, was dedicated to finding a *new interpretation of the theater*. As we have seen, Brecht's epic theater was an effort to find a new way of writing, acting, and staging plays. When Brecht worked with actors on the production of his own plays, he constantly struggled against the old tendencies of empathic identification as he tried to establish the

Bertolt Brecht was one of the most influential people in the theater in this century. He is here directing an "epic" production of his *Mother Courage* **at the Munich Kammerspiele. Note the obvious lighting equipment and the absence of pictorial scenery.**

alienation effect. His purpose was to induce the spectators to evaluate critically the onstage events and to relate them to the social and economic conditions of the real world, so that they might work for change. One of his favorite ways of explaining to his casts the quality of playing he wanted was to cite the example of a witness describing a traffic accident. The acting was "not to cast a spell over anyone, but to repeat something which had already occurred"; that is, "the incident *has* taken place, the repetition is taking place."

In the notes that he prepared for the production of *Mother Courage,* Brecht described the business in detail for each of the characters involved. In Kattrin's drumming scene he provided a complete scenario of action for the soldiers, peasants, and Kattrin, including the kind of actions and the attitudes of the participants.

Kattrin's action must "steer free of heroic cliché," Brecht said, and the scene must avoid "wild excitement." To counteract the temptation toward emotional involvement, he suggested that the soldiers should appear apathetic, Kattrin's drumming should be interrupted, and the peasants' dialogue should be spoken as though secondhand. For example, one peasant says, "The watchman will give us warning." Brecht was attempting to avoid the immediate impression of "unique, actual horror" to give the effect of repeated misfortune: "Fear must show through the ceremony in this scene." But despite these efforts to achieve objectivity, Brecht had to admit, "Spectators may identify themselves with Dumb Kattrin in this scene; they may project their personality into this creature; and may happily feel that such forces are present in them, too."

At the end of the play, when Mother Courage, completely alone in an unfriendly universe, drags her wagon into the gathering darkness, Brecht intended the audience to see her as an object lesson of one whose life and energies have been wasted in the traffic of war, of which she is a willing part. But the solitary image was so loaded that at the premiere in Zurich, it created a strong empathic response of compassion. Brecht is reported to have rewritten the part in an effort to make Courage less sympathetic.

Despite the fact that he was never able to reconcile completely his theories with the effects his plays created in the theater, Brecht gave the modern director a new and provocative way of using the actors and the stage.

Others in the New Theater

Sam Shepard, one of the most imaginative of the contemporary American playwrights, worked with an ensemble in San Francisco on *INACOMA*, a play depicting the struggle for survival of a young woman who has been seriously injured in an accident. Shepard, in a program note, describes his open approach in shaping the production:

> I've tried to make use of every influence that has moved me. From vaudeville, circuses, the living theater, the open theater, and the whole world of jazz music, trance dances, faith healing ceremonies, musical comedy, Greek tragedy, medicine show, etc. Our approach has been to include as much information as possible, coming from the material on every level we could find. To try to remain open to any new possibilities and at the same time discard what was unnecessary.[15]

Joseph Papp has become an increasingly important force in the U.S. theater. He began working with an actors' workshop in a church basement in an effort to develop a style of playing Shakespeare that was realistic and credible, without destroying the poetic style. From that background, Papp began his New York Shakespeare Festival in Central Park, which was given a permanent out-door home in the Delacorte Theater. Summer festivals offered free to the public a series of three plays. By 1970 Papp was involved with four companies, but his most important contributions have been with the Shakespeare Festival and the Public Theater, which has a resident company of actors. Papp is important in the contemporary American theater because, more than any other individual, he has opened the doors of opportunity for designers, playwrights, and actors. His willingness to experiment with all kinds of material and talent has had a salutary effect. Although his reputation does not depend on his directing ability, his hand is evident in many of the productions.

In order to present classical plays in a natural way to an unsophisticated audience, Papp says:

> We look for the answer in our casting. In the choice of the actor, we determine the style of our productions. . . . . We seek blood-and-guts actors, those who bring spice and vitality to the production—actors who have the stamp of truth on everything they say or do.[16]

Directors in the new theater work with a free hand. In the past, the director aimed at bringing the text to life by giving the lines a careful reading; searching the text for meaning; selecting and training the actors for accurate, credible characterization; and using the technical resources of production to present a dramatic work as a cohesive whole.

The new director is more interested in the performance than in the play; the text has no validity of its own. Unity and coherence give way to the moment-by-moment sporadic sensations that come partially from the actors and partially from sound, light, scenery, and costume. The emphasis is on images, on creating a dynamic montage, often with multiple focus and simultaneous action.

The vehicle for performance may be a truncated or fragmented classic. Stephen Willems eliminated all but the love story of *A Midsummer Night's Dream*, and of the mechanicals, only Bottom was retained. Michael Grüber cut *Faust I* to an hour and a half and used four actors instead of fifty. At the Berkeley Shakespeare Festival, the director reduced the cast from forty odd roles to eleven and changed the witches to street punks, who joined Macduff and Banquo in disposing of Macbeth at the end of the play.

One of the striking features of many contemporary directors is the manner in which they work with actors. In addition to rehearsals of the script, workshops that include exercises, improvisations, and experiments with sound, movement, and style are a part of the preparation process. Sometimes the workshops contribute materially to the play and its interpretation, as in the case of Chaikin's Open Theater production of *Vietnam* and Mnouchkine's *1789*.

Some critics resent the authority that directors now wield over the production of a play, but the temper of our times suggests that the strong-minded individual with original ideas will continue to have a free hand. Innovations of recent years, particularly those in which directors emphasize performance over fidelity to the text, point toward even more emphasis on theatricalism—ritual, total theater, environmental theater, epic theater, open theater, and even anti-theater. Although the traditionalist may be wary of some of the chances the daring director takes, it is from the inspiration of such leaders that much of the most exciting theater has come.

PLAYS TO READ AND SEE

F = Film available; V = Videotape available

F	V	William Shakespeare, *A Midsummer Night's Dream*
F	V	Tennessee Williams, *A Streetcar Named Desire*
F	V	Anton Chekhov, *The Cherry Orchard* (Olivier directs)
F	V	Arthur Miller, *Death of a Salesman* (Hoffman)
F	V	John Osborne, *Look Back in Anger*
F		Peter Weiss, *Marat/Sade*
F		Carson McCullers, *Member of the Wedding*
F		Samuel Beckett, *Rockaby* (Schneider directs)

FILMS AND VIDEOTAPES ON DIRECTING

F	V	Directing a Film: Ionesco's *The New Tenant*
F	V	*Drama: Play, Performance, and Perception* (series)
F	V	*The Dresser*
F	V	*Houseman Directs Lear*
F	V	*Ingmar Bergman*
F	V	*The Producer*

BIBLIOGRAPHY

BENEDETTI, ROBERT L. *The Director at Work.* Englewood Cliffs, N.J.: Prentice-Hall, 1985. (This is a log of *Hamlet,* directed by Benedetti at the Oregon Shakespeare Festival.)

BRAUN, EDWARD. *The Director and the Stage: From Naturalism to Grotowski.* New York: Holmes and Meier, 1982.

CHEKHOV, MICHAEL. *To the Director and the Playwright,* compiled by Charles Leonard. New York: Limelight Editions, 1984.

CLURMAN, HAROLD. *On Directing.* New York: Macmillan, 1972.

COLE, TOBY, and H. K. CHINOY, eds. *Directors on Directing.* Indianapolis: Bobbs-Merrill, 1964.

GUTHRIE, TYRONE. *In Various Directions.* New York: Macmillan, 1965.

HOUGHTON, NORRIS. *Moscow Rehearsals.* New York: Harcourt, Brace & Co., 1936.

HOUGHTON, NORRIS. *Return Engagement.* New York: Holt, Rinehart & Winston, 1962.

KOTT, JAN. *Theater Notebook.* New York: Doubleday, 1968.

SAYLER, OLIVER M. *Max Reinhardt and His Theater.* New York: Brentano's, 1924.

SELBOURNE, DAVID. *The Making of A Midsummer Night's Dream.* London: Methuen, 1982.

STANISLAVSKI, CONSTANTIN. *My Life in Art.* New York: Theater Arts Books, 1924.

TAIROV, ALEXANDER. *Notes of a Director.* Coral Gables, Fla: University of Miami Press, 1969.

NOTES

1. Tyrone Guthrie, *In Various Directions* (New York: Macmillan, 1965).

2. Konstantin Sergeevich Alekseev, *Stanislavski Produces Othello,* trans. Helen Nowak (London: Bles, 1948). Reprinted by permission of Geoffrey Bles, Ltd., London.

3. Norris Houghton, *Moscow Rehearsals* (New York: Harcourt, Brace & Co., 1936).

4. Raikin Ben-Ari, "Four Directors and the Actor," *Theater Workshop,* January–March 1937.

5. Harold Clurman, *On Directing* (New York: Macmillan, 1972), p. 254.

6. Ibid., p. 230.

7. Elia Kazan, quoted in Toby Cole and Helen Krich Chinoy, *Directing the Play* (New York: Macmillan, 1972).

8. Robert L. Benedetti, *The Director at Work* (Englewood Cliffs, N.J.: Prentice-Hall, 1985).

9. Tyrone Guthrie, "An Audience of One," in Toby Cole and Helen Krich Chinoy, eds., *Directors on Directing* (New York: Macmillan, 1964). By permission from Macmillan Publishing Company.

10. Peter Brook, Foreword to Charles Marowitz, *Prospero's Staff* (Bloomington: Indiana University Press, 1968), p. xii.

11. Ibid., p. xi.

12. Charles Marowitz, *Prospero's Staff,* pp. 4–5.

13. Clive Barnes, *New York Times,* August 28, 1970, 15:1.

14. Mike Steele, *Minneapolis Star,* 1981. Reprinted by permission.

15. Sam Shepard, program note, *INACOMA,* 1977.

16. Joseph Papp, quoted in Cole and Chinoy, *Directors on Directing,* p. 432. By permission of Macmillan Publishing Company.

ten
The Actor

Two of the finest performers in the contemporary theater are Judith Anderson and John Gielgud, seen here as Queen Gertrude and Hamlet in the New York production.

When Thespis became the first actor in the sixth century B.C., he introduced the idea of impersonation—of becoming someone else—of changing from Thespis to the god. By that audacious and remarkable action, Thespis invented the idea of acting.

The word *impersonation* comes from the Latin *persona,* a mask. We remember that Thespis first appeared wearing a white linen mask, not only to identify the role for the spectators, but also to assist him in possessing or being possessed by the god. In Greek, the word for this act of complete identification is *enthousiasm,* to be possessed by the god.

Through impersonation, Thespis (and every actor since) assumed a dual role—that of the actor and that of a character, both at the same time. This is a curious phenomenon in the theater, where the actor becomes his or her own artistic medium. Actors do not work on marble or clay, or with paint, nor do they play pianos, violins, or horns. *They work on themselves.* This means operating at two levels at once. In life, you have the experience of handling two or three levels of consciousness at the same time. You may plug a language cassette into the tape machine in your car and start memorizing French irregular verbs, while threading your way through a traffic snarl, meanwhile thinking ahead to the date who awaits you at the end of your trip.

Actors go beyond this ordinary experience when they deal simultaneously with separate identities as real persons and as the characters they are playing. Acting involves presenting a fictitious character in such a convincing way that the audience believes and responds emotionally to the role as if there were genuine persons, not simply an act of deception, calculated to fool the audience. Actually, it is the process of creating a credible aesthetic illusion—and it is no more deceptive that a Van Gogh landscape. The actor, like all other artists, works within the parameters and conventions of his or her art.

An actor's effectiveness in creating a convincing or moving performance is not a matter of realism. Plays in all styles, from many periods, are capable of affecting an audience, despite their obvious dissembling. I remember watching a Noh play performed in the shell of a bombed-out theater in Tokyo years ago. It was a reenactment of the ghost of an old fisherman whose small son had drowned when his father was fishing in illegal waters. The single actor, in a long black robe, wearing an enormous white wig and a mask with a fixed expression of suffering, glided across the polished floor to the area where the accident occurred. He spoke in a subdued voice, which gradually became louder and more violent. Meanwhile, his dance followed his voice, the beat of the drums, and the sharp sounds of a flute. He grew more and more agitated, stamping the floor. Then he suddenly stopped and, in dead silence, turned and made a slow exit. I didn't understand a word, and the conventions of the theater and the performer were completely foreign to me, but the impact of this stylized performance is fresh in my mind to this day. We are quite capable of accepting conventionalized performance as an authentic experience.

Shakespeare, in *Hamlet,* presents a striking example of how a skillful actor simulates genuine emotional involvement. In Act II, Scene 2, a traveling troupe of actors are brought to Elsinore. Hamlet welcomes them as old acquaintances and requests that the First Player recite a passage he remembered hearing him perform.

Hamlet: Come, give us a taste of your quality; come, a passionate speech.

The actor proceeds to play Aeneas' tale to Dido with such complete conviction that Hamlet is astonished at his ability to identify himself in the part.

Hamlet: Is it not monstrous that this player here,
But in a fiction, in a dream of passion,
Could force his soul so to his own conceit
That from her working all his visage wann'd,
Tears in his eyes, distraction in's aspect,
A broken voice, and his whole function suiting
With forms his own conceit? And all for nothing![1]

Hamlet's speech is an interesting commentary on Elizabethan acting, because the description of the First Player's performance is one of such convincing identification with the part that he turned pale, shed tears, appeared distracted, and spoke with a broken voice—and all without benefit of scenery, costume, or a supporting cast! The illusion of reality in the theater is a venerable one.

In this Royal Shakespeare Company production, Hamlet meets the touring company of actors to arrange for his "Mousetrap" insertion into their performance.

In most plays, the actor is called upon to create a believable character who is expected to speak, move, and generally behave in a consistent manner. The audience accepts as real the character that the actor presents to them. The playwright, director, and actor have taken great pains to create convincing characters in their speech, action, motivations, appearance, and general behavior.

Meanwhile, the actor inside the character is aware of such technical matters as interaction with other characters, timing crosses and speeches, projecting lines and business, and being alert to the audience response. Throughout the play, the actors maintain this dual responsibility, always kept in control, so that the character and the emotions do not run away with the show.

The performers' tasks may be further complicated when they are called upon to double by playing several characters in the same play. Even more demanding is a play like Gurney's *The Dining Room*, in which each of the actors plays five or six different roles without benefit of makeup or costume changes.

THE ACTOR'S CONTRIBUTION

The life force of the theater is the actor's living presence before an audience. Sometimes a performer will find a part that is especially remarkable. When Maggie Smith brought the London hit comedy *Lettice and Lovage* to Broadway, the *Los Angeles Times* drama critic observed:

> Smith won the Tony award because she gets away with every bit of personal shtick for which she has ever been condemned, reviled, and adored. It is a positively unconscionable performance, in which you wouldn't want to change a tittle or a jot.[2]

Clive Barnes of the *New York Times* was moved to make this comment on George C. Scott's Willy Loman in *Death of a Salesman:*

> There is nothing on earth like the magic of great acting. An actor takes off—his words fly up, image and reality become one, the actor creates a patch of humanity on the quietly empty stage, a rustle runs through the theater, a breeze of awareness, a special alertness. One of the world's few renewing miracles flickers into life. Great acting. The kind you can never forget. The kind you tell your grandchildren about. The kind that leaves you in a state of grace, enables you to jump beyond yourself, to see something that perhaps even the playwright himself only dimly perceived.[3]

Our technically adept age may find ways to record actors' voices and movement on film or on tape and ship their likenesses from here to there in a can or cassette, and their images may be projected in enormous colored enlargements on wide screens in immense drive-in lots, or their range of action may be reduced to a twenty-one-inch frame in our living rooms, but genuine theater begins and ends with the actors' living presence. Their creations and interpretations give the theater its special quality. More than the stage settings or the director's skill in organization, sometimes more than the drama itself, the actors give to the theater

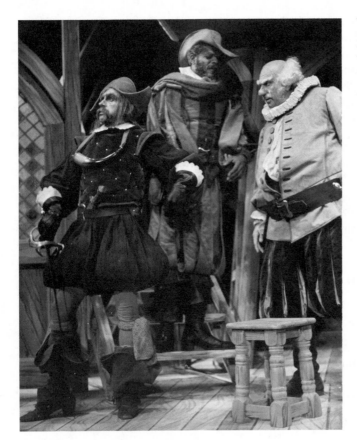

The actor's appearance is important in establishing character, as is apparent in these comic figures from the American Conservatory Theater production of *The Merry Wives of Windsor.*

its reason for existence. It is their histrionic sensibility that induces the audience to live imaginatively in the characters and drama before them. It is the actors who ignite the spark and fan the flame that warms and illuminates the audience.

As we have seen earlier, the impulse to imitate, to impersonate, to act is a very old one in the race and a very early one in our own lives. Because of the peculiarly subjective and intimate nature of acting, the creative processes of the actor are difficult to define and describe. Since acting is a private creation, actors may work through intuition and the unconscious, by means that they do not fully comprehend themselves. Actors, like other artists, vary widely in their methods of approach. Some actors insist that they must have complete emotional identification with the characters they are playing; others are equally adamant that acting is a matter of technique. Interestingly, exponents of both extremes can cite examples of brilliant actors in defense of their position.

Not only do approaches to roles vary with individuals, but also actors in the past have been prisoners of their times, and especially the kind of drama and theater in which they appeared. This did not mean a lack of variety, for an actor such as Richard Burbage in Shakespeare's company played a wide range of leading roles, from Hamlet to Prospero. An Athenian actor in the fifth century B.C. might have been called upon to play two or three roles in three different plays. He might play a hero who dies offstage and then come on as a messenger and narrate his own death! In our theater today an actor may play in a variety of periods, as well as different media. Dustin Hoffman played Tootsie in the movies, then Willy Loman on stage, and then Shylock in *The Merchant of Venice*. Jessica Tandy began her career in London, playing classic roles such as Titania in *A Midsummer Night's Dream*, Cordelia in *King Lear*, and Ophelia in Gielgud's *Hamlet*. Then she appeared on Broadway with Marlon Brando in *A Streetcar Named Desire*, and, when she was eighty, she won an Oscar for the film version of *Driving Miss Daisy*.

Jack Lemmon describes the difference in films versus the stage:

> I think that the healthiest thing about theatre versus film is basically the discipline, the demands are absolutely intrinsic to theater. It's much more demanding to do one concentrated show for a few hours than it is to work all day long in film. One is a piece of cake compared to the other. . . . One of the problems of film acting is to be able to sustain it. Yes, that is a separate problem. But overall, for a variety of reasons, stage is much more demanding. Once that curtain is up, that is it! There are no retakes, obviously, and nobody can help you, nobody's going to edit anything.[4]

In a hit show on Broadway, the actors' chief problem may be how to keep their performances as spontaneous and credible on the three hundredth night as on the first. The same actors working in motion pictures may satisfy the director if they can give a series of satisfactory performances of a few seconds' duration in two to six takes over a period of two weeks. There is no one approach that can be applied to all acting roles, from Oedipus to Willy Loman, Scapin to Salieri, Lady Macbeth to Blanche, Medea to Liza Doolittle, Mrs. Malaprop to Lady Bracknell. There is no one acting style suitable for the naturalism of Gorki, the stylized Kabuki drama of Japan, the neoclassicism of Racine, the romantic comedy of Shakespeare, the sophisticated comedy of Congreve, the expressionism of Strindberg, the epic parables of Brecht, the open theater of Chaikin, the sensual, frenetic style of a rock musical, or the impersonal puppets who become part of the scenery in Wilson's visual displays. The actors' performances vary with the conditions under which they work; and although no rigid formula can be applied, especially for the new theater that has evolved since World War II, certain traditional elements pertain. We will begin with conventional factors and deal with the new ones later.

REQUISITES OF THE ACTOR

The first requisite concerns the actor's physical equipment. With the wide variety of roles available in drama, actors may be almost any size and shape; but whatever their physical endowments, they must control their bodies as precisely as violinists control their fingers and instruments. Actors should move and gesture easily and

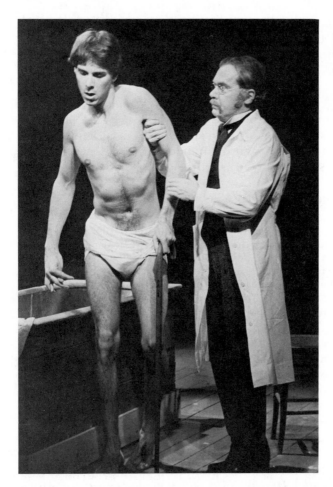

In Bernard Pomerance's *The Elephant Man,* enormous physical demands are placed upon the actor, who must convey the impression of a grotesquely deformed character without the use of makeup. Shown here are Phillip Anglim as John Merrick and Kevin Conway as Dr. Frederick Treves.

in a variety of ways to fit the demands of different kinds of characters and plays. They should be as comfortable playing on a bare stage picked out in a cone of light as they are in a modern living room with chairs, cocktails, and cigarettes. They must have a feeling for movement that is expressive and meaningful, not only in their overt gestures, but also in a constant stream of subtle, nearly hidden images that reveal character and motivation to the audience. Their movements must not be mere posturing; the first law of stage deportment is that every movement should have a meaning and purpose. Actors should be imaginative in the invention of business by which they enrich the characters, indicate the mood, create atmosphere, or reveal emotions. They should be able to handle their props and costumes not only in authentic ways but also in reinforcement of the meaning of their lines and characters. Stanislavski, who is generally thought of in terms of character motivation, insisted that the actors train their bodies so that they would be supple and expressive instruments. In a class session with his students, he

Zoë Caldwell and Hume Cronyn, two of the most versatile and accomplished performers today, are seen here in Molière's *The Miser*. *(Directed by Douglas Campbell, Guthrie Theater)*

demonstrated his skill with a fan to convince them of the need for control over the "language of objects." Nikolai Gorchakov, a visiting director in Moscow, describes Stanislavski's demonstration:

> Then he showed us how one should talk with a fan. The fan quivered in his hand like the wings of a wounded bird, revealing his excitement. Stanislavski's figure, face, and half-closed eyes were seemingly calm. Only the movement of his hand and a slight trembling of the closed fan showed his inner excitement. Then the fan opened with a sharp impulsive movement, flying up and hiding his face for an instant, and just as suddenly it lowered and closed. We understood that in this brief moment the face hidden by the fan had time to give vent to feeling and time for a deep sigh or a short laugh. And it was possible that the hand lightly brushed away a tear with the aid of the fan. Then the fan, with scarcely a noticeable movement, ordered someone supposedly nearby to come closer and sit next to him. The fan stopped trembling. It opened calmly and began to sway softly in his hand as though listening attentively to the person sitting next to him. Then the fan smiled and even laughed. "We swore to him later that that's exactly what we heard." The fan closed again for a second and lightly struck the hand of the person next to him as though saying, "Oh, you are mean!"—and then suddenly covered the blushing face. Now his eyes entered the conversation. First they sparkled under the lace-edged fan; then they looked over the fan and half hid behind it.[5]

Dramatizations of novels have been successfully brought to the stage, such as the Steppenwolf Theater Company's version of *Grapes of Wrath*, produced in Chicage and at La Jolla. The nature of the material made special demands on the large cast.

A second requisite of the actor is clear and flexible speech. The performer's voice should be free from tension, monotony, and unpleasantness, and it should carry easily to all parts of the theater. Actors must be able to read a range of materials, from the verses of Shakespeare and Sophocles to the terse colloquialism of Pinter. They must communicate the full intellectual and emotional content of each line as it relates to their characters and the play as a whole. They must sustain long narrative passages and soliloquies or engage in the rapid repartee of smart comedy with precise timing that maintains the pace without stepping on laughs. They must be part of an ensemble, reading their lines in context with other players in the appropriate action and reaction.

The importance of disciplined control of the voice and speech is evidenced by Ekkehard Schall, the leading actor of the Berliner Ensemble and the foremost Brechtian actor in the world. He spends four to five hours on vocal exercises and script work every day, even when he performs a full play in the evening.

The speaking skill of an excellent performer is apparent from critic Eliot Norton's description of Zoë Caldwell's performance as Cleopatra at the Ontario Stratford Festival production of Shakespeare's *Antony and Cleopatra*.

> Miss Caldwell has an astonishing voice. She can purr like a lioness, hiss like an adder or, when anger shakes her Cleopatra, bellow out words with the power of a boat whistle. . . . She did many remarkable things. Her Cleopatra, for example, spoke

most of the time quite rapidly, which is fair and reasonable, for the woman's mind works rapidly and her eloquence is unlimited. Yet she was at all times easily and clearly audible. Whether brooding or bellowing, her Cleopatra made her points with exquisite clarity and with the kind of music which is present in the verse.[6]

Finally, the actor must possess a quality difficult to define, which the great French actor François-Joseph Talma referred to as an "excess of sensibility." He meant by this a vivid imagination and an acute awareness, which is indicated by the actor's insight into the role, an understanding of what the play and the character are all about, and in performance, a keen sense of the effect on the audience and the other members of the cast. One of the deadliest defects of actors is the inability to assess the effect of their performance, especially in comedy; in striving too hard to "milk" laughs, insensitive actors unconsciously destroy themselves. The actors' sensibility enables them to perceive the response they are receiving and to communicate the playwright's full meaning in performances that are highly personal and unique, yet fitting and compelling.

Beyond these attributes, the actor must have the ability to adapt to a variety of styles and playing conditions. In a repertory company, it is common for the performer to appear in a leading role one night and a supporting role the next, and to move freely from Greek drama to Elizabethan to Restoration to modern— each requiring a special style of playing. In today's theater, the performers must be open to learning because the playwright may have them perform on trapezes, roller skates, skateboards, motorcycles, swings, and other gymnastic equipment. They may have to dance in a variety of ways, tumble, and play instruments.

In addition, many people would suggest that the actor needs a spark, a magnetism, a personality that projects out to the audience and wins it. Many of our popular stars, especially in television and motion pictures, have this spark as their basic talent.

THE EVOLUTION OF MODERN ACTING

Until modern times, actors learned their trade mostly by observation and experience. In the past, stage-struck youths watched the stars in action, became apprentices, and worked their way up from spear carriers or servants to speaking parts, assimilating what they could by contact with the veterans. The beginner might be taken under the wing of an experienced actor or a sympathetic manager and be given pointers about acting. But in general, newcomers were left pretty much to their own inspiration, imagination, and powers of observation. A number of published works appeared from time to time on elocution, oratory, rhetoric, and stage deportment, chiefly emphasizing oral interpretation and the use of the voice. There were occasional attempts to define characteristic emotional states and to relate them to specific postures, gestures, vocal qualities, and facial expressions, but these were entirely subjective and mechanical. The great teacher was the theater itself, where, through trial and error, actors groped for interpretation and perfected their techniques. Those who struck the public's fancy at their first attempt in the major theatrical centers were fortunate. Others, like Molière and Mrs. Siddons, two of the greatest performers of all time, met with initial failure and had to spend years in the outlying provincial theaters mastering their craft, before making triumphant returns to Paris and London.

In the latter half of the nineteenth century, as a part of the scientific revolution in which nearly everything was examined, classified, and catalogued, the Frenchman François Delsarte devised an elaborate system of acting based on purely mechanical techniques. He found in each person a trinity, consisting of the torso, the "vital zone"; the head, the "intellectual zone"; and the face, the "moral zone." Each zone and every part of the mechanisms were in turn divided into trinities, each producing its own specific expression. The student of Delsarte learned to act by memorizing and utilizing the appropriate gestures, vocal qualities, and inflections.

This artificial and external school of acting was opposed by another approach, based on the inner life of the character being portrayed. In part, this new method resulted from the contemporary interest in psychology; but the strongest impulse came from the new drama of realism and naturalism, in which playwrights took their cues from the scientist, attempting to record with strict fidelity the observed facts of human existence, even though they showed an individual in commonplace or sordid surroundings. Because the new science taught that a person was conditioned by environment, naturalistic playwrights depicted the physical surroundings in accurate detail as a causal force on their characters' motivation and behavior.

In 1877, Henri Becque, responding to the new influence, wrote a naturalistic play called *The Vultures*, a somber study of what happens to domestic life when the forces of the economic jungle prey on helpless and unsuspecting victims. In 1882, the Comédie Française was persuaded to give the play a production; but unfortunately it was played in the traditional style of acting, in which the performers declaimed with exaggerated gestures and inflections, rising from their chairs for their speeches and directing much of their dialogue to the audience, thus destroying the atmosphere of Becque's play. It was not until 1887, when Antoine gave *The Vultures* a sympathetic and effective performance at the Théâtre Libre, that the full impact of the drama was realized. Antoine recognized the need for a new way of acting in the new plays, and he demonstrated his ideas in performances in which he and his casts attempted to become completely absorbed in their roles, using such unconventional stage behavior as turning their backs on the audiences and speaking in a conversational manner with the fragmentary gestures of real life.

Antoine's ideas took root, and a revolution occurred in the theater, driving out the old inflated bombastic acting with its pyrotechnic displays of the stars. The ground was ready for the modern style of acting, but it was not a one-sided victory. Although the old exhibitionist school of acting had its faults in its wallowing emotionalism, it was also true that traditional actors could make verse sing, and they knew how to win and hold an audience in the palm of their hands. The virtue that Antoine brought to modern acting was a style that was simple, restrained, and uncluttered with mannerisms and posturing. But in relinquishing the old traditions, many contemporary actors lost much of their unique flair and flavor. John Mason Brown aptly referred to the new style as the "transom school of acting," in which there are "teacup comedians and gas-jet tragedians."

The playwrights who wrote in a naturalistic or realistic manner introduced a new type of character to the audience. The protagonists were no longer picaresque heroes, romantic adventurers, or highbrow ladies and gentlemen in evening clothes. They might be middle- or lower-class protagonists—often the victims of their environments or their passions. Many of these characters were psychologically complex because the primary purpose of the new dramatists might be the revelation of conflicting desires that resulted in aberrant conduct. Strindberg indicates the complex motivation of his protagonist in *Miss Julie:*

> And what will offend simple brains is that my action cannot be traced back to a single motive, that the viewpoint is not always the same. An event in real life—and this discovery is quite recent—springs generally from a whole series of more or less deep-lying motives, but of these the spectator chooses as a rule the one his reason can master most easily. A suicide is committed. Bad business, says the merchant. Unrequited love, say the ladies. Sickness, says the invalid. Crushed hopes, say the shipwrecked. Now it may be that the motive lay in all or none of these directions.[7]

The Stanislavski Method of Acting

With the demands of this new kind of characterization, it was inevitable, as Antoine insisted, that new methods of acting should be devised. The most famous and most important innovator was Constantin Stanislavski, who not only wrote at length about his method of acting but also demonstrated his ideas through his teaching, his directing, and his own acting. The great Russian actor-director worked out his system at the Moscow Art Theater, of which he was one of the founders. As the result of years of experience in the theater and his self-analysis and the observation of others, he formulated his method of acting during the first decade of the twentieth century. His ideas were made known in his three books, *My Life in Art, An Actor Prepares,* and *Building the Character,* and through his work with his students and actors, a number of whom became teachers, spreading his gospel throughout the theatrical world.

The Stanislavski "method" is not an eccentric style of acting for psyched-up performers who are off on an emotional jag. It is not based on sheer raw feeling without consideration of the techniques and skills of movement and speech. These common misconceptions about the method are the result of the notoriety of some of the actors who have misunderstood, misapplied, or distorted the basic tenets that Stanislavski formulated.

Stanislavski's purpose was to devise an objective, regularized technique by which actors could gain control of their bodies and emotions for the appropriate interpretation of the characters and the play. Instead of depending on haphazard inspiration, Stanislavski searched for a system with basic principles by which the

The 1901 production of *The Three Sisters* at the Moscow Art Theater featured Chechov's wife, Olga Knipper (left), as Masha.

actors could discipline their art. Much of his emphasis was on *preparing to act* by means of a conscious technique for causing inspiration as a conditioned response. His books are full of examples through which he sought the practical application of his techniques as he worked with students and actors.

In the following excerpt, Stanislavski is explaining his method to Gorchakov:

> Now what are these basic principles of my method? First, my method gives no recipes for becoming a great actor or for playing a part. My method is the way to the actor's correct state of being on the stage. The correct state is the normal state of a human being in life. But it's very difficult for an actor to create this state on the stage. He must be physically free, must control his muscles, and must have limitless attention. He must be able to hear and see on the stage the same as he does in life. He must be able to communicate with his partner and to accept the given circumstances of the play completely.
>
> I suggest a series of exercises to develop these qualities. You must do these every day, just as a singer or pianist does his scales and arpeggios.
>
> My second principle concerns the correct state of being on stage. This calls for the

correct actions in the progressive unfolding of the play: inner psychological actions and outer physical actions. I separate the actions in this manner intentionally. It makes it easier for us to understand each other during rehearsal. As a matter of fact, every physical action has an inner psychological action which gives rise to it. And in every psychological inner action there is always a physical action which expresses its psychic nature; the unity between these two is organic on the stage. It is defined by the theme of the play, its idea, its characters, and the given circumstances. In order to make it easier for himself, an actor must put *himself* into the given circumstances. You must say to yourself, "What would I do *if* all that happens to this character happened to me?" I believe this *if* (I call it jokingly the magic *if*) helps an actor to begin to *do* on the stage. After you have learned to act from yourself, define the differences between your behavior and that of the character. Find all the reasons and justifications for the character's actions, and then go on from there without thinking where your personal actions end and the character's begin. His actions and yours will fuse automatically, if you have done the preceding work as I suggested.

The third principle of the method—the correct organic (inner plus outer)—will necessarily give rise to the correct feeling, especially if an actor finds a good basis for it. The sum of these three principles—correct state of being, actions and feelings— will give to your characters and organic life on the stage. This is the road which will bring you closest to what we call metamorphosis. Of course this takes for granted that you have understood the play correctly—its idea and its theme—and that you have analyzed the character accurately. And beyond all this, the actor must have a good appearance, clear and energetic diction, plastic movement, a sense of rhythm, temperament, taste, and the infectious quality we often call charm.[8]

To develop the ability to control the state of being, Stanislavski prescribed a rigorous program of training, which in addition to dance, fencing, movement, and voice and diction, included a series of exercises on concentration, observation, imagination, and improvisation. Considerable emphasis was also given to the analysis of plays and characters, seeking out the basic meanings and objectives as the so-called *spine* of interpretation.

A factor contributing to the misinterpretation of the Stanislavski method was that his book *An Actor Prepares* appeared in English translation thirteen years before *Building the Character* was available. The earlier book emphasizes an internal approach to acting, and it was this aspect to which many actors and teachers gave their attention. Although *Building the Character* stresses much more the technique and training of the voice and body, it was not as widely read and followed as the earlier volume; therefore, the method was often incomplete or distorted in practice.

Stanislavski in his early work developed the technique of "emotional memory," by which the actor is supposed to be able to draw on personal experience to re-create its emotional content for a performance. It is an intriguing idea, but the technique has its drawbacks—the actor's recall lacks spontaneity, or the memory of the emotion may be faulty. Stanislavski himself abandoned the technique, but it is remarkably persistent and has its advocates to this day; they find in it a valid rehearsal technique for character analysis and sometimes for therapy. Another way to attack character motivation and emotional states that was popularized by Stanislavski is the use of improvisations as a rehearsal procedure. Actors spontaneously create actions and conditions similar to those in the play under rehearsal. It was Stanislavski's way of extending the actors' background and understanding of the conditions in the play's environment.

Although the central idea of the Stanislavski system is control, an admirable objective for any actor, the use of the method for all kinds of drama and all styles of production is of dubious value. His approach to the production of realistic plays, which permit long periods of rehearsal and experimentation, may be eminently successful, but the method is quite inappropriate for the training of a Japanese Kabuki actor, whose objectives at times may be to simulate the movement and gestures of a puppet. Nor is his system applicable to Meyerhold's acrobatic style of performance, nor does it seem suitable for farce or high comedy. Moreover, in the new theater of the twentieth century, emphasis on character identification is often replaced by a performance that is frankly theatrical or presentational in style.

One of Stanislavski's main contributions to acting was in stressing the importance of the *subtext,* to the hidden life of characters in what he called "the deep sea-currents of meaning." In a realistic theater, in which language is reduced to the commonplace, a dramatist is forced to rely on what he must leave unsaid. The Moscow Art Theater's emphasis on the silent implications of an action, the subtext, was relentlessly pursued.

The value of Stanislavski's ideas has been discussed widely. Most of the criticism of the method centers on its abuse. Too many disciples and performers have exaggerated feeling and inspiration and paid too little attention to the originator's insistence on the importance of technique. Those who emphasize technical training point out that the actors must have complete mastery of their voices and bodies so that they are free to move and speak in an expressive, projectile, and appropriate way. It is not enough for Romeo to feel like fighting a duel; he must also know how to fence. In reading a comic line, it is not enough to think that the dialogue is funny; the delivery requires skillful timing. Long before Stanislavski, generations of outstanding actors gave compelling performances based on their own intuitive approaches. All actors must find their own procedures. The value of the Stanislavski system is that it has helped many actors to regularize their way of working.

After Stanislavski, other avenues to realistic acting have focused on the action that accompanies the emotion rather than the emotion itself. Barrault suggested that actors cannot really play emotional states, but only the actions that accompany them, and it is through their behavior that they express their feelings. Robert L. Benedetti echoes the James-Lange theory that emotions tend to follow the action—we are afraid because we run rather than the reverse. This approach recognizes the *gestalt* concept of the individual as a whole person, whose mind and body are integrated. Feelings are, therefore, a part of a total configuration, not separate entities. So the actor focuses on the actions and the feelings will follow.

One of the most provocative innovators of the new approach to acting, Brecht flatly rejected the Stanislavski system and its identification of character. Brecht wanted onstage the objectivity of a scientist giving a lecture and pointing out the evidence. Hence, Brechtian acting is cool, detached, objective. Brecht's opposition to Stanislavski's brand of acting was based on his rejection of realistic and naturalistic dramas; he regarded them as highly personalized accounts of individuals rather than important documents of social and economic reform.

Lee Strasberg and the Actors' Studio

When the Moscow Art Theater toured the United States in 1923, its ensemble style of acting and its character identification were a revelation. Two of Stanislavski's actors remained in New York and helped set up the American Laboratory Theater, where American actors were introduced to the so-called method or Stanislavski system of acting. Three students who worked at the American Laboratory Theater were to become major influences on the American stage: Lee Strasberg, Stella Adler, and Harold Clurman. They were prime movers in what became an outstanding company—the Group Theater, starting

One of Jessica Tandy's outstanding performances in a long and distinguished career was as Blanche in *A Streetcar Named Desire*.

in 1931, which was associated with the career of Clifford Odets, because his domestic and social plays were well suited to Stanislavski's approach to acting.

In 1947 Lee Strasberg launched the Actors' Studio as a place for professional actors to work on their acting, which was heavily influenced by the Stanislavski system. A notable example of Strasberg's style was *A Streetcar Named Desire*, starring Marlon Brando with his macho style, slovenly speech and dress, and crass behavior. Although the kind of acting that came out of the Studio was criticized for its lack of technical skills and control, Strasberg made an important impact through his emphasis on "inner truth." As realism began to yield to theatricalism in new experimental plays, the Actors' Studio's influence abated, but it made its mark on a generation of many of our outstanding American actors.

THE ACTOR'S WAYS OF WORKING

Actors' ways of working are highly personal since they are the result of their imagination, talent, and physical attributes; but whatever their procedure, they face intriguing tasks. Says Peter Brook:

> Acting is in many ways so unique in its difficulties, because the artist has to use the treacherous, changeable and mysterious material of himself as his medium. He is called upon to be completely involved while distanced—detached without detachment. He must be sincere, he must be insincere; he must practice how to be insincere with sincerity and how to lie truthfully.[9]

The way an actor approaches a new play and builds a character has been the subject of endless conjecture and controversy. Actors themselves freely acknowledge their inability to describe what actually happens to them in performance. The literature of the art of acting is filled with conflicting statements, indicating that the process is too personal for clear-cut intellectual analysis. To quote Brook again:

> Outstanding actors like all real artists have some mysterious psychic chemistry, half conscious, yet three-quarters hidden, that they themselves may only define as "instinct," "hunch," "my voices," that enables them to develop their vision and their art.[10]

The actor places faith in feelings. This point is made again and again in a series of interviews that Lillian Ross conducted with outstanding stage and motion picture performers for the *New Yorker,* in which are found such statements as these:

> It's when you start to rehearse, with other people, that things begin to happen. What it is exactly I don't know, and even don't want to know. I'm all for mystery there. Most of what happens as you develop your part is unconscious. Most of it is underwater. [Kim Stanley][11]

Once you set things you do and make them mean certain things, you then respond to the stimuli you yourself set up. Then you *feel*. [Maureen Stapleton]

Joanne Woodward describes her experience in these words:

Acting is rather like stringing a bead necklace. Each bead you put on is a moment, and when you act, it's moment to moment. . . . Whatever feels right, I do.[12]

Ben Kingsley, who created one of the most memorable portraits of an historical figure in *Gandhi,* describes his way of approaching an acting assignment:

I only take parts where I am sure the leap between the part and myself will be successful. Now that leap is no guarantee of success; I'm not saying it is. But you know as well as I do that the leap is an actual appreciable chemical experience inside one's body that you know, for better or for worse, that you have created the character. You also know, for the worse, when you have failed to create a character.[13]

Acting places heavy demands on an individual. Talent is not enough. Although some performers seem to get by with little or no background because of their personal charm, the genuine actors who can play a variety of roles in a variety of ways almost invariably come through a rigorous program of training and experience before they make their mark. Joanne Woodward makes this point in describing her early career.

"My acting teacher, Sandy Meisner, used to tell me," said Joanne, "that you have to learn to be an actor the way you learn to play a violin. The moment finally comes when you're playing the violin and you don't have to think about where to put your fingers. The same thing should happen to an actor. There's a moment you don't have to say to yourself, 'What is my motivation for this scene? Where am I going and what am I doing?' That is when you have it."[14]

The veteran British stage and screen actor Michael Redgrave, when asked in an interview, "How do you control emotion?," responded,

I think the best description of how that is controlled is the one by Joseph Jefferson, the American actor of many years ago, who, when asked his opinion about the so called Coquelin controversy (Coquelin believing that an actor shouldn't feel anything at all, and Irving believing that the actors should appear to be the very things he's talking about), said very meekly, "As for me, I find that I act best when my heart is warm and my head is cool.[15]

In working on a new play, many actors testify to an initial period of trial and error before the image becomes clear. Geraldine Page, an outstanding American actress, sees her role developing like a jigsaw puzzle, a small piece at a time. Apparently many actors go through a similar experience until all at once "a bell rings" or "there is a spark" or "suddenly there is a click." Page makes an interesting observation concerning character identification:

> When you take the character over and use the character, you wreck the fabric of the play, but you can be in control of the character without taking the character over. When the character uses *you*, that's when you're really cooking. You know you're in complete control, yet you get the feeling you didn't do it. You have the beautiful feeling that you can't ruin it. You feel as if you were tagging along on an exciting journey. You don't completely understand it, and you don't have to. You're just grateful and curious.[16]

This statement suggests the interesting dichotomy of the actor who, although assuming the role of another character, still remains in complete control. Whether the actor's approach is emotional or sheerly technical, it must be recognized as a very personal and highly individualized process that defies complete definition or understanding. Nevertheless, there are certain general steps that may be followed.

Like the director, the actor's initial approach to a play is that of analysis—the search for the core idea, the spine. What does the play mean? What is the effect supposed to be on the audience? How is each role related to the complete play? Under the guidance and stimulation of the director, each performer analyzes the play to establish its basic interpretation.

Glenda Jackson, a courageous and tough-minded actress who has triumphed both on stage and in film, talks about the challenge of playing Ibsen:

> I found working on *Hedda Gabler* fascinating. We used a literal translation of the original Norwegian which I found was an extremely spare language with very few adjectives. The characters have a limited range of expression, they repeat themselves constantly, and they sit around and discuss life endlessly. They behave like a literary debating society with words and the expression of emotion. Through their words are the be-all and end-all of life. I've always wondered why I found them rather dull—interesting but dull—but they're not dull at all. They are absolutely meticulous pictures of what it's like to live in a small town in a country that is dark and cold . . . and it's marvelous. And all that black, black humour . . . zinging through.[17]

Jessica Tandy begins working from the text. Her blueprint for creating a part starts with reading a script as though she is reading a story, as an audience would read it.

> Then I go back, if I'm intrigued at all, and read the part again and see what it suggests. I get all kinds of pictures in my mind. It's those constant pictures and memories that evoke things. I find parallels in my life. Then I listen to the other actors. I don't think about it really, it just happens.[18]

The actor will want to know the style of the play and the production. By style is meant the *manner* of production, the *quality* of the actions and images. For example, it is obvious from the opening lines of *Hamlet* that the play is elevated in style, the language dignified and poetic, the action controlled. There is nothing

Ibsen's *Hedda Gabler,* one of the most challenging roles in modern drama, was performed at the Hartman Theater Company by Jane Alexander.

trivial or folksy about the guards and Horatio when they confront the ghost. Contrast *Hamlet* with the opening lines of *Death of a Salesman*—its ordinary characters and colloquial language. Its style suggests a domestic environment, with a husband and wife in a commonplace situation.

The style of the particular production is usually determined by the director, who may elect to stage the play in a manner other than the original one; for example, *The Taming of the Shrew* might be set in the wild West in the nineteenth century, or a Molière comedy may be done in a style that suggests the commedia dell'arte. Even when a play is done "straight," the author may see the characters playing at different levels simultaneously in order to convey both text and subtext.

Another view of acting style was suggested by Roger Planchon, the outstanding French director of Le Théâtre de la Cité in the suburbs of Lyons. He is primarily interested in bringing the experience of the theater to the common people. When asked by Planchon what kind of stories they would like to see, the factory workers suggested *The Three Musketeers*. A dramatization of Alexander Dumas's historical romance was made and proved to be an enormous hit. The play became a joyful vehicle for demythologizing a rigid view of French history. Played with great élan, the swashbuckling intrigue included movie techniques of Westerns and slapstick comedies—incongruous homely touches, such as Richelieu frying real eggs on stage and menials interrupting a royal ceremony to change the candles in the chandeliers. Planchon described the acting style he was seeking in these terms:

> I am trying to define a certain style, but it's very fine, very French, if you like, very . . . humorous to play the kind of theater I want. I need, as Brook has also said he needs for his kind of threater, *very intelligent actors*. The more intelligent they are, the more they can play what I want them to play. And another thing: my style is absolutely stripped bare of pathos. I think the Living Theater and others like them are fatally tempted by pathos. Not me, absolutely not. I've no taste for it at all, excess repels me. When I see an actor plunging into pathos, I always feel he is lying. In this I'm very Brechtian. I want someone to tell me a story I can watch smoking my pipe, and I don't want to have to ask myself questions about *feelings*. . . . I love relaxed performances.[19]

The analysis of the play should lead the actor to an understanding of the pervading atmosphere of the play. Does it suggest the hot, sensual quality of *A Streetcar Named Desire*? Is the mood one of menace, as if some alien force were trying to break in, as in many of Pinter's plays? Does the environment require the tempo and flavor of big-city corruption, as in some of Brecht's works? The dominant atmosphere of the play gives the actor clues to interpretation and the method of playing—the tempo, use of props, and business. From a study of the total play, the actor not only sees the relationship of one character to the action as a whole, as a part of a larger metaphor, but also finds many sources of inspiration for the interpretation of the spirit and quality of the playwright's creation.

After a performer has a clear comprehension of the play's structure, atmosphere, style, and basic interpretation, he or she studies the individual character, perhaps approaching the character from the outside—making an inventory of age, occupation, appearance, manner of speaking and moving, physical condition, posture, movement, carriage, and dress. Observations may be directly from life; if it is a period play, it will be profitable to study historical pictures showing the costume, architecture, and manners of the time. Stein, working with his excellent ensemble at the Hallenschen Schaubühne in West Berlin, found it worthwhile to spend considerable time getting acquainted with the cultural background of the play and the playwright through readings, seminars, and discussions.

The actor will find in the script four main sources of information about character: description, lines, actions, and reactions of others. The modern playwright frequently provides a character description, which includes some of the details just listed. Some playwrights, like Shaw, provide very complete portraits, down to the color of the nostrils. Some contemporary playwrights may simply give the actor the barest hint—"a waiter," "a young man of twenty-four," "a tramp." In period plays, the dramatist usually gives no character description at all.

The second source of information comes from the lines the actor speaks.

The playwright has usually taken great pains to write dialogue that represents and delineates the character. Lines, of course, are susceptible to a variety of interpretations, and it is obvious that two actors playing the same role may reveal marked differences in the reading of the dialogue. Indeed, the same actor may give a variety of interpretations of the same lines in different performances. The skillful playwright goes beyond the literal meaning of the words, using dialogue as a means of revealing character as well as advancing the plot. The actor, therefore, must search the lines for their essential meaning, in reference not only to the immediate context, but also to the revelation of the total character.

A third clue in the analysis of acting roles is the characters' actions. Are the individuals active agents or are they acted upon? What change do they undergo during the course of the play? What emotions are aroused? What are their primary objectives, and how do they go about reaching them? How much of the inner life is revealed by what the performers do? To what extent do they understand their own motives? What choices and decisions do they make and how do these affect their fortunes? Do their actions make them sympathetic characters? Playwrights must convey the inner lives of their characters in clear and concise ways, and very often the actions are more revealing than the words. The essential actions are usually created by the dramatist, but the director and performers also invent stage business that is significant in interpreting the roles. In any case, all the action in a performance should be relevant and essential to the meaning of the play.

A pertinent example occurs in *Sly Fox*, a modern revision of Ben Jonson's *Volpone;* it is based on the deceptive actions of Sly, who pretends to be dying in order to elicit gifts from his greedy acquaintances, who are hoping to become his beneficiary. The play opens with an action that is repeated throughout—Sly's feigned illness. He is heard groaning offstage; then he enters, supported by his valet, Able, and three servants. Sly appears to be at death's door, but when the servants leave, he is miraculously "cured."

Sly: *(Standing up on the bed)* No one's better! No one's more fit! *(Getting out of bed)* I've got enough health to start another man!

George C. Scott romped through the role of Sly, alternating his dying act with a vigorous contrast of ebullient life. His actions revealed his true character to the audience.

The actor's *way of acting* reveals character—not just what is done but *how* it is done. Many accomplished performers bring to their roles a wealth of detailed actions—pieces of business that give dimension and sharpness to the portraits they create. A case in point occurred in a production of David Rabe's play *The Basic Training of Pavlo Hummel,* a play about a misfit who hopes to find his manhood in Vietnam. (This is another part of Rabe's Vietnam War trilogy.) Using the metaphor of basic training and military service, Rabe builds up a vivid picture of a character who symbolizes all of life's unnoticed young men. Critic Jack Kroll describes Al Pacino's way of playing the part:

Like Ted Williams waiting for a pitch, Pacino builds potential energy out of a thousand jittery movements. He's one actor you want to film in slow motion. What you'd see would be a flow of behavioral hieroglyphics—jounce the pelvis, touch the hip, rub the face, swing the head, purse the mouth, shift the foot, paw the hair. Even the words come out reshaped by inner tension—the vowels mauled and flattened, the phrases syncopated with savage sensitivity.[20]

Finally, the actor learns a good deal about a role from the reactions of others. The actor must understand the character's dramatic purpose in the action, which is often revealed by the lines of another character. Shakespeare sometimes delineates characters sharply in this way: "Yon, Cassius, hath a lean and hungry look." Coriolanus was captured in one sentence: "When he walks, he moves like an engine, and the ground shrinks before his treading; he is able to pierce a corselet with his eyes, talks like a knell, and his hum is a battery." But it is mostly in the interactions of characters that the playwright indicates their motivations.

Rehearsals

The actor does not work in isolation; most preparation takes place in rehearsal with other members of the cast under the guidance of the director. It is in the rehearsal period that actors test their preliminary analysis of the role. By putting the characters on their feet in action, the actors find the valid basis for performance. Rehearsal is a time of learning and exploration. Many directors augment the work on the text by exercises and improvisations designed to open the text and explore the actors' potential. Selbourne's account of Brook's *Midsummer Night's Dream* rehearsals show how important experiments on sound, rhythm, and style were in shaping the production.

Rehearsals are periods of experimentation and discovery. Actors have the resources of the text, the director, the rest of the cast, and their own personal backgrounds on which to draw. It can be a complicated, frustrating, and fascinating experience because there are so many factors involved. In a professional production, the actor comes with a background of training and experience, so that he or she can concentrate on working with the rest of the company to interpret and communicate the play. In the educational or amateur theater, there may be many other problems to solve that involve basic work on speech and movement.

In any case, rehearsals are designed to solve problems. Through discussion, experimentation, and preliminary blocking, the director guides the efforts of the cast. Each individual works on an outline of the role, in keeping with the overall play and the style and interpretation set by the director. During these sessions, the director may work away from the text on training exercises, such as improvisation, in order to free the actor or stimulate the imagination. Rehearsals can be a painful time of floundering until an image comes clear.

Jessica Tandy talks about her experience in working on a play.

I'm always amazed when I start rehearsing a play. I go through a period of time when I haven't found anything, when I feel this is so boring, nothing is falling into place, nothing is happening. Why am I an actress? God, I've got to retire, do something else. I get through that searching stage and I've found a lot of things. Then I start throwing them out. Then: simplify, simplify, simplify. A part is never in place for me until opening night. It takes being gauged by the educated eye of the director, and then two or three weeks in front of the audience. Even after a year of playing a part, I find it interesting. I still discover new aspects. And when the play is over I continue to think about it.[21]

Once the problems of interpretation have been solved, actors are guided by the director in the process of communication, to make sure that the actors can be seen and heard, that the blocking reinforces the basic interpretation of the text, and that the actors are all playing in the same style. In short, the framework of the play has been filled in.

Then the tension of rehearsals gives way to the anxiety of how the play will work before an audience. Dress rehearsals and previews are used to see whether the play has achieved its goal.

Improvisation

One of the most effective tools for training actors from Stanislavski's time to the present is the use of improvisations. They are spontaneous inventions by the performers of actions, dialogue, and characters, usually around a basic idea, situation, or theme. Sometimes they are used to build a character—for example, to create imaginary scenes that are not in the play: Hamlet and the pirates, the Loman family picnic, Oedipus and his father at the crossroads, what happens at Helmer's when Nora leaves. Improvisations are useful in working on characterization away from the script, and help the actor to visualize a character more fully.

The interest in improvisation, especially at the college level, was due to the teaching methods of Viola Spolin, described in her text *Improvisation for the Theater* (1963). This is not a professional manual but, rather, a guide to group communication and cooperation. Spolin's games and exercises are effective ways of introducing a person to the performing arts without damaging the ego. A typical exercise is a group building game, in which one member begins constructing something with imaginary materials. Others join in the project as soon as they recognize what is going on. Another example is that of establishing an environment or specific place. One individual begins by pantomiming an action appropriate to the locale. A girl pretends to arrive at a bus station with a piece of luggage. Another person becomes the ticket seller, another is the janitor, another the relief driver, another a person waiting for a friend. The action continues until everyone is involved. The aim is a joint effort, with no one trying to dominate or star. Criticism is not personal but is directed at the total effect.

A very simple exercise is playing a game of tennis or volleyball without any equipment—first at normal speed, then in slow motion, then underwater, then as if you were blind, or old, or a small child.

Nowadays, improvisations may be public performances by skilled ensemble units, especially in playing revue material. Subjects and characters may be suggested by the audience, and the actors make up their dialogue and actions on the spur of the moment. Such groups, however, prepare for improvisation by working together for a long time in order to perfect their teamwork and to stimulate one another's imagination. Notable groups working with improvisations are the Premise, Second City, El Teatro Campesino, and Paul Sills's Story Theater.

ACTING IN THE NEW THEATER

Since the new theater rejected traditional drama and theater practices, it had to find new ways of acting. Sometimes it made this search by working on individual plays; in other instances, workshops were formed to find fresh ways of looking at theater, which meant either making up their own material or revising established plays to suit their needs. Most of the innovative work in the theater came out of groups that were dedicated to experimental acting techniques or politically motivated companies whose productions demanded unconventional methods.

At the Royal Shakespeare Company, Peter Brook began by conducting an actors' workshop with Charles Marowitz to investigate the potential of the "theater of cruelty" and to expose the actors to Artaudian techniques essential for Weiss's play. Similarly, Brook experimented freely with styles of performance in his famous production of *A Midsummer Night's Dream*. His rehearsals became a laboratory for investigating sounds, rhythms, and images to suit his vision of the drama's magical world. Rehearsals also became training periods for acquiring the circus skills that Brook imposed on the actions.

Joseph Chaikin's Open Theater began in 1963 in New York as a workshop to explore the art of acting. It was intended to be a private studio with no interest in public performance. Its aims were quite different from those of the professionally slanted school, in that the members were not primarily concerned with developing themselves for Broadway consumption. They rejected the psychoanalytical orientation to drama and to method acting. They were dedicated to ensemble play, to the interaction of one performer with another, and to the group as a whole. Said Chaikin, "The actor has to be willing to wake himself up out of this mesmerized state of being where he is unable to distinguish between a person and a picture of a person."

At the center of Chaikin's work was the actors' need to establish "presence"— an awareness of their own body; a sensitivity to the presence of others; and an acute consciousness of the meeting of lives at a specific moment and space, "a visceral confrontation." The actors must go beyond their "prepared responses" in order to *open up*. As Chaikin said, "We must open up to our deepest despair, to coldness around the heart, to the secret wishes about God."

C. W. E. Bigsby described Chaikin's efforts in this way:

In exploring the full potential of the actor, he was seeking simultaneously to assert the infinite capacities of man; in stressing not only the physical accomplishments of the actors and their ability to communicate across a wide range of emotions and through a wide variety of channels, but also their intellectual involvement in the creation of the drama which they perform, he was also offering a model of the integrated sensibility, a self restored to its own lost unity.[22]

Grotowski's "poor theater," the Polish Laboratory Theater, was an actor-oriented workshop whose methods won a worldwide reputation in the late 1960s and 1970s. Grotowski's actors had little interest in communication. Their emphasis was on developing discipline through acting techniques that free the body and mind. Avoiding the customary supporting production elements of scenery, lighting, and costuming, the actors sought to transform themselves before a small audience, selected for their seriousness of interest. By mastering a rigid control of all their faculties, and thereby eliminating the traditional blocks, the actors achieved a new awareness. Grotowski's kind of theater did not generate a wide following, but many young actors experimented with his exercises and found them useful in achieving ensemble integration and discipline.

Brook invited Grotowski and his company to visit London in 1967, and the impact on the workshops of the Royal Shakespeare Company was considerable. In 1969 the Laboratory Theater visited the United States, where it attracted a great deal of attention. Perhaps Grotowski's most direct influence in this country was in the Performance Group of Schechner, who had worked briefly with the Laboratory abroad.

Capitalizing on his experience with Grotowski, Schechner set up a series of exercises aimed at exploring personal potential, which was in a way a kind of group therapy, by exchanging "touches, places, ideas, anxieties, words, gestures, hostilities, rages, smells, glances, sounds, loves." When the group began rehearsing its version of Euripides' *The Bacchae,* intended to be "a dance, an ecstasy," in which the audience would participate, it was also an attempt to be an encounter with oneself.

Performances began with exercises derived from Grotowski, which were incorporated into a production. The text of the play was shortened, and words were sometimes split into syllables or prolonged as wails and elemental sounds. Actions became rituals, such as one based on a New Guinea tribal ceremony of rebirth. The performers enacted the roles in an ancient Greek play, but they also played themselves in an attempt to go beyond the mask to a kind of psychotherapy. Schechner challenged his actors to include the audience in a communal event—not just to tell a story but to search "for themes and gestures, for sounds and dances *vis-à-vis* audience and with ourselves."

In the Performance Group's production of *Commune* in 1970, the material came out of the players' personal backgrounds, their experiments in acting, and a study of American history, joined together in a collage arranged to investigate their roots.

The performers begin with improvised singing and talking; they tell in overlapping speeches of their personal background in relation to the Performance Group; then the evening erupts into a rapid pattern of transformations that defies time and demands the spectator's engagement. As the performers reenact their personal beginnings, they discover archetypal beginnings; out of animal sounds and undefined movements, they become a boat and its inhabitants, as water is scooped and dripped from the tub; they sing revival songs, play cops and robbers, feed and become monkeys, act out scenes from *Lear, Richard III, The Tempest,* and *Moby Dick.* All of these are discovered as part of their matrices; they are not cute memorabilia, but metaphors for finding meaning, performed by a people digging out their own roots.[23]

This work reminds us of Mnouchkine's Théâtre du Soleil's experiments in developing styles for *1789,* which showed the "rough" kind of performing of the common people as a contrast to the highly artificial, genteel style of the aristocracy; we also think of their productions of Shakespeare's *Twelfth Night* and *Richard II,* which featured an assortment of techniques from Japanese Noh, Kabuki, and Bunraku; Indian dancing; and suggestions of the commedia dell'arte.

Similar experiments with exotic styles were used by Ludlow's Theater of the Ridiculous, the San Francisco Mime Troupe, and the Mabou Mines Company, ranging from spoofs of romanticized cinematic acting, puppetry, soul and rock performances, Italian comedy, circus and carnival shows, and nineteenth-century flamboyant melodrama to the burlesquing of the high styles of French neoclassicism and Elizabethan and Greek theater.

Although many experimental groups have come and gone, the impact of their work has not been lost. Today there is a much freer, more eclectic attitude toward actors and their training, and inevitably, their influence has been felt not only in offbeat plays but also in productions of drama in the mainstream.

Sam Shepard has been especially demanding, because his plays are such mixtures of vivid and often incongruous images, intuitive creations reflecting a wide spectrum of influences—the "car culture" of the young, science fiction, Westerns, television in its pop or junk aspects, circuses, ceremonials, medicine shows, hallucinatory experiences, magic, graphic arts, and popular music of various kinds. Somehow, Shepard manages to integrate this welter of pop and outercultures. Although he is not an absurdist, his affinity to Beckett, Pinter, and Ionesco is apparent in his rejection of linear construction, logically developed sequences, diction with precise meanings, and unified or consistent characterization.

In his preface to *Angel City* in 1976, Shepard made this revealing statement:

> The term "character" could be thought of in a different way when working on this play. Instead of the idea of a "whole character" with logical motives behind his behavior which the victor submerges himself into, he should consider instead a fractured whole with bits and pieces of character flying off the central theme. In other words, more in terms of collage construction or jazz improvisation.[24]

Such an explanation from the playwright brings with it a new perspective to the actor.

Shepard's contribution to the new theater is that he is in time with the revolutionary and experimental fervor of those searching for fresh ways of using the stage. He is a catalytic force in breaking down the boundaries of the established patterns of playwriting. In his efforts he has, of course, taken risks. His spontaneous, volatile, and often unorganized methods make his work seem fragmented and incomplete, but the compensation is in the vigorous and vivid spirit that animates all his plays. His plays are collages of powerful images for performance, and this is why he is the most important American playwright in the new theater.

As performers in the new theater reject many of the practices of the past, they search for a style based on theatricalism. Actors often become *agents of the action,* with the meaning residing in the performance, not in the person who performs it. For example, in watching a double play in a baseball game, the fan's interest is in how the shortstop fields the ball and tosses it to the second baseman, who in turn fires it to first base. There is little or no thought about the psychological significance behind the actions. Likewise, during a concert, the listener's attention is engaged by the pianist or vocalist as a performer, not as a complex character whose playing reveals his or her psyche. Similarly, in the current theater, the actor may simply play the *action,* not the *role.* The style may be cool, detached, or even flat—without emotional content.

The acting style may be frankly theatrical, like that of a storyteller in front of children. Or actors may engage in transformations, like a person assuming several roles while telling a joke. Actors may suggest several parts simultaneously, exchange roles with one another, go through warm-up exercises before the play begins, change costumes and makeup before the audience, and set the stage and move the furniture. Although *Amadeus* is not a play for the new theater (it has a clear narrative and a beginning, middle, and end, and the characterization is coherently developed), it nevertheless exhibits the new theatricalism; for example, Salieri, who talks directly to the audience throughout the play, begins Act I, Scene 2, as a man of seventy in a wheelchair and, a few minutes later rises, takes off his dressing gown, and becomes a young man in the prime of life—a handsomely dressed, successful composer of the 1780s.

Actors in the new theater may improvise their dialogue and actions, speak a synthetic language, use gibberish or animal sounds, speak simultaneously or mouth tape recorded dialogue, or create a cacophony of unintelligible sounds. They may stress mime and dance, simulate puppets, begin actions that are never completed, avoid moving altogether, or make changes without transitions. They may play deadpan, play behind clown faces or masks, or appear as ciphers without motivation or meaning. In an attempt to go beyond the literal word, performers may present a welter of sensory signals that many traditional theatergoers cannot or will not follow. But despite the disparity between the old style of acting and the new, one essential binds them together: the living presence of the performers; only they can make theater.

Three versatile actors, Walter Matthau, Maureen Stapleton, and Jack Lemmon, appeared together in Sean O'Casey's *Juno and the Paycock* at the Mark Taper Forum. All three are equally at home on stage or before a camera.

FILM ACTING

In the movies, the star is the most important box office attraction. Occasionally, a story or director may generate primary interest, but by and large, film depends on its stars. Their names are household words, their lives are always hot copy— they, along with our sport stars, are about the only aristocracy we have.

Most actors who go from stage to screen comment that the main difference is the absence of a live audience. Stage actors are familiar with playing to a live audience and adapting their performance to the circular response that takes place only in the theater. A second difference is due to the nature of the medium. On film, the basic unit is the *shot* or *take*—a short segment of the action recorded by the camera. The editor combines these into segments of the narrative, called *sequences,* which resemble the chapters in a book. Shots may be of a few seconds' duration, such as those of horror-stricken faces of witnesses of an accident. Or they may be of considerable length—such as a leisurely view of a canoe gliding across placid waters.

Because a film is the composite of many shots, each one made separately, it is not necessary to shoot the film in its final narrative form. The editor organizes the shots. Films are not rehearsed in their entirety like stage plays. Usually, scenes or shots are rehearsed separately, each one just before a take. The director rehearses the actors until he gets what he wants, and then several takes are made. The director views the daily "rushes" and decides if the shots were satisfactory. The shooting sequence is determined by a number of factors, such as the various locales used and the availability of the actors. The actor may have to play his most important scenes first. This lack of an orderly sequence requires the actor to make full use of his imaginative concentration, so that each shot is consistent to the character and expressive enough to create the desired effect. Film actors have the advantage of making numerous shots before they get it right.

In film acting, the actor's face is very important, because the camera can make close-ups that magnify the image and reveal subtleties of expression not seen from a stage. Moreover, the flexibility of the camera can do a great deal to reinforce the actor's performance by using bright or soft lighting, varied angles, and different tempos. Such acting demands a face that has great vitality. Although the director and technical staff can do a great deal to support the actors, ultimately the actors themselves create the total effect through every frame, by every word they speak and every movement they make. The notion that anyone with good looks can walk on the set and become a star is a myth. Most of the top film stars have an extensive background of learning their craft on the stage: Jessica Tandy, Peggy Ashcroft, Maggie Smith, Joanne Woodward, Katharine Hepburn, Glenda Jackson, Meryl Streep, Shirley MacLaine, Geraldine Page, Jack Lemmon, George C. Scott, Marlon Brando, Paul Newman, Gene Hackman, Richard Dreyfuss, Dustin Hoffman, Ben Kingsley, and William Hurt.

PLAYS TO READ AND SEE

F = Film Available; V = Videotape Available.

F		Jerzy Grotowski, *Akropolis* (16 mm B&W)
F	V	*Approaches to Hamlet*
F	V	Edmund Rostand, *Cyrano de Bergerac*
F	V	*Exploring a Character* (Shakespeare)
F	V	William Shakespeare, *Hamlet, Henry V, Othello, King Lear* (Royal Shakespeare Company)
F		*Marat/Sade* (RSC)

F   V   *Preparing to Perform Shakespeare*
F   V   *Rehearsing the Text* (Royal Shakespeare Company on Film for the
Humanities)
David Rabe, *Sticks and Bones*
F   V   Anton Chekhov, *The Three Sisters* (directed by Laurence Olivier)
(Two interesting films about theater are *The Dresser* and *The Producers*.)

BIBLIOGRAPHY

BENEDETTI, ROBERT L. *The Actor at Work*, 3rd ed. Englewood Cliffs, N.J.: Prentice-Hall, 1981.

BOLESLAVSKY, RICHARD. *Acting: The First Six Lessons*. New York: Theater Arts Books, 1933.

CHAIKIN, JOSEPH. *The Presence of the Actor: Notes on the Open Theater*. New York: Atheneum, 1972.

COLE, TOBY, and HELEN KRICH CHINOY. *Actors on Acting*. New York: Crown, 1980.

FRANKLIN, MIRIAM A., and JAMES G. DIXON III. *Rehearsal: The Principles and Practices of Acting for the Stage*. Englewood Cliffs, N.J.: Prentice-Hall, 1983.

FUNK, GEORGE, and JOHN E. BOOTH, eds. *Actors Talk about Acting*. New York: Random House, 1961.

GAM, RITA. *Actors: A Celebration*. New York: St. Martin's Press, 1988.

GAM, RITA. *Actress to Actress*. New York: Nick Lyons Books, 1986.

GLENN, STANLEY. *The Complete Actor*. Boston: Allyn and Bacon, 1977.

HETHMON, ROBERT, ed. *Strasberg at the Actors' Studio*. New York: Viking Press, 1965.

KURITZ, PAUL. *Playing: An Introduction to Acting*. Englewood Cliffs, N.J.: Prentice-Hall, 1982.

LEWIS, ROBERT. *Advice to the Players*. New York: Harper & Row, 1980.

SAINT-DENIS, MICHAEL. *Training for the Theater, Promises and Promises*. New York: Theater Arts Books, 1982.

SPOLIN, VIOLA. *Improvisation in the Theater*. Evanston, Ill.: Northwestern University Press, 1983.

SPOLIN, VIOLA. *Theater Games for the Classroom: A Teacher's Handbook*. Evanston, Ill.: Northwestern University Press.

STANISLAVSKI, CONSTANTIN. *An Actor Prepares*. New York: Theater Arts Books, 1963.

STANISLAVSKI, CONSTANTIN. *Creating a Role*, trans. E. R. Hapgood. New York: Theater Arts Books, 1961.

NOTES

1. William Shakespeare, *Hamlet*, Act II, Scene II.

2. Sylvia Drake, *Los Angeles Times*, June 9, 1990.

3. Clive Barnes, *New York Times*, June 27, 1975.

4. Jack Lemmon, interviewed by Rita Gam in *Actors: A Celebration* (New York: St. Martin's Press, 1988), p. 14.

5. Nikolai M. Gorchakov, *Stanislavski Directs*, trans. Miriam Goldina (New York: Funk & Wagnalls, 1958).

6. Eliot Norton, quoted in *The Stratford Scene, 1959–1968*, ed. Peter Raby (Toronto: Clarke, Irwin, 1968).

7. August Strindberg, Preface to *Miss Julie*, in *Plays of Strindberg*, Vol. 1, trans. Edith Oland and Warner Oland (New York: Bruce Humphries. 1912).

8. Gorchakov, *Stanislavski Directs.*

9. Peter Brook, *The Empty Space* (New York: Atheneum, 1969).

10. Ibid.

11. Lillian Ross, "Profiles: The Player," *New Yorker,* October 21, 1961; October 28, 1961; November 4, 1961. Copyright © 1961 The New Yorker Magazine, Inc., October 26, 1961. Reprinted by permission.

12. Joanne Woodward, interviewed by Rita Gam in *Actress to Actress* (New York: Nick Lyons Books, 1986), p. 11. Copyright © 1986 by Rita Gam.

13. Ben Kingsley, interviewed by Rita Gam in *Actors: A Celebration,* p. 124.

14. Joanne Woodward, in Gam, *Actress to Actress,* p. 116.

15. Michael Redgrave, interviewed by Richard Findlater in *Great Acting,* ed. Hal Burton (New York: Hill and Wang, 1967).

16. Ross, "The Player."

17. Glenda Jackson, in Gam, *Actress to Actress,* p. 83.

18. Jessica Tandy, in Gam, *Actress to Actress,* p. 153.

19. Roger Planchon, interviewed by Michael Kustow in "Creating a Theater of Real Life," *Theater Quarterly,* 2(5), January–March 1972.

20. Jack Kroll, *Newsweek,* May 9, 1977.

21. Jessica Tandy, in Gam, *Actress to Actress,* p. 155.

22. C. W. E. Bigsby, *Twentieth Century American Drama,* Vol. 3 (Cambridge: Cambridge University Press, 1985).

23. William L. Trilby, "Commune," *Educational Theater Journal,* May 1971.

24. Sam Shepard, Preface to *Angel City, Curse of the Starving Class, and Other Plays* (New York: Urizen Books, 1976).

eleven
The Designer

One of the outstanding contemporary scenographers is Ladislaw Vychodil. His design for Janacke's *Makropolus* shows the concept of a stage setting as an assemblage of varied elements. (Slovak National Theater, Bratislava, Czechoslovakia)

You go to the theater to *see* a play; it is a *show*. Your hungry eye expects to see fascinating people involved in action supported by dramatic lighting, sound, scenery, and costuming. Years ago, radio was our most popular means of communication, but television superseded it because we like to see what is going on, as well as hear it. We can empathize with the action. Reading a newspaper can be a satisfactory way to learn what is happening in the world, but listening to the radio cannot compete with *watching* the news. The box score is no substitute for a live ball game.

Although film has taken over the main burden of satisfying the public's craving for the spectacular, in such efforts as *Star Trek, Raiders of the Lost Ark, Dark Shadows, Outer Limits, 2001: A Space Odyssey,* and *The Hunt for Red October,* the live theater does not neglect visual appeal, as almost any musical demonstrates. Think of, *Cats, Gypsy, Les Miserables, City of Angels, Grand Hotel,* and *Phantom of the Opera.*

Although most plays begin as words, written texts, a large part of the appeal of the theater comes from the visual aspects: the performers in action, scenery, lighting, and costumes. Greek and Elizabethan dramatic productions made little use of stage scenery as we know it, but they were filled with eye-catching costumes, dances, movement, and pageantry. During the Italian Renaissance, the scenery ran away with the show; and in the eighteenth and nineteenth centuries, striking stage settings were often such a feature of the productions that admission prices were raised because of their sensational appeal.

THE PICTORIAL TRADITION

The convention of pictorial representation of the dramatic environment is only a few centuries old. Medieval drama, with its manifold stations, often was staged with elaborate attention to realistic detail to secure the maximum amount of identification from the spectator, especially in the scenes from Paradise and Hell. Essentially, however, our scenic tradition stems from the Renaissance innovation of the proscenium arch at the Farnese Theatre in Parma, Italy (1618). This theater exerted an enormous influence on playwriting and on all phases of production, especially on stage design, which continues to affect our practice today.

Two factors were especially influential in the kinds of sets that appeared in the new proscenium arch theaters. First, the Italian painters were intrigued by the potential of design with linear perspective, by which they could produce the illusion of depth on a flat surface. This development led to the construction and painting of scenery built of wood and canvas, in direct imitation of architecture and natural phenomena. Verisimilitude and solidity were given to the settings by making those units nearest to the audience three dimensional and gradually reducing the space between set pieces until the upstage area was completely two dimensional. As time went on, perspective settings became more and more elaborate, until they became astonishing mazes of corridors, fountains, pillars, and buildings so huge and spectacular that the actor was completely dwarfed onstage.

The Bibiena family inaugurated the use of several vistas by running their perspective scenery at divergent angles, thus making possible overwhelming visual displays.

The second factor influencing stage decoration was the custom of creating extravagant "effects"—floats and arches for court pageants and festivals. This taste for ostentatious display and the novelty of perspective scenery were combined in the theater when designers swamped the stage not only with eye-filling scenery but also with all manner of sensational mechanical stunts, such as great floating clouds and chariots, dazzling practical fountains, and enormous fires that were frighteningly real. Although at first the perspective set served as a neutral background for the production of many plays, under royal and aristocratic patronage the practice was to create specific scenery and effects for specific plays and occasions. Thus, the tradition was established of illusional picture settings—a tradition from which the theater has not entirely escaped to this day.

As the public stage grew and professional companies were forced to make their own way financially, it was impossible for many theaters to afford the expense of extravagant scenery. Furthermore, the action of many plays demanded scenery that could be shifted rapidly. A mechanical system was developed, consisting of backdrops and wing-pieces on which were painted a variety of scenes. Wings were portable screens of wood and canvas that could be slid in and out of grooves at the sides of the stage. Rows of these wings, set parallel to the footlights, lined the acting area. Entrances and exits were made by simply walking between the wings. A series of backdrops was flown at the rear of the stage, completing the vista of the setting. Overhead, borders of canvas masked the flies from the spectator. Although these stock pieces were obviously two-dimensional painted contrivances, they satisfied the audience's taste for reality. Not only were individual pieces of scenery standardized, but every theater owned a series of stock sets, such as an Italian garden, a prison, a mountain pass, a drawing room, a woodland glade, a kitchen, and a palace. These stock sets were used again and again as the various plays demanded. Occasionally, extra care and money were expended to design and construct scenery for specific productions, at which time this fact became a special point of publicity.

In England, Charles Kean, at the Princess Theater (1850–1859), set a new standard for staging plays that were carefully rehearsed and lavishly mounted and costumed. Often called the "illustrator" of Shakespeare's plays, Kean used every opportunity to achieve spectacular effects with scenery, properties, and costumes that were historically correct. His example was influential, especially in the Shakespearean productions of Henry Irving. But by and large, most drama in the eighteenth and nineteenth centuries was performed in stock sets of standardized units of wings and backdrops.

In the chapter on realism we noted the effort in the nineteenth century to achieve authentic environment, not only for visual appeal, but also as a conditioning force on character. The naturalists, in particular, went to great lengths to make their settings as credible as possible. In Paris, Andre Antoine went so far as to hang raw meat onstage for a scene in a butcher shop. The naturalists' excessive concern with imitating the surface aspects of life led to clutter when they attempted to implement the idea of the "significant trifle."

The realists were more moderate, emphasizing simplification and selectivity. In their production of Robertson's plays (1870s), the Bancrofts marked a new approach to realism on the English stage with stage settings that gave the appearance of the appropriate environments, coupled with an acting style that emphasized character and accurate stage business. Their productions won approval for the box set and for the convention of the "fourth wall"—the performers created the illusion that there was an invisible wall across the stage frame, and there was no direct communication with the audience.

A box set consists of three walls of framed canvas and usually a ceiling to enclose the playing area, inside of which the performance takes place. It is usually set with furniture to create the effect of a room, and it is provided with practical doors for exits and entrances.

As an example of a box set, here are Ibsen's stage directions for the setting of his *An Enemy of the People:*

Renaissance perspective settings with their ornate style of decoration nearly dwarfed the performers. The designer Giuseppe Bibiena was a member of a family of designers who dominated the stages of Europe in the seventeenth and eighteenth centuries.

Evening. Dr. Stockmann's sitting-room; simply but neatly decorated and furnished. In the wall to the right are two doors, the further one leading to the hall, the nearer one to the Doctor's study. In the opposite wall, facing the hall door, a door leading to the other rooms of the house. Against the rear wall stands the stove; further forward a sofa, and behind it an oval table with a cover. On the table, a lighted lamp, with a shade. In the back wall an open door leading to the dining-room, in which is seen a supper-table, with a lamp on it.[1]

In the United States, David Belasco (1854–1931) achieved a reputation for his realistic staging by such ventures as reproducing onstage a Child's restaurant, which was daily stocked by the firm with food, and by buying and bringing onstage, for *The Easiest Way*, the contents of a boarding house, including the wallpaper. Belasco was also an innovator in new lighting effects, and his handling of crowd scenes was outstanding.

The effect of wiping out the tradition of painted perspective scenery brought a new sense of the material rightness of things, and the stage was filled with casual objects of daily living. Most important, the idea was accepted that scenery should serve as the specific and appropriate environment for the action of the play.

However, with all arts, there is a constant ebb and flow, an action and a reaction. Realism was no sooner the accepted way of staging drama than it was challenged by the appearance of plays written in defiance of realistic practices, as in the works of Maeterlinck, Claudel, Yeats, and Hauptmann. But even more significant was the appearance of two pioneering spirits, endowed with poetic fervor and imagination, who led the way toward new stagecraft, Gordon Craig and Adolphe Appia.

Gordon Craig

Although Gordon Craig was trained and experienced in the English legitimate theater, his contribution does not lie in the practical aspects of scene painting and construction but rather in his point of view, which was that of a visionary who crusaded for an ideal art of the theater. He castigated the contemporary stage for its shabbiness, for its exaggeration of realistic detail, and most of all for its lack of artistic purpose and direction. Craig conceived of the theater as an aesthetic unity in which all aspects of production would be harmonized. Toward this end, he called for a director who would achieve this unified concept. Impatient with actors, Craig even suggested replacing them with supermarionettes. His concept of design was based on the selection of a few simple, symbolic set pieces and properties, as his description of a designer illustrates:

And remember he does not merely sit down and draw a pretty or historically accurate design, with enough doors and windows in picturesque places, but he first of all chooses certain colors which seem to him to be in harmony with the spirit of the play, rejecting other colors as out of tune. He then weaves into a pattern certain objects—an arch, a fountain, a balcony, a bed—using the chosen objects which are mentioned in the play, and which are necessary to be seen.[2]

A drawing by Adolphe Appia for Wagner's opera *Die Walküre,* 1892. Atmosphere is created by skillful use of light and the plastic quality of the setting.

     Craig sought to replace imitation with suggestion, elaboration with simplicity. He insisted on the spiritual relationship between setting and action. He pointed out the emotional potential of figures moving in design, of shifting light and shadow, of the dramatic values of color. He emphasized that the theater was above all "a place for seeing." Craig illustrated his ideas with a series of provocative designs, and he sought to demonstrate his theories in production; sometimes these were doomed to failure because of impracticability, but sometimes they were brilliantly successful. Craig's contribution was not, however, in the utilitarian aspects of the theater; his real significance was in his dream, which he persuaded others to see by the compelling force of his enthusiasm and argument.

Adolphe Appia

The other pioneer of modern staging was the Swiss Adolphe Appia, who in 1899 published his seminal work *Die Musik und die Inscenierung,* in which he called for reforms in the theater. Appia began with the actor and insisted that the design must be in harmony with the living presence of the performer. When a forest was required onstage, for example, it was not necessary to give an accurate representation but only to create the atmosphere of a person amid the trees. The attention of the audience should be focused on the character, not distracted by detailed branches and leaves. Painted stage settings are incompatible with the actor because of the contrast between the actor's plasticity and the flatness of the scenic surroundings:

> The human body does not seek to produce the illusion of reality *since it is in itself reality!* What it demands of the *decor* is simply to set in relief this reality. . . . We must free staging of everything that is in contradistinction with the actor's presence. . . . Scenic illusion is the living presence of the actor.[3]

Appia suggested two tenets of good design: the lighting should emphasize the plasticity of the human form, rather than destroy it, and a plastic scene should give the actor's movements all their value. Implicit in Appia's theories is the fundamental unity of all phases of production, the major emphasis being on the actor. Appia enforced his arguments by applying them to a series of designs for the production of Richard Wagner's operas, fashioning uncluttered settings of simple forms in which skillful lighting created a remarkably appropriate and effective atmosphere. Appia's theories were well timed, since they coincided with the invention in 1879 of the electric light, which gave theatrical production a marvelous dimension in design. Until that time, stage lighting was an awkward and dangerous aspect of production, in which almost all effort went into merely getting enough light on the stage so that the audience could see. With electricity, lighting could be used for its evocative potential in creating and enhancing the mood of the play. Appia was the first to demonstrate this new force aesthetically.

The sparks kindled by Craig and Appia ignited, and the "new stagecraft" made its appearance, based on the generally accepted point of view that scenery should augment and reinforce the atmosphere and meaning of the play and that it should give the actor a serviceable environment. This point of view is apparent from the following representative statements: John Gassner regards the function of the setting as a "psychological frame of reference"; Marc Blitzstein says that scenery "should be used to pull the play along its intended course"; and Harold Clurman stresses its practicability—"A set is a utensil which cannot be judged until its worth is proved in practice by the whole course of the play's development onstage."

In discussing modern staging, it is important to distinguish between two points of view. First, *representationalism* endeavors to create the illusion of actuality. The characters and events onstage for the moment are intended to convey real life. The second attitude, *presentationalism*, frankly admits that the theater is make-believe and that the actors are only pretending. Though less familiar to Western audiences, presentational staging has a long tradition, notably in the oriental theater, where symbolic conventions are readily accepted. Two coolies, carrying banners on which are painted wheels, become a carriage; a stick becomes a horse when an actor mounts it; a table may be a bridge, a bed, or a mountaintop.

Wilder was the first to successfully introduce presentationalism to the Broadway stage with *Our Town* (1937); he blended the theatricalist elements of absence of scenery and a combined stage manager, narrator, and bit player with a

In the 1938 production of *Our Town* that pioneered presentational staging, the environment was suggested by a few pieces of furniture, properties, costuming, and lighting. This is the setting for George's funeral.

foundation of realistic characterization. Williams followed with *The Glass Menagerie* (1945), in which Tom sets the perspective of the "memory play" as the drama begins by talking directly to the audience and then moving back and forth between playing the role of the brother in the action and stepping outside the fourth wall as narrator and commentator.

Realistic, representational staging is appropriate only to those plays, beginning with Ibsen, written in the realistic mode and intended by the playwright for performance on the picture-frame stage. Dramas written outside the realistic mode are presentational by virtue of their creation for such conventions as the masked male actors of the Greek theater and the poetry, soliloquies, and open, flexible platform stage of the Elizabethans. These conventionalized forms of theater created a unified illusion without self-conscious deception. The spectators were aware that they were in a theater and that what was taking place before them was an arbitrary, aesthetic invention, but nevertheless, one powerful enough to arouse deep feelings.

The impact of an action in the theater does not depend on its accuracy so much as on the quality of the performance. An obviously artificial and stylized piece of business can be enormously affecting—for example, in *Equus* when the boy stabs out the eyes of the horses, which are actors wearing sculptured wire heads.

Meyerhold and Constructivism

One of the most important innovators in the modern theater was the Russian Vsevolod Meyerhold. Although he was not a designer, he was known for his bold theatricalism—using a presentational approach to staging, especially his *constructivism*. Inspired by the machine and reacting against the ostentatious décor of the czarist regime, the constructivist created stage settings of skeletonized ramps, staircases, bridges, and similar structural forms. The spectator saw the bare bones of the setting against the backstage brick wall, unrelieved by any decorative or aesthetic intention. The set was based entirely on its practicability as a tool for action. Its advantages were that it was frankly theatrical, it gave the performer extraordinary opportunities for movement and the use of space, and it invited fluent and uninterrupted action. Meyerhold made full use of these advantages, even to developing a style of acting, "biomechanics," suited to the machine age, a style that included training in acrobatics, circus movement, and ballet.

EPIC THEATER

One of the most interesting efforts in experimental drama was the *epic theater,* which began in the 1920s as a result of the work of Piscator and Brecht. As we have seen, Brecht, in addition to being a director, was also a playwright who put his theories into practice, even to inventing a new approach to acting, like Meyerhold. Epic theater workers revolted against the tradition of Ibsenian realism. They were not concerned with the domestic problems of a husband and wife in a home; epic drama called for a larger arena of action, showing the dynamics of social forces at work. Hence, the epic theater playwright and designer demanded a stage that would serve for many fragments of action, some of them occurring simultaneously.

In 1928, Piscator's production of *The Good Soldier Schweik* offered a brilliant and stimulating example of the new style. A dramatization of a novel, the play concerns the life of a private soldier ground down by the stupidity and brutality of war. His story is told in a kaleidoscopic arrangement of scenes, recitations, songs, and explanations. In addition to the usual facilities of the stage, Piscator used slides, posters, charts, maps, graphs, a treadmill for moving scenery and actors, and a motion picture screen on which were projected cartoons, captions, and film sequences—all joined together in a welter of sights and sounds.

Gorelik describes the nature of Piscator's production:

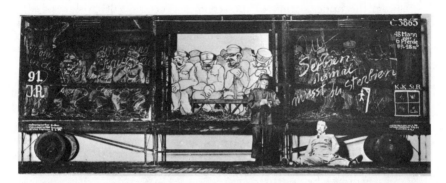

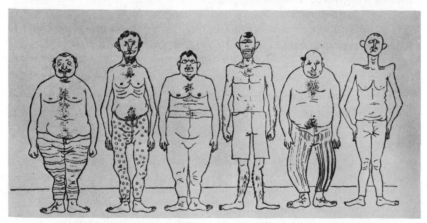

Erwin Piscator's "epic" staging of _The Good Soldier Schweik_ in Berlin, 1927, used all elements of staging in a presentational style.

"I'll do my duty for the Emperor to the end," adds Schweik. On the screen a Russian soldier is swimming in a pond. A bush rolls on with the Russian's uniform hanging on it. "A souvenir," thinks Schweik. He puts it on. A shot rings out, and a Hungarian patrol rushes on and seizes him in loud Hungarian tones. "What do you mean, prisoner?" Schweik demands. "I'm on your side . . ." A shell bursts. Schweik falls. From the upper corner of the screen a procession of crosses starts toward the audience. As the crosses, growing nearer in perspective, reach the lower edge of the screen, a muslin drop, lowered downstage, catches them once more, bringing them still closer to the spectators. A rain of crosses falls upon this wry comedy as the lights begin to go up.[4]

Brecht's *The Private Life of the Master Race,* another epic play, dramatizes the experiences of a German Panzer crew, moving across Europe from the early stages of World War II until it is defeated by the Russians. The play is really a series of one-acts, depicting the effects of Nazism and warfare on the crew. The various threads are knit together by lyrical passages. The play begins with this stage direction:

> (*A band plays a barbaric march. Out of the darkness appears a big signpost:* To Poland *and near it a Panzer truck. Its wheels are turning. On it sit twelve to sixteen soldiers, steel helmeted, their faces white as chalk, their guns between their knees. They could be puppets. The soldiers sing to the tune of the Horst Wessel Song.*)[5]

There follows a series of scenes such as "The Betrayal," "The Jewish Wife," and "The Informer," dramatizing various phases of Nazi terrorism until the Panzer is bogged down in Russia. The sequences are bridged by voices out of the darkness and the roar of the armored car.

Brecht's presentational style rejected the realistic theater of illusion and the notion of ornamentation and display. Scenery was spare and skeletal; the lighting was used to illuminate the stage so that everything was clear, not to create atmosphere through suggestive colors and shadows. No attempt was made to conceal light sources; instruments were mounted in galleries, boxes, or pipe battens, in full view of the audience. Since attending the theater was educational, Brecht used visual aids such as projected slides, maps, charts, and diagrams. Working in the Berliner Ensemble (1947–1956), Brecht demonstrated in his own plays, as well as in a dozen others, his approach to the theater in such a compelling way that he is regarded as one of the most influential forces in the modern theater.

STAGE SCENERY

Stage scenery has three purposes. The primary function of the setting is to create a *useful playing area* for the actor. The set, like domestic architecture, must be designed for the people who use it. In the theater, this means placing the entrances for effective use, providing ample space for all the movement and staging of important scenes—and for any special needs, such as a collapsing barber chair in *Sweeney Todd,* or a steep step unit for *Noises Off,* or a fold-up bed as in nearly any Feydeau farce.

In designing an Ibsenian interior for a few characters, the utilitarian setting is no problem. But when the script calls for a great deal of action, as the nineteenth-century melodramas did, it is difficult to take care of actors' needs when they must climb trestles, leap off bridges, or get caught in storms and train wrecks. That is why film was invented.

In our current theater, the designer is especially challenged in musicals, which reflect their melodramatic backgrounds—in chases, kidnappings, battles, and escapes in such productions as *The Phantom of the Opera* and *Les Misérables.* Another current trend of dramatizing novels like *Nicholas Nickleby* and *The Grapes of Wrath,* with their frequent changes in locale, also necessitates designing sets that are utilitarian.

Secondly, scenery must create the *appropriate mood* or atmosphere. We have just seen how Ibsen's *Ghosts* calls for a set that is cold and brooding, created by the use of pictorial elements of the fjord and the rain. At the very outset of *Macbeth,* an eerie atmosphere must be created for the appearance of the three witches, as it must, in *Hamlet* for the entrance of the King's Ghost.

John Lee Beatty's experience in designing Henley's offbeat *Crimes of the Heart* shows how the designer is involved in setting the mood.

> I started working on the ground floor plan. There's a bed in the kitchen—makes no sense. There's a door to the grandfather's bedroom off the kitchen—it doesn't make any sense. Then I finally realized, "Oh, it doesn't make any sense"; and then it was clear to me. Once I understood that it was all crazy, I intentionally tried to make it seem thrown together, even though it is a realistic box set.[6]

In addition to the use of line, shape, and proportion, the present-day designer has a marvelous tool for evoking mood in the use of light. Today's equipment is extremely flexible in its use of color, intensity, direction, and movement.

A third function of scene design is to locate the *time and place* of the action. In the Greek theater, playwrights paid little attention to the locale, except in general terms—and there was no scenery. For *The Suppliants,* Aeschylus simply calls for "a sacred precinct near the shore in Argos." For *Oedipus Rex,* Sophocles notes, "Before the palace of Oedipus at Thebes." Similarly, in the Elizabethan theater, there was no pictorial scenery. *Hamlet* requires several different locations in Act I: "Scene 1—Elsinore. A platform before the Castle"; "Scene 2—A Room of State in the Castle"; "Scene 3—A Room in Polonius' House"; "Scene 4—The Platform"; "Scene 5—Another Part of the Platform." Shakespeare's audiences were expected to use their imagination—stimulated, of course, by superb language.

During the Renaissance, with the introduction of the proscenium arch and pictorial scenery, the stage setting became one of the features of the theater. Since it was a common practice to use stock sets, the dramatists often simply stipulated: "Scene 1—A Garden"; "Scene 2—A Tavern"; "Scene 3—A Hall"; and so on. Stock sets were used, and the other requirements of place might be met by costuming or the dialogue of the play. When special scenery was introduced, theater managers raised admission prices. As we have seen earlier, when melodrama became popular in the nineteenth century, the stage scenery became one of the most important aspects of production, not so much to locate the place as to create sensational effects and to accommodate the actors' violent performances. For the upper classes, Charles Kean, in the mid-nineteenth century, made a fetish of staging productions of Shakespeare with elaborate and greatly detailed settings.

With the coming of realism, stage sets became specific for another reason. All at once, people became conscious of the conditioning influence of the environment. Plays that dealt with sociological issues needed to show the formative influences on the characters' behavior. Thus, Ibsen's *Ghosts* calls for a set with a glass wall through which "a gloomy fjord-landscape is faintly visible, veiled by a steady rain." At the end of the play, Oswald, who had fled from this dismal atmosphere to Paris in search of *joie de vivre*, returns home, a victim of hereditary venereal disease. The last words he can utter are, "Mother, give me the sun, the sun."

In his *Doll's House*, Ibsen requires a domestic interior of a middle-class family in Norway in 1890. The play opens when Nora, vivacious and charming, enters through the door laden with Christmas presents, humming gaily. Two hours later, shaken by her husband's cowardice and lack of compassion, she leaves him and goes out the door—alone.

It is obvious that Ibsen and his fellow realists and naturalists created their plays with a strong sense of place. That emphasis has persisted pretty well throughout the century for many playwrights. We think of the very definite place requirements of such plays as *The Piano Lesson, Buried Child, Crimes of the Heart, The Odd Couple, Sticks and Bones,* and *A Streetcar Named Desire,* to name a few.

Place does not necessarily mean creating a replica of a room with all of its furniture. Often it is enough to suggest the environment by a fragment of scenery, the lighting, costume, or property.

THE SCENE DESIGNER AT WORK

The scene designer today is neither an interior decorator nor merely a skilled craftsperson who is obliged to follow the producer's orders in the construction and arrangement of set pieces on the stage. Like directors and actors, scenographers these days are members of a team that shares the challenge of bringing the script to life. Not only do they locate the place of the action, but above all, they reveal the significance of the play.

René Allio, an outstanding European designer who is associated with Planchon's notable Théâtre de la Cité in Lyons, describes his function in the theater:

To invent a sort of visual language for each play, that, within a chosen expressive style, underscores its various meanings, extending and echoing them, sometimes in a precise and almost critical way, sometimes more diffusely and subtly in the manner of a poetic image where fortuitous meanings are no less important than those that are sought.[7]

The scenographer begins work on a specific play by studying the script, perhaps recording initial impressions during or after a first reading. Ben Edwards, one of the foremost U.S. scenographers, tells how he begins:

I try not to think about the scenery too much when I read the play. I try to think of the play itself and what it is saying, and somehow, have the scenery evolve from the play. If you don't get a lot from the script, it's a very difficult job to design it.[8]

Oliver Smith, who has gained an enviable reputation for his designs, especially for such musicals as *West Side Story, Camelot, Sound of Music,* and *My Fair Lady,* describes his initial steps:

What I do is read the material, listen to the score, and if it's present, read the script. And then I do a lot of thinking. I don't draw a line, I just brood—concentrate. I might make tiny sketches on envelopes or pieces of paper, just as idea sketches, but not anything I plan to use particularly. If it is a project that requires research, I do a thorough research and collect a large body of it, which I study carefully. Then when I start to work, I put all the research away, forget it. I mean, it has to be absorbed subconsciously. . . .[9]

During this early preparation, the scenographer is not primarily concerned with problems of construction, painting, and lighting, though of course the fact that the set must be capable of being built and used cannot be ignored. In the early planning, the questions are likely to be these: What images dominate the action? What is the atmosphere of the environment? What are the important scenes, and what kinds of performance areas are needed?

When Boris Aronson was asked about his approach to the scenery for *Fiddler on the Roof,* he said,

Fiddler on the Roof is the title of a very famous painting by Marc Chagall. Both the director and producer felt that the lightness, the playfulness of mood found in Chagall's work should be incorporated into the design. This contribution was to the atmosphere, but was not the solution to the design itself. I reread the Sholom Aleichem stories. . . . Tevye's house was described as a circle within a circle. I designed it as two revolving stages . . . one large, and one small. *Fiddler* was an attempt to show the beauty of nature, growing even within poverty.[10]

Mordecai Gorelik searches for the "poetic image of the scene" by making numerous small sketches. He pays no attention to the practicalities of the staging. For example, in his designs for *Golden Boy,* Gorelik began with the concept of a prize ring, even though the playwright, Clifford Odets, did not call for such a scene in his play; however, the basic image influenced the designs of all the scenes. An illuminating example of Gorelik's thinking is indicated in his approach to Chekhov's *Three Sisters:*

> It is the *dramatic metaphor*, probably, which sums up, for each setting, all the thoughts which the designer may have. Thus, the attic bedroom of *The Three Sisters* is not only an attic, not only a bedroom, not only a girl's room, not only a European room, not only a room of the period of 1901, not only a room belonging to the gentlefolk whom Chekhov wrote about. On top of all that, and including all that, it may be for the designer, the scene of a raging fever.[11]

Still another example shows how Donald Oenslager captured the atmosphere of *Hamlet:*

> Hamlet dwells in a dual world, the everyday world of external events which is the life of Court, and the haunted, brooding world of the imagination which is the inner world of an avenging Prince, who drifts down endless corridors of dark, fir-bordered streams. . . . It is the conflict of these two worlds that unbalances his mind and goads him on to indecisive action and helpless frustration.
>
> The way he distorts the external world through the eyes of his own inner world of the imagination must determine the nature and appearance of the scenes. Just as he sees the events of the Court in the curving mirror of his own brooding conjectures, so the scenes which he inhabits must appear as indefinite embodiments of his own inner preoccupations. The members of the Court must seem to be resolved into dewy shadows of this "too, too solid flesh" and cloaked in veiled fragments of reality. . . . For all the Castle scenes bare, chalky walls are pierced with tall tragic doors—always three, whose depth beyond is as black as Hamlet's sable suit. They must be high, very high, to admit his anguish and his spirit. Only flashes of red, the red of blood, livens the scenes—washed over walls, or splotched on characters' clothing.[12]

When Oliver Smith designed *West Side Story,* his overall conception came from the dominant image of the rumble.

Sometimes a designer is faced with a particular difficulty because of the playwright's handling of his or her materials. Miller uses more than forty scenes in *Death of a Salesman,* but he wanted them played without interruption and flowing freely from the present to the past and to the present again. The scenographer Jo Mielziner describes how he approached Miller's play by trying to visualize the action as if he were a member of the audience. Then he made a "breakdown" of the scenes and determined where each one could be played. He arrived at this basic concept:

> One thought came to me: In the scene where the Salesman mentally goes back to the early years of his marriage, when his boys were young and the house was surrounded by trees and open country, I had to create something visually that would make these constant transitions in time immediately clear to the audience. My next thought was that, even if we ended up with a big stage, with plenty of stagehands, and I was able to design some mechanism for handling the large number of individual scenes, the most important visual symbol in the play—the real background of the story—was the Salesman's house. Therefore, why should that house not be the main set, with all

Jo Mielziner's design for *Death of a Salesman* created various acting areas within the framework of the home. The downstage level was used for flashback scenes.

the other scenes—the corner of a graveyard, a hotel room in Boston, the corner of a business office, a lawyer's consultation room, and so on—played on the forestage? If I designed these little scenes in segments and fragments, with easily moved props and fluid lighting effects, I might be able, without ever lowering the curtain, to achieve the easy flow that the author clearly wanted.[13]

Mielziner went on to design one of the most remarkable sets of the modern American theater.

Although most designers begin with sketches, some prefer working with models, scaled replicas constructed in three dimensions. Many directors prefer the models because the plasticity gives them a clearer idea of the shapes and spaces they will be using. The model is also helpful in planning the shifting of scenery as well as the lighting. Robert Randolph, who designed such hits as *Bye, Bye, Birdie, The King and I,* and *Gypsy,* comments, "You'll never know what it looks like until it is in a model." Viennese designer Rouben Ter-Arutunian adds,

> I always make models and I do not always make a painted sketch in terms of a pretty picture. . . . The spatial relationships are far more important to present to a director and technical departments than a picture.[14]

The next step in design is the preparation of working drawings through which the sketch and model are translated into actual scenery by the carpenters

This model of a setting for Behan's *The Hostage* at the Bern State Theater shows scenic elements projecting beyond the proscenium arch into the auditorium.

and painters. The working drawings usually include a scaled and dimensioned floor plan, elevations of the walls, a hanging chart of flying pieces, and detail drawings of special set pieces and properties. Complete specifications are a part of the drawings. In the professional theater, the designer may make only the sketches and the model, turning the preparation of the working drawings over to a draftsman, and the construction over to the professional scene builders and painters. In educational and community theater, the scene designer often works through all steps of the design, from the preliminary sketches to the actual construction, painting, and mounting of the set.

Perhaps one of the most interesting ways of showing designers at work is to consider their efforts on the same play. The following are descriptive passages of three designers' approaches to *Macbeth*. The first is a celebrated statement by Craig, which illustrates his intuitive and aesthetic feeling for design:

> Come now, we take *Macbeth*. We know the play well. In what kind of place is that play laid? How does it look, first of all to our mind's eye? Secondly to our eye?
>
> I see two things. I see a lofty and steep rock, and I see the moist cloud which envelops the head of this rock. That is to say, a place for fierce and warlike men to inhabit—a

Gordon Craig's design for *Macbeth*.

place for phantoms to nest in. Ultimately this moisture will destroy the men. Now then, you are quick in your question as to what actually to create for the eye. I answer as swiftly—place there a rock! Let it mount up high. Swiftly I tell you, convey the idea of a mist which hugs the head of this rock. Now, have I departed at all for one-eighth of an inch from the vision which I saw in the mind's eye?

But you ask me what form this rock shall take and what color? What are the lines which are the lofty lines, and which are to be seen in any lofty cliff? Go to them, glance but a moment at them; now quickly set them down on your paper; the *lines and their directions*, never mind the cliff. Do not be afraid to let them go high; they cannot go high enough; and remember that on a sheet of paper which is but two inches square you can make a line which seems to tower miles in the air, and you can do the same on your stage, for it is all a matter of proportion and nothing to do with actuality.

Set design by Robert Edmund Jones for the banquet scene in *Macbeth*.

You ask about the colors? What are the colors that Shakespeare has indicated for us? Do not first look at Nature, but look in the play of the poet. Two: one for the rock, the man; one for the mist, the spirit.[15]

The second description is of the banquet scene as it appeared in Max Reinhardt's production of *Macbeth,* designed by Ernest Stern. Ludwig Lewisohn's account of the production emphasizes the overall severity:

Take the scene of the banquet in *Macbeth.* Every line is a straight line, every angle a right angle. All form is reduced to a barbaric severity. But the two rectangular windows in the background through which the cold Northern stars glitter are narrow and tall—so unimaginably tall that they seem to touch that sky of doom. The torches turn the rough brown of the primitive walls to a tarnished bronze. Only on the rude table lie splashes of menacing yellow. There is something barren and gigantic about the scene—a sinister quiet, a dull presage.[16]

The eminent theater critic Stark Young described the celebrated designs of Robert Edmond Jones:

This design for *Macbeth* was the most profoundly creative decor that I have ever seen in the theater. There was a stage enclosed with a background of black, flat so that no light was caught to break the complete darkness of it. Drawings or photographs can give at least a suggestion, and only a suggestion of the gold frames, or sharp gold lines, or the forms like Gothic abstractions, or however we may define them, which, standing alone against the black, defined the scenes. Three great tragic masks were hung to the front, high above the action, and from them vast daggers of light poured down, crossed, pierced, flooded the action below, as in the witches' scene or the banquet. The banquet hall with its gold and light figures moving, and above all else, Lady Macbeth's robe, in which a hidden combination of many shades, an unheard-of intensity of red was discovered, defied any conveyance in words.[17]

Each of these designs is valid in its own right. We see the designer's efforts to evoke the appropriate atmosphere of the play; to intensify its emotional content through judicious use of line, color, lighting, and texture; and to create the environment for the action. Each represents the approach of the designer in helping to interpret the play.

CONTEMPORARY SCENE DESIGN

The bulk of modern drama up to World War II was written in the realistic mode. It dealt with the problems and frustrations of contemporary human beings against an authentic environment of daily life. Hence, its style was representational—performers simulated real people, often shaped or trapped by their immediate environments. The stage designer was obliged to capture the atmosphere and meaning of the play with scenery that served the needs of the performers. As time wore on, a strictly realistic attitude toward the theater lost its hold; then designers began to produce stage settings that were increasingly selective and imaginative and less dependent on overwhelming detail.

Robert Edmond Jones, a moving force in American scenography, struck a note that echoes to this day in the theater:

> Stage designing should be addressed to this eye of the mind. There is an outer eye that observes, and there is an inner eye that sees. . . . The designer must always be on guard against being too explicit. A good scene, I repeat, is not a picture. It is something seen, but it is something conveyed as well; a feeling, an evocation. Plato says somewhere: It is beauty I seek, not beautiful things. That is what I mean. A setting is not just a beautiful thing, a collection of beautiful things. It is a presence, a mood, a symphonic accompaniment to the drama, a great wind fanning the drama to flame. It echoes, it enhances, it animates. It is an expectancy, a foreboding, a tension. It says nothing, but it gives everything.[18]

The result was *selective realism,* by which is meant that the scenery conveys the impression of reality without reproducing it. Designers take artistic license in asking the spectator to join in the imaginative process of production by working from simplified settings and properties chosen for their evocative power.

Selective realism often uses "space staging." Working either within the proscenium arch or on a thrust platform, the designer no longer defines the environment of the action by a box set or scenic enclosure. Instead, the playing area, scene after scene is picked out of darkness by a pool of light, with either portable furniture and properties, or by moving from one space to another in a permanent set that offers a variety of places and levels. All the properties and furniture, as well as the fragments of scenery, are chosen for their power to locate the action and to create the appropriate atmosphere.

In adapting John Steinbeck's *The Grapes of Wrath* for the stage, designer Kevin Rigdon was obliged to suggest a variety of locales and an ingenious vehicle to travel from one to another. *(Steppenwolf Theater Company and La Jolla Playhouse)*

One of the most compelling productions of recent years was the Chicago-based Steppenwolf's ensemble-generated adaptation of John Steinbeck's *Grapes of Wrath*. Steppenwolf has earned a reputation for its acting style. Sheridan Morley of the *International Herald Tribune* says, "There is a raw strength here . . . which ranks this company with the best in the world."

The Grapes of Wrath was widely acclaimed when it played Chicago, La Jolla, London, and Broadway. Jack Tinker, critic of the *London Daily Mail*, commented, "as shatteringly perfect a piece of American theater as you are likely to experience in a lifetime."

Adapting the novel to the stage posed several interesting technical problems. In the setting for the play, director Frank Golati wanted the basic elements of earth, fire, and water. He told his designer that he wanted fire as a focal point for gathering together, and water for rain and the river. Designer Kevin Rigdon met these needs by providing three small traps for gas jets and a larger trap with water. These were built into the orchestra pit. The water was used to represent the Colorado River in the first act, and a flooding creek in the second. When the script called for a rain effect, the designer's ingenuity was further taxed when he had to devise a track for a moving truck that could pivot and move from one wing of the stage to the other.

Fuller's *Soldier's Play* was written in a realistic style, with a unit set designed to serve as various areas in the Army camp at Fort Neal. This is the playwright's description of the set:

> (Scene: *The inner shell of the stage is black. On the stage, in a horseshoe-like half circle, are several platforms at varying levels.*
>
> *On the left side of this horseshoe is a military office arrangement with a small desk (a nameplate on the desk reads:* CAPTAIN CHARLES TAYLOR*), two office-type chairs, one straight-backed, a regimental, and an American flag. A picture of F. D. R. is on the wall.*
>
> *On the right side of the horseshoe, and curved toward the rear, is a barracks arrangement, with three bunk beds and footlockers set in typical military fashion. The exit to this barracks is a free-standing doorway on the far right. (This barracks should be changeable—these bunks with little movement can look like a different place.) On the edge of this barracks is a poster, semi-blown up, of Joe Louis in an army uniform, helmet, rifle, and bayonet. It reads:* PVT. JOE LOUIS SAYS, "WE'RE GOING TO DO OUR PART—AND WE'LL WIN BECAUSE WE'RE ON GOD'S SIDE."
>
> *On the rear of the horseshoe, upstage center, is a bare platform, raised several feet above everything else. It can be anything we want it to be—a limbo if you will.*
>
> *The entire set should resemble a courtroom. The sets, barracks and office, will both be elevated, so that from anywhere on the horseshoe one may look down onto a space at center stage that is on the stage floor. The levels should have easy access by either stairs or ramps, and the entire set should be raked ever so slightly so that one does not perceive much difference between floor and set, and the bottom edges of the horseshoe. There must also be enough area on both sides of the horseshoe to see exits and entrances.*[19]

The experimentalists have left their mark on the theater. Staging is increasingly presentational, both in writing and in design. The traditional conventions of the representational style have been changed to accommodate a more frankly theatrical perspective; today, even in box set commercial hits, characters may address the audience in monologues or asides, time sequences may be altered by flashbacks, and scenery may be shifted in full view of the audience by the crew or even the performers.

During the 1985 season, one of the highlights of the London theater was the premiere of *Wild Honey,* a play based on an old manuscript by Chekhov that was found in a Moscow bank after his death. Michael Frayn cut and revised the lengthy manuscript, and it was produced at the National Theater. Although Chekhov's reputation rests on his skillful delineation of sympathetic but frustrated people, usually in Russian drawing rooms, *Wild Honey's* theatrical debut owed a great deal to its sensational staging. The dialogue, situations, and characters have the quality of Chekhovian drama, but the stage effects, which feature a train, made a powerful impact in the theater. Here is the sequence leading up to the stunning climax.

In Act I, Scene 2, which is set in a garden, a distant train whistle is heard, and then another a little closer, with the faint sound of a locomotive. The second act begins with the sound of a freight train clanking and whistling as it passes by, its red taillight receding in the distance. At the end of Scene 1, Act II, Osip, the local ne'er-do-well, crazed by jealousy, tries to commit suicide by lying across the level crossing just as the headlight of an approaching train appears. He is dragged clear of the track just as the train whistle screams to a crescendo. At the end of the play, Platnovov, a philanderer, is caught in the arms of another woman by two of his former conquests. When they threaten to shoot him, Platnovov jumps out of the window. The stage directions read,

> (*In the instant while they automatically look around for four rubles, Platonov jumps out of the window.*
>
> *Sofya and the others rush to the window after him. As they do so there is the sound of an approaching train whistle, and they all turn, struck by the same thought. They run out of the door; and the world falls apart. Amidst the gathering roar of the train the rear wall of the house moves aside and the lights go down. The forest and the railway line of the previous scene are revealed beyond. Stumbling towards us between the rails is Platonov. He stops, blinded by the brilliant headlight of a train approaching from behind the heads of the audience, its whistle screaming. He staggers back a step or two, trying to wave the train away like the flies. Then sudden blackness, and the great roar of the train, its note falling as it passes us. The red tail light of the train appears at the front of the stage and dwindles rapidly into the smoke left by the locomotive. There is a smell of sulphur in the air. Blackout.*)[20]

Modern technology provides scenography with a broad spectrum of new materials. Lightweight metal pipes and tubing enable the designer to erect scaffolding high above the floor, spanning twenty-five to thirty feet, and with the addition of wooden platforms, this makes possible a variety of stairways and ramps. Pressed decorative metal plates are used for ceiling and walls. Other useful metal materials are expanded mesh wire, sheeting, and corrugated iron.

Sheets of Mylar allow highly reflective surfaces on walls, floors, or frameworks. Sculptured props and surface decorations are made by using latex and silicone molds and fast-setting plaster bandages. Carved and shaped ornaments are constructed from polyurethane foam.

In Chapter Eight on theatricalism and the new theater, we pointed out that the Dadaists and surrealists made their creations out of incongruous combinations of objects and figures, simultaneous action, fragmentation, and distortion. More than sixty years later, we see this tendency at work in contemporary scene design.

When John Bury became scene designer for Joan Littlewood's East End Theater Workshop in 1954, he was obliged to work on an austere budget, so he designed from the available materials he found in the shop or elsewhere rather than from the drawing board. Hence, he resorted to "real" materials like rusted corrugated iron and used lumber. Later, when Bury worked as a designer with Peter Hall at the Stratford-upon-Avon Theater, he continued to use "found" materials. A notable example was the set he prepared for Shakespeare's history plays, known as the *War of the Roses,* for which he employed expanded metal, textured by acids and copper solutions and lighted directionally to enhance the quality of the material. His central image, the steel of war, created the impression of a hard and dangerous world. On a floor of sheet steel, tables became daggers, staircases axeheads, and doors the traps of the gallows. Everything contributed to the creation of a steel-clad, enclosing prison. Even the trees in the background were harsh with iron foliage.

One of the most creative designers is the Czechoslovakian Josef Svoboda, whose combination of aesthetic and technical talents has enabled him to provide stunning examples of the new uses of the stage. He sees the theater as providing "a vivid sense of separate elements imaginatively combined to express new insights into reality." He considers that his purpose as a designer is not to provide substitutes for décor or delineation of locale but to create new stage space. His designs exploit the theatrical possibilities of kinetic scenery and multiple images, which can react to or against the live performer on stage.

For his production of *Hamlet* in Brussels (1965), director Ottomar Krejca based his interpretation on the idea that the ghost is a fiction of Hamlet—his alter ego—and that the play is concerned with this dual role. Svoboda's technical solution was to use a mirror whose reflections he could control to reveal not only the protagonist's state of mind but the disparity of his surrounding world as well. For a production of the Capek brothers' *The Insect Comedy,* he used two mirrors, twenty-five feet square, placed at an angle to reflect the decorated area of the stage floor, which contained a turntable. No regular scenery was used, and only the stage floor was lighted. Svoboda's set design for *Romeo and Juliet* at the National Theater in Prague (1963) was made up of architectural components that moved in a variety of ways—rising, sinking, and sliding laterally or forward and back to accommodate the action.

Josef Svoboda's setting for _Oedipus Rex_ at the National Theater, Prague. _(Directed by M. Machecek)_

It is particularly in the use of projections that Svoboda has made such interesting contributions, for he is at once an artist and an engineer. One of his devices, the _diapolyekran,_ is a complex screen on which simultaneous and synchronous slides and films can be shown and controlled to exploit the interplay between the images. His Laterna Magika is a multiscreen device designed for use onstage with the live actor. It enables the director to work with a visual collage of background or supporting material in a new way—as director Jan Grossman put it, to show "the multiplicity and contrariety of the world in which we live." Svoboda describes the use of projections in his designs for Gorki's _The Last Ones:_

We stacked things, people, scenes behind each other; for example, action around the wheelchair downstage, above that a girl in a tub being stroked by twigs, "in front" of her a boy being flogged on the screen; then suddenly, a drape covering part of the screen opens and we see a small, live orchestra playing a waltz, with pomp—an image of the regime. A space collage using a triptych principle, truly a dramatic poem—what I wanted to do. A clear spatial aesthetic is formed by the contrast of stage action, flat projection, and live orchestra behind the screen on which the images are projected. It's all structured like music, and a law is present. Break it and a new one is set up. This is what attracts me—leitmotifs and repetitions, then sudden contrast; plus tempo indications. Themes disappear only to crop up again later.[21]

Josef Svoboda's setting for *Das Susannchenspiel* at the Frankfurt State Theater. The scenery is a collage.

For Luigi Nono's *Intolerance,* Svoboda employed five large screens on which were projected images of intolerance, such as piles of bones and bodies in a concentration camp; a frozen, bloody corpse; a chained black, tied to a tree while being whipped; an angry mob. The effect was to create a montage like a night-mare, shifting from one brutal reality to another.

Another Czechoslovakian scenographer who has won an international rep-utation for his striking designs for stage plays and operas is Ladislav Vychodil. He has been an influential force in the contemporary theater not only for his settings, but also for his prestigious Bratislava School of Scenography, which has attracted talented designers from all over the world. Vychodil's approach to theatrical design is to interpret the playwright's meaning through arresting combinations of scenic elements, lighting, projections, painting, and space that often take the form of collages or assemblages that include human images.

As we have seen, one of the interesting developments of theatrical stag-ing comes from a fresh interpretation of an established play: Stein's *Peer Gynt,* Svoboda's *Hamlet* and *Romeo and Juliet,* or Brook's *A Midsummer Night's Dream.* One

John Napier's design for the English staging of the musical *Cats.* **The center of the theater was cleared out for the playing area, and it was mechanized so that it could revolve. The oversize junkyard properties suggest the cat's-eye view. The setting is virtually an assemblage.** *(Directed by Trevor Nunn)*

of the striking features of the last was the use of trapezes. Sally Jacobs, the designer, explains that it was decided to delimit a small-sized acting area to a neutral place, where the various elements of the play could be introduced. She describes the solution to the problem of placing performers:

> There are points, for instance, where people are "sleeping" while action is taking place. At first, we wanted the actors stuck on the walls, but didn't know how to do it. Then I suddenly realized that we already had a marvelous mechanism—the flies—for lifting people up and down, and so the trapezes came in. They also accentuated the floating and dreaming aspect of the play. We could use the stage vertically as well as horizontally.[22]

Stage designers explore the new theater in a variety of ways. They respond to the revolution and experimentation in the visual arts by expanding the areas of perception, relating the external image to the unconscious, juxtaposing disparate objects and experiences through simultaneous viewing and the combination of media, and showing the dynamic nature of creation through mobile forms and kinetic objects.

John Napier, one of the most successful British designers (*Nicholas Nickleby, Equus,* and *Cats*) views himself not as a maker of pictures for scenic background but as a creator of spaces for the performers and spectators. He says:

> I want to wrap and involve people in the experience that's going on. I want to break down the usual distance between audience, stage, performers, and public, partly because I'm not pictorial, not a painting person.[23]

Napier demonstrated what he meant in his designs for *Cats.* For the London production, he revamped an old theater by transforming the arena into a three-sided audience area, which enclosed a huge, circular stage—a cluttered junkyard that could revolve 180 degrees. The set became a vast assemblage, which he described as

> . . . the accumulation and proliferation of tangible, recognizable materials and artifacts of a given time and place, a highly littered environment which, along with the complex activity of the performers, creates a specific, fictive world and atmosphere.[24]

Maria Björnson has been a stage designer in England for two decades. Her reputation, until recently, was mostly with opera, but *The Phantom of the Opera* brought her into the spotlight. *The Phantom* is based on a novel of 1911, which was made into four motion picture versions, the most famous being that of Lon Chaney in 1925.

Since the setting is in the Opera House, Björnson visited the site and took over 300 pictures. The building was designed by Charles Garnier in 1875 and took fifteen years to complete. One of the workmen, named Erik, who worked on the project from the beginning, persuaded the authorities to allow him to live there. Thus, the legend of the phantom began. Erik's name is preserved as the leading role in the musical version. The Opera House is seventeen stories high, seven of them being below the stage level, with a lake at the bottom, as well as a burial ground and stables for horses, which were used at one time to move winches for the scenery. There are twelve miles of corridors and two special features used in the musical—the chandelier and the grand staircase.

In shaping her design, Björnson said that the most important element was the lake. She was fascinated by the beauty-and-the-beast myth, and for her the lake became a subconscious sexual metaphor, which she tried to suggest in the Phantom's mysterious, dark journey to the lake. "What interests me," says Björnson, "is the ability to move the audience without their realizing it."

Director Harold Prince suggested that he saw the show in terms of dark corners, lots of curtains, and heaviness. From these ideas, Björnson fashioned an overpowering, lush musical that dazzled the audiences on both sides of the Atlantic. She provided dark nooks and crannies for Andrew Bridge's lighting, as well as dimly lit caverns, huge drapes, and a baroque candelabra. One of the many striking moments was the simulated boat ride of the Phantom and Christine cross a lake of dry ice and smoke machines, while floating candles gleaming in the mist rise from the floor to become candelabra.

In the musical version, they were not able to pull off the stunt used in Lon Chaney's film, when the huge chandelier in the auditorium fell on the audience. But they came as close as safety regulations would permit by lowering the chandelier rapidly over the heads of those in the front rows to come to rest on the stage. Other notable scenes were the grand staircase modeled after the original, the rooftop, the Phantom's subterranean lair, and the spooky tombs in the desolate underground graveyard.

Bringing *The Phantom* to New York involved some complications. The Majestic Theater in New York was ten feet shallower than the London stage. Over $1 million was spent in renovating the Majestic by adding a false proscenium, reinforcing the grid over the stage, rigging the chandelier, and installing ninety-six small traps for smoke and fog in the stage floor. It was also necessary to create 150 costumes for the cast of thirty-two performers. It is estimated that it cost $8 million to mount *The Phantom* on Broadway, but with a $10 million presale at the box office, the success of the venture was assured.

For a long while, American scene designers lagged behind their English and European contemporaries. In part, this was due to the fact that the Americans lacked the continuity of production made possible by state-subsidized theaters. The one-shot system of each production on Broadway was not conducive to establishing a solid basis for design. Now, with the remarkable proliferation of regional and university theater programs throughout the country, many theater workers, especially designers, remain for several years with an established company so that they are able to develop their ideas and talents more freely. Many of them also now design for a variety of productions—Broadway, off-Broadway, opera, ballet, television, and regional theaters—giving them excellent opportunities for all kinds of designs.

Although Ming Cho Lee has not been associated with any Broadway blockbuster hits, he has been the most influential scenographer in the United States for the past two decades. He began his career working as an assistant to Jo Mielziner, the leading postwar Broadway designer, who specialized in poetic settings of painted backgrounds, combined with fragmentary set pieces.

As an independent, Lee had experience with opera at the Peabody Institute of Music in Baltimore, and the New York Shakespeare Festival conditioned him to work on low-budget productions with multiple sets. He learned to strip plays down to their bare essentials by staging them in a *presentational* manner, exploiting frank theatricality instead of illusion, after the example of Bertolt Brecht's Berliner Ensemble. One of his favorite materials is pipe framework, which he uses for towers and walls, sometimes decorated with shields, panels, or statues, or often left bare. Lee has a great feeling for texture, and he experiments freely with interesting materials, such as rough planking, metal surfaces, mylar, and urethane foam. Ming Cho Lee has been especially successful in his approach to opera, rejecting the nineteenth-century romantic tradition, in which the cast played in front of stage pictures. Instead, he fashioned sculpturesque environments that enclosed the performers.

When he begins a new assignment, Lee reads the script just once, to get the basic idea. Then he sets it aside, because he wants to work first with the total effect, not details. Then he sketches. As a young man (he was born in Shanghai), Lee studied Chinese watercolors, so he has the knack of suggesting the essentials. Sketches are followed by rough models, and these are used as the basis of discussions with the director and the technical staff. After this, an accurate scale model is made, which is used to make plans for construction, shifting, and lighting.

One of Lee's most satisfying designs was his set for *Electra*. Heavily textured, sculpturesque units made of urethane foam were mounted on a pipe framework, facing a symmetrical playing area, broken up into varied levels by irregularly shaped platforms and ramps. The massive decorative central door offered a major focal point. This set is noteworthy for its presentational style and its combination of textured elements that evoke a sense of primitive strength, reflecting the basic theme of revenge that dominates the play.

Marjorie Bradley Kellogg is one of the leading realist designers in our contemporary theater, with notable designs for *Requiem for a Heavyweight, Heartbreak House, Present Laughter,* and *American Buffalo* (at the Long Wharf Theater). Kellogg says she is "a maker of places." The purpose of scenery "is to put the audience in the proper frame of mind and in the right place." Research is the prime requisite for Kellogg's preparation of a design. "When you know the atmosphere, the realities, the texture, the color, the spaces, the smells—when you know all those things about a space, then you can really put it on stage."[25]

John Lee Beatty has made a reputation for small-scale settings that have a touch of "poetic realism." They feature curved lines and soft lighting. His best known designs were for *5th of July, Talley's Folly,* and *Crimes of the Heart.* Beatty enjoys the collaboration with directors and playwrights. "I love the other people's ideas," he says. "It's always a wonderful feeling when you break through you own resistance and realize the other person's way works."

Santo Loquasto is noted especially for his sculpturesque sets, which he designs because of his concern with the interaction between the space and the performer. His work reflects his experience in dealing with unusual theater shapes. At the Guthrie Theater in Minnesota and the Beaumont in New York, he worked with thrust stages which demand that you "push the action forward." At the Arena in Washington, D.C., the center stage with a bare floor surrounded by the audience challenged Loquasto to find new ways to break up the space, such as by breaking up the floor with a variety of levels and step units. At the outdoor Delacorte Theater for the New York Shakespeare Festival, he was confronted with a very wide stage and the need to screen off the light of the city in the background. He enlarged the scale of his sets so that he regularly used flats that were at least thirty feet high.

The combination of Liviu Ciulei's direction and Santo Loquasto's sets made

In John Lee Beatty's design for *Talley's Folly* at the Circle Repertory he began with a bull's-eye focus on the actor's faces and bodies and worked outward in concentric circles.

the Guthrie Theater production of *Peer Gynt* a highly theatrical event. Ibsen's play is a loose, episodic plot that moves around freely in time and space. Loquasto's design was a unit, set with mirrors surrounding the playing areas. The large mirror at the back was made of stretched vinyl and was hinged so that it could reflect from below. The mirrored surfaces reflected the moving images, sometimes normal and at other times distorted. Grills in the floor covered trapdoors that were used for entrances, light, and smoke. A throwback to the nineteenth century was the shipwreck scene, making use of stagehands underneath a "sea-cloth" to simulate waves.

Robin Wagner is one of the most successful designers in terms of popular appeal, with such hits as *Hair, Chorus Line,* and *42nd Street.* He began working with the Actors' Workshop in San Francisco. When that group took over the Lincoln Center in 1965, he came to New York City. Wagner, like several of his contemporaries, profited from his experience at the New York Shakespeare Festival and the Arena Stage in Washington, D.C., where he learned to design for unusual kinds of theater.

Wagner is known for three basic strengths:

1. He is concerned with using space—all of it. Painted scenery has little appeal

Douglas Schmidt's set for the New York Shakespeare Festival production of *The Death of von Richtofen as Witnessed from Earth.* This ingenious design provided several acting areas, as well as floating bodies, explosions, battles scenes, and the means for flying Richtofen's plane on and off.

for him, so he breaks up the stage area through the use of multileveled towers, bridges, and structures.

2. He constantly searches for interesting materials, such as chrome, Formica, ceramic tile, and Mylar. He says, "When I have a show in my head, I'm always looking for something that will reflect the basic nature of the show. Certain textures and substances are very expressive.

3. He views scenery as dynamic—as part of ongoing action. So he developes kinetic settings in a cinematic style. He creates designs for movement—" dancing scenery," not static places.

Wagner is probably best known for his *Chorus Line,* which reduced the setting to a minimum, with a white line on the floor and a mirrored wall in the background.

Sometimes, an attempt to achieve spectacular theatricalism does not pay off at the box office. Douglas Schmidt's setting for *Dr. Frankenstein* in 1981 included a scene toward the end of the play that was located in Dr. Frankenstein's laboratory, which collapsed in a blaze of lightning, flames, smoke, and debris. The curtain came down on chaos, only to rise five seconds later on an empty stage. The production thrilled preview audiences, but it was a flop financially. The show used thirteen scenes, including the North Pole, a cemetery, a forest, a series of interiors, and the laboratory.

To facilitate set changes, twenty-five electric winches were used, and some of the shifts were made by using a revolve that was hidden in a fog bank. Despite all of this gimmickry, *Dr. Frankenstein* closed after one performance, at a loss of over $2 million, the most gigantic loss in the history of Broadway. (Since then, the musical *Legs Diamond* failed even more spectacularly—it lost $7 million!)

THE LIGHTING DESIGNER

In the production staff, there is one person above all others for the actor to cultivate—the lighting designer. He or she can make or break you. Lighting is an essential element for establishing time, place, weather, season—but most of all, the mood. In the opening scene of *Hamlet,* the light designer sets the atmosphere by controlling the direction, color, and intensity of the light and the area that is to be lit. It must be the appropriate environment for a ghost, stalking the tower at midnight. The second scene changes to the King's court—a much bigger area, with more illumination to see all of the cast and, of course, a brighter atmosphere. Then to a smaller area in Polonius' house. For each change, the lighting is very important in creating the right mood. If the play is given in a skeletal set or on a bare stage, the lighting may be the most essential element in the design.

Lighting *Hamlet* is, of course, quite a contrast to lighting a production of a comedy like Neil Simon's *The Odd Couple,* which requires bright, warm, cheerful illumination, with good visibility throughout. In musicals like *Phantom of the Opera,* the light designer works especially closely with the scene designer, because together they must work out the playing areas; the atmosphere of each scene; and the texture, color, and shape of all aspects of the production.

The playwright indicates specific requirements in the script. For example, at the beginning of *Ghosts,* Ibsen calls for a rainy, gloomy day; a mystery writer, as another example, specifies cues, such as blackouts and lightning. But the general orchestration is the creative job of the designer, who generally works out a plot for every moment of the production.

THE COSTUME DESIGNER

Costuming is an integral part of the production. Like the scenery, it is a basic element of the total visual design. Moreover, since the costumes are worn and used by the actors, they are part of the live performance and can become the most important part of the overall picture. Many productions these days use abstract or neutral scenic backgrounds, or none at all, and depend on the costuming and the text to carry the show. Costumes can make or break a performance because they are so fundamental in establishing the time and place of the action, the social status of the cast, and the overall style of the production. They are also invaluable

An indispensable part of the hit musical *Cats* is the costuming and makeup.

in establishing the individuality of each character. Hamlet speaks of his "inky cloak," Lear refers to the "loop'd and window'd ruggedness" of the miserable creatures of the storm, and Malvolio's great comic scene depends on his cross-gartered costume.

The costumer must have a complete knowledge of the play and the director's interpretation of it. Costumers must know the period, the kind of furniture, properties, and accessories used in it; the etiquette, manners, and behavior patterns; and the kinds, textures, and colors of fabrics. They must work in close collaboration with the set and lighting designers, stay within the budget, and be ready to adapt to any change right up to curtain time.

It is apparent that the trend toward a more theatrical theater will encourage the elimination of the gaps between performer and spectator, playing space and auditorium. With a more open climate for playwriting, designers will be increasingly concerned with the total environment. With the availability of new materials and facilities, the only limitation will be the designer's imagination.

FILMS TO SEE FOR OUTSTANDING DESIGN

F = Film available; V = Videotape available

F	V	Peter Shaffer, *Amadeus*
F	V	Edmond Rostand, *Cyrano de Bergerac*
F	V	Peter Shaffer, *Equus*
F	V	William Shakespeare, *Henry V*
F	V	Rod Steiger, *The Pawnbroker*
F	V	Stephen Sondheim, Hugh Wheeler, *Sweeney Todd*
F	V	Anton Chekhov, *The Three Sisters* (design by Svoboda)
F	V	Jerome Robbins, Leonard Bernstein, *West Side Story*
F	V	Ingmar Bergman, *Wild Strawberries*

BIBLIOGRAPHY

APPIA, ADOLPHE. *The Work of Living Art,* trans H. D. Albright. Coral Gables, Fla.: University of Miami Press, 1961.

ARONSON, ARNOLD. *American Set Design.* New York: Theater Communications Group, 1985.

BABLET, DENIS. *The Revolution of Stage Design in the 20th Century.* Paris: Leon Amiel, 1977.

BURDICK, ELIZABETH B., PEGGY C. HANSEN, and BRENDA ZANGER. *Contemporary Stage Design, U.S.A.* Englewood Cliffs, N.J.: Prentice-Hall, 1974.

BURIAN, JARKA. *The Scenography of Josef Svoboda.* Middletown, Conn.: Wesleyan University Press, 1971.

CRAIG, EDWARD GORDON. *Theater Advancing.* Boston: Little, Brown, 1963.

GILLETTE, A. A. *Stage Scenery.* New York: Harper & Row, 1972.

GORELIK, MORDECAI. *New Theaters for Old.* New York: Samuel French, 1940.

HAINAUX, RENÉ, ed. *Stage Design Throughout the World, 1970–1975.* New York: Theater Arts Books, 1976.

JONES, ROBERT EDMOND. *The Dramatic Imagination.* Middletown, Conn.: Wesleyan University Press, 1941.

OENSLAGER, DONALD. *The Theater of Donald Oenslager.* Middletown, Conn.: Wesleyan University Press, 1978.

PARKER, OREN W. *Scene Design and Stage Lighting.* New York: Holt, Rinehart & Winston, 1980.

PECKTAL, LYNN. *Designing and Painting for the Theater.* New York: Holt, Rinehart & Winston, 1975.

SIMONSON, LEE. *The Stage Is Set.* New York: Theater Arts Books, 1963.

NOTES

1. Henrik Ibsen, *An Enemy of the People,* trans. William Archer (New York: Charles Scribner's Sons, 1911).

2. Gordon Craig, *On the Art of the Theater* (London: Heinemann, 1905).

3. Adolphe Appia, *The Work of Living Art and Man Is the Measure of All Things* (Coral Gables, Fla: Florida University Press, 1964).

4. Mordecai Gorelik, *New Theaters for Old* (New York: Samuel French, 1940).

5. Bertolt Brecht, *The Private Life of the Master Race,* trans. Eric Bentley (Norfolk, Conn.: New Directions, 1944).

6. John Lee Beatty, quoted in Arnold Aronson, *American Set Design* (New York: Theater Communication Group, 1985).

7. René Allio, quoted in Denis Bablet, *The Revolution of Stage Design in the 20th Century* (Paris: Leon Amiel, 1977).

8. Ben Edwards, quoted in Lynn Pecktal, *Designing and Painting for the Theater* (New York: Holt, Rinehart & Winston, 1975).

9. Oliver Smith, quoted in Pecktal, *Designing and Painting for the Theater.*

10. Boris Aronson, quoted in Pecktal, *Designing and Painting for the Theater.*

11. Mordecai Gorelik, quoted in John Gassner, ed., *Producing the Play* (New York: Holt, Rinehart & Winston, 1975).

12. Donald Oenslager, *Scenery Then and Now* (New York: W. W. Norton, 1936).

13. Jo Mielziner, *Designing for the New Theater* (New York: Bramhall House, 1965).

14. Rouben Ter-Arutunian, quoted in Pecktal, *Designing and Painting for the Theater.*

15. Craig, *On the Art of the Theater.*

16. Ludwig Lewisohn, *The Drama and the Stage* (New York: Harcourt Brace Jovanovich, 1922).

17. Ralph Pendleton, ed., *The Theater of Robert Edmond Jones* (Middletown, Conn.: Wesleyan University Press, 1958).

18. Robert Edmond Jones, *The Dramatic Imagination* (New York: Duell, Sloan and Pierce, 1941).

19. Charles Fuller, *A Soldier's Play* (New York: Hill and Wang, 1981). Copyright © 1981 by Charles Fuller. Reprinted by permission of Hill and Wang, a division of Farrar, Straus and Giroux, Inc.

20. Anton Chekhov and Michael Frayn, *Wild Honey* (London and New York: Methuen, 1984). Copyright © 1984 by Methuen London.

21. Jarka Burian, "Joseph Svoboda: Artist in an Age of Science," *Educational Theater Journal,* 22(2), May 1970.

22. Sally Jacobs, quoted in René Hainaux, ed., *Stage Design Throughout the World, 1970–1975* (New York: Theater Arts Books, 1976).

23. John Napier, in Jarka M. Burian, "Contemporary British Scene Design: Three Representative Scenographers," *Theater Journal,* May 1983.

24. Ibid.

25. Marjorie Bradley Kellogg, quoted in Arnold Aronson, *American Set Design* (New York: Theater Communications Group, 1985), p. 60.

twelve
Theater Architecture

The Greek theater was an admirable architectural solution in bringing an audience of 6,000 or more in close proximity to the acting area, so that everyone was part of a communal gathering. (Theater at Epidaurus, where annual festivals are held featuring the Greek National Theater)

The physical theater exerts a considerable influence on those who work in it. The form, organization, and size of the playhouse affects the conventions of staging, the style of production, and the structure of the drama. For example, the Kabuki and Noh drama theaters of Japan, with their long passageways to the stage, capitalize on effective entrances and exits in a manner unknown in Western drama. The unlocalized platform of the Elizabethan stage, combined with the inner and upper alcoves, gave to Shakespeare and his contemporaries a stage of exceptional versatility for presenting a complicated and animated plot in a way unknown in our present theater, except in motion pictures. To understand the drama of any period, it is helpful to know something of the characteristics of the theater that housed it.

A theater building, like a play, is the result of an interaction of various forces. Architecture is not a mere matter of styles and forms; it has a life of its own. A building reflects the propensities of those who created and occupy it, and they in turn are influenced by the architecture they have produced.

The basic requisites for a theater are that the performers must have a place to play and the audience must be able to see and hear. Two of the outstanding dramatic periods in theater history, the golden ages of fifth-century B.C. Greece and Elizabethan England, began by using improvised surroundings, such as marketplaces, threshing floors, inn yards, and banquet halls. However, as drama became more mature and complex, it was necessary to design and construct theaters specifically suited to dramatic production. In both instances the forms that evolved were extraordinarily successful in serving the drama written for them.

THE GREEK THEATER

The first Greek theater was built on the slopes of the Acropolis in Athens at the beginning of the fifth century B.C. It consisted of three parts: (1) the *theatron* for the audience; (2) the *orchestra*, or dancing circle, for the performer; and (3) the *skene*, or stagehouse, for the background of the action. The theatron, first with wooden seats, later replaced by stone, seated about 16,000 spectators and had eighty rows of seats arranged in a semicircular pattern around the orchestra. Although the theatron was large, the absence of barriers between players and spectators gave the effect of a close relationship. Most authorities agree that all the performers—actors as well as chorus—played in the orchestra, a large, earthen circle about twenty meters across with an altar in the center. Passageways at either side of the orchestra, called *paradoi*, made possible spectacular and lively entrances and exits. Actors could also enter from three openings in the skene. There was no stage, as such, although the actors would have been well served by a platform with steps in front of the skene as a place for speeches, debates, and entrances and exits. In the orchestra circle were three acoustical centers, at which the actors could most easily be heard. One center was at the very middle, where an altar was placed, and the other two were about five meters to either side. In festival productions at Epidaurus, these centers affected the blocking of the action because directors and actors learned to capitalize on them during many of the most telling moments of the play. The style of acting in the Greek theater demanded broad gestures because of its immense size, but because of the excellent acoustics, voices did not require extensive volume. As a result, the acting style was probably neither stagey nor bombastic.

Although the Greeks used some scenery, it is a mistake to think of elaborate settings that enclosed the action. Because the audience wrapped around the playing area, it was impossible to surround the actors with scenery. There was probably a simple iconographic suggestion of locale mounted on the back wall, but as in present-day revivals in Athens and Epidaurus, much of the performance was played well out in the orchestra, often in close contact with the chorus. The huge orchestra provided one of the best solutions for an acting area in theater history because it allowed striking entrances and exits and gave the chorus and actors a very large and flexible playing space for movement, dance, and ensemble groupings. Despite the minimal use of scenery, the Greek theater was a spectacular one, with striking masks and costumes, and the movement and dancing of the performers took place in a handsome structure in a picturesque setting.

Just as Roman drama was based on Greek originals, theater architecture was

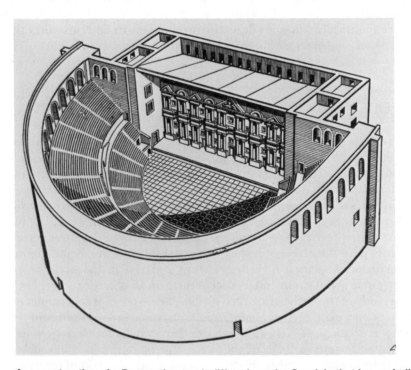

A reconstruction of a Roman theater. It differs from the Greek in that is was built on a level site rather than a mountainside. Note the elaborate scenic background and stage, and the semicircular shape of the orchestra and auditorium.

derived from the Greeks. Unlike the Greeks, the permanent Roman theaters did not come until a century or two *after* the three playwrights Plautus, Terence, and Seneca.

The first permanent theater in Rome was the Theater of Pompey, during the first century B.C. It was quickly followed by two others, the most notable being the Marcellus in 11 B.C. Eventually, there were some 150 Roman theaters built during the Empire, in widely scattered places, including France, Spain, Asia Minor, and North Africa. The Romans also reconstructed extant Greek theaters to serve their needs, so that no complete, original Greek theater has survived.

The Roman theaters were not built on slopes, but from a flat surface. The tiered seats were divided by aisles that were reached by covered stairways and corridors. The tiered-up seats rose to the colonnade at the rear, while in front they came up against a half-circle orchestra that was often used to seat dignitaries. At the back of the orchestra, a very large stage, from 20 to 40 feet deep and 100 to 300 feet wide, was backed by a three-storied stage house covered with pillars, statues, and architectural ornamentation. The stage was about five feet high and had five large doors in the rear wall and a pair of doors in the side wings. The stage house served as the scenic background for the plays.

The Romans were fond of shows and displays of all kinds, and no doubt the theaters, which catered to the public, not to the gods, were used for all kinds of entertainment besides drama.

THE MEDIEVAL THEATER

Medieval drama was first performed in the church when dramatic episodes were used to augment such celebrations as those of Easter and Christmas. The faithful were shown scenes from the Bible—the Three Wise Men coming to the manger, the three Marys discovering the empty tomb. As the reenactment of the stories became more and more popular, various stations of the cathedral were utilized for each segment of the story, until in the thirteenth century drama became so expansive and secular that it was moved outside of the church, and laymen of the craft guilds took over the responsibility of dramatic production. Three elements of the improvised performances in the church were retained—the episodic structure of the plays, the representation of specific locales, and the convention of moving the action from station to station.

On the continent *stations* or *mansions* were used for *simultaneous staging*. That is to say, separate representational structures were built and painted for each specific locale utilized in the play. At Mons in 1501, *The Mystery of the Passion* employed sixty-seven mansions (stations) and required forty-eight days of rehearsal. In front of the stations, a common playing area called the *platea* or platform was used by the actor who made his entrances and exits through the appropriate structure. The stations might be arranged in a single line as they were at Valenciennes in 1547 on a stage 130 feet long, with Heaven at one end of the stage and Hell-mouth at the other. In between were a variety of other stations,

In Lucerne, medieval plays were performed at various "stations" in the marketplace.

such as a Temple, the House of the High Priest, and a marketplace. An analogy might be made with the stock setting for a western movie, which consists of a block-long series of stations such as a saloon, a general store, the jail, another saloon, a livery stable, and still another saloon. In the street in front of this façade, the actors move about from place to place according to the requirements of the plot. Another arrangement for simultaneous staging involved locating the mansions around a central area such as a courtyard, in much the same fashion as separate booths are set up for circus side shows or carnivals. The audience occupied the center area and accompanied the action from one station to another.

Another solution for staging medieval drama was to bring the scene to the spectator by means of a wagon or *pageant stage*. The audience gathered at convenient places through the town, and the pageants appeared one at a time like floats in a parade. This method was particularly popular in England where over a hundred towns and villages used pageant stages for dramatic productions.

The graphic representation of specific locale combined with the neutral playing area of the platea, had two interesting effects on subsequent dramatic development. In France, the pictorial tradition continued, but when drama went indoors again, the size of the theater made it impossible to show but a few mansions at one time. This coupled with the misinterpretation of Aristotle by classical scholars in insisting on the unities, imposed a rigid structure on French playwriting which profoundly affected the future of their drama. In England, the reverse was true. The Elizabethan theater capitalized on the freedom of the platea as the main acting area, and virtually ignored the need for representational background. This flexible physical theater gave to Shakespeare and his contem-

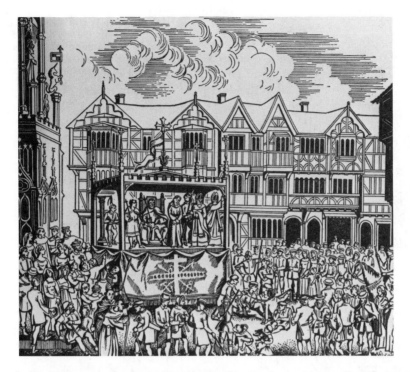

In England, pageant wagons brought the plays to the spectators. Each segment of the play was performed at a different site. This scene shows Jesus before Pilate.

poraries the opportunity to continue the medieval tradition of using a complicated plot, and putting much of the essential action of their stories on stage before the eyes of their audience.

THE ELIZABETHAN THEATER

The lack of primary evidence about the Elizabethan theater has caused an endless amount of conjecture and controversy. It is enough for our purposes to know that the playhouses used by Shakespeare and his contemporaries were covered, wood-framed, three-storied buildings; round, octagonal, or square in shape; enclosing an open yard or pit. The galleries in the enclosure were provided with benches. A large (about twelve to fourteen meters wide) raised platform projected into the pit; this stage was partially covered by "the heavens" as protection against inclement weather for stage machinery, mostly for flying objects or people, and it also housed musicians and equipment for sound effects. Usually the roof was supported by large pillars, although in some cases it was cantilevered from the structure behind the stage.

The area behind the stage is the subject of most argument; although all

Johannes de Witt, a visitor to London during Shakespeare's time, made this sketch of the interior of the Swan Theater. The accuracy of de Witt's drawing has been debated endlessly.

agree that it had at least a two-storied façade, some authorities suggest that the spectator galleries completely surrounded the yard, including the backstage. There were two large doors at either side, at the stage level; some scholars argue for a curtained alcove in between that would be useful for storing properties or even for staging some action. In another version a pavilion projected out from the center area, whereas others insist that there was only a blank wall between the doors.

There are also conflicting theories about the "inner above," an alcove at the second-story level, which could have been used for scenes requiring elevation, such as those with a balcony. Some authorities contend that all the action could be accommodated on the large stage and that there was no need for an elevated alcove. Actually, Elizabethan practice may have been as diverse as scholarly conjecture. Given the sightlines of the Elizabethan theater, there was no possibility of backing the performers with illusionistic scenery.

The Elizabethan theater was a highly successful architectural solution for the plays it housed. Working with a playhouse that held as many as 2,000 spectators in close proximity to the performers, dramatists were able to exploit the possibilities of the language to the full, and the unlocalized stage allowed enormous flexibility for the lively action of a complicated plot that moved from scene to scene without interruption.

The architecture of the Greeks and Elizabethans makes the point that a theater must be suitable for the drama it serves. We have had to learn this lesson through trial and error. Efforts to produce Shakespeare for over three centuries in the pictorial tradition of the proscenium arch theater have demonstrated the inevitable loss of fluency so essential to Elizabethan staging. Likewise, the performance of Greek tragedy in the cramped area of our end stage modern playhouses is awkward, not only because our taste for illusion is at odds with the conventions of the ancient theater, but also because the limitations of sightlines and space make it difficult to accommodate the chorus. A part of the difficulty in designing a playhouse today is that it is expected to accommodate all kinds of plays. In an attempt to achieve flexibility, we risk the danger of constructing a theater that does not serve any drama very well.

Most contemporary drama is written for production in theaters that follow the pictorial tradition of the Renaissance. It is important that we understand how that tradition began and what its implications are today.

PROSCENIUM ARCH THEATER

In Italy during the latter part of the fifteenth century, interest in the revival of classical drama led academies and wealthy nobles to the performance of ancient plays. Part of the interest in the revival of drama came from the Roman architect Vitruvius (first century B.C.), whose *De Architectura* was discovered in 1414 and published in 1486. Vitruvius' description of the Roman stage included settings for three kinds of plays: tragedy, comedy, and pastoral. Interest in Vitruvius was coupled with the Italian fascination for perspective painting, especially as demonstrated in the work of Filippo Brunelleschi (1377–1446). This Florentine architect showed how it was possible to suggest spatial relationships on a flat surface from a fixed point of view. Efforts were made to capitalize on perspective scenery, but it was not until Sebastiano Serlio (1475–1554) that the idea gained popular attention. His *Architectura* (1545) included three celebrated drawings of the settings described by Vitruvius. Serlio's settings for tragedy, comedy, and pastoral were perspective scenery with a central vanishing point. They were made up of four sets of wings at the sides, slightly raked except for the rear ones. Behind the wings, the scene was completed with a painted backdrop. The settings were fixed in place on a temporary stage at the end of a great hall. The front of the stage was used by the performers, whereas the back half was sloped to add an illusion of depth.

Two important Renaissance theaters were constructed in "antique" style to satisfy the vogue of classical revivals. The oldest of these extant theaters is the Olympic Theater at Vicenza, built by the Olympic Academy, which was founded in the mid-sixteenth century to foster interest in classical literature. It was de-

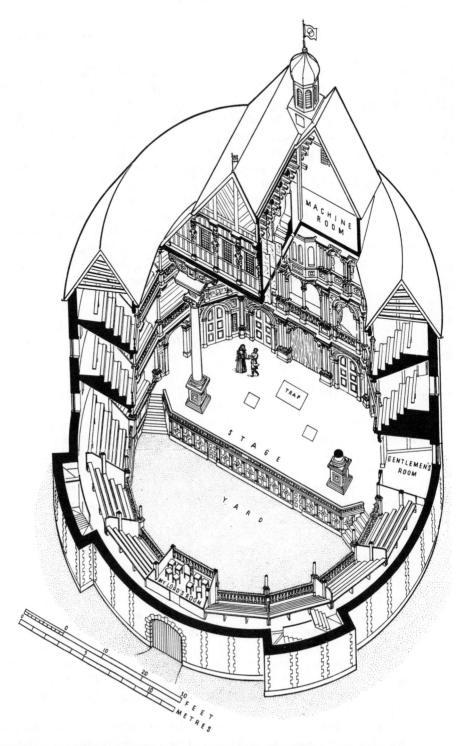

The second Globe Theater, 1614, as reconstructed by Richard Leacroft. This view shows the large platform stage projecting into the yard, providing the versatile theater so necessary for Shakespearean production.

352

The Olympic Theater at Vicenza, Italy, designed by Palladio in 1579, with perspective vistas down the five openings. The auditorium is essentially a Roman theater with a roof over it.

signed by Andrea Palladio (1508–1580), who attempted to follow Vitruvius' plans. However, the Olympic Theater has semielliptical tiered-up seating, constructed around an orchestra, also a semiellipse. It is a roofed-over theater, seating about 3,000, with a colonnade at the rear. The most interesting feature is the stage—a long, narrow platform, backed by a decorative façade in the Roman tradition of pillars, niches, arches, and statuary. The central arch is at least five meters high. There are four other openings in the façade in which Vicenzo Scamozzi (1552–1616), after the untimely death of Palladio, placed permanent perspective scenes, creating the illusion that the stage is a city square from which five streets disappear into the distance. The Olympic Theater opened in 1585 with Sophocles' *Oedipus Rex,* which was sung before a gala crowd.

The Farnese Theater at Parma was designed by Aleotti and completed in 1618, but it was not used for performances until a decade later. The Farnese is important because it is the oldest extant theater with a proscenium arch. There is considerable dispute over this feature, since some scholars believe the framing arch to have evolved from the visual arts; others, from triumphal arches; still others, as an expansion of the center doorway of the ancient Roman theater as anticipated at the Olympic Theater. In any case, the proscenium arch served an important function: The frame made it possible to use changeable scenery. During the seventeenth century, the proscenium arch became a standard theatrical feature, which continues to this day along with the tradition of pictorial scenery. The Farnese Theater is the forerunner of the stage with a proscenium arch, but the development of the auditorium came from the opera house.

In the early part of the seventeenth century, Italian opera's enormous popularity profoundly affected architecture; many of the theaters erected on the continent for the next century and a half were intended for the production of elaborate musical spectacles. These were often public structures, so the auditoriums were large, usually accommodating from 2,000 to 3,000 spectators. The auditorium assumed a narrow horseshoe shape so that spectators could see the stage area behind the arch. Architects soon learned that tiers of galleries along the walls of the auditorium would enlarge the seating capacity. From three to seven galleries were built, supported by posts that separated the galleries into boxes. Until this time, in court celebrations, members of the royalty occupied seats on the floor level, directly in front of the stage but several meters back. No one could sit in front of these seats for fear of obstructing the view. In the new auditorium of the Renaissance, a royal box was placed in the center of the first gallery, allowing a clear view of the stage and making it possible to increase the capacity of the auditorium by adding seats to the floor level, which was sloped to improve the angle of vision.

The stage house became gigantic in size and complex in organization because scene designers and playwrights required increasingly spectacular sets and effects. For example, the Salle des Machines, erected in Paris in 1660, had a stage more than forty meters deep. Ingenious equipment was devised for producing all manner of sensational visual displays. The basic settings were made up of side wings, backdrops or shutters, and overhead borders.

At first, scenery was changed manually, but Giacomo Torelli (1608–1678) developed the "chariot-and-pole" system in Venice in the 1640s. At the stage level, scenery was attached to poles that were inserted in slots cut in the stage floor. Underneath the stage, the poles were fastened to pulleys on tracks. When the chariots were rolled toward the center, the scenery moved onstage. The scenery was removed from view by moving the chariot toward offstage. The chariots and poles were rigged by a series of ropes and pulleys to a single winch, enabling a stagehand to change all of scenery simultaneously. Torelli's system became the standard method of handling scenery in the major theaters until well into the nineteenth century. Another mechanical innovation was flying machinery, used to create all kinds of spectacular effects, especially the magnificent entrances of performers or patrons on clouds, chariots, or other fantastic elements. The perspective of the single vanishing point gave way to multiple vistas, especially in the lavish scenery of the Bibiena family. All kinds of visual displays were created in an attempt to satisfy the audience's craving for novelties—fires, earthquakes, storms, and disasters. By the end of the eighteenth century, Italian-style theaters and scenery extended over the continent and England.

The audience that was attracted to these public theaters was made up of the upper and middle classes. Their taste in theater fare was not so much for spoken drama as it was for opera, ballet, and spectacular exhibitions. Moreover, the play was not always the thing, since the theater was considered a social center. Boxes became private drawing rooms for gossip and entertainment, flirtation, and ostentatious show. In attempting to make the theater décor as impressive as possible, extravagant ornamentation was used. Walls were covered with baroque contortions of entablatures, wreaths, cornucopias, statues of nymphs and cupids, and fat rolls of swirling and gilded plaster.

When the public theaters of the late eighteenth century became too crowded with the irksome hoi polloi, there was a resurgence of smaller private theaters, more suitable for tasteful performances given to the genteel people of quality. However, the general characteristics of the European theater through the nineteenth century followed the pattern of the Italian Renaissance opera house.

The general effect of the picture-frame Renaissance theater was to encourage spectacle and music. The dramatist was compelled to create plays in which there was ample opportunity for lavish pageantry and show. Drama was often grandiose in style. As a consequence of the huge size of the auditorium and the competition of the scenery, actors faced a difficult task in making themselves seen and heard. Such a theater was not conducive to the development of spoken drama. It was the smaller, private court theaters that gave the playwright a more congenial atmosphere in which to work.

DEVELOPMENT OF THE MODERN THEATER

Architects in the nineteenth century protested against the traditionalism that dominated the theater. Gottfried Semper (1803–1879) and his associates made a major breakthrough in the design for Wagner's Bayreuth Festival Theater (1876). Most of the innovations were in the auditorium, in which Wagner wanted to have a "classless" audience. So there were no side boxes and no gallery. Instead, there was a single bank of thirty rows of seats arranged like a fan to enable every spectator to get a good view of the stage. The rows of seats were widely spaced in what has since become known as "continental seating." This arrangement eliminated the need for a center aisle because spectators could reach their seats without disturbing those already seated. Another feature of this theater was an orchestra pit partially under the apron and deep enough to conceal the musicians. A double proscenium arch framed the illusionary scenery and created a "mystic gulf" between the audience and performer.

The deep, straight slant of the seats did not completely solve the sightline problem, so other innovations were tried—the most successful being a "dished" floor, which greatly improved the visibility.

During the nineteenth century the impact of science was felt on architecture as well as on dramatic material. A most important technical advance growing out of the scientific revolution was made possible by the use of steel. Architects could design large cantilevered balconies extending at the rear and sides and over the lower-level amphitheater like half-opened drawers. Because of the strength of the material, the balconies needed few or no supporting pillars. Thus, it became

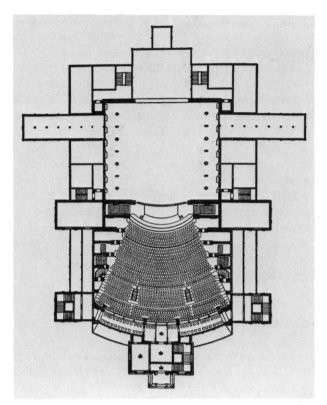

Floorplan of Wagner's theater at Bayreuth, 1876. Note that the audience is in one bank of seats without boxes or aisles. This theater was influential in modern theater architecture.

possible to pack a great many people into a limited area—a fundamental consideration in New York and London, where the cost of real estate limited the size and shape of the theater.

Another major technical advance was made in lighting. For centuries theaters were inadequately (and dangerously) lit by oil lamps, mostly from chandeliers over the stage and the auditorium. In 1817 gas was used for the first time in the Drury Lane Theater in England; it was quickly installed in most theaters not only because it gave better illumination but also because it could be controlled from a central position, often by the prompter, who could run a series of valves and stopcocks. Such gas systems became quite complicated. In a French opera house in 1880, there were no fewer than twenty-eight miles of gas piping, with eighty-eight valves controlling 960 gas jets.

The major breakthrough in lighting came with Edison's invention of the incandescent lamp in 1879. That same year, the California Theater in San Francisco became the first to use electricity for stage lighting. Within a decade, electricity was installed in most theaters throughout the world.

Adolphe Appia was the first to envision the possibilities of electric lighting, and his ideas and designs have been the basis for most lighting design since. His

Steele MacKaye, an American theater manager, designed this elevator stage at the Madison Square Theater, 1880, for making rapid stage shifts.

aesthetic theory reflected his view that since the actor was a three-dimensional agent, it was incongruous for him to play before flat, painted scenery. Artistic use of lighting could achieve the plasticity desired. Not only was Appia a theoretical visionary, but he was also a practitioner who showed how stage lighting could enhance the performance by creating atmosphere, emphasizing the actor, and following the shifting patterns of meaning. He demonstrated the means for breaking up the light and diversifying its direction, intensity, and color. During the twentieth century, vast improvements have been made in the quality and control of stage lighting, and it is universally recognized as a most important element of theatrical design.

Many of the changes in theater design during the first part of this century were made possible by the availability of electric power. For generations, scenery consisted mostly of two-dimensional painted drops and wings that could be readily shifted. A system of ropes and pulleys enabled stagehands to raise and lower the units, most of which were lightweight in construction because the emphasis was on illusionistic painting. But when scenery became three dimensional and solid, some other means had to be devised for moving sets quickly, noiselessly, and economically. Steele MacKaye demonstrated his elevator stage at the Madison Square Theater in New York in 1880. MacKaye's ingenuity was widely admired, but its cost was prohibitive for most theaters. The use of mechanical facilities was more prevalent in Europe, especially where government support enabled many cities to build permanent plants for residential companies with generous work and rehearsal spaces as well as bars, restaurants, and lobbies for the public. In Germany especially, theaters were equipped with hydraulic lifts, turntables, winches, and lighting equipment—all electrically controlled so that the scene technician nearly needed to be a trained engineer.

Some theater practitioners opposed the proscenium arch. In 1893 William Poel constructed his version of the Fortune Theater on the stage of the Royalty Theater in London and produced *Hamlet* with no interruptions and no scenery. He continued with other Shakespearean plays at Gray's Inn and the Middle Temple, proving his point that a bare, unlocalized stage was more satisfactory for the production of Elizabethan drama than the proscenium arch playhouse with its changeable scenery.

Jacques Copeau, at the Vieux-Colombier in Paris, eliminated the arch from an old hall so that the stage and auditorium were an organic whole. There were no footlights and no barrier between performer and audience. On the stage, at several levels, Copeau placed screens, props, and backings to suggest the environment for each play. In this theater, he produced an extensive range of drama with

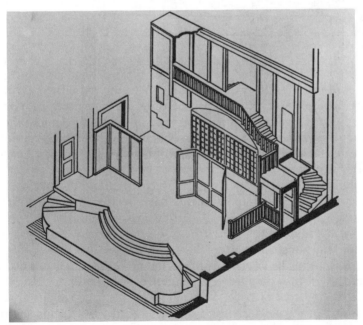

Jacques Copeau's Théâtre du Vieux Colombier in Paris provided a notable experiment in staging, working with limited scenic pieces in a permanent architectural arrangement.

exemplary simplicity and clarity that made Copeau one of the greatest forces in the French theater during the first half of the twentieth century.

In Berlin in 1919, Reinhardt also proved it was theatrically sound for the players and the audience to share the same space. His circus style structure featured a vast horseshoe-shaped auditorium around a large, projecting fore-stage, backed by a revolving stage with a plaster dome. It seated 3,500 spectators. Although Reinhardt was working on a large scale, his efforts to put the action close to the audience, as in the Greek theater, gave his productions a sense of participation and immediacy.

THE SPACE STAGE

During much of the twentieth century, commercial theaters in New York and London produced plays in inadequate buildings, crammed into parcels of expensive land, whose cost usually dictated the size and arrangement of the structure. Since playhouses are frequently rented for single productions, and there is limited work space, scenery is very often built elsewhere and trucked in, and many rehearsals are held outside the theater. These theaters are usually proscenium arch buildings with the traditional separation of performer and spectator. Instead of building new theaters, the practice has been, especially in New York, to revise the old ones by moving the acting area forward and installing new equipment for sound and light as well as for changing scenery.

Progress in lighting has given designers and directors an enormous amount of flexibility, both within the arch and on platforms projecting into the auditorium. Now the acting areas can be defined by light, which is known as the "space stage." A front curtain is no longer needed because, to begin a scene, the performance space is picked out of the darkness, and the scene is ended with a fade-out or blackout.

The size and shape of the playing area is readily controlled, and one scene can follow another virtually without interruption because it is possible to use skeletal settings and a minimal amount of properties and furniture. Sometimes a play is mounted in a large sculpturesque, permanent setting with a variety of spaces and levels, and the action proceeds from one scene to another by illumination of the area needed. For example, a setting suggesting the castle at Elsinore can be designed and lighted to accommodate the scenes of *Hamlet*—a platform, a churchyard, a plain in Denmark, the Queen's closet, and various rooms and halls.

Another advantage of the space stage is its suitability for the use of projections on the cyclorama, on free-standing screens, on pieces of material hung from the flies, or on the performers themselves. Such imagery can accompany the action, expand the environment, make a comment on it, or serve as counterpoint.

Space staging is eminently suitable for multiple-scene plays because no bulky scenery needs to be changed. Hence, the action continues without interruption. Period plays, such as Restoration comedies and those of Molière, can be set with a few pieces of furniture and perhaps a few screens, with the acting area established by the lighting. Although the space may seem bare, well-chosen properties and colorful costumes, supported by an orchestrated light plot that follows the action and constantly changes to fit the play's atmosphere, provide an entirely satisfactory visual experience.

As for realistic plays originally intended to be played in authentic-looking rooms with complete walls and ceiling and with a full complement of furniture as well as practical doors and windows, experience has demonstrated the efficacy of staging with almost no scenic support except for a few pieces of furniture, the minimal suggestion of locale, and most important, the light. The space stage has the great virtue of focusing the audience's attention where it usually belongs—on the actors.

A good example of the flexibility of the space stage can be seen in *Amadeus*, which opened in the National Theater in London in 1979. Act I contains twelve scenes; the second act, nineteen. It spans a period from 1781 to 1823. Peter Shaffer wanted continuous action from one scene to another. Partially, this was accomplished by having Salieri act as a narrator as well as the leading character, so he bridges the gaps and provides the necessary exposition. But in part, the continuity was assured by the use of space staging.

The set consisted of a large rectangle that represented interiors: Salieri's salon, Mozart's last apartment, reception halls, and opera houses. At the rear, an imposing decorative arch supported curtains that parted to reveal an inner alcove with varied backdrops on which were projected theater boxes, walls of mirrors, landscapes, figures and silhouettes of Viennese citizens and courtiers, and a huge fireplace.

Scene and time changes were indicated by changes in the lighting. The continuity of the action was enhanced by the appearance of liveried servants to change the props and furniture between scenes.

THE THRUST STAGE

Since World War II, there has been a persistent attack against the proscenium arch in favor of the thrust stage—a bare platform, projecting into the audience area, which encloses it on three sides.

Guthrie designed a thrust stage theater that proved to be such a successful arrangement for staging Shakespeare and other playwrights that it has been widely influential. The stage, which often has steps leading to the audience level, is reached by entrances from the sides, the rear, and below, allowing great variety in movement. Because of the sightline problems, scenery is often fragmented or eliminated altogether, so the actor is no longer confined by canvas wall.

The Mark Taper Forum in Los Angeles is limited because it was designed not for theatrical production so much as for chamber music and lectures; however, the auditorium and thrust stage have proved to be exemplary for an intimate style of production, so directors and designers have learned to live with

The Guthrie Theater in Minnesota is one of the oldest and most influential theaters in the country, with an enviable record of outstanding productions.

the limited backstage space. One of the directors with considerable experience at the Mark Taper, Edward Parone, described the use of the stage:

> The most difficult plays to stage are realistic, naturalistic, etc. . . . Chekhov can and has worked on this stage, but it is not easy, particularly with scene changes. We have severely limited backstage space and almost no storage space for one thing. Then too, sets must be changed in full view of the audience. . . . In a production of *Major Barbara* which I directed, I changed time periods as part of the production concept, and I staged the changing of the sets. It worked. And with Shaw, all the talk works very well on the thrust stage; it is rather like a platform for debate, discussion, speeches, and pronouncements. The problem then is to get everybody else out of the way.
>
> The Greeks and Shakespeare of course are a minimum of trouble.
>
> The truly exciting challenge of the thrust stage is that it *looks its best with nothing on it.* Nothing, that is, except the actor and the words of the play. Whatever looks sculptural, simple and three-dimensional acquires a richness and purity that, with the right play, can be breathtaking.[1]

Another director with extensive experience with the thrust stage is Michael Langham at the Stratford Theater, Ontario:

> I am convinced that one can achieve a greater imaginative bond between actor and audience with a thrust stage theater. In a picture-frame theater, I think the tendency is for the actor to pretend to play to his colleagues where in fact he is playing to the audience. This is an impossibility on a thrust stage—the actor is forced to play to the actor and consequently the relationships that develop between characters are deeper and draw the audience more fully into the experience.[2]

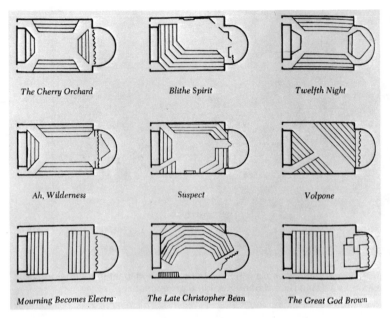

The Cherry Orchard   *Blithe Spirit*   *Twelfth Night*

Ah, Wilderness   *Suspect*   *Volpone*

Mourning Becomes Electra   *The Late Christopher Bean*   *The Great God Brown*

Ralph Freud at the University of California, Los Angeles, pioneered central staging with his flexible workshop theater. Movable banks of seats made it possible to vary the audience and playing areas from play to play.

THEATER-IN-THE-ROUND

A widespread form of theater architecture, particularly among campus and civic organizations, is the arena stage, also referred to as "theater-in-the-round" or "central staging." Glenn Hughes, at the University of Washington, led the way in this venture with his Penthouse Theater. He simply placed a few rows of seats around an acting area in a large room. Locale was defined by props, furniture, and costumes; and the only separation between performer and spectator was an attempt to keep the latter in the dark, although it was difficult to keep the light from spilling onto the audience from the playing area. The advantages of arena staging were immediately apparent—it was more economical, it gave the audience a fresh kind of theatrical experience, and it was excellent training for the actor in concentration and ensemble play.

At first, central staging was considered suitable only for drawing-room plays, but Margo Jones, in her Dallas theater in the 1950s, demonstrated that many other kinds of drama could be performed successfully—except for those with too much violent action. The original Arena Stage in Washington, D.C., demonstrated that theater-in-the-round could be used for professional productions in a theater that seated 750 people and that nearly any kind of play was

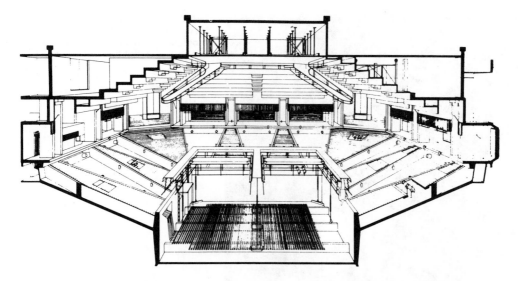

The Arena Stage in Washington, D.C. has a rectangular playing area surrounded by tiers of seats for 752 spectators. Part of the seating is movable for various productions, and a catwalk overhead and a trapped floor give added flexibility.

possible. The idea spread, especially to tent and music theaters. Now most college and university campuses have some version of arena staging; various arrangements have been tried, such as placing the audience on two or three sides and including a considerable amount of scenery.

COLLEGE AND UNIVERSITY THEATERS

In the United States, a unique development in the twentieth century was the rise of college and university theaters. Since these buildings generally grew out of the needs of dramatic arts or theater arts departments and were designed as an extension of the academic program, a distinctive kind of architecture emerged. Freed from the pressure to make box office appeal the primary target, the academic theater was able to construct buildings that had auditoriums well suited for spoken drama and excellent facilities for production in terms of space and equipment.

One of the first university theaters in this country was built at the University of Iowa in 1935. It included an auditorium with continental seating for 500 spectators, a double proscenium, and, most important, a great deal of offstage space for shops and storage. This theater set the standards, emulated by scores of other academic institutions.

The University of Michigan's Mendelssohn Theater has a projecting semicircular stage. Note the variety of lighting positions.

FLEXIBLE AND MULTIPLE THEATERS

A persistent problem of theater buildings occupied by residential repertory companies on a permanent basis is that of providing suitable staging for plays intended for varied playing conditions—from Greek orchestra to Shakespearean thrust to nineteenth-century proscenium arch to contemporary avant garde. In general, attempts to serve all needs result in serving none well.

The Malmo Municipal Theater, built in 1941 in Sweden, is a fairly successful attempt to design a multipurpose structure. The front of the orchestra is provided with elevators, which make the area usable for a thrust stage, for an orchestra pit, or for seating. Another interesting feature is the flexible auditorium, which can be varied in size by the use of large, movable panels, so that the building is suitable for large concerts and musical productions; when reduced in size, it is an effective house for spoken drama. As a civic structure, it is exemplary because of its spacious lobbies, working and rehearsal areas, experimental theater, and parklike setting.

Another, much more satisfactory solution to the problem of various production conditions is the multitheater, which includes a proscenium, thrust, and/or arena as experimental stages. Many American universities and regional theaters have found this a satisfactory solution.

An excellent example of the multitheater is the National Theater in London. After 125 years of planning, it was finally opened in 1976. It includes three kinds of theater. The Olivier has a thrust stage in the corner of a two-tiered, fan-shaped auditorium that holds 1,160. The Lyttelton is an adjustable prosce-

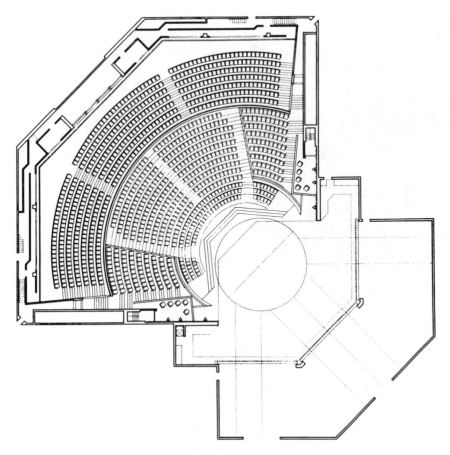

The large platform stage of the Olivier Theater in London projects into the fan-shaped auditorium, which seats 1160 people. The rear of the stage can be opened to give additional depth.

nium theater with continental seating for 895. Experimental productions are given in the Cottsloe, a flexible studio space with galleries around three of the four walls that range in capacity from 200 to 400, depending on the arrangement of the playing space. A most attractive feature of this plant are the supporting facilities for the audience's convenience and comfort—terraces, foyers, exhibition spaces, bars, restaurants, and parking facilities.

ARTAUD'S THEATER

We have seen how Antonin Artaud's ideas affected playwriting and acting; he also had an enormous influence on staging. His views are worth quoting at length

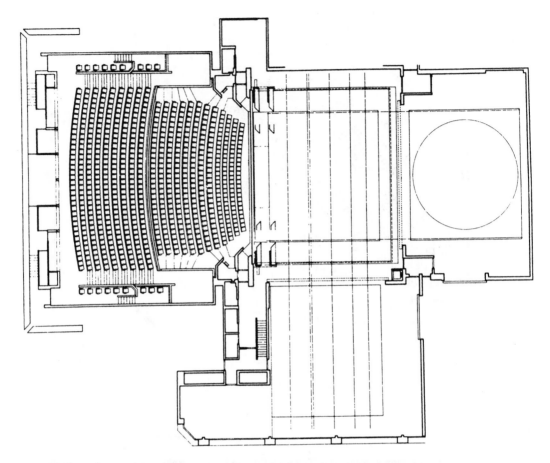

The Lyttleton Theater of the English National Theater is a proscenium arch structure that seats 895 people in two tiers. It has spacious areas in the wings and backstage, one equipped with motorized scenery wagons, and scenery can also be flown overhead.

because in them are the seeds that have since reached fruition in the experimental theater:

The Stage—The Auditorium: We abolish the stage and the auditorium and replace them by a single site, without partition or barrier of any kind, which will become the theater of action. A direct communication will be reestablished between the spectator and the spectacle, between the actor and the spectator, from the fact that the spectator, placed in the middle of the action, is engulfed and physically affected by it. This envelopment results, in part, from the very configuration of the room itself.

Thus, abandoning the architecture of present-day theaters, we shall take some hangar or barn, which we shall have reconstructed according to processes which have culminated in the architecture of certain churches or holy places, and of certain temples in Tibet.

In the interior of this construction special proportions of height and depth will prevail. The hall will be enclosed by four walls, without any kind of ornament, and the public will be seated in the middle of the room, on the ground floor, on mobile chairs which will allow them to follow the spectacle which will take place all around them. In effect, the absence of a stage in the usual sense of the word will provide for the deployment of the action in the four corners of the room. Particular positions will be reserved for actors and action at the four cardinal points of the room. The scenes will be played in front of whitewashed, wall-backgrounds designed to absorb the light. In addition, galleries overhead will run around the periphery of the hall as in certain primitive paintings. These galleries will permit the actors, whenever the action makes it necessary, to be pursued from one point in the room to another, and the action to be deployed on all levels and in all perspectives of height and depth. A cry uttered at one end of the room can be transmitted from mouth to mouth with amplifications and successive modulations all the way to the other. The action will unfold, will extend its trajectory from level to level, point to point, paroxysms will suddenly burst forth, will flare up like fires in different spots. And to speak of the spectacle's character as true illusion or of the direct and immediate influence of the action on the spectator will not be hollow words. For this diffusion of action over an immense space will oblige the lighting of a scene and the varied lighting of a performance to fall upon the public as much as upon the actors—and to the several simultaneous actions or several phases of an identical action in which the characters, swarming over each other like bees, will endure the onslaughts of the situations and the external assaults of the tempestuous elements, will correspond the physical means of lighting, of producing thunder or wind, whose repercussions the spectator will undergo.

However, a central position will be reserved which, without serving, properly speaking, as a stage, will permit the bulk of the action to be concentrated and brought to a climax whenever necessary.[3]

THEATER ARCHITECTURE REVISED

Another attempt to find new relationships between audience and players has been found in the radical revision of the buildings themselves. Performers have moved out into the audience's areas, in the auditorium, lobbies, cloakrooms, and rehearsal spaces. Spectators have found themselves onstage or confronted by players all over the theater.

Some designers today consider it their prerogative to change the structure of the building as well as to design the stage space. John Napier, in designing *The Comedy of Errors* in 1976, extended the two top galleries of seating beyond the proscenium to surround the acting area of the stage, which became a public square in Corfu, with souvenir shops and bistros. Some of the audience occupied side tables on the stage level.

Napier made an even more radical transformation of the architecture for the musical *Cats* in 1981. The New London Theater had a spotty record as a musical hall, conference center, theater, and television studio. Napier changed the arena space into a three-sided circular seating arrangement around a raised, circular platform. A variety of ramps provided access from the stage to the auditorium so that the performers could mingle with the audience. The first four

When the musical *Candide* moved from off-Broadway to the Broadway Theater, the designers removed the seats and rebuilt the ground floor, joining the audience and actors together by a series of ramps and platforms.

rows of seats and the acting platform were mounted on an immense turntable that moved 180 degrees when the performance began. For the New York production, it was necessary to open up the roof of the Wintergarden Theater to allow the heavenly ascension of the cat Grizabella, astride a huge tire.

Eugene Lee, in designing a double-decked framework for Baraka's *Slaveship* for the Chelsea Center Theater in New York, ripped up the seats and leveled the floor of the auditorium. In the center, he built a larger platform set on rockers. The spectators could see into the narrow space below, where the tortured, frightened slaves were chained. Brook reconstructed the Théâtre des Bouffes du Nord for his production of Shakespeare's *Timon of Athens* (1975). He took up the seats of the orchestra and put in a concrete slab floor, which became the primary playing area. The raised stage was removed and replaced by a pit six meters deep, reached by a wide set of steps. The orchestra pit was covered by a wooden platform, part of which was removed to serve as Timon's cave. Spectators sat on rows of seats under the balcony at the sides of the playing area. The decaying walls of the old theater remained unchanged and unpainted to suggest Timon's decaying universe. When Brook produced *Carmen* in 1983 at the Beaumont Theater in New York, the first thing the spectators saw when they entered was a mound of dirt and gravel in the center of the auditorium, surrounded by a board fence to convey the sense of earthiness.

When designers Franne and Eugene Lee moved Harold Prince's produc-

Mnouchkine's Théâtre du Soleil plays in an abandoned munitions factory in Vincennes, near Paris. Spectators stand in the center or are seated in the raised gallery and watch the action on three large table platforms.

tion of *Candide* from the Chelsea Theater in Brooklyn to the Broadway Theater, they began by eliminating the seats and rebuilding the ground floor. Then they closed off the balcony and installed seats around new platforms and ramps, thus putting part of the audience in the acting areas. British designers remodeled theater buildings extensively for *Cats* and *The Phantom of the Opera.* Likewise, *Starlight Express,* with its roller skating tracks surrounding the audiences, required substantial remodeling of existing theaters in London and New York.

FOUND SPACES

Another attempt to find greater freedom from traditional forms of production is to reject the playhouse altogether. Avant garde experimentalists wanted to get away from a theater of illusion—painted scenery and actors on display like commercial products. They believed that all aspects of production should make their own statements, not merely support the words of a dead text. The quest for new environments led to making performance areas out of "found spaces," adapting productions to existing structures, or performing in the open air.

Schechner's Performance Group adapted an old garage by moving scaffolding and platforms around the interior. Mnouchkine's Théâtre du Soleil occupies an abandoned cartridge factory. Stein moved from his theater in Berlin to an exhibition hall for *Peer Gynt;* Schumann's Bread and Puppet Theater plays in the streets or in the Coney Island concession hall formerly occupied by a freak show; Serban, Garcia, and Brook have staged productions in an ancient Persian monument.

In part, this exodus from the theater stems from the experimental groups' limited budgets. (Antoine began the Théâtre Libre in Paris in a room over a billiard parlor, and O'Neill's early one-act plays were tried out in a Provincetown living room before they were shifted to a warehouse on the wharf.)

Among noteworthy theater experimentalists, Grotowski rejects traditional architecture because he wants a "poor theater," free from décor, and because he insists that the emphasis should be on the actor. Grotowski calls for limited, elite audiences who are willing to go through self-analysis as they participate in the explorations of the performers. For this action, he prescribes a minimal, but variable, performance area:

> We have practically renounced the stage. The only indispensable thing is an empty area where a space can be shaped for the audience and the actors, and in a different way for each new production so that the most diverse relationships are made possible. The actors can perform in the pathways formed between spectators. . . .[4]

And so we have come full circle. Long ago, Thespis made theater from a bare space by the act of performing. So today, in many places, actors and directors, in their effort to reduce their art to its basic essentials, emphasize performance—and, in the process, remind us that theater is not architecture or set design but players in action before an audience. You with your imagination will take care of the rest.

FILMS AND VIDEOTAPES ON THEATER ARCHITECTURE AVAILABLE ──────

F = Film available; V = Videotape available.

F		*Drottningholm Court Theater*
F	V	*Shakespeare and His Stage*
F	V	*Shakespeare and the Globe*
	V	*The Serpent*—An Open Theater Production

BIBLIOGRAPHY

BIEBER, MARGARETE. *The History of the Greek and Roman Theater.* Princeton, N.J.: Princeton University Press, 1961.

BURRIS-MEYER, HAROLD, and EDWARD COLE. *Theaters and Auditoriums,* 2nd ed. New York: Van Nostrand Reinhold, 1964.

HODGES, C. WALTER. *The Globe Restored.* New York: Coward, McCann & Geoghegan, 1968.

IZENOUR, GEORGE C. *Theater Design.* New York: McGraw-Hill, 1977.

LEACROFT, RICHARD, and HELEN LEACROFT. *Theater and Playhouse.* London: Methuen, 1984.

MULLIN, DONALD C. *The Development of the Playhouse.* Berkeley: University of California Press, 1970.

NICOLL, ALLARDYCE. *The Development of the Theater,* 5th ed. New York: Harcourt Brace Jovanovich, 1966.

SCHEVILL, JAMES. *Breakout! In Search of New Theatrical Environments.* Chicago: University of Chicago Press, 1972.

SILVERMAN, MAX, and NED A. BOWMAN. *Contemporary Theater Architecture.* New York: New York Public Library, 1965.

WICKHAM, GLYNNE. *Early English Stages, 1300–1660.* New York: Columbia University Press, 1959–1963.

NOTES

1. Edward Parone, *Theater Quarterly,* 3(11), July–September 1973.

2. Michael Langham, *Theater Quarterly,* 3, (11), July–September 1973.

3. Antonin Artaud, *The Theater and Its Double,* trans. Mary Caroline Richards (New York: Grove Press, 1958). Translated by Mary C. Richards.

4. Jerzy Grotowski, *Towards a Poor Theater* (New York: Simon & Schuster, 1968).

thirteen
The Audience

This drawing of a seventeenth-century English audience shows that the audience's interest was not entirely confined to the play.

The playwright has an idea and sits down to write a play. He or she contacts a producer who is intrigued with putting it on stage. Funds are accumulated, a theater is rented, and a director is hired who happens to know some talented actors, perfect for the show.

Auditions are held to fill out the cast, designers are recruited, and the director puts the play into rehearsal. There is a tremendous outpouring of talent as the director and the actors work together on the interpretation and playing style; there are endless consultations on the set, costume, lights, and sound. Finally, everything comes together.

All of this planning and preparation have been done—just for *you*, the audience. At every step of the process, from the first word to go down on paper to the dress rehearsal, everyone is conscious that ultimately what really counts is you. Your response makes or breaks the show. Without your positive reaction, all the expenditure of time, talent, and money means nothing.

It is one of the fascinating and bewildering aspects of the theater that, despite years of experience in production, no one knows for sure how you are going to respond.

Alfred Uhry thought his modest little play, *Driving Miss Daisy,* would run for a few weeks off-Broadway. It ran for 854 performances on Broadway, captured the Pulitzer Prize for the best American play, 1987–1988, and, as a movie, won Oscars for Uhry as a writer and for Jessica Tandy as an actress. Recently, New York producers thought they had surefire hits in their musicals, *Carrie* and *Legs Diamond.* They both lost $7 million! When Ming Cho Lee worked on *Hair,* the technical staff thought it was a disaster that would fold in one week. It played 1,750 performances in New York and ran for two years in London!

Nearly all playwrights will tell you that the most difficult times they have in the theater are on opening nights, when you tell them whether or not their brain children will survive. All too frequently, you bedevil those who work in the theater with your fickleness, because sometimes you pick up their cues as planned, and sometimes you sit on your hands, or stay away in droves.

As Samuel Johnson observed:

> The drama's law the patrons give,
> And we who live to please, must please to live.

Seeing a play is a social occasion, a group effort. Its full effect is realized only when the production becomes a dynamic, communal celebration that brings about a union of all aspects of the theater—a coming together.

Throughout theater history, most plays have been written for immediate consumption, the obvious way of measuring success—the box office. This influences both playwrights and producers, who are well aware that they must create a work that gains instant acceptance from a sufficient number of customers to pay the bills and perhaps show a profit. In these days of astronomical production costs in the commercial theater, a play must pack the house every night for months just to break even. It was estimated that *Phantom of the Opera* needed to play to full capacity for two years just to meet expenses. Off-Broadway productions now may run as high as $500,000. When *Cats* moved from one theater to another, the estimated cost was $650,000. Nevertheless, *Cats* is reported to have made a profit of $44 million in the United States alone. This kind of high finance is for musicals. Straight plays are far less expensive, but the income is seldom enough to break even.

The result of box office pressure over the years has resulted in an emphasis on entertainment such as musicals and comedies, because that is what the New York audiences will pay for. The list of long-run hits on Broadway reveals that seventy productions ran over 1,000 performances. Of these, thirty-eight were comedies. Not one play among the most popular fifty was by a major playwright. As we shall see a bit later, however, the development of regional, nonprofit theaters is an encouraging feature of recent years, because new audiences are ready and willing to accept more substantial material.

It should be remembered that many masters of drama in the past transcended the problems of catering to the lowest common denominator of the audience. Sophocles, Aristophanes, Shakespeare, Molière, Jonson, Lessing, Schiller, and Sheridan satisfied public taste while creating landmarks of dramatic literature. But popularity itself is no criterion of lasting value; many plays of enormous popularity are very thin, and, conversely, some of the masterpieces of the theater are not major attractions. As educational, civic, and regional theaters continue to grow, they are developing audiences for all kinds of theatrical experiences, including literary, provocative, and experimental plays.

THE NATURE OF ATTENTION

To create a play and a performance that will evoke an appropriate response, it is essential for the playwright and the theater worker to know something about the nature of attention. Attention comes in short spurts. Concentration requires constant renewal because it is impossible for us to fix our attention on a single object and hold it there as we might a spotlight. Ordinarily, an audience arrives with the expectation of giving full attention to the play, but if the drama is dull and the performance monotonous, if attention is not captured and sustained, the spectators make their escape into a world of their own imagining.

There are two kinds of attention—voluntary and involuntary. Voluntary attention implies that spectators look and listen by an act of will; they make an effort. Involuntary attention, on the other hand, requires no conscious effort; it results from responding to stimuli, for example, a scream in the night, a fascinating story, or our name spoken aloud by another. Theater workers are interested in securing our involuntary attention. They employ such devices as bright lights and colors, movement, emotional stimulation, space and elevations, sound, and visual focus. Directors combat monotony by varying the groupings of characters, by changing the pace, by making sure that actors do not imitate one another's pitch patterns, by inventing business and action—in short, by every possible means of renewing attention. They aim to control and direct every instant of our attention throughout the course of the play. This is one of the director's most difficult tasks because the play, by its very nature, is a stream of complex visual and auditory stimuli; attention constantly flits from one character to another and back again. Motion picture directors have far greater control of the spectator's attention because of their ability to focus the camera on one object, one person, one face at a time, eliminating all extraneous elements, and to edit a film after it has been shot, ordering retakes if necessary. But stage directors must find other ways to achieve much the same effect.

Part of the problem of controlling attention is avoiding the distractions that plague a theatrical performance, such as late arrivals, rustling of programs, foot shuffling, coughs and wheezes, and the vicissitudes of production that may occur onstage—missed cues, long waits, poor costumes, obvious makeup, scenery that shakes when the door is slammed, a crooked picture on the wall, and light-reflecting surfaces. Some aspects of the production itself may destroy the audience's concentration, such as an unexpected novelty that arouses surprise and comment in the audience, scene shifts that take too long or involve too much noise, spectacular special effects, or an unexpected laugh. In a well-managed theater, every effort is made to focus and control the audience's interest so that their voluntary attention becomes involuntary as they become thoroughly engrossed in the action and the play.

THE AUDIENCE AS A CROWD

Most members of the audience come to the theater to be entertained, to be stirred emotionally, to be amused by the foibles of their fellow mortals, to be enlightened by fresh insights into the human condition, or to be in the same room with talented, interesting people.

As a reader, you simply have to pick up the text of a good play, find a quiet place, and enjoy yourself. If you are an art buff, you meander through a gallery at your own pace, pausing before a painting that arrests your attention and passing by those that do not appeal to you. But if you go to the theater, usually you must plan in advance, obtain tickets, and arrange your schedule to fit that of the performance. Then you will be herded into a darkened room, along with hundreds of strangers, most of whom you have never seen before in your life and never will see again. The theater audience is usually a varied mix—all ages, occupations, backgrounds, and races. Your gathering together is mostly accidental. You are together because of one reason: You hope to find a meaningful theatrical experience.

The lights go down, the curtain opens, and you see before you a place you have never seen before occupied by a small group of make-believe people, going through an artificially contrived plot. All of you know you are being deceived. You know that the handsome room is made of painted canvas, that the gun fires only blanks, that the innocent-looking blonde lead is in litigation over her third

An eighteenth-century English audience at Covent Garden, 1763, got involved in the action when they protested the raising of admission prices. Note the boxes at the side of the stage.

sensational divorce, and that the murdered victim will appear smiling and bowing for the curtain call. Astonishingly enough, you and your fellow theatergoers are fully aware that you are being successfully duped, and at the end you will join in enthusiastic applause to show your appreciation of how well the deception has been carried out.

Although you came together as isolated individuals, an audience quickly becomes a group. Through willing suspension of disbelief, individual differences melt away, you become a crowd, and the nature of your response changes, too. Social psychologist Emory Bogardus, in his discussion of crowd behavior, points out:

> A heightened state of suggestibility is characteristic of a crowd. The preponderance of feelings over reason heightens suggestibility. The excitement that frequently prevails in a crowd throws persons off their guard. The force of numbers is overwhelming.[1]

Thus, a theater audience loses some of its sense of personal responsibility. There is a temporary release from restraint, with the result that in a crowd people may respond to stimuli that would leave them untouched as isolated individuals. For example, they may laugh in the theater at salacious humor they would consider vulgar in their own living rooms. There is the pressure to conform, the

An eighteenth-century English audience in rustic surroundings, as visualized by
James Wright. This may be a scene from *Macbeth* during the sensational entrance of
the three witches. Note the by-play of some members of the audience.

contagion to join in. These psychological phenomena are at least a partial explanation of how the effectiveness of a play may be enhanced by a responsive
audience, which willingly suspends its disbelief and succumbs to the emotions of
the play.

TYPES OF AUDIENCES

Anyone experienced in theatrical production can testify to the fact that audiences
vary from performance to performance. A Saturday night crowd will almost
invariably outlaugh a Monday night one. A matinée audience with a preponder-
ance of shoppers or tourists reacts quite differently from one dominated by
travelers. Audiences likewise differ from place to place. A performer meets a

different reception in Las Vegas than in Boston. University theatergoers are a marked contrast to those in a community theater. Spectators may find their responses to a play varying according to the stimulation they receive from others, the way they feel, the temperature of the auditorium, and the location of their seats. They will also notice that their reactions to a motion picture in a crowded theater are not the same as their response to a film seen in the seclusion of their own home.

Different kinds of plays attract different kinds of audiences. Compare an audience that attends an opera with those at a musical comedy, or note the difference between the spectators attending a farce and a tragedy. A striking example of variation may be seen in Japan, where the archaic, restrained Noh drama is met with dignified, nearly reverent attention, whereas the popular Kabuki audience may have a noisy and enthusiastic response. Spectators at an experimental production are often a strange mixture; some are sympathetic to any kind of provocation, whereas others may remain aloof—baffled, shocked, or offended by what is going on.

As a social institution, the theater has at times served as a tribunal, propaganda agency, house of the devil, temple of worship, meeting place for disreputable characters, showcase for ostentatious display, and place for intellectual stimulation. Its status and function have depended on the audience that patronized it. Consider, for example, four representative audiences.

The Greek Audience

The theater of Greece was a religious institution, which every free male attended during the two main festivals; the Lenaia, primarily a local celebration since the seas were rough for travel in winter, was especially important for comedy. Since most of the audience were Athenians, Aristophanes took great delight in satirizing local situations and prominent people, and even the audience itself. The City Dionysia, which offered competition in tragedies, satyr plays, and choral singing, was a more serious occasion, though still a celebration. The audience came to share in the great searching problems of mankind—problems that elevated the human spirit through suffering.

Athenian audiences were remarkable because of their great zest for living and thinking. Art, literature, philosophy, and logic were not mere subjects of contemplation for them. They were an active, inquiring people with an unquenchable thirst for learning. Because their interests and tastes ranged widely, their infrequent dramatic productions could accommodate the tragic grandeur of Aeschylus and the comic irreverence of Aristophanes, whose uninhibited shafts of ridicule are a commentary on the amazing tolerance of Greek society.

The Greeks were a knowledgeable audience, steeped in their literary heritage, with keen ears for the rhythm and texture of language, and so thoroughly familiar with the plays of their time that they could identify specific passages of Euripidean and Aeschylean dialogue in Aristophanes' comedy *The Frogs*. Such an audience invited dramas of great ideas and magnificent language. The culture that produced the idea of the golden mean—moderation in all things—led to a drama that was clear and logically organized and usually free from the excesses of pathos and sentiment. The Athenians' search for truth in life resulted in drama that was unflinchingly and relentlessly honest in confronting evil, suffering, and catastrophe. Their intellectual tolerance and sense of balance enabled them to see the sense and nonsense of the Aristophanic satire that scathingly attacked the follies of the time. The Athenians of the fifth century B.C. were astonishingly civilized human beings, and their level of culture is nowhere reflected so admirably as in the dramas created for their pleasure and edification.

In Rome, by contrast, the character of the audience was the chief handicap to the playwright, who wrote for a miscellaneous rabble who had no taste for poetic diction, subtle characterization, or refined humor.

The Elizabethan Audience

Like the Greeks, the Elizabethans had an enormous enthusiasm for life. Shakespeare's time was one of remarkable intellectual ferment, with great interest in language, literature, music, and politics. The Elizabethans viewed human beings as creatures of great potential. The spirit of the times was positive, dynamic, tumultuous.

The theater reflected the climate of the age. More than 30,000 customers a week flocked to see half a dozen professional, competing companies in London offer the richest concentration of dramatic fare the world has ever known. The theater appealed to the public's taste for pageantry and action, which elsewhere manifested itself in masques, processionals, and bear-baiting. The plays capitalized on the audience's interest in language, and the Elizabethan playwright enthusiastically followed the practice of medieval drama in putting as much vigorous and vivid action onstage as possible. Such a combination of words and action enlarged the appeal of drama so that all the motley audience could find something to suit its pleasure in the play. For the groundlings, there was exciting and violent action and raucous comedy. For the discriminating, there was delight in the magnificent language and food for thought in the elevated ideas. The Elizabethan audience's interests and tastes covered a wide range, and for it the playwright wrote both serious and comic dramas that were full-bodied, exuberant images of a turbulent and heady age.

One of the interesting attributes of the Elizabethans was their willingness to use their imaginations in viewing a play. Writing for a bare stage, Shakespeare and his contemporaries were nevertheless able to transport their audiences to distant times and places without benefit of illusionistic scenery.

Shakespeare's *Henry V* offers a striking example of how the playwright captured the spectators' imagination. The action of the play includes "England, afterwards France," with such locales as the King's Palace in London, a castle in Rouen, and the field of battle at Agincourt, where savage fighting takes place—all

The audience at the Globe Theater, as visualized by C. Walter Hodges in *Shakespeare's Theater*. This view looking toward the stage shows the spectators standing in the pit, while others occupy the galleries. The drawing conveys the feeling of intimacy that characterized the Elizabethan playhouse.

in imaginary settings supplied by the audience. The play begins when the Chorus (a single narrator) comes forward and addresses the theatergoers:

> *Chorus:*   Can this cockpit hold
> The vast fields of France? or may we cram
> Within this wooden O the very casques
> That did affright the air at Agincourt?
> O, pardon! since a crooked figure may
> Attest in little place a million;
> And let us, ciphers to this great accompt,
> On your imaginary forces work,
> Suppose within the girdle of these walls
> Are now confin'd two mighty monarchies;
> Whose high upreared and abutting fronts
> The perilous narrow ocean parts asunder;
> Piece out our imperfections with your thoughts;

Le Petit-Bourbon, the first court theater in France, 1577, was shared by Molière's troupe and another company. This view shows King Louis XIII and Cardinal Richelieu seated behind the arch on a raised stage during a performance.

> Into a thousand parts divide one man,
> And make imaginary puissance;
> Think, when we talk of horses, that you see them
> Printing their proud hoofs in the receiving earth;
> For 't is your thoughts that now must deck our kings,
> Carry them here and there, jumping o'er times
> Turning the accomplishment of many years
> Into an hour-glass.[2]

The Restoration Audience

The Restoration audience offers a sharp contrast to the Elizabethan. When Charles II returned to the throne, the theater became the preoccupation of the court. The audience was made up of fashionable wits, fops, beaux, parasites, and women of easy virtue. So limited was the audience that only two theaters were active in London, despite the fact that the population had doubled since Elizabethan times. For twelve years, one theater was sufficient to accommodate this narrow following. The theater was a plaything for fashionable people. Such patronage resulted in drama that was artificial and deliberately unconcerned with the stern realities of life. When the Restoration playwright attempted to write serious heroic dramas, the result was exaggerated and false pseudoclassical plays, full of excessive emotion. The special achievement of the period was high comedy, which dealt with the foibles of social conduct rather than ethics. Puritan morality was satirized. Comedies dealt with the complications of intrigue and the defects of manners. The level of the playwrights' subject matter was offset by their brilliant use of language. They achieved a high polish in their repartee and their eloquence of style. The limited audience allowed the playwright to capitalize on personal invective and local and timely allusions. Restoration comedy is a particularly explicit example of the effect of an audience on the drama.

Thus we see that people come to the theater for a variety of purposes and that they constitute a vital force on the writing and production of plays.

The Modern Audience

Part of the driving force toward a new theater was the dissatisfaction with the audience–actor relationship. Brecht and Artaud were outspoken about the need for new kinds of audiences, suitable for their concepts of theater. Although they represented entirely different points of view, both made an enormous impact on the changing view of what the audience in the theater should be.

Brecht was dedicated to finding a new actor–audience relationship based on an objective attitude. At the center of his dramatic theory was the idea of "alienation," which rejected the emotional attachment of the Stanislavski illusionistic theater; Brecht believed this theater lulled the spectators into a fantasy land of make-believe and shut off the rational, critical judgments necessary for evaluating the social problems put before them.

Brecht makes this contrast between realistic, "dramatic" theater and his epic theater:

> The audience in the dramatic theater says: Yes, I have felt that way too.—That's how I am.—That is only natural.—That will always be so.—This person's suffering shocks me because he has no way out. This is great art: everything in it is self-evident.—I weep with the weeping, I laugh with the laughing.
>
> The audience in the epic theater says: I wouldn't have thought that.—People shouldn't do things like that.—That's extremely odd, almost unbelievable.—This has to stop.—This person's suffering shocks me, because there might be a way out for him.—This is great art: nothing in it is self-evident.—I laugh over the weeping, and I weep over the laughing.[3]

At the other end of the spectrum, Artaud, in *The Theater and Its Double*, called for a radical departure that would place the audience and the actors in the same space, sharing a common experience that would completely engage the spectators in a communal ceremony. Artaud describes the desired response:

It is a question, then, of making the theater, in the proper sense of the word, a function; something as localized and as precise as the circulation of the blood in the arteries or the apparently chaotic development of dream images in the brain, and this is to be accomplished through involvement, a genuine enslavement of the attention.[4]

Perhaps, the most notable example of Artaud's influence was Brook's

A contemporary audience gathers for a performance at the Olivier Theater, part of the National Theater in London.

Marat/Sade production at the Royal Shakespeare Theater. Artaud's notion of a "theater of cruelty" made an important impact, especially in some of the highly inventive offerings in the new theater.

Although the actor was at the matrix of the Polish Laboratory Theater, Grotowski was also dedicated to developing a special kind of audience, which came to a performance as serious participants in a demanding experience. Working without the customary technical support of scenery, costuming, lighting, or even makeup, the Laboratory actors gave themselves fully to the performance with a kind of religious fervor. Grotowski, like Artaud, sought a special kind of involvement:

> We do not cater to the man who goes to the theater to satisfy a social need for contact with culture: in other words, to have something to talk about to his friends and be able to say that he has seen this or that play and that it was interesting. We are concerned with the spectator who has genuine spiritual needs and who really wishes, through confrontation with the performance, to analyze himself . . . toward a search for the truth about himself and his mission in life.[5]

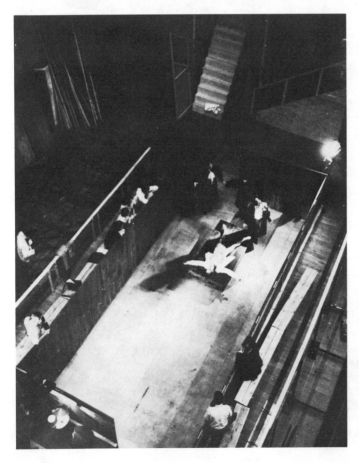

The set designed by Jerzy Gurawski for Grotowski's *Constant Prince* at the Polish Laboratory Theater deliberately kept the size of the audience restricted, and in this instance, kept it behind a fenced enclosure that surrounded the playing area.

Grotowski was keenly interested in controlling the audience as well as the players, and he often specified the place of performance and the number of spectators to be admitted. An example of how he included the audience in his production design for the *Acropolis* is described by James Roose-Evans:

> The production is set on a large rectangular stage standing in the middle of the audience. The platform is piled high with scrap metal. A ragged violinist appears and summons the rest of the cast, who hobble on in sacks and wooden boots. The action takes the form of daydreams in the breaks, between work. The seven actors attack the mound of rusting metal, hammering in unison, and fixing twisted pipes to struts over the audience's heads. The audience, however, is not involved. They represent the dead. . . . At the end of *Acropolis* there is an ecstatic procession following the image of the Saviour (a headless corpse) into a paradise which is also the extermination chamber.[6]

It was inevitable that the political and cultural rebellion in the 1960s in the United States should include new views of the audience, stemming not only from

Director Adrian Hall, in this production of *Billy Budd* at the Trinity Square Repertory Company, Providence, brought the action out into the audience. Eugene Lee's setting provided a flexible environment with a shipyard atmosphere.

Brecht, Artaud, and Grotowski but also from experimental groups with their own original ideas. Disdainfully opposed to the "canned entertainment" of movies and television, as well as popular Broadway hits aimed at bored or tired business people, the new theater workers wanted to capitalize on live, kinetic, highly energized performances that could jolt the spectators out of their seats. Director Tom O'Horgan, who gave the new audience the "tribal rock musical" *Hair,* described his view of the way to handle an audience: "You have to keep nudging the audience; to say, 'You're alive. You do exist, right now.' You try to make the audience feel that it's not something that's nailed to a chair."

One of the striking features of the Living Theater was Beck's strenuous efforts to engage the audience as participants in a form of political activism. As a part of the performance, the actors encroached on the audience's area. For example, before the plays began, actors in street clothes circulated in the auditorium, sometimes buttonholing individuals directly, sometimes in warm-up exercises. Audiences were invited onstage, where they might join in a pile of bodies of other spectators and performers in a communal gesture. Or spectators joined a circle with the actors onstage, moving and chanting as one voice. At the end of the performance, the cast would at times come down the aisles and invite the audience to join them in the streets in celebrations that occasionally led to protest marches, demonstrations, or riots. In some instances, Beck's intentions were successfully realized, and audiences freely participated in the action, but at other times the blatant aggression was counterproductive.

Chaikin's Open Theater began as a private workshop for actors exploring their potential for new ways of working, but inevitably actors need a response to test the effectiveness of their playing. At first, the public was admitted to observe workshops of improvisations and exercises, but the need was felt to create a full-scale production. The Open Theater did not attract an ordinary audience, looking for momentary diversion. People came to share an experience or to see new ways of performing.

Chaikin's workshop and his book were centered on *The Actor's Presence.* He was acutely concerned with developing ensemble play or interrelationships of one actor with another and with the group. But his sensitivity also expanded to include the audience:

> The confrontation is with that delicate but powerful pulse of people assembled in the same room. For this reason, it is the rhythm and dynamic responses, rather than the confrontation of attitudes between the actor and the audience, which is important. This special task is possible in the particular context of the *anonymous intimacy* between players and audience, and through it the main theme, which is the confrontation of our mortality.[7]

Schechner, under the strong influence of Grotowski's Laboratory Theater and its methods, aimed at involving the audience in communal events with the Performance Group. In an attempt to enlist the audience in the performances, some of which were intended to be rites or celebrations, the Group members would usher their patrons into the theater one at a time, invite them to remove their shoes, and ask for donations of small pieces of paper that were later burned during a ritualistic fire in the performance.

The politically radical San Francisco Mime Troupe views its audience as a potential human resource to mobilize in its battle against social injustice. The Troupe specializes in broad comedy and sharp satire, using both as weapons for promoting social change. It works in parks, marketplaces, fairgrounds, and any other place it can gather up a crowd. Schumann's Bread and Puppet Theater is also a street theater, working wherever it can find an audience. Although its huge, awesome puppets frequently appeared in parades and protest marches during the time of the Vietnam War, its underlying drive seems to be toward a restoration of a traditional moral order and beneficent humanism. Because it performs without ticket sales and with no regular place for playing, Schumann's theater performs with childlike clarity and simplicity, making its points with impressive images and gestures.

The audience of the new theater very often sees a different kind of drama than the theatergoer in the commercial playhouse. The story line gives way to sensory experience often multilayered, with multifocused and simultaneous action. Instead of following clearly defined characters involved in a plot, spectators respond to the moment-by-moment stimuli that impinge on them. They are interested in what is happening now, rather than what will happen next. Lighting, scenic effects, film, projections, and sound are often used as separate entities as well as for support. The theater worker operates in a permissive world since there are almost no barriers on subject matter, nudity, obscenity, and behavior. Anything goes. As a result, there is a good deal of straining for effect and an exaggerated use of novelty and sensational devices, often without control or taste.

Once upon a time, when you went to the theater, you settled back in the darkness and drifted off to some never-never land in a vicarious adventure that freed you from your mundane cares. Now you may sit on the floor or in bleachers or on scaffolding, with no assurance that you will remain aloof from the show. You may be invited to participate in a group exercise; you may be queried or argued with; you may be teased, insulted, fondled, whispered to, embraced. Experimental performance seeks immediacy, intensity, and exuberance in an effort to reach all levels of your consciousness. These changes are directed at the narrow concept of drama as middle- and upper-class amusement and toward theater as a means of enlightenment and release, a place of celebration, fulfillment, and wonder.

OPPORTUNITIES FOR THE AUDIENCE

In this country, we have no permanent dramatic tradition, no national theater, no classical repertory of American plays. We do have a rich history of professional theatrical activity, especially before World War I. At the turn of the century, more than 300 traveling companies brought stars and productions to every corner of the country, but the coming of film and television has taken over much of the public's hunger for popular entertainment.

Even in New York City theatrical conditions are not encouraging. In 1929, there were seventy-five theaters that offered 233 new shows in a single season. Now, only about a third of the playhouses remain, and there are only about thirty-five new offerings each year—mostly musicals, revivals, or foreign plays. Increased production costs and soaring ticket prices do not make the Broadway situation any brighter.

In London, by contrast, more than forty theaters offer a wide variety of fare that features the two jewels of the British crown, the Royal Shakespeare Company and the National Theater, both occupying excellent facilities supported by substantial government subsidies, as are about thirty other English theaters, many of whom are repertory companies. The virtue of a residential repertory company is that a theater can have a stabilized, continuous program with a full complement of actors, technicians, and management personnel to offer a diversified bill of plays—revivals of the classics, experimental styles of productions, and new plays. Such a company develops an audience that is willing to take the risk of seeing new and innovative performances, and it reduces the box office pressure from management. Because of the diversification of the repertory system, the English theater has an enormous advantage in training new talent in all aspects of production. It is no wonder that more than two million American tourists visit the English theaters in the summer and account for 80 percent of their business.

In the United States, we took a brief fling at government-subsidized theater as a means of combating unemployment in 1935. The Federal Theater Project, under Hallie Flanagan, employed more than 10,000 theater workers and brought plays to audiences in forty states. It developed a highly theatricalized style of production, "the living newspaper"—dramatic documentaries of scenes and excerpts of speeches and articles, resembling Brecht's epic theater in form. One of its productions, Sinclair Lewis's *It Can't Happen Here* (1936), played simultaneously in twenty-one theaters throughout the country to people paying admission prices from a dime to a dollar. When the project was forced to close because Congress felt the plays were too political in tone, it is estimated that one-fourth of the entire population had seen live theater, most for the first time.

To fill the vacuum left by the Broadway theatrical decline since World War II, the off-Broadway movement has made an important contribution. Newcomers searching for a place to train and exhibit their talents began forming groups, which usually occupied small houses, to be able to negotiate with unions for actors and stagehands. Limited by scanty resources, they made theaters of old movie houses, lofts, cafés, and churches. Their efforts followed the pattern of two early experimental companies, the Provincetown Playhouse and the Washington Square Players, which had as early as 1916 served as showcases for promising talent. From the Provincetown Players came such outstanding figures as Eugene O'Neill and Robert Edmond Jones, the United States' foremost playwright and designer. The Washington Square Players became the Theater Guild, which played to subscription audiences and gave to New York a high standard of production of innovative and noncommercial plays.

Following these two examples, the burgeoning off-Broadway theaters of the 1950s and 1960s proved to be excellent training grounds and showcases for new actors, including Dustin Hoffman, Al Pacino, George C. Scott, Geraldine Page, Meryl Streep, and William Hurt. Off-Broadway also was an important development for attracting and conditioning new audiences open to fresh approaches.

In 1959 another movement began with the introduction of off-off-Broadway theaters that were not primarily "farm clubs" for training rookies for the big leagues of Broadway. This new movement was more inclined to develop its own kind of theater, without one eye on the scouts and critics. These venturesome theater workers wanted their own identity, and although audiences' acceptance was appreciated, their goal was not box office or an ambition to become part of the "show-biz" scene.

Off-off-Broadway began with Joe Chino's Coffee House, followed by Ellen Stewart's Café La Mama. Both these theaters were dedicated to giving new writers a chance to be heard without worrying about the commercial feasibility of their work. They provided opportunities for dozens of playwrights to see their plays in performance before audiences, an invaluable experience for the writer.

A generation ago, the only way for most Americans to see a professional play was to visit New York or wait for an infrequent touring company to play in the nearest metropolitan theater. The other available producing groups were community, college, and university theaters, whose casts were mostly amateur actors.

In 1950 there were only about a dozen professional regional theaters. Now, a national organization, the Theater Communications Group, serves as a network for 314 regional theaters in forty-three states. These ventures have given the American theater a remarkable new vitality that was sorely needed. Scores of groups feature new native playwrights and U.S. premieres of outstanding foreign imports.

One of the most heartening aspects of this regional growth is the development of new audiences who are willing to back fresh material. Season ticket holders support experimentation as an act of faith by buying out two-thirds of the tickets, even though they know little or nothing about the playwrights. A world premiere is an exhilarating opportunity. This exciting phenomenon has opened up opportunities for American playwrights as never before, because many regional theaters actively solicit new work and offer prizes, subsidies, play readings, and play development projects. It is not coincidental that most of the new plays now produced on Broadway were first produced and developed at such regional theaters as the Seattle Repertory Company, Steppenwolf in Chicago, the Louisville Actors Theater, South Coast Repertory, Yale, Hartford Stage, the Arena, and the Old Globe, to name just a few.

The emergence of these nonprofit theaters has also provided employment for hundreds of actors, designers, directors, technicians, and staff. Designers whose works were once seen only on Broadway (or not at all) are active now in regional theaters, sometimes on a one-shot basis, sometimes for several years. The same thing is true of the rest of the creative talent, so there is a very positive kind of mutual stimulation and interchange going on.

One feature of the regional theaters that augurs well for the future is their active campaigns for building audiences. There are such educational programs as tours of the theater, special performances and demonstrations, and preshow and postshow discussions with actors, directors, and playwrights. Some theaters sponsor overseas tours. There is a wealth of educational material, such as play outlines, detailed study guides, and visits by performers to schools. Many theaters offer a variety of courses in all phases of production, and some have full-time two- and three-year professional programs. Some offer seminars, workshops, and conferences. In short, there is an enormous burgeoning of interest in theater at all levels all over the country. The benefits of this development are encouraging because it enables theaters to plan for an entire season instead of for a single play; it provides the opportunity to develop an effective staff and a cohesive company of actors and technicians; it provides a basis for financial security; it has led to the renovation or building of excellent physical plants; it has made the theater an intrinsic part of the community; and it has encouraged a fresh approach to the selection and production of all kinds of plays.

For a long time, those in the arts have been lamenting the absence of continuity in American dramatic production. Lacking a national theater with a permanent residential company, we have had to put up with the Broadway

Regional theaters are building audiences for the future. Tom Haas, director of the North Carolinian Playmakers Repertory Company, talks to high school students following his production of *Macbeth*.

pattern of commercial productions put together for each show in a rented theater. We have looked enviously at the state-supported theaters of England and Europe, where for generations there have been permanent theaters with residential companies. As a result, in those countries theater became a habitual part of the social life of a large audience who knew the theater as an ongoing communal resource. Now, U.S. regional theaters are building audiences that are bringing a measure of continunity to their efforts.

Augmenting the professional scene are an impressive number of college and university theaters, many of them with exemplary physical plants. They offer extensive training in all phases of dramatic literature and production, supplemented by ambitious programs of theatrical performances. At least forty of them sustain resident companies, and more than two hundred offer professional training.

You may be a student at such a university, with all of the opportunities it affords. Or, if dramatic arts is not a major offering, you are sure to find on your campus courses and activities related to the theater which will give you a chance to try your hand at acting, painting scenery, running lights, writing a play, or taking tickets—an opportunity that is sure to leave its mark, because the theater is a beguiling creature—once she smiles on you, she will be difficult to ignore.

BIBLIOGRAPHY

BLAU, HERBERT. *The Impossible Theater: A Manifesto.* New York: Macmillan, 1964.
CORRIGAN, ROBERT. *The Making of the Theater.* Glenview, Ill.: Scott, Foresman, 1981.
JACOBS, SUSAN. *On Stage: The Making of a Broadway Play.* New York: Knopf, 1972.
LEE, VERA G. *Quest for a Public, French Popular Theater Since 1945.* Cambridge, Mass.: Schenckman, 1970.
MCLUHAN, MARSHALL. *Understanding Media.* New York: McGraw-Hill, 1964.
SCHECHNER, RICHARD. *Public Domain.* Indianapolis: Bobbs-Merrill, 1969.
SONTAG, SUSAN. *Against Interpretation.* New York: Farrar, Straus & Giroux, 1966.
STYAN, J. L. *Drama, Stage and Audience.* Cambridge: Cambridge University Press, 1975.
YURKA, BLANCHE. *Dear Audience: A Guide to the Enjoyment of the Theater.* Englewood Cliffs, N.J.: Prentice-Hall, 1959.

NOTES

1. Emory Bogardus, *Sociology* (New York: Macmillan, 1949).

2. William Shakespeare, *Henry V,* Prologue.

3. Bertolt Brecht, "Theater for Learning or Theater for Pleasure." trans. Edith Anderson, *Mainstream, 11,* June 1958.

4. Antonin Artaud, *The Theater and Its Double* (New York: Grove Press, 1958). Translated by Mary C. Richards.

5. Jerzy Grotowski, quoted in *Time,* October 24, 1969.

6. James Roose-Evans, *The Experimental Theater* (New York: Universe Books, 1970).

7. Joseph Chaikin, "Closing the Open Theater," *Theater Quarterly,* November 1974–January 1975.

fourteen
Playwriting

William Shakespeare (1564—1616) is universally acclaimed as the foremost playwright of the theater. His genius extended from broad comedy to magnificent tragedy. He acquired his craft as a playwright by working in the theater as an actor at the Globe in London. This Droeshut portrait appeared in the *First Folio*—the first collected works of Shakespeare.

In the beginning is the word—the text. Theater begins with the play. In the theatrical revolution that has taken place since World War II, all kinds of experiments have been made, including assaults on plays and playwriting. Efforts have been made to improvise a script or to put one together as a team creation. Old plays have been ransacked, hacked up, patched together, cut to the bone, or changed entirely by idiosyncratic interpretations. Rebels may still echo the war cry, "No more masterpieces," but the truth is that the greatest single need in the theater today is for quality playwrights and plays.

Every year, the search goes on for good new plays, and although there are a multitude of competent and promising writers, the paucity of truly outstanding plays remains a fact of life. This shortage is the more striking, despite unparalleled opportunities for new writers, because many regional and university theaters are actively searching for new playwrights, and there is a groundswell of support for original work.

The theater has always been a difficult medium to write for, because of the special conditions of production—and without production, the writer's creation is incomplete. As you will see, authors work in a wide variety of ways, but everyone is conscious of the fact that the ultimate test occurs when the curtain goes up and the actors walk on stage. Although present-day playwrights have a much freer hand in writing for a flexible theater, the art of creating a fine play remains the most demanding and difficult form of writing.

A BRIEF HISTORY OF PLAYWRITING

We have already credited Thespis with being the first actor; we should also recognize him as the first playwright, because we know that he introduced his "tragedies" in Athens. Aeschylus added a second actor, and Sophocles a third. Their plays were written in competition with one another and consisted of three tragedies and a satyr play. It is estimated that between 500 B.C. and 400 B.C. more than a thousand tragedies were written; only thirty-one are extant. All of the surviving comedies of the fifth century B.C. were written by Aristophanes, who satirized Greek politics, society, and literature. Whereas the tragic writers were treated as venerable men, Aristophanes, because of his barbed comedies, was frequently in trouble with the authorities.

Roman drama was secular, and the playwrights, especially the comic ones, Plautus and Terence, wrote for the rabble. Their plots were taken from the Greeks. Seneca rewrote the tragic dramas of the Greeks, but his rhetoric lacked the elevation of the original, and the result was striking melodrama. These Romans are remembered because they influenced the Elizabethans in England and the Renaissance dramatists in France.

With the decline of Rome, the theater disappeared for hundreds of years. It was not until the tenth century that drama began to develop again, this time as part of the liturgy of the Church. Unknown clergy added episodes to the services, and eventually they developed miracle, mystery, and morality plays that were aimed at promoting religious doctrine and the gospel of salvation.

The humanism of the English Renaissance provided fertile soil for the development of the astounding burgeoning of playwriting talent that included Shakespeare, Marlowe, Jonson, Kyd, Greene, and Lyly, most of whom wrote for professional theater companies competing with one another for the lively Elizabethan audience. For the most part, they followed no rules, but freely mixed high characters with low and produced a marvelous assortment of tragedies, light and dark comedies, chronicle and history plays. They borrowed freely from the classics and from one another and wrote plays for flexible stages, talented companies of actors, and exciting audiences. Their Jaccobean successors, especially John Webster, were so offensive in their agnosticism that the Puritans closed the London theaters in 1642.

Meanwhile in France, Corneille and Racine were hemmed in by the misinterpretation of classical rules, but nevertheless managed to produce admirable plays. Molière, actor-manager and playwright, wrote comedies suited to the talents of his company. His ridicule of authorities usually delighted the king but alienated his enemies, and he ended up in an unmarked grave—one of the greatest comic talents of all time.

The Renaissance in Spain saw the emergence of the prolific Lope de Vega and Calderon de la Barca, an ordained priest. After the Restoration in England in 1660, when Charles II returned from France, he brought with him a taste for drama. The theaters were opened again, heavily influenced by the French and now with the added fillip of female performers—which, of course, profoundly affected playwriting, not to mention production. Drama exploited marital and extramarital relationships in drawing room comedies featuring bright repartee. William Congreve, William Wycherly, and George Farquhar wrote for a limited and sophisticated audience; in the eighteenth century, however, when the taste for theater reached the masses, Richard Sheridan and Oliver Goldsmith broadened their comedy to meet a more plebeian taste.

In late-eighteenth-century Germany, Goethe spearheaded the revolutionary Sturm und Drang movement that prompted his own Romantic plays, especially *Goetz von Berlichingen* and those of Schiller and Lessing. As a playwright, Goethe profited from his personal experience as a director and actor as well as from his association with the actor Schröder. Victor Hugo's success with *Hernani* in France in 1830 reflected the Romantic spirit in France, but the popular drama of the day became melodrama, especially in the plays of Pixerécourt. In England, Boucicault also wrote melodramas that captured the public fancy, as did Kotzebue in Germany. Melodrama has always had a facility for pleasing a wide audience with its strong conflicts between good and evil and the use of spectacular action and sensational stage effects.

The enormous social and political changes and the technical advances of the Industrial Revolution in the nineteenth century brought about profound differences in the ways of looking at the world. In the theater this social upheaval was reflected in the plays of Ibsen, Strindberg, Chekhov, Shaw, Gorki, Pirandello, and O'Neill—to mention just a few who were concerned with the individual's attempt to adjust to a complex and confusing new world.

The two world wars and the Depression compounded this situation, and again playwrights dramatized the problems of survival in an alien world, as in the works of John Osborne, Harold Pinter, Arthur Miller, Bertolt Brecht, Tennessee Williams, Edward Albee, Samuel Beckett, Eugene Ionesco, and Jean Genet. The drastic changes in the post–World War II period resulted in revolutionary ways of looking at all aspects of the theater.

Perhaps there has never been a more perplexing time for a playwright, or a greater opportunity for plays of genuine vision and insight. Dramatists may work alone as individuals, but they are inextricably tied to the society that provides the material and outlet for their creations.

RESTRICTIONS OF PLAYWRITING

One who writes for the theater faces certain restrictions unknown to the novelist or film writer. These stem from the final form of a play—production in the theater before an audience.

A play must be compact. It is limited in time, place, and characters. An occasional production like *Nicholas Nickleby* or the *Mahabharata* may succeed in drawing an audience despite playing for eight or nine hours, but throughout theater history the consistent format is two to four hours of playing time.

Unity of place is not essential, especially nowadays, when staging and lighting are so flexible, but there is a solid basis for limiting the locale because of the gain in concentration. Shakespeare's plays, with their multiple scenes, work in performance if they are staged in Elizabethan or open style; but any attempt to place the action in pictorial, changeable scenery is courting disaster. Changing the set invites distraction. Reversing Aristotle's elements by giving top priority to spectacle and music may work for musical comedy, but not for serious drama.

Another factor in making a play compact is the use of a limited number of characters. Most successful plays concentrate the attention on two or three main roles. After all, how many strangers can you really get to know in two or three hours? Since much of drama depends on conflicts, the usual practice of focusing on two or three adversaries is a sound one. Furthermore, in the professional theater, large casts are expensive. Every time you add a character to a cast you add a salary, costume expense, and probably additional rehearsal time. Is it any wonder that producers look for plays with a small cast and a single set?

The restrictions on time and place these days have often yielded to more flexible production techniques, such as having actors play transformations or multiple roles, and using minimal staging techniques with a few set pieces, or projections, or just changing lights, properties, and costumes. But the generalization still holds true: Dramatic art is a compact one.

A third essential fact about playwriting is that the script is almost all dialogue—with a few lines of stage directions. The audience gets its clues from the characters themselves. A fiction writer can go inside the person's head or write a paragraph of description, but the actor on stage must talk.

Take the problem of exposition. When the curtain rises, the audience faces a handful of strangers. Somehow, if we are to get interested, we must get background material on who these characters are and what they are up to. Mostly, this is a matter of words. Today we have a much freer stage, which allows actors to talk directly to the audience to give them expository material. Matt in *Talley's Folly* (p. 47) walks down to the footlights and tells the audience directly about how he met Sally. Similarly, Tevye, in *Fiddler on the Roof* (p. 155), talks to God for a moment and explains his predicament. But in general, playwrights observe the convention of the "fourth wall"—pretending that the audience is not there—and provide exposition unobtrusively in the dialogue and action, as in Willy Loman's first few lines in *Death of a Salesman* (p. 4).

A playwright works under pressure. The dialogue must be dynamic, continually moving forward to create the momentum of the play. There is no time for digression or wool-gathering. The characters' speech must be consistent and seem natural, even though it is concentrated. Furthermore, it must be clear at once to the spectator, because there is no time for repetition or turning back. In short, writing good dramatic dialogue is a very special talent.

Finally, the playwright is confronted with the restriction that the theater is a collaborative enterprise. When the script is completed, his or her problems may just be beginning. There is the basic problem of getting the play produced in the theater with all its attendant complexities—finding a suitable director, casting the roles, working out the interpretation with the director and designers—and, finally, attracting an audience. Each of the collaborators—director, actor, and designer—is a creative artist in his or her own right, so there is a good deal of give and take that is absolutely essential if the play is to succeed.

CREATING A PLAY

The sources of creation in any art are always mystifying and often very personal, so it is very difficult to nail down the specific steps of creating a play. In general, most successful playwrights had first-hand, practical experience in working in the theater before they wrote plays.

In playwriting, it is customary to think that a play begins with a specific process. A spate of examples shows that playwrights work in a variety of ways and that they depend a good deal on intuition and inspiration.

Charles Fuller, who wrote *A Soldier's Play*, says he wants to tell a story that no one else has ever told. The most important part of the play is the opening scene, which he might try a hundred times before he gets it right (see p. 21); ". . . if I don't get you in those first few minutes, I've lost you." After he has a beginning, Fuller says, he creates the story as it comes along: "The process is one of discovery from beginning to end."

Tennessee Williams also relates how he sometimes writes a page or two of dialogue as a starter mechanism:

> Something on a page or two of dialogue will spark in the way of characters or situation, and I just go along from there. I am a very wasteful writer. I go through several drafts, as many as four or five, before I finish a work.[1]

Asked how he begins working on a play, Williams made this response:

> It's almost impossible to pinpoint the start of the play, for I think that all plays come out of some inner tension in the playwright himself. He is concerned about something, and that concern begins to work itself out in the form of creative activity.[2]

Harold Pinter says he works in a similar way:

> I don't know what kind of characters my plays will have until they . . . well, until they *are* . . . I don't conceptualize in any way. Once I've got the clues, I follow them— that's my job, really, to follow the clues.[3]

Edward Albee follows the intuitive approach, which he describes in these terms:

> The process goes something like this: I discover that I have gotten an idea somewhere. I never *get* an idea—I discover that I *have* one. Then over the next six months or a year or two years, it gradually, slowly develops. I think about it occasionally. The characters are forming at that time, and eventually after a certain period of time, when the idea seems both vague enough and clear enough to start working on, and the characters seem three-dimensional enough to carry the burden of work by themselves, then I go to the typewriter. So the actual writing time is very short— anywhere from a month to three months. But the prewriting process—which is a form of writing, I suppose—takes a good deal of time.[4]

Luis Valdez, who made such a reputation with the Teatro Campesino and his play *Zoot Suit,* works his way into a play by random thinking:

> . . . When I begin, I allow myself at least a month of free association with notes. I can start anywhere. I can start with an abstract notion, a character . . . it's rarely dialogue or anything specific like that. More often than not, it's just an amorphous bunch of ideas, impressions and feelings. I allow myself to tumble in this ball of thoughts and impressions, knowing that I'm heading toward a play and that eventually I've got to begin dealing with character and then structure.[5]

David Hwang, whose *M. Butterfly* caused such a sensation in the 1987 season in New York, commenting on his development as a playwright, says that in his early plays, *FOB, Dance and the Railroad,* and *Family Devotions* (1981), he wrote them with no preplanning. All he had as a germ idea was this: What would happen if these two gods met in Torrance, California? "I had no idea what the next word would be." But when he hit upon the idea for *M. Butterfly,* based on a true story, he became far more aware of structure, and he knew what "the arc of each scene was going to be" before he started it.

Many playwrights go through a period of experimentation, once the germ idea is identified. David Rabe, who won the Pulitzer Prize for his *Sticks and Bones*, describes what happens to him:

> With an impulse or a situation or sometimes just a fragment of dialogue that begins to expand once you work on it. Something sticks in my mind—it could be a real person or a real exchange of dialogue or a fragment that just pops into my head. It doesn't have to have any historical basis. I'll decide to work on it and it'll either expand or it won't. It's just a feeling I have, when it's going well. I do best if I don't get too conscious too soon. Usually the best things happen when they develop in ways you hadn't anticipated. So I try to work in a way that will allow that to happen, which isn't easy—your mind is always jumping ahead. Some people work from an outline or notes but I find them more of a block that stops me from following these impulses when they show up.[6]

Henrik Ibsen

Henrik Ibsen, whose plays are generally credited with the advent of realism, was an interesting playwright because of the written record he left behind. The process of actually writing a play was preceded by a period of thinking and experimentation. Ibsen said, "I am forever creating, or, at any rate, dreaming of something, which, when in the fullness of time it ripens, will reveal itself as a creation."

When he began to think about *Hedda Gabler* (1890), he wrote in a letter to a young lady he met in Austria: "A new poem begins to dawn on me." And then this note of anticipation: "I will execute it this winter, and try to transfer to it the bright atmosphere of the summer. But I feel it will end in sadness—such is my nature."

During this preparation, Ibsen jotted down notes, character descriptions, and fragments of dialogue to help him with his thinking. His first note about Hedda foreshadows the final character: "The pale, seemingly cold beauty. Great demands upon life and upon the joy of life." He translates this into more specific terms by his observation that she felt that she had wasted earlier years in supporting her father, and now, at twenty-five or twenty-six, she was on the point of going downhill unmarried. "This becomes her motivation for her unsatisfactory marriage to Tesman, who was an 'insignificant person'."

Earlier, when Ibsen was writing *Ghosts* (1881), he began with such notes to himself as this:

> Among us we place monuments over the dead, for we recognize duties toward them; we allow people only fit for the hospital to marry: but their offspring—? The unborn—?[7]

From such preliminary thinking, Ibsen translated the problem into human form in the characters of Mrs. Alving, Oswald, Pastor Manders, and Regina.

Ibsen's revision of *A Doll's House* (1879) offers an interesting example of a playwright at work. He wrote three drafts of the play. In the first two, he treats his characterization and plot in a melodramatic fashion, after the style of the French. But in the final version, he shows his development by stressing the conflict between Nora and Helmer. The key scene is no longer Nora's talk of suicide or dancing the tarantella, but the confrontation between husband and wife when they attempt to communicate for the first time. This conflict is epitomized in the change in a line from the first draft. When Krogstad returns the forged bill to Helmer, he cries out: "You are saved, Nora! You are saved!" In the final version, Ibsen changed the line to read: "I am saved, Nora! I am saved!"

In these three plays, the plots centered on memorable characters: Nora, Mrs. Alving, and Hedda. Ibsen professed not to be interested in the "woman movement," but rather in individuals. However, it is clear from his preliminary notes that Ibsen was deeply conscious of the plight of women in the social situation:

> These women of today, ill-treated as daughters, as sisters, as wives, not educated according to their gifts, withheld from their vocation, deprived of their heritage, embittered in mind—these it is who furnish the mothers of a new generation. What will be the consequence?[8]

Out of such questioning, Ibsen found plot ideas that revolutionized the theater.

In Ibsen's *An Enemy of the People*, Dr. Stockman alienates his fellow townspeople when he testifies that their public baths are polluted. They turn on him because they fear the loss of the tourist trade. *(Directed by Yvonne Shafer, University of Colorado)*

Eugene O'Neill

O'Neill was the first American playwright to achieve an international reputation. He was a serious playwright, who spent his career trying to write plays with important themes. Among his most important works are *A Long Day's Journey into Night, Anna Christie, Desire under the Elms,* and *Mourning Becomes Electra.* The latter play was written in response to a question that O'Neill posed for himself: Is it possible to write a modern tragedy based on Greek sources?

When he set out to answer this question in 1926, O'Neill kept a revealing diary of his thoughts during the process of writing and rewriting the play over a period of five years. The first steps show O'Neill's disciplined approach to playwriting, much like that of a scholar writing a history book:

October, 1928. Use story of Electra as a base.

November, 1928. Give Electra a tragic ending worthy of the character. Greek unsatisfactory.

April, 1929. Use modern history as a base. Civil War.

April, 1929. Use New England seaport. Puritan idea of sin and punishment useful. Agamemnon—Mayor, General. Departure from Greek. Electra loves 1. Father,

Alla Nazimova and Alice Brady in Eugene O'Neill's *Mourning Becomes Electra.*

2. Brother, 3. Paramour of Mother. Work out motivation and conflicts from these.

May, 1929. Characters' names.

May, 1929. Title: "Mourning Becomes Electra."

May, 1929. Make trilogy. Each play a title.

May, 1929. Technique: Write first draft in straight realism.

June, 1929. Finished scenario of first play.[9]

O'Neill goes on to write second and third scenarios at three-week intervals. Then he starts on the first draft, which takes three and a half months, followed by a period of revising, cutting, and experimentation, during which the playwright is painfully self-critical, but finds that some things work. For example, his entry on February 7, 1931, reads:

> Read over—don't like most of the new stuff—all right but introduces too many added complications—trying to get added values has blurred those I had—too much of a muchness—would need another play to do it right—and would be wrong even then! Can't crowd intuitions all hidden aspects of life form into one work! I better throw this new stuff out.[10]

Mourning Becomes Electra opened in New York in October 1931. It was admired for the grandeur of the concept but criticized for its language, which failed to reach tragic heights, and for its negative ending, which lacked the exaltation and catharsis of classic tragedy.

Arthur Miller

When Arthur Miller decided that the seventeenth-century Salem witch hunts among the Puritans offered a modern parallel to the McCarthy hearings in the Senate in the 1950s, he carefully researched New England history and based his play *The Crucible* on actual events and characters. He had a completely different experience in writing *All My Sons*, when he was suddenly struck by an idea during an innocuous conversation with a lady visitor from the midwest. She told him the story of a neighbor whose family had been destroyed by the father's corrupt practice during the war of selling defective military machinery. Miller was impressed by the fact that the father was convicted through the testimony of his own daughter. The playwright immediately found in this conversation the root idea for the conflict between father and son that is so powerfully developed in *All My Sons*. When he wrote *Death of a Salesman*, Miller says he began with the root idea of the character of Willy. All the playwright knew when he started was that Willy would destroy himself.

Obviously, creating a play is a highly individual matter. The playwright faces a variety of choices that often are made intuitively during the course of writing. Several of the most prominent playwrights have kept notes or diaries during the process of creation, and it is worth looking at some of their comments.

A striking element of Arthur Miller's *The Crucible* is the group of Salem girls who become "possessed" by evil spirits, which leads to witch hunts. *(Pacific Conservatory of Performing Arts)*

Friedrich Duerrenmatt

Friedrich Duerrenmatt's *The Visit* was first performed in his native Switzerland in 1956 at the Zurich Schauspielhaus. It created an immediate sensation and became one of the most popular plays by a European playwright since World War II. The playwright's efforts in creating *The Visit* are a revealing commentary on writing for the theater.

His first version of the germ idea was a novel in which a young man flees from his European village because his rival has taken his childhood sweetheart from him. He becomes very wealthy and returns to his village to get revenge. He offers the villagers a fortune if they agree to kill his enemy. The villagers are incensed at the idea and set up a plot to destroy the millionaire by having him killed by a falling tree.

Duerrenmatt was dissatisfied with his novel and decided to put his idea into a play. He began by changing the wealthy man into a rich widow, Madame Zachanassian, who in her early years had fallen in love with a young man, Anton Schill. When she became pregnant, Schill abandoned her. She was brought before the local court and charged with prostitution. Her lover bribed two false witnesses to testify that the girl was indeed a prostitute. Schill washed his hands of the matter and she was driven from the town. She married a wealthy man, and,

Lynn Fontanne as Madame Zachanassian and Alfred Lunt as Schill in *The Visit.* She has returned to her native village to take the life of the man who betrayed her.

after amassing a fortune, she determined to return to her native village and avenge her ill-treatment by offering a billion marks to the villagers for killing Schill.

In making a theater piece out of his story, Duerrenmatt was faced with the problem of staging. How could he show the village of Güllen, and how could he show in dramatic terms that this once prosperous village now suffered economic blight? The townspeople must be poor so that they would be more susceptible to a bribe. In the novel there was no problem of establishing these conditions by a page or two of description. But on stage he was limited to dialogue, action, and setting. Duerrenmatt decided to show that the village was impoverished by the fact that the prestigious trains no longer stopped at Güllen—a metaphor that prosperity had passed them by.

Here is the opening scene of *The Visit:* As the house lights begin to dim, you hear the clanging of a railway crossing bell and then an approaching train. The curtain goes up and you see on one side a small, run-down railway station, with a faded sign that says "Güllen." Nearby is a baggage wagon. On the other side is a shabby waiting room, with signs for restrooms—"Manner" and "Damen." Along the wall, there is a wooden bench on which four poorly dressed idlers sit watching a man kneeling on the floor painting a sign that reads, "Welcome, Clara." There is the suggestion of distant rooftops and a tower of the village in the background.

The stationmaster, in an old, faded uniform, comes out and salutes as the imaginary train thunders across the stage. The five men follow it with their eyes.

Before there is a single word of dialogue, you know the environment—a small, dilapidated town somewhere in Europe. The time is the present, and the characters are ordinary people who have seen better days. From their first few lines, you learn that this is a familiar routine:

First Man: The "Emperor," Hamburg-Naples.

Second Man: Then comes "The Diplomat."

Third Man: Then "The Banker."

Fourth Man: And at eleven twenty-seven, the "Flying Dutchman," Venice-Stockholm.

First Man: Our only pleasure—watching trains.

> *The bell rings, the Station Master comes out and salutes another train as it rushes through.*[11]

Now the playwright gives you additional clues and starts to build up anticipation for the entrance of Madame Zachanassian:

Fourth Man: Once upon a time, the "Emperor" and the "Flying Dutchman" used to stop here in Güllen. So did the "Diplomat," the "Banker," and the "Silver Comet."

Second Man: Now it's only the local from Kaffigen and the twelve-forty from Kalberstadt.

Third Man: The fact is, we're ruined.

First Man: What with the Wagonworks shut down . . .

Second Man: The Foundry finished . . .

Fourth Man: The Golden Eagle Pencil Factory all washed up . . .

First Man: It's life on the dole.

Second Man: Did you say life?

Third Man: We're rotting.

First Man: Starving.

Second Man: Crumbling.

Fourth Man: The whole damn town.

> *(The station bell rings.)*

Third Man: Once we were a center of industry.

Painter: A cradle of culture.

Fourth Man: One of the best little towns in the country.

First Man: In the world.

Second Man: Here Goethe slept.

Fourth Man: Brahms composed a quartet.

Third Man: Here Berthold Schwarz invented gunpowder.

Painter: And I once got first prize at the Dresden Exhibition of Contemporary Art. What am I doing now? Painting signs.

> *(The station bell rings. The Station Master comes out. He throws away a cigarette butt. The men scramble for it.)*

First Man: Well, anyway, Madame Zachanassian will help us.

Fourth Man: If she comes . . .

Third Man: If she comes . . .

Second Man: Last week she was in France. She gave them a hospital.

First Man: In Rome she founded a free public library.

Third Man: In Leuthengau, a bird sanctuary.

Painter: They say she got Picasso to design her car.

First Man: Where does she get all that money?

Second Man: An oil company, a shipping line, three banks, and five railways—

Fourth Man: And the biggest string of geisha houses in Japan.[12]

In this short scene, the playwright specifies the economic decline of this once prosperous village, and then raises the prospect of a possible savior—Madame Zachanassian. Will she come? Who is she? What will she do? Duerrenmatt carries our interest forward. He also creates a sense that some odd things are about to happen. You did not really see a train go through, but you are willing to accept his way of suggesting it. Besides, it is not the train you want to see. It is Madame Zachanassian. Then, too, the dialogue is not altogether realistic, with its little clipped exclamations. You are getting the feeling that the playwright is setting you up for something quite extraordinary.

In a moment, a group of poorly dressed townspeople appears, led by the Burgomaster, the Pastor, Schill (a prominent citizen), a Teacher with a children's chorus, and the village band. All are excited about the prospect of having a mysterious visit from the wealthy widow, even though they know the train is not supposed to stop here. Suddenly, another train approaches, goes through, slams on its brakes, and stops down the tracks! The crowd is astonished when Madame Zachanassian enters. Duerrenmatt describes her:

> *(From the right Claire Zachanassian appears. She is an extraordinary woman. She is in her fifties, red-haired, remarkably dressed, with a face as impassive as that of*

an ancient idol, beautiful still, and with a singular grace of movement and manner. She is simple and unaffected, yet she has the haughtiness of a world power. The entire effect is striking to the point of the unbelievable. Behind her comes her fiance, Pedro Cabral, tall, young, very handsome, and completely equipped for fishing, with creel and net, and with a rod case in his hand. An excited Conductor follows.)[13]

The conductor scolds her for stopping the train, but she promptly pacifies him with a personal bribe. The rest of Madame's retinue appears, including two blind servants, two bodyguards, a black panther in a cage, and an empty casket. Notice how the playwright immediately establishes Madame Zachanassian's eccentric character by specific symbols.

Duerrenmatt goes on to develop the plot around Madame Zachanassian's sensational proposal, which she announces at a village feast put on in her honor. She will give the town one billion marks, half a billion for the community and half a billion to be divided up equally among the citizens. In return, she demands the life of Anton Schill. The town, at first outraged by her barbarous proposal, rejects the offer, but soon insidious greed begins to show. The playwright shows again, by concrete signs, the evidence of the villagers' avarice. Anton Schill, a shopkeeper, soon notices that his customers are beginning to charge more items. Citizens are beginning to dress better, in finer clothes and new shoes. Even Schill's children reject their father, and in the end a mock town meeting is held and the townspeople decide to clear up the injustice of the past. The men of the village surround Schill, and he dies. The scene returns to the railway station, now freshly painted, glowing with neon lights and surrounded by garlands, posters, and bright flags—tangible evidence of the change in status to the townspeople of Güllen. The train stops, and a procession arrives with Madame Zachanassian, her retinue, and the coffin. The train moves off as the villagers gather to watch her exit.

In assessing *The Visit* as a successful theater piece, it is worth remembering Brunètiere's observation that the action must be developed around a character striving for a goal. Madame Zachanassian has a clear objective and a strong motive—vengeance on a man and a village that shamefully wronged her in the past. When she announces her goal, the villagers are incensed and reject her proposal. But the initial conflict between the widow and Güllen erodes when greed corrupts the citizens. The conflict changes to the town versus Anton Schill. Ultimately, this culminates in Schill's death at the hands of the townspeople, and Madame Zachanassian makes her exit, having gained her revenge, not only on Schill but also on the villagers of Güllen, who silently watch her go away in the train, leaving them to their thoughts of what they have done.

Madame Zachanassian is not a proper Aristotelian tragic heroine, because of her motivation, but she is an arresting theatrical figure, not only in her appearance and action, but also in the bizarre way her mind works. Duerrenmatt has fashioned a remarkable theatrical vehicle with its striking characters and grotesque actions. In *The Visit*, Duerrenmatt demonstrates his mastery of the theater by the way he develops his plot in specific and memorable signs.

Peter Shaffer

Peter Shaffer is an English playwright with an exceptional sense of the theatrical. He has written a variety of plays, but in each one he has demonstrated his gift for creating remarkable, dramatic actions, and images. Examples are *The Royal Hunt of the Sun, Black Comedy, Equus,* and *Amadeus.*

Shaffer's lively comedy *Lettice and Lovage* (1987) offers an excellent example of how something dull can be transformed into highly theatrical material by vivid language and action. In the first four short segments of Scene 1, Shaffer shows how a frustrated, but imaginative, tour director of an old English Trust House livens up her performance from a drab, factual account to a thoroughly captivating one. Lettice leads a bored group of tourists on a rainy day to view a staircase in the old house, where she describes an incident that occurred during the Elizabethan period in the sixteenth century, when the Queen came on a visit.

Segment A:

Lettice: To mark the occasion, Fustian caused a banquet to be laid here in this hall, and himself stood by the Queen's side at the top of the stairs to escort her down it. However, as Her Majesty set foot on the first stair, she tripped on the hem of her elaborate dress, and would have fallen, had not her host taken hold of her arm and saved her.

Segment B:

Lettice: Her Majesty arrived at John Fustian's feast, emerging from the bedchamber at the head of the stairs. She was wearing a dazzling dress with a hem on to which had been sewn one hundred pearls, dredged from the Indian Ocean by an Ottomite Sultan! Alas, so heavy was this hem that she tripped on the first step and would have fallen all the way down had not her host, who was standing near the middle of the staircase—on the seventh stair from the top, can you see it?—. . . had he not rushed up and caught her in the very nick of time.

Segment C:

Lettice: . . . Suddenly she appeared—Gloriana herself, the Virgin Queen of England—encrusted from bosom to ankle with a blaze of diamonds presented to her by the Czar Ivan the Terrible, who had seen a portrait of her in miniature and lost a little of his icy heart to her chaste looks! Smiling, she set foot upon the first stair, up there! Alas, as she did so—at that precise moment—she slipped and would have plunged headlong down all fifteen polished and bruising steps had not her host—standing precisely where I stand now, *at the very bottom—leapt in a single bound,* the whole height of the staircase to where she stood and saved her! Imagine the scene! Time as if suspended! A hundred beribboned guests frozen like Renaissance statues, arms outstretched in powerless gesture! Eyes wide with terror in the flare of torches! . . . And then suddenly John Fustian moves! He who up to that moment has lived his whole life as a dull and turgid yes-man, breaks the spell! Springs forward—upward—rises like a bird—like feathered Mercury—*soars* in one astounding leap the whole height of these stairs, and at the last possible moment catches her in his loyal arms, raises her high above his head, and rose-cheeked with triumph, cries up to her: "Adored Majesty! Adored and *En*dored Majesty! Fear not! You are safe!—And your hedgehogs await.[14]

In Segment D, Lettice changes the story from the Queen to an exquisite bride who is knocked over the banister by a wolfhound. She is crippled for life and spends the rest of her days confined to her chamber. Lettice is discharged for her exaggerated performance, but in the end her infectious imagination contaminates her employer as well. While these passages from *Lettice and Lovage* are examples of comic hyperbole, they also show how drab material is enlivened through the use of striking imagery.

August Wilson

By now you should be familiar with the name of August Wilson, who first became known in 1984 with *Ma Rainey's Black Bottom,* to be followed by his hits, *Fences, Joe Turner's Come and Gone,* and *The Piano Lesson.* His approach to starting a new play is quite unique. He takes a pad of paper, sits down in a bar or restaurant, begins with a patch of dialogue, and lets his characters talk—and from that process, he writes a play.

"The foundation of my playwriting is poetry. . . . The mental process is poetic: you use metaphor and condense." Wilson wrote poetry for twenty years before he became interested in the theater.

Wilson says he begins a play with an idea, "with something I want to say." The idea in *The Piano Lesson,* for example, was, "Can one acquire a sense of self-worth by denying the past?" Wilson got the title from a painting by Romare Bearden, a picture of a piano instructor with a child. The painting triggered his writing:

From the painting I had a piano, and I just started writing a line of dialogue and I had no idea who was talking. First, I had four guys moving the piano into an empty house. I discarded that because people would be offstage too much, getting other pieces of furniture.

Someone says something to someone else, and they talk, and at some point I say, "Well, who is this?" and I give him a name. But I have no idea what the story line of the play is. It's a process of discovery . . . I knew there was a story, but I didn't know what the story was. I discovered it as the characters began to talk: one guy wants to sell the piano, the sister doesn't want to. I thought, why doesn't she want to sell it? Finding all these things out helped the story. I put off writing the history of the piano—one character tells the whole story—until I found it out in the process of writing the dialogue.[15]

Les Myers in August Wilson's Pulitzer Prize-winning *The Piano Lesson,* **another in his series of plays on the black experience in urban America.** *(Directed by Lloyd Richards, Yale Repertory Theater)*

Wilson's way of working is highly individual. It is as if he conjures up in his mind a set of characters and listens to them talk—and from their dialogue, he picks up clues on how he writes his play.

It is no accident that many of our most successful playwrights have had firsthand experience in the theater. Wilson lacked that background, but he began picking it up when his first play, *Ma Rainey's Black Bottom,* was tried out at the O'Neill Theater Center.

Wilson comments: "The O'Neill made me more conscious of what theater is about. There's nothing like encountering the problems of costume, lighting, set design. What do you mean by this? Where is this? Where is the window?—which make you more aware of the totality of what you are doing. . . . I've become conscious of things like that and it's made me a better playwright. But I don't want to lose the impulse, the sense as with *Ma Rainey,* that anything goes, that you can do whatever you want to do."

Another valuable lesson that Wilson learned as the result of *Ma Rainey* at the O'Neill was how to work on a play:

> I learned to rewrite. Not just patchworking here and fixing there, but exactly what the word means—rewriting. When you write, you know where you want to go—you know what a scene, a particular speech is supposed to accomplish. Then I discovered that it's possible to go back and rewrite this speech, to find another way to say it.
>
> . . . Nobody writes a perfect play by just sitting down and writing. You find out what's there when the actors begin to move around in the space.[16]

The most difficult art of the theater is playwriting. In every age there is a constant search for playwrights who are able to bring before the audience interesting and remarkable characters engaged in actions that are meaningful and stimulating. Today, more than ever, the theater offers great opportunities to the potential playwright.

PLAYS TO READ AND SEE

F = Film available; V = Videotape available

F	V	Peter Shaffer, *Amadeus, Equus*
F	V	Henrik Ibsen, *A Doll's House*
		August Wilson, *Fences, The Piano Lesson*
		Eugene O'Neill, *Mourning Becomes Electra*
F	V	Friedrich Duerrenmatt, *The Visit*
		Edward Albee, *Zoo Story*
		Luis Valdez, *Zoot Suit*

BIBLIOGRAPHY

BECKERMAN, BERNARD. *Dynamics of Drama.* New York: Knopf, 1970.
COLE, TOBY, ed. *Playwrights on Playwriting.* New York: Hill and Wang, 1960.
PACKARD, WILLIAM. *The Art of the Playwright.* New York: Paragon, 1987.
SAVRAN, DAVID, ed. *In Their Own Words.* New York: Theater Communications Group, 1988.
WAGER, WALTER, ed. *The Playwrights Speak.* New York: Delta Books, 1967.
"The Woman Playwright Issue." *Performing Arts Journal, 21*(3), 1983.

NOTES

1. Tennessee Williams, interviewed in *The Playwrights Speak,* ed. Walter Wager (New York: Delta Books, 1967), p. 225.

2. Ibid., p. 224.

3. Harold Pinter, interviewed in Wager, *The Playwrights Speak,* p. 187.

4. Edward Albee, interviewed in Wager, *The Playwrights Speak,* p. 187.

5. Luis Valdez, interviewed by David Savran, *In Their Own Words,* p. 74.

6. David Rabe, interviewed by David Savran, *In Their Own Words,* p. 198.

7. Henrik Ibsen, *The Collected Works of Henrik Ibsen,* ed. William Archer (New York: Charles Scribner's Sons, 1911), p. 195.

8. Ibid., p. 196.

9. Eugene O'Neill, in *Chief European Theories of Drama,* ed. Barrett H. Clark (New York: Crown, 1947), p. 835.

10. Ibid., p. 837.

11. Friedrich Duerrenmatt, *The Visit*, trans. Maurice Valency. Copyright © 1958 by Maurice Valency. Reprinted by permission of Random House, Inc.

12. Ibid.

13. Ibid.

14. Peter Shaffer, *Lettice and Lovage* (New York: Harper & Row, 1987), Act I.

15. August Wilson, interviewed by David Savran, *In Their Own Words*, p. 294.

16. Ibid., p. 293.

General Bibliography

ARNOTT, PETER. *The Theater in Its Time.* Boston: Little, Brown, 1981.

BECKERMAN, BERNARD. *Dynamics of Drama: Theory and Method of Analysis.* New York: Knopf, 1970.

BENTLEY, ERIC. *The Life of the Drama.* New York: Barnes & Noble, 1967.

BIGSBY, C. W. E. *Twentieth Century American Drama.* 3 vols. New York: Cambridge University Press, 1982–1985.

BROCKETT, OSCAR G. *The Essential Theater.* New York: Holt, Rinehart & Winston, 1980.

BROCKETT, OSCAR G. *Modern Theater: Realism and Naturalism to the Present.* Boston: Allyn and Bacon, 1982.

BROOK, PETER. *The Shifting Point, 1946–1987.* New York: Harper & Row, 1988.

CHINOY, HELEN KRICH, and LINDA WALSH JENKINS. *Women in American Theater: Careers, Images, Movements.* New York: Crown, 1982.

ESSLIN, MARTIN, ed. *The Encyclopedia of World Theater.* New York: Charles Scribner's Sons, 1977.

GREENBERG, JAN. *Theater Careers: A Comprehensive Guide to Non-Acting Careers in the Theater.* New York: Holt, Rinehart & Winston, 1980.

HARTNOLL, PHYLLIS. *The Oxford Companion to the Theater.* New York: Oxford University Press, 1967.

HUERTA, JORGE A. *Chicano Theater.* Ypsilanti, Mich.: Themes & Forms, 1982.

JACOBS, SUSAN. *On Stage: The Making of a Play.* New York: Knopf, 1972.

KOTT, JAN. *The Theater of Essence.* Evanston, Ill.: Northwestern University Press, 1984.

MALPEDE, KAREN, ed. *Women in the Theater: Compassion and Hope.* New York: Drama Book Publishers, 1983.

MARRANCA, BONNIE. *American Playwrights: A Critical Survey.* New York: Drama Book Publishers, 1981.

MATES, JULIAN. *America's Musical Stage.* Westport, Conn.: Greenwood Press, 1985.

MITCHELL, LOFTEN. *Black Drama: The Story of the American Negro in the Theater.* New York: Hawthorne Books, 1967.

NICOLL, ALLARDYCE. *The Developments of the Theater.* London: Harrap, 1966.

ROOSE-EVANS, JAMES. *Experimental Theater from Stanislavski to Peter Brook.* London: Routledge and Kegan Paul, 1984.

SELDES, MARIAN. *The Bright Lights: A Theater Life.* New York: Limelight Editions, 1984.

SPOLIN, VIOLA. *Theater Games File.* Evanston, Ill.: Northwestern University Press, 1988.

STANISLAVSKI, CONSTANTIN. *My Life in Art,* trans. J. J. Robbins. New York: Meridian Books, 1956.

STYAN, J. I. *The Dramatic Experience: A Guide to Reading Plays.* London: Cambridge University Press, 1965.

TAYLOR, J. R. *The Penguin Dictionary of the Theater.* London: Penguin Books, 1966.

TRAPIDO, JOEL. *An International Dictionary of Theater Language.* Westport, Conn.: Greenwood Press, 1984.

VINSON, JAMES, ed. *Contemporary Dramatists.* New York: St. Martin's Press, 1977.

WALKER, ETHEL PITTS. *The Theater of Black Americans.* Englewood Cliffs, N.J.: Prentice-Hall, 1980.

Glossary

Acting area. Traditionally, that part of the theater occupied by the performers. Usually the stage, but in experimental productions it may be any area used by the actor.

Aesthetic distance. The physical and psychological detachment between a work of art and those who respond to it. Experimentalists are now trying to eliminate this area of separation.

Alienation. A technique used by Bertolt Brecht in his "epic dramas" to negate the emotional involvement of his audience to make an intellectual appeal for his message.

Antagonist. The character or force in opposition to the protagonist or hero.

Apron. The forestage extending beyond the proscenium arch.

Arena stage. An arrangement for "central staging" of plays with the acting area in the middle of the room, surrounded by the audience.

Aside. A dramatic convention in which the actor speaks private thoughts aloud, unnoticed by the other actors.

Automatism. A theory by Henri Bergson based on mechanical or repetitious actions or language.

Backing. Stage scenery used to mask the openings to prevent the audience from seeing the offstage areas.

Beat. A basic unit for rehearsal.

Blocking. The director's organization of the stage movements of the cast.

Bourgeois drama. Pseudoserious plays involving middle-class society, with the general emphasis on pathos and morality.

Business. The individual actions of the characters in a play, for example, taking a drink, smoking a pipe, writing a letter.

Catharsis. The act of purging, cleansing, or purifying, usually associated with tragedy.

Chorus. In Greek drama a group, varying in size from 12 to 50, that recited lines in unison. As the first element to develop in Greek drama, it provided information and, in its most elaborate state, commentary on past actions and forebodings about future ones. With the invention of the second and third actors, the chorus gradually became less important.

Classical drama. Usually refers to the dramas of ancient Greece and Rome. *See also* Neoclassicism.

Climax. The strongest point of emotional tension. Most plays have a series of climaxes culminating in a major climax.

Comedy. Drama designed to amuse the audience, often showing human frailties and foibles; usually ends happily.

Comedy of humours. Comedy of character based on a dominant trait, such as greed or jealousy. Popularized by the Elizabethan playwright Ben Jonson.

Comedy of manners. Social comedy wittily satirizing characters in terms of their shortcomings as measured against a specific code of conduct—for example, *The School for Scandal*.

Commedia dell'arte. Improvised Italian comedy of the sixteenth, seventeenth, and eighteenth centuries put together out of stock roles in formula situations. Performed by small companies of professional actors who were very popular all over Europe.

Confidant(e). A minor character paired with a major one, who shares the latter's confidences, usually for expository purposes.

Constructivism. An approach to staging developed by the Russians in the 1920s that was antidecorative and antiillusionistic. The setting was a framework for action.

Conventions. Common agreements between theater worker and spectator concerning the manner of production, that is, certain "ground rules" that determine how the game is played, for example, the physical separation of actor and spectator.

Crisis. A time of decision; a turning point.

Cycle plays. Medieval plays dealing with scriptural stories from the Creation to the Last Judgment.

Cyclorama. Drapery or canvas usually hung in a half circle to mask the wings and backstage areas. It often represents the sky, or it may be a simple drapery.

Denouement. The resolution or unraveling of a plot so that an equilibrium is usually restored.

Deus ex machina. In the Greek theater, a "god from a machine"; a mechanical device used for the intervention of some outside agent to resolve the plot. As a general term, it refers to the intervention of any outside force to bring about a desired end.

Diction. Aristotle's fourth element—the language of the play; the words that the actors speak.

Discovery. The revelation of important information about the characters, their motivations, feelings, and relationships. Discovery is often accompanied by recognition (*anagnorisis*), when a character learns the truth about him- or herself.

Doubling. One actor playing more than one character in a single play. In the ancient Greek theater, the actor usually doubled.

Downstage. The area of the stage closest to the audience.

Drame. Any play that deals seriously with themes, characters, and ideas of the present day.

Dress rehearsal. A rehearsal conducted under complete performance conditions, including all technical aspects.

Eccyclema. A movable platform in the Greek theater thought to have been positioned in the central opening of the *skene*, usually to show corpses.

Empathy. Literally, "feeling into"; the imitative motor response of the spectator.

Environmental theater. The performers play around, above, behind, and among the spectators. Any environment can be used as a theater that has enough space for performing and viewing. Often takes place in "found spaces."

Epic theater. The nonillusionistic theater of Piscator and Brecht, dealing with broad themes, with loosely organized plots presented in a frankly theatrical style.

Exposition. Dramatic techniques for acquainting the audience with antecedent information and background material.

Expressionism. A style of drama that attempts to present "inner reality," the person beneath the skin. Often distorts the normal to present symbolic action in dreamlike sequences.

Farce. Low comedy, written for amusement, usually enphasizing physical action.

Flat. The most useful element of stage scenery, consisting of a wooden frame generally covered with muslin or canvas to represent walls.

High comedy. A general term referring to comedy that evokes thoughtful laughter through its concern with character, ideas, and dialogue.

Histrionic sensibility. The spectator's ability to perceive and discriminate actions and visual symbols, just as in music the trained ear discriminates sounds.

Illusionistic theater. Any theater that attempts to create the effect of an actual experience—authentic places, real people, and genuine situations.

Imagery. Communication by means of concrete and particular meanings through language devices such as metaphors, similes, and clusters of related words.

Improvisation. Spontaneous invention by the performers of actions, dialogue, and characters usually around a basic idea, situation, or theme. Although widely used for actors' rehearsal and training, it is now employed in happenings, performances, and other experimental forms of theater.

Incongruity. A comic theory based on contrast.

Irony. A discrepancy between what a character plans or anticipates and what actually occurs.

Linear plot. A plot that follows a carefully articulated sequence of action generally organized in chronological order.

Magnitude. The elevation that Aristotle says should characterize tragedy. May refer to character, thought, diction, and spectacle.

Mask. To conceal the backstage, wings, or flies from the spectator's view.

Melodrama. Pseudoserious drama that is played at the game level, employing exciting action aimed at audience involvement. Usually ends with poetic justice. Popular in the nineteenth century but still stageworthy in present-day mystery and suspense plays.

Method acting. Stanislavski attempted to devise a systematic approach that enabled actors to gain more control over themselves and their performance. Involves control of the voice and body, the "correct state of being" onstage, and inner psychological response as the basis for outer physical actions.

Mise-en-scène. All of the visual aspects of the staged production.

Mixed media performances. Experiments that may involve a combination of the arts and technical equipment, such as tapes, slides, and films.

Motivation. Logical justification, or the giving of plausible reasons, for the behavior of the characters in a play.

Myth. Archetypal stories that suggest widespread cultural beliefs, events, and feelings.

Naturalism. An exaggerated form of realism that emphasizes a sordid and deterministic view of life. First appeared in France in the late nineteenth century as a response to the scientific revolution.

Neoclassicism. An attempt in the sixteenth, seventeenth, and eighteenth centuries to "regularize" dramatic techniques by following scrupulously what were thought to be practices of the ancients—for example, adherence to the "unities," use of a chorus, preservation of "decorum" in language and action, avoiding acts of violence onstage, and use of only royal or noble characters.

Objective. A dramatic character's goal.

Open stage. Sometimes an attempt to break away from the proscenium arch theater to play as close as possible to the audience. Also, experimental productions freed from the strictures of a prepared script.

Orchestra. In the fifth-century B.C. Greek theater, the large circle (approximately 22 meters across) that served as the playing area. Located between the *theatron* and the *skene*.

Pathos. The "suffering" aspect of drama, especially that quality that evokes pity.

Peripetia. In ancient Greek tragedy, a reversal, usually in the protagonist's fortunes.

Pity and fear. The emotions aroused and purged in tragedy. Pity goes beyond pathos to include compassion and shared grief; fear goes beyond fright to include awe and wonder.

Plot. The structure of the incidents; the formative agent of drama; dramatic composition.

Point of attack. The moment in a play when a precipitating force sets the mechanism in motion and disrupts the equilibrium; the first complication.

Practical. Functional, utilitarian—for example, doors and windows that are workable, not simply decorative.

Presentational staging. Production that is frankly theatrical, free from the illusion of reality. The performer confronts the audience directly.

Probability. An attempt by the playwright to establish credibility or, as Aristotle says, to make the action of a play seem "necessary and probable."

Project. Vocally, to increase the volume so as to be heard by the entire audience; technically, to show enlarged slides or films on backgrounds as a part of the scenery.

Prologue. The introduction to a play, sometimes a monologue delivered by an actor directly to the audience. In classical drama, that part of the play preceding the chorus's entrance.

Properties (props). Includes objects used by the actors in the production of a play, such as letters, weapons, and food.

Proscenium arch. The architectural frame through which the spectator views the stage.

Protagonist. The chief character in a play.

Purgation. *See* Catharsis.

Rake. To slant the stage floor so that it is higher away from the audience to aid in the perspective illusion. Also, the slant of the auditorium floor, designed to give all of the audience a good view.

Realism. Drama that attempts to establish authenticity through the use of the observed facts of daily existence.

Recognition. *See* Discovery.

Representational staging. Production that imitates experience, that seeks to create the illusion of reality.

Reversal. An Aristotelian critical term (*peripetia*) referring to a sudden change in the fortunes of the protagonist.

Ritual. Social customs, events, and ceremonies whose repeated actions are directed toward specific goals.

Romanticism. Concerns itself with adventurous, emotionally loaded characters in remote and exotic circumstances; in contrast to classical drama.

Satire comedy. Uses wit as a weapon to correct antisocial behavior.

Scenario. The skeletal outline of the plot.

Setting. The scenic environment of the action.

Skene. Originally a small hut at the back of the orchestra in the Greek theater, which later became the stagehouse.

"Slice of life." Attempt to give the impression of unorganized actuality without an apparent beginning, middle, or end. Used principally in naturalistic drama.

Soliloquy. A "solo" speech of a single character, which is usually taken to be introspective analysis; a character's internal thoughts.

Spectacle. The visual aspects of a produced play.

Spine. Stanislavski's idea of "line of through-action" of an acting role. A means of connecting motivations and objectives of all parts of a play.

Stage left or right. Left or right side of the stage from the actor's point of view facing the audience.

Stylization. Theatrical production that usually emphasizes the visual aspects and the manner of performing.

Subtext. Interaction beneath the surface of the spoken language of a play.

Surrealism. A literary movement that began in France in the 1920s, exploiting the irrational and unconscious with emphasis on dreams.

Sympathetic magic. Primitive ceremonies used in an attempt to enlist the help of the gods by enacting the desired objectives.

Theatricalism. The direct use of all aspects of the theater to exploit the play as a staged work.

Theatron. The seating area in the Greek theater.

Theme. The general subject of the playwrights' concern; their interpretation of the meaning of their action.

Thought. Aristotle's third element. The reasoning aspect of drama—the argument, the theme, the meaning.

Thrust stage. A platform or "open stage" projecting into the auditorium, bringing the performer in close proximity to the audience.

Tracking. An approach to performance in which several elements develop simultaneously in parallel tracks, such as music, images, and mime. The elements may remain separate from one another.

Tragic flaw. An Aristotelian concept of an "error in judgment," or missing the mark. A frailty in an otherwise good and prominent character that accounts for his or her downfall.

Tragic hero. The central figure in a tragedy. Aristotle described the hero as a prominent person "not preeminently virtuous and just, whose misfortune is brought upon him not by vice and depravity but by some error of judgment."

Tragicomedy. That form of drama that is serious and evokes apprehension for the fate of the protagonist but ends happily.

Transactions. An approach to action through the "games theory" of Eric Berne, which analyzes behavior in terms of the social, or overt, level and the psychological, or concealed, level.

Unity of action. Aristotle stipulated that all parts of a plot should be essential and organic to make a complete whole, free from digressions or subplots.

Unity of place. All action occurs in a single locale. By convention, the Greeks usually observed this unity.

Unity of time. The action of a play takes place, as Aristotle suggested, "within the single revolution of the sun." Covers a short span of time.

Upstage. The acting area farthest from the audience.

"Well-made play." Dramatic technique associated with French playwrights Scribe and Sardou, in which all aspects of plot are carefully worked out in a logical cause-and-effect relationship.

Wings. The area offstage of the acting area.

Photo Credits

417

Bern, Switzerland. **325** Victoria and Albert Museum, London. **326** University Press of New England. **328** Courtesy of La Jolla Playhouse and Steppenwolf Theater Company. **332** Dr. Jaromir Svoboda, Prague National Theater. **333** Courtesy of Prague National Theater. **334** Courtesy of Professor J. Burian. **338** Gerry Goodstein. **339** Martha Swope. **341** Martha Swope.

CHAPTER TWELVE: 344 D.A. Harissiadis. **346** Courtesy of Professor William Melnitz. **348** Courtesy of Professor William Melnitz. **349** Courtesy of Professor William Melnitz. **350** Victoria and Albert Museum, London. **352** Richard Leacroft. **353** Courtesy of Professor William Melnitz. **356** Courtesy of Professor William Melnitz. **357** Theater Arts Prints. **358** Courtesy of Professor William Melnitz. **361** Courtesy of Guthrie Theater. **362** University of California at Los Angeles. **363** Courtesy of Arena Stage. **364** University of Michigan. **365** Architectural Press, London. **366** Architectural Press, London. **368** Martha Swope. **369** Courtesy of Théâtre du Soleil.

CHAPTER THIRTEEN: 372 Victoria and Albert Museum. **376** Victoria and Albert Museum. **377** *Theatre Annual* (1906) **380** Walter C. Hodge, *Shakespeare's Theater.* **381** Courtesy of Professor William Melnitz. **383** Architectural Press, London. **384** Courtesy of Jerry Grotlowski. **385** Courtesy of Trinity Square Theater. **390** Courtesy of North Carolina Playmakers.

CHAPTER FOURTEEN: 392 Droeshout print, University of California, Santa Barbara Library. **399** Jack Valari, University of Colorado. **400** New York Public Library. **402** Tom Smith, Pacific Conservatory of Performing Arts. **403** New York Public Library. **409** Gerry Goodstein.

COLOR INSERT: *The Visit,* University of California, Santa Barbara. *Crime and Punishment,* Stockholm State Theater. *Pacific Overtures,* Santa Barbara City College. *The Roar of the Greasepaint,* Paper Mill Playhouse. *Peer Gynt,* Christopher Briscoe. *The Phantom of the Opera,* Clive Barda. *Ghosts,* Pacific Conservatory of Performing Arts. *Mahabharata,* Martha Swope.

Index